D0860852

Early praise for *Property-Based Testing with PropEr, Erlang, and Elixir*

Property-based testing through PropEr and QuickCheck is one of the most powerful, yet underutilized, testing approaches of the Erlang Ecosystem. Fred, through his book, has reduced the barrier to entry, making property-based testing accessible to everyone. This book is unarguably a must-have if you are serious about Erlang and Elixir. A long time coming!

➤ **Francesco Cesarini**
  Director, Erlang Solutions Ltd.

In his inimitable and engaging way, Fred lays out a strong case for why property testing is a revolutionary idea in software testing and, throughout the book, masterfully teaches readers how to become proficient in property testing. As we move toward property testing at Bleacher Report, *Property-Based Testing with PropEr, Erlang, and Elixir* is our indispensable guide. For anyone considering property testing, it should be yours, too.

➤ **Ben Marx**
  Software Architect, Bleacher Report

Fred Hebert has crafted a text with breadth and depth in his inimitable approachable style. *Property-Based Testing with PropEr, Erlang, and Elixir* thoroughly demystifies property testing with detailed examples and practical tips in a way that is useful to beginners and experts alike.

➤ **Sean Cribbs**
  Staff Software Engineer, Postmates Inc.

Fred breaks these topics down in understandable ways and provides a lot of insight into how to think about property-based testing. There's a real emphasis on ensuring that your tests are working to find the hidden bugs and not just generating random data.

➤ **Chris Keathley**
  Senior Engineer, Bleacher Report

This book is an excellent resource if you want to introduce property-based testing to your Erlang or Elixir project. It will guide you from the basics to the challenges of applying property-based testing in practice, giving invaluable advice on how to get your tests correct and efficient.

If you want to get started with property testing—you need look no further!

➤ **Dr. Annette Bieniusa**
  Senior Researcher and Lecturer, University of Kaiserslautern

Property-Based Testing with PropEr, Erlang, and Elixir

Find Bugs Before Your Users Do

Fred Hebert

The Pragmatic Bookshelf

Raleigh, North Carolina

Our Pragmatic books, screencasts, and audio books can help you and your team create better software and have more fun. Visit us at *https://pragprog.com*.

The team that produced this book includes:

Publisher: Andy Hunt
VP of Operations: Janet Furlow
Managing Editor: Susan Conant
Development Editor: Jacquelyn Carter
Copy Editor: L. Sakhi MacMillan
Indexing: Potomac Indexing, LLC
Layout: Gilson Graphics

For sales, volume licensing, and support, please contact *support@pragprog.com*.

For international rights, please contact *rights@pragprog.com*.

ISBN-13: 978-1-68050-621-1
Book version: P1.0—January 2019

Contents

Acknowledgments ix

Introduction xi

Part I — The Basics

1. **Foundations of Property-Based Testing** 3
   Promises of Property-Based Testing 5
   Properties First 7
   Property-Based Testing in Your Project 10
   Running a Property 14
   Wrapping Up 16

2. **Writing Properties** 17
   Structure of Properties 18
   Default Generators 22
   Putting It All Together 24
   Wrapping Up 31

3. **Thinking in Properties** 33
   Modeling 33
   Generalizing Example Tests 37
   Invariants 38
   Symmetric Properties 42
   Putting It All Together 44
   Wrapping Up 47

4. **Custom Generators** 51
   The Limitations of Default Generators 52
   Gathering Statistics 53
   Basic Custom Generators 61
   Fancy Custom Generators 72
   Wrapping Up 83

Part II — Stateless Properties in Practice

5.	**Responsible Testing**	91
	The Specification	92
	Thinking About Program Structure	92
	CSV Parsing	95
	Filtering Records	106
	Employee Module	116
	Templating	128
	Plumbing It All Together	131
	Wrapping Up	132
6.	**Properties-Driven Development**	133
	The Specification	134
	Writing the First Test	135
	Testing Specials	140
	Implementing Specials	148
	Negative Testing	152
	Wrapping Up	166
7.	**Shrinking**	167
	Re-centering with ?SHRINK	168
	Dividing with ?LETSHRINK	172
	Wrapping Up	175
8.	**Targeted Properties**	179
	Understanding Targeted Properties	179
	Targeted Properties in Practice	186
	Thinking Outside the Box	193
	Wrapping Up	197

Part III — Stateful Properties

9.	**Stateful Properties**	201
	Laying Out Stateful Properties	202
	How Stateful Properties Run	204
	Writing Properties	205
	Testing a Basic Concurrent Cache	210
	Testing Parallel Executions	224
	Wrapping Up	230

10. **Case Study: Bookstore** 233
 Introducing the Application 233
 Writing Generators 245
 Broad Stateful Testing 247
 Precise Stateful Modeling 253
 Refining the Tests 265
 Debugging Stateful Properties 273
 Parallel Tests 278
 Wrapping Up 280

11. **State Machine Properties** 281
 Laying Out State Machine Properties 282
 How State Machine Properties Run 284
 Writing Properties 285
 Testing a Circuit Breaker 289
 Modeling the Circuit Breaker 292
 Adjusting the Model 305
 Wrapping Up 310

A1. **Solutions** 311
 Writing Properties 311
 Thinking in Properties 311
 Custom Generators 316
 Shrinking 320
 Stateful Properties 323

A2. **Elixir Translations** 325
 Thinking in Properties 325
 Responsible Testing 326
 Stateful Properties 329
 Case Study: Bookstore 331
 State Machine Properties 339

A3. **Installing PostgreSQL** 343
A4. **Generators Reference** 345
 Index 349

Acknowledgments

I want to thank everyone who offered their time to review this book: Sean Cribbs, Chris Keathley (who also has been a huge cheerleader of this work on the Elixir Outlaws podcast), Gabrielle Denhez, Jamu Kakar, Maurice Kelly, Xavier Shay, Ben Wilson, Evan Vigil-McClanahan, Ben Marx, Bruce Williams, Kim Shrier, and folks who got the beta versions of this book and then sent feedback or filed errata, or both.

There's also an obvious list of people to thank at PragProg, including Andy, Bruce Tate, and more particularly Jackie Carter, who edited this book and without whom it wouldn't be nearly as readable as it is.

I need to thank Jenn, who tolerated me writing this on weeknights on and off for over a year. I should finally thank Drew Fradette, who suggested I pitch my early draft to PragProg, which started the whole process of turning it into this book.

Introduction

When I finished my first book, *Learn You Some Erlang*, I told myself "never again." There's something distressing about spending months and years of work writing a book, spending all bits of free time you can find on it, putting aside other projects and hobbies, and rewriting your own texts close to a dozen times. You reach the point where before you're even done, you're tired of writing about the topic you chose to write about.

I knew all of that was waiting for me if I ever wanted to write another book. I decided to do it anyway because I truly believe property-based testing is something amazing, worth learning and using. In fact, part of the reason why I wanted to write a book was that I wanted to use property-based testing in projects at work and online, and it's generally a bad idea to introduce a technology when only one person in the team knows how it works.

It's a better compromise to spend all that time and effort writing a book than never using property-based testing in a team when I know what it can do and bring to a project. Hopefully, you'll feel that learning about it here is worth your time as well.

Who Is This Book For

If you know enough of Erlang or Elixir to feel comfortable writing a small project, you're fit for this book. There're a few things that might be a bit confusing, but you should be able to pull through.

If you have experience with unit testing and TDD, you'll feel comfortable with most of this book's testing concepts. While the text does not advocate using TDD or not (we avoid this whole debate), techniques that use properties to help design your programs are still shown and constitute a valuable option to explore a new problem space.

If you are, like me, one of these grumpy people who are annoyed with the quality of software and feel that you can't trust yourself to deliver high-quality code every time—you know your code will come back to haunt you sooner or later—then you will probably consider property-based testing a godsend.

Why Both Elixir and Erlang

The Erlang and Elixir communities possibly suffer from a kind of *narcissism of minor differences*; a kind of hostility exists based on small differences between the two languages and how developers do things, despite Elixir and Erlang being so much closer to each other than any other language or platform out there.

This book represents a conscious effort to bridge the gap between the two communities and see both groups join strengths rather than compete with each other; it is one small part, attempting to use one property-based testing tool, with one resource, to improve the code and tests of one community.

What's in This Book

This book covers pretty much everything you need to get started, up to the point where you feel confident enough to use the most advanced features of PropEr. We'll start smoothly, with the basic and foundational principles of property-based testing, see what the framework offers us to get started, make our way through thinking in properties, write our own custom data generators, and then really start going wild. You'll see how property-based testing can be used in a realistic project (and where it should not be used) and learn various techniques to make the best use of it possible to get the most value out of it. We'll also cover properties to test more complex stateful systems, a practice that is useful for integration and system tests.

Those are the topics covered, but more than anything, you may get a set of strategies to think about new approaches to test your software. Rather than just writing repetitive examples for tests, or just generating random data to throw at the code, you'll learn new techniques to find new bugs you never thought could be hiding in your code. You'll also gain tools to reason about how to build software, how to explore the problem space, and how to evaluate the fitness of the solutions you choose.

How to Read This Book

You should feel comfortable just reading all chapters in order. The first part of the book contains truly essential material to get your fundamentals right and get started properly. The second part applies properties in more realistic scenarios to gain comfort, and the last part covers stateful tests.

But really, it's easiest to read things in order. Some chapters have questions and exercises at the end. You can skip these if you want, but going through them will be a good way to reinforce your understanding of the material covered.

The exercises are added particularly when a lot of theory is introduced in the chapter and when the material will come back again and again in following chapters. Going through them may sometimes be tricky, but they will make the following chapters easier to go through. And because exercises left for the reader with no guidance are annoying as hell, all solutions are provided.

About the Code

Code is provided in both languages in most places where it makes sense to do so. Code samples may look like the following:

Erlang   code/path/to/file.erl

```erlang
%% This is some random code for demonstration purposes
path(_Current, Acc, _Seen, [_,_,_,_]) ->
    Acc;
path(Current, Acc, Seen, Ignore) ->
    frequency([
        {1, Acc}, % probabilistic stop
        {15, increase_path(Current, Acc, Seen, Ignore)}
    ]).
```

Elixir   code/path/to/file.ex

```elixir
# This is some random code for demonstration purposes
def path(_current, acc, _seen, [_,_,_,_]) do
  acc
end
def path(current, acc, seen, ignore) do
  frequency([
    {1, acc}, # probabilistic stop
    {15, increase_path(current, acc, seen, ignore)}
  ])
end
```

Code references such as ❶ will be used to point to locations in both languages at once.

Exceptions to this norm will include code that should be treated as pseudo-code, shell session output (which will be in Erlang only), and longer code samples that would take a lot of space, which will instead be located within an appendix to ease the reading flow. Otherwise, things should be quite readable for both languages at once.

When mentioned, file names for a code snippet point to where you should put the code if you're following along. Frequent reminders about this will be added, just in case. Downloadable code for this book contains the final code for each module and may not contain intermediary steps shown in the text.

Online Resources

The apps and examples shown in this book can be found at the Pragmatic Programmers website for this book.[1] You'll also find a link there where you can provide feedback by submitting errata entries.

The book relies on the PropEr[2] library. Its online documentation[3] will invariably prove useful.

Elixir users will use the PropCheck[4] wrapper library, which also has its own online documentation.[5]

Fred Hebert
January 2019

---

1.   https://pragprog.com/book/fhproper/property-based-testing-with-proper-erlang-and-elixir
2.   https://github.com/proper-testing/proper
3.   https://proper-testing.github.io/
4.   https://github.com/alfert/propcheck
5.   https://hexdocs.pm/propcheck

Part I

The Basics

First things first. This part contains all you need to give you a solid foundation on which to build and includes important material explaining what property-based testing is, how to get set up, and information to let you get familiar with thinking in properties and the tools the framework provides for you.

## CHAPTER 1

Foundations of Property-Based Testing

Testing can be a pretty boring affair. It's a necessity you can't avoid: the one thing more annoying than having to write tests is not having tests for your code. Tests are critical to safe programs, especially those that change over time. They can also prove useful to help properly design programs, helping us write them as users as well as implementers. But mostly, tests are repetitive burdensome work.

Take a look at this example test that will check that an Erlang function can take a list of presorted lists and always return them merged as one single sorted list:

```erlang
merge_test() ->
    [] = merge([]),
    [] = merge([[]]),
    [] = merge([[],[]]),
    [] = merge([[],[],[]]),
    [1] = merge([[1]]),
    [1,1,2,2] = merge([[1,2],[1,2]]),
    [1] = merge([[1],[],[]]),
    [1] = merge([[],[1],[]]),
    [1] = merge([[],[],[1]]),
    [1,2] = merge([[1],[2],[]]),
    [1,2] = merge([[1],[],[2]]),
    [1,2] = merge([[],[1],[2]]),
    [1,2,3,4,5,6] = merge([[1,2],[],[5,6],[],[3,4],[]]),
    [1,2,3,4] = merge([[4],[3],[2],[1]]),
    [1,2,3,4,5] = merge([[1],[2],[3],[4],[5]]),
    [1,2,3,4,5,6] = merge([[1],[2],[3],[4],[5],[6]]),
    [1,2,3,4,5,6,7,8,9] = merge([[1],[2],[3],[4],[5],[6],[7],[8],[9]]),
    Seq = seq(1,100),
    true = Seq == merge(map(fun(E) -> [E] end, Seq)),
    ok.
```

This is slightly modified code taken from the Erlang/OTP test suites for the lists module, one of the most central libraries in the entire language. It is boring, repetitive. It's the developer trying to think of all the possible ways the code can be used, and making sure that the result is predictable. You could probably think of another ten or thirty lines that could be added, and it could still be significant and explore the same code in somewhat different ways. Nevertheless, it's perfectly reasonable, usable, readable, and effective test code. The problem is that it's just so repetitive that a machine could do it. In fact, that's exactly the reason why traditional tests are boring. They're carefully laid out instructions where we tell the machine which test to run every time, with no variation, as a safety check.

It's not just that a machine *could* do it, it's that a machine *should* do it. We're spending our efforts the wrong way, and we could do better than this with the little time we have.

This is why property-based testing is one of the software development practices that generated the most excitement in the last few years. It promises better, more solid tests than nearly any other tool out there, with very little code. This means, similarly, that the software we develop with it should also get better—which is good, since overall software quality is fairly dreadful (including my own code). Property-based testing offers a lot of automation to keep the boring stuff away, but at the cost of a steeper learning curve and a lot of thinking to get it right, particularly when getting started. Here's what an equivalent property-based test could look like:

```
sorted_list(N) -> ?LET(L, list(N), sort(L)).

prop_merge() ->
    ?FORALL(List, list(sorted_list(pos_integer())),
        merge(List) == sort(append(List))).
```

Not only is this test shorter with just four lines of code, it covers more cases. In fact, it can cover hundreds of thousands of them. Right now the property-based test probably looks like a bunch of gibberish that can't be executed (at least not without the PropEr framework), but in due time, this will be pretty easy for you to read, and will possibly take less time to understand than even the long-form traditional test would.

Of course, not all test scenarios will be looking so favorable to property-based testing, but that is why you have this book. Let's get started right away: in this chapter, we'll see the results we should expect from property-based testing, and we'll cover the principles behind the practice and how they influence the way to write tests. We'll also pick the tools we need to get going, since, as you'll see, property-based testing does require a framework to be useful.

Promises of Property-Based Testing

Property-based tests are different from traditional ones and require more thinking. A lot more. Good property-based testing is a learned and practiced skill, much like playing a musical instrument or getting good at drawing: you can get started and benefit from it in plenty of friendly ways, but the skill ceiling is very high. You could write property tests for years and still find ways to improve and get more out of them. Experts at property-based testing can do some pretty amazing stuff.

The good news is that even as a beginner, you can get good results out of property-based testing. You'll be able to write simple, short, and concise tests that automatically comb through your code the way only the most obsessive tester could. Your code coverage will go high and stay there even as you modify the program without changing the tests. You'll even be able to use these tests to find new edge cases without even needing to modify anything.

With a bit more experience, you'll be able to write straightforward integration tests of stateful systems that find complex and convoluted bugs nobody even thought could be hiding in there. In fact, if you currently feel like a code base without unit tests is not trustworthy, you'll probably discover the same phenomenon with property testing real soon. You'll have seen enough of what properties can do to see the shadows of bugs that haven't been discovered yet, and just feel something is missing, until you've given them a proper shakedown.

Overall, you'll see that property-based testing is not just using a bunch of tools to automate boring tasks, but a whole different way to approach testing, and to some extent, software design itself. Now that's a bold claim, but we only have to look at what experts can do to see why that might be so. An example can be found in Thomas Arts' slide set[1] and presentation[2] from the Erlang Factory 2016. In that talk, he mentioned using QuickCheck (the canonical property-based testing tool) to run tests on Project FIFO,[3] an open source cloud project. With a mere 460 lines of property tests, they covered 60,000 lines of production code and uncovered twenty-five important bugs, including:

- Timing errors
- Race conditions

---

1. http://www.erlang-factory.com/static/upload/media/1461230674757746pbterlangfactorypptx.pdf
2. https://youtu.be/iW2J7Of8jsE
3. https://project-fifo.net

- Type errors
- Incorrect use of library APIs
- Errors in documentation
- Errors in the program logic
- System limits errors
- Errors in fault handling
- One hardware error

Considering that some studies estimate that developers average six software faults per 1,000 lines of code, then finding twenty-five important bugs with 460 lines of tests is quite a feat. That's finding over fifty bugs per 1,000 lines of test, with each of these lines covering 140 lines of production code. If that doesn't make you want to become a pro, I don't know what will.

Let's take a look at some more expert work. Joseph Wayne Norton ran a QuickCheck suite[4] of under 600 lines over Google's levelDB to find sequences of seventeen and thirty-one specific calls that could corrupt databases with ghost keys. No matter how dedicated to the task someone is, nobody would have found it easy to come up with the proper sequence of thirty-one calls required to corrupt a database.

Again, those are amazing results; that's a surprisingly low amount of code to find a high number of nontrivial errors on software that was otherwise already tested and running in production. Property-based testing is so impressive that it has wedged itself in multiple industries, including mission-critical telecommunication components,[5] databases,[6] components of cloud providers' routing and certificate-management layers, IoT platforms, and even in cars.[7]

We won't start at that level, but if you follow along (and do the exercises and practice enough), we might get pretty close. Hopefully, the early lessons will be enough for you to start applying property-based testing in your own projects. As we go, you'll probably feel like writing fewer and fewer traditional tests and will replace them with property tests instead. This is a really good thing, since you'll be able to delete code that you won't have to ever maintain again, at no loss in the quality of your software.

---

4. http://htmlpreview.github.io/?https://raw.github.com/strangeloop/lambdajam2013/master/slides/Norton-QuickCheck.html

5. http://www.erlang-factory.com/conference/ErlangUserConference2010/speakers/TorbenHoffman

6. http://www.erlang-factory.com/upload/presentations/255/RiakInside.pdf

7. http://www2015.taicpart.org/slides/Arts-TAICPART2015-Presentation.pdf

But as in playing music or drawing, things will sometimes be hard. When we hit a wall, it can be tempting (and easy) to tell ourselves that we just don't have that innate ability that experts must have. It's important to remember property-based testing is *not* a thing reserved for wizard programmers. The effort required to improve is continuous, and the progress is gradual and stepwise. Each wall you hit reveals an opportunity for improvement. We'll get there, one step at a time.

Properties First

Before jumping to our tools and spitting out lines of code, the first thing to do is to get our fundamentals right and stop thinking property-based testing is about tests. It's about *properties*. Let's take a look at what the difference is, and what thinking in properties looks like.

Conceptually, properties are not that complex. Traditional tests are often example-based: you make a list of a bunch of inputs to a given program and then list the expected output. You may put in a couple of comments about what the code should do, but that's about it. Your test will be good if you can have examples that can exercise all the possible program states you have.

By comparison, property-based tests have nothing to do with listing examples by hand. Instead, you'll want to write some kind of meta test: you find a rule that dictates the behavior that should always be the same no matter what sample input you give to your program and encode that into some executable code—a *property*. A special test framework will then generate examples for you and run them against your property to check that the rule you came up with is respected by your program.

In short, traditional tests have you come up with examples that indirectly imply rules dictating the behavior of your code (if at all), and property-based testing asks you to come up with the rules first and then tests them for you. It's a similar distinction as the one you'd get between imperative and declarative programming styles, but pushed to the next level.

The Example-Based Way

Here's an example. Let's say we have a function to represent a cash register. The function should take in a series of bills and coins representing what's already in the register, an amount of money due to be paid by the customer, and then the money handed by the customer to the cashier. It should return the bills and coins to cover the change due to the customer.

An approach based on unit tests may look like the following:

```
%% Money in the cash register
Register = [{20.00, 1}, {10.00, 2}, {5.00, 4},
            {1.00, 10}, {0.25, 10}, {0.01, 100}],
%% Change                  = cash(Register, PriceToPay, MoneyPaid),
[{10.00, 1}]               = cash(Register, 10.00, 20.00),
[{10.00, 1}, {0.25, 1}]    = cash(Register,  9.75, 20.00),
[{0.01, 18}]               = cash(Register,  0.82,  1.00),
[{10.00, 1}, {5.00, 1}, {1.00, 3}, {0.25, 2}, {0.01, 13}]
                           = cash(Register,  1.37, 20.00).
```

At ❶, the test says that a customer paying a $10 item with $20 should expect a single $10 bill back. The case at ❷ says that for a $9.75 purchase paid with $20, a $10 bill with a quarter should be returned, for a total of $10.25. Finally, the test at ❸ shows a $1.37 item paid with a $20 bill yields $18.63 in change, with the specific cuts shown.

That's a fairly familiar approach. Come up with a bunch of arguments with which to call the function, do some thinking, and then write down the expected result. By listing many examples, we try to cover the full set of rules and edge cases that describe what the code should do. In property-based testing, we have to flip that around and come up with the rules first.

The Properties-Based Way

The difficult part is figuring out how to go from our abstract ideas about the program behavior to specific rules expressed as code. Continuing with our cash register example, two rules to encode as properties could be:

- The amount of change is always going to add up to the amount paid minus the price charged.

- The bills and coins handed back for change are going to start from the biggest bill possible first, down to the smallest coin possible. This could alternatively be defined as trying to hand the customer as few individual pieces of money as possible.

Let's assume we magically encode them into functioning Erlang code (doing this for real is what this book is about—we can't show it all in the first chapter). Our test, as a property, could look something like this:

```
for_all(RegisterMoney, PriceToPay, MoneyPaid) ->
    Change = cash(RegisterMoney, PriceToPay, MoneyPaid),
    sum(Change) == MoneyPaid - PriceToPay
    and
    fewest_pieces_possible(RegisterMoney, Change).
```

Given some amount of money in the register, a price to pay, and an amount of money given by the customer, call the cash/3 function, and then check the change given. You can see the two rules encoded there: the first one checking that the change balances, and the second one checking that the smallest amount of bills and coins possible is returned (the implementation of which is not shown).

This property alone is useless. What is needed to make it functional is a property-based testing framework. The framework should figure out how to generate all the inputs required (RegisterMoney, PriceToPay, and MoneyPaid), and then it should run the property against all the inputs it has generated. If the property always remains true, the test is considered successful. If one of the test cases fails, a good property-based testing framework will modify the generated input until it can come up with one that can still provoke the failure, but that is as small as possible—a process called *shrinking*. Maybe it would find a mistake with a cash register that has a billion coins and bills in it, and an order price in the hundreds of thousands of dollars, but could then replicate the same failure with only $5 and a cheap item. If so, our debugging job is made a lot easier by the framework because a simple input means it's way easier to walk the code to figure out what happened.

For example, such a framework could generate inputs giving a call like cash([{1.00, 2}], 1.00, 2.00). Whatever the denomination, we might expect the cash/3 function would return a $1 bill and pass. Sooner or later, it would generate an input such as cash([{5.00, 1}], 20.00, 30.00), and then the program would crash and fail the property because there's not enough change in the register. Paying a $20 purchase with $30, even if the register holds only $5 is entirely possible: take $10 from the $30 and give it back to the customer. Is that specific amount possible to give back though? In real life, yes. We do it all the time. But in our program, since the money taken from the customer does not come in as bills, coins, or any specific denomination, there is no way to use part of the input money to form the output. The interface chosen for this function is wrong, and so are our tests.

Comparing Approaches

Let's take a step back and compare example-based tests with property tests for this specific problem. With the former, even if all the examples we had come up with looked reasonable, we easily found ourselves working within the confines of the code and interface we had established. We were not really testing the code, we were describing its design, making sure it conformed to expectations and demands while making sure we don't slip in the future. This is valuable for sure, but properties gave us something more: they highlighted a failure of imagination.

Example-based unit tests made it easy to lock down bugs we could see coming, but those we couldn't see coming at all were left in place and would probably have made it to production. With properties (and a framework to execute them), we can instead explore the problem space more in depth, and find bugs and design issues much earlier. The math is simple: bugs that make it to production are by definition bugs that we couldn't see coming. If a tool lets us find them earlier, then production will see fewer bugs.

To put it another way, if example-based testing helps ensure that code does what we expect, property-based testing forces the exploration of the program's behavior to see what it can or cannot do, helping find whether our expectations were even right to begin with. In fact, when we test with properties, the design and growth of tests requires an equal part of growth and design of the program itself. A common pattern when a property fails will be to figure out if it's the system that is wrong or if it's our idea of what it should do that needs to change. We'll fix bugs, but we'll also fix our understanding of the problem space. We'll be surprised by how things we thought we knew are far more complex and tricky than we thought, and how often it happens.

That's thinking in properties.

Property-Based Testing in Your Project

What we need now is a framework. As opposed to many testing practices that require a tiny bit of scaffolding and a lot of care, property-based testing is a practice that requires heavy tool assistance. Without a framework we have no way to generate data, and all we're left with are encoded rules that don't get validated. If you use a framework that doesn't generate great data or doesn't let you express the ideas you need, you'll find it very hard to get as high a quality in your tests as you would with a good one.

As the book title implies, we will use PropEr. It can be used by both Erlang and Elixir projects, and integrate with the usual build tools used in both languages. There are other frameworks available, namely QuickCheck framework by Quviq,[8] and Triq. These two frameworks and PropEr are similar enough to each other that if your team is using any of them, you'll be able to follow along with the text without a problem. This remains true if you're using Elixir. You might have heard about StreamData,[9] which is a property-based testing framework exclusive to Elixir (although PropEr has fancier features

---

8. http://quviq.com/
9. https://github.com/whatyouhide/stream_data

than StreamData, particularly in relation to stateful testing). The concepts should not be hard to carry over from framework to framework in any case.

PropEr is usable on its own through either manual calls or command line utils. This is fine for some isolated tests and quick demos, but it's usually nicer to be able to get the framework to fit your everyday development workflow instead.

Erlang Workflow

We'll first get things going in Erlang. You should have the language installed along with the rebar3[10] build tool. If you've used the Common Test or EUnit frameworks before, you may know that you can use rebar3 ct or rebar3 eunit to run the tests for your project. To keep things simple, we'll use a PropEr plugin that will let us call rebar3 proper and get similar results. That way, everyone feels at home even with brand-new tools.

If you're one of the folks who enjoy putting unit tests along with the source code, you need to know that PropEr requires a different approach, more in line with Common Test's vision: tests are in a separate directory and don't become part of the artifacts that could ever end up in production.

Fear Not the GPLv3 License

PropEr is licensed under the GPLv3. People are often worried about having to attach and ship GPL-licensed code with their projects. Placing the tests and dependencies that are related to PropEr in their own directory means that they are only used as development tools in a testing context, and never in production. This is true with rebar3 and for mix as well in Elixir.

As such, whenever you build a release with code to ship and deploy, none of the test code nor PropEr itself will be bundled or linked to your program. This tends to put most corporate lawyers at ease, without preventing the authors from getting contributions back in case the tool is modified or used at the center of a commercial product.

Let's make a fake project out of a template:

```
$ rebar3 new lib pbt
===> Writing pbt/src/pbt.erl
===> Writing pbt/src/pbt.app.src
===> Writing pbt/rebar.config
===> Writing pbt/.gitignore
===> Writing pbt/LICENSE
===> Writing pbt/README.md
$ cd pbt
```

---

10. http://www.rebar3.org/

That's a regular library project named pbt. The PropEr plugin and dependency must be added to the configuration of each individual project you want to use them with. You do this by editing the rebar.config file so it contains the following:

About the Code

 In the snippets that follow, code is labeled with both the language (Erlang and Elixir) and the file where you should put the code if you're following along.

Erlang	code/Foundations/erlang/pbt/rebar.config

```erlang
%% the plugin itself
{project_plugins, [rebar3_proper]}.

%% The PropEr dependency is still required to compile the test cases,
%% but only as a test dependency
{profiles,
    [{test, [
        {erl_opts, [nowarn_export_all]},
        {deps, [proper]}
    ]}
]}.
```

This sets up the PropEr plugin for rebar3 so that we can invoke it from the command line, and sets up the framework as a dependency for our test builds only, and only, within that project. Let's first check that the plugin works by invoking any command:

```
$ rebar3 help proper
≪automatically fetching and building plugin≫
Run PropEr test suites
Usage: rebar3 proper [-d <dir>] [-m <module>] [-p <properties>]
                     [-n <numtests>] [-v <verbose>] [-c [<cover>]]
                     [--retry [<retry>]] [--regressions [<regressions>]]
≪a lot more help output≫
```

The build tool fetches the things it needs, and everything is now available within that directory. We're now ready to write a property, which we can do in the next section, after going over the equivalent setup for Elixir.

Elixir

If you're more familiar with Elixir, you can still use PropEr with mix,[11] Elixir's build tool. By adding the propcheck[12] package to your project configuration, mix will be able to find and execute PropEr properties within the same files as

---

11. http://elixir-lang.github.io/getting-started/mix-otp/introduction-to-mix.html
12. https://hex.pm/packages/propcheck

those that contain standard Elixir test cases written in ExUnit, the language's default test framework.

Once again we'll start by setting up a standard project, this time in Elixir.

```
$ mix new pbt
* creating README.md
* creating .gitignore
* creating mix.exs
* creating config
* creating config/config.exs
* creating lib
* creating lib/pbt.ex
* creating test
* creating test/test_helper.exs
* creating test/pbt_test.exs

Your Mix project was created successfully.
You can use "mix" to compile it, test it, and more:

    cd pbt
    mix test

Run "mix help" for more commands.
$ cd pbt
```

Within that project, modify the mix.exs file to include propcheck dependency for tests:

Elixir	code/Foundations/elixir/pbt/mix.exs

```
# Run "mix help deps" to learn about dependencies.
defp deps do
  [
    {:propcheck, "~> 1.1", only: [:test, :dev]}
  ]
end
```

This makes PropEr available to the tool, and also lets properties be perceived like regular ExUnit unit tests. As such, there's no need to use special commands, just the regular ones you may be used to. To get going we just have to remember to fetch the dependencies:

```
$ mix deps.get
«fetching package»
$  mix test
==> proper
«build information»
==> propcheck
«build information»
==> pbt
«build information»
```

Alright, things seem to be in place there as well. We can now run a property.

Running a Property

The properties we've seen so far were pseudocode-like and left a lot to imagination. Now that we have a stand-in directory structure with a structure similar to what we'd have in a real project, we're going to tie everything together. We'll add a property to the project and execute it. The property will be basic and test nothing of significance, but it'll give you a brief idea of what things look like and how they should all fit together.

Erlang

As mentioned earlier, PropEr's properties are not located within the same module as your production source code. Instead, we'll enforce a strict separation of production code and test code by forcing all properties to be placed in standalone modules under the test/ directory, right next to your Common Test and EUnit test suites, if you have any.

Properties must be added to modules that have a name starting with prop_ (so that the rebar3 plugin picks them up), and are otherwise regular Erlang code. You can add a module named prop_foundations under test/prop_foundations.erl, or you can also use templates to do the same thing for you by calling the following within the pbt/ directory:

```
$ rebar3 new proper foundations
===> Writing test/prop_foundations.erl
```

The file should contain Erlang code similar to the following:

Erlang	code/Foundations/erlang/pbt/test/prop_foundations.erl

```erlang
-module(prop_foundations).
-include_lib("proper/include/proper.hrl").

prop_test() ->
    ?FORALL(Type, term(),
        begin
            boolean(Type)
        end).

boolean(_) -> true.
```

That's what a property looks like. It's regular Erlang code—although a bit macro heavy. Calling the prop_test() function from the shell or any other bit of Erlang code wouldn't do anything useful, but when PropEr gets its hands on it, we have a test. That property always returns true and will always pass.

We'll go through how they work in Chapter 2, *Writing Properties*, on page 17, but for now, let's just ask our build tool to run it:

```
$ rebar3 proper
«build information»
===> Testing prop_foundations:prop_test()
.......................................................................
......................
OK: Passed 100 test(s).
===>
1/1 properties passed
$ rebar3 proper -n 10000
«build information»
===> Testing prop_foundations:prop_test()
.......................................................................
......«a lot more dots»
OK: Passed 10000 test(s).
===>
1/1 properties passed
```

And alright, that's a test. Well, many of them. Each period is a specific test sample, and there are a hundred of them. As you can see in the second command, we can run as many as we want by using the -n argument. We've got 10,000 test cases in ten lines of code! Everything is definitely in its right place.

Elixir

For Elixir, a similar mechanism is required. Properties go in the test/ directory under regular test modules. Open up the file at test/pbt_test.exs that mix created for us, and replace its code with the following:

Elixir	code/Foundations/elixir/pbt/test/pbt_test.exs

```elixir
defmodule PbtTest do
  use ExUnit.Case
  use PropCheck

  property "always works" do
    forall type <- term() do
      boolean(type)
    end
  end

  def boolean(_) do
    true
  end
end
```

The use instructions load the macro definitions that are required, and instead of the test "description" do ... end format required by ExUnit, we use property "description" do ... end to write properties. Within that property, you can probably see the parts that are in common with Erlang.

You can ask mix to run the property for you through the mix test command:

```
$ mix test
  1 defmodule PbtTest do

.

Finished in 0.05 seconds
1 property, 0 failures

Randomized with seed 189382
```

While Erlang's build tool happily writes out one period per property sample, mix will group all of them under a single one if they pass. Aside from that, things are roughly the same. A hundred executions have all been bundled together.

Wrapping Up

We've now gone through a little bit of an overview of what property-based testing asks of us and offers in return, and have things working in a typical project structure for both Erlang and Elixir. You have your toolbox in order, and even though we've successfully run a property (and over 10,000 tests), chances are you're not quite at a point where you feel like you really understand what goes on in the framework and how we could write arbitrary properties.

That's fine, though, because the next chapter will get us there. We'll look into the specific format of properties, how we can tell the framework what data to generate for them, how to interpret test results, and so on.

## CHAPTER 2

Writing Properties

Property-based testing requires us to approach testing differently from what we're used to. As we've seen earlier, the core of properties is coming up with rules about a program that should always remain true. That's the hard part. But just having that will not be enough: we'll need to find a way to turn these rules into executable code, so that a specific framework (PropEr in our case) can exercise them. We will also need to tell the framework about what kind of inputs it should generate so that it can truly challenge the rules, something we call a *generator*. Once we take the rules encoded as code, the generators, and then put them together through the framework, we have a property.

Properties come in multiple flavors, but the two main categories are stateless properties and stateful properties. In traditional example-based testing, it's usually a good idea to start with simple unit tests. In property-based testing, stateless properties are their equivalent. Stateless properties are a great fit to validate components that are isolated, stateless, and without major side effects. They are still usable for more complex stateful integration and system tests, but for those use cases, stateful properties (seen in Chapter 9, *Stateful Properties*, on page 201) are more appropriate.

The properties we've seen and discussed in the previous chapter were all stateless, albeit a bit abstract. In this chapter, we'll make everything concrete and see how stateless properties are structured so that we can read and understand them. We'll also see what data generators are offered out of the box by PropEr, with some ways of composing them together. Finally, we'll run some more properties. This will give us the opportunity to figure out how to read the results of failing test cases and to see how to fix them.

Structure of Properties

Even though this chapter will focus on stateless properties, do know that *all* properties will share a common basic structure. Fancier stateful properties will only add content and special calls, but the core will remain the same. All properties go into files that contain an Erlang (or Elixir) test module, and must respect a specific format. What we'll be looking for here is the structure we'll use within these modules to let PropEr know what the rules to test are, and to let it know how to generate the data it should use to test them.

File Structure

Let's start by taking another look at the code generated within an existing project when using the templates provided by rebar3's PropEr plugin, so that you get a feel for the general way properties should be laid out. In the root of any standard Erlang project, call the following command:

```
$ rebar3 new proper base
===> Writing test/prop_base.erl
```

The generated file contains the prop_base module, a test suite that is divided in three sections: one section for the many properties we will want to test, one for helper functions, and one for custom data generators:

About the Code

 In the snippets that follow, code is labeled with both the language (Erlang and Elixir) and the file where you should put the code if you're following along.

Erlang   code/WritingProperties/erlang/pbt/test/prop_base.erl

```erlang
-module(prop_base).
-include_lib("proper/include/proper.hrl").

%%%%%%%%%%%%%%%%%%%%
%%% Properties %%% %
%%%%%%%%%%%%%%%%%%%%
prop_test() ->
    ?FORALL(Type, mytype(),
        begin
            boolean(Type)
        end).

%%%%%%%%%%%%%%%%
%%% Helpers %%%
%%%%%%%%%%%%%%%%
boolean(_) -> true.
```

```
%%%%%%%%%%%%%%%%%%%
%%% Generators %%%
%%%%%%%%%%%%%%%%%%%
mytype() -> term().
```

The section starting at ❷ is for properties. You can have many properties per module, each within a dedicated function starting with the prop_ prefix. It's usually a good idea to put all the properties at the top of the file, so that whoever maintains your code will have an easy time seeing what's being tested exactly. Here we only have the prop_test() property, but before digging into that one, let's see the other sections of the file.

The two other sections are mostly there to help us organize our code whenever we have multiple properties, and jamming everything into each of them would be too repetitive or unreadable. Here the second section contains helper functions. We'll typically use this part of the file to extract functions that are common to multiple properties, or code that is simply long enough that it hurts readability of the properties themselves. When you have few properties or they're all short, you may want to omit this section.

The last part of the module contains generators. Each generator is a function that returns metadata representing a given type. This is a high-level recipe for data generation, which PropEr knows how to interpret. By default, PropEr provides a bunch of them, but eventually we'll write custom generators. This section's purpose is therefore similar to the helpers sections, but it's dedicated to custom data generators. Whenever the data we need the framework to generate for us becomes fairly complex or shared across properties, moving these generators there will be helpful. We won't need this section for now, but in Chapter 4, *Custom Generators*, on page 51 we'll make use of it.

When a module's main purpose is to expose a bunch of tests or properties, we tend to call it a *test suite*. Not all property test suites have exactly the same structure as the one here, and while some people will prefer a different code organization, this one is the default recommended by the rebar3 templates.

For Elixir users, files can have a similar structure:

Elixir	code/WritingProperties/elixir/pbt/test/pbt_test.exs

```
defmodule PbtTest do
  use ExUnit.Case
  use PropCheck
```

```
# Properties
property "description of what the property does" do
  forall type <- my_type() do
    boolean(type)
  end
end

# Helpers
defp boolean(_) do
  true
end

# Generators
def my_type() do
  term()
end
end
```

But since Elixir properties get to run within the existing ExUnit files your project might have, you will probably want to make the properties work with your existing test module structure instead.

Property Structure

Let's take a look at the prop_test() property. Standing out is the ?FORALL Erlang macro, which has been imported through the module attribute at ❶. The macro has this form:

Erlang

```
?FORALL(InstanceOfType, TypeGenerator,
        PropertyExpression).
```

Elixir

```
property "some description" do
  forall instance_of_type <- type_generator do
    property_expression
  end
end
```

The data for the test case is generated by the functions we will enter in the TypeGenerator position, called the *generators*. The framework will take these generators, execute them, and turn them into actual data, which will then be bound to the InstanceOfType variable. This variable is then made available within PropertyExpression, a piece of arbitrary code that must return true if the test is to pass, or false if it is to fail. Since PropertyExpression is a single expression, you'll frequently see begin...end blocks used in that area to wrap more complex sequences of expressions into a single one.

We can translate the ?FORALL macro:

```
proper:forall(TypeGenerator, fun(InstanceOfType) -> PropertyExpression end).
```

This may feel less magical, and it removes the need for the begin … end expression. But since all property-based testing frameworks in Erlang implement the ?FORALL macro interface, we'll use that format to make sure everyone feels at home.

Execution Model

To figure out what the macro ends up doing at run time, let's see the prop_test() property being tested by the framework:

```
$ rebar3 proper
«build output»
===> Testing prop_base:prop_test()
...........................................................................
```

In this output, PropEr finds our test suite (the prop_base module), finds all the properties it contains—only prop_test() for now—and executes them. Every period represents an instance of PropEr taking our property and testing it against some input. So we have one property run a hundred times, succeeding at every attempt. For each run, PropEr did the following:

1. It expanded the generator (which was defined with the term() function provided by PropEr) to a given piece of data.

2. It passed the expanded data to the property, binding it to the InstanceofType variable.

3. It validated that the actual PropertyExpression returned true.

That term() generator isn't a standard in Erlang. That's where property-based testing frameworks do a bit of magic. The include file directive at the top of the file is causing all of it:

```
-include_lib("proper/include/proper.hrl").
```

The included proper.hrl file contains macro code and inlines and imports multiple functions provided by PropEr. The term() function is actually shorthand for the proper_types:term() function call. Try playing with it in the shell:

```
$ rebar3 as test shell
«build output and shell prelude»
1> proper_types:term().
{'$type',[{env,[{'$type',[{env,{inf,inf}},
                          {generator,{typed,#Fun<proper_types.7.91186128>}},
                          {is_instance,{typed,#Fun<proper_types.8.911818>}},
                          {shrinkers,[#Fun<proper_types.9.91186128>]},
                          [...]
```

This is a high-level recipe for data generation, which PropEr knows how to interpret. To debug generators in the terminal, you can ask PropEr to materialize an instance of the data type through the proper_gen:pick(Generator) function call. Play with it a bit in the shell to get a feel for how things work:

```
2> proper_gen:pick(proper_types:number()).
{ok,-6}
3> proper_gen:pick(proper_types:term()).
{ok,{30,'iPMÒR\237M\203',[],0,-2.3689578345518227,{},
    [[],4,{}],
    -0.04598152960751201}}
4> proper_gen:pick(proper_types:term()).
{ok,['^ l&\212iåx\210\n',1.5133511315056003,
    -8.964623044991622,-49.99970474088979,
    {<<1:1>>,1,5.666317902012531,{}},
    3.799206557402714,-0.5871676980812601,3]}
```

To experiment with Elixir, you should instead call mix deps.get, then MIX_ENV="test" iex -S mix to get a shell, and then call :proper_types.term() and :proper_gen.pick().

Here, each sample is returned in a tuple of the form {ok, Data}. In the first case, number() returns -6. For the two other cases, since term() represents almost *any* Erlang data type (PIDs, for example, are not generated), what we get as a result is utter garbage, which can nevertheless be useful in some cases. The ability to get some sampling of the data generated will prove useful when debugging generators, especially when they grow in complexity later on.

We've just seen number() and term(), but those are only two from a large generator zoo. We should get familiar with more of them, since they end up being pretty critical in properly exercising properties.

Default Generators

Generators are a huge part of where a property-based testing framework's magic comes from. While we do the hard work of coming up with properties, the efficiency with which they will be exercised entirely depends on what kind of inputs will be passed to them. A framework with bad generators is not an interesting framework, and great generators will directly impact how much trust you can put in your tests.

Generators are functions that contain a bunch of internal parameters that direct their randomness, how the data they create gets more or less complex, and information about other generators that can be used as parameters. We really don't need to know how their internals work to use them; from our point of view, they're just functions that can be combined. Being familiar with what data they can generate is, however, important, since it lets us create all the kinds of Erlang data we might need. You'll likely even want to use generators outside of a testing context because they are just that nifty.

PropEr comes with quite a few basic data generators out of the box. They tend to represent all the relevant basic data types of the language (aside from opaque data like PIDs, references, or sockets), with some special ones that allow you to do things such as making sure integers are in a given range, or making one generator that actually represents multiple other generators.

Here are a few of the important ones. A full list is available in Appendix 4, *Generators Reference*, on page 345—it would be a good idea to get familiar with them.

Generator	Data Generated	Sample
any()	Any Erlang term PropEr can produce. Same as term()	any of the samples below
atom()	Erlang atoms	'ós43Úrcá\200'
binary()	Binary data aligned on bytes	<<2,203,162,42,84,141>>
boolean()	Atoms true or false. Also bool()	true, false
choose(Min, Max)	Any integer between Min and Max inclusively. Same as range(Min, Max)	choose(1, 1000) => 596
float()	Floating point number. Also real()	4.982972307245969
integer()	An integer	89234
list(Type)	A list of terms of type Type	list(boolean()) => [true, true, false]
non_empty(Gen)	Constrains a binary or a list generator into not being empty	non_empty(list()) => [abc]
number()	A float or integer	123
range(Min, Max)	Any integer between Min and Max inclusively	range(1, 1000) => 596
string()	Equivalent to list(char()), where 'char()' returns character codepoints between 0 and 1114111 inclusively	"^DQ^W^R/D" (may generate weird escape sequences!)
{T1, T2, ...}	A literal tuple with types in it	{boolean(), char()} => {true, 1}

You don't need to know all of these by heart. Just put a bookmark in the appendix so you have a handy reference, or look at the online documentation for PropEr[1] or Quickcheck[2] when you need to find generators. However, it

---

1. https://proper-testing.github.io/
2. http://quviq.com/documentation/eqc/index.html

may be useful to play with the generators in the Erlang shell to get familiar with them. Try to see the results of typing the previous generators in the shell, and try some of those in the appendix as well:

```
$ rebar3 as test shell
1> proper_gen:pick(proper_types:range(-500,500)).
{ok,-64}
2> proper_gen:pick({proper_types:bool(), proper_types:float()}).
{ok,{true,0.8565227550368821}}
3> {ok,F} = proper_gen:pick(proper_types:function(3, proper_types:list())).
{ok,#Fun<proper_gen.31.64457461>}
4> F(1,2,three).
[[-7,'(\226\212_J',-3,[<<0:3>>,{},[[]],53,'',{[]},-5],á,-1]]
5> proper_gen:pick(proper_types:non_empty(
5>    proper_types:list(proper_types:number())).
{ok,[-38.585674396308065,17,9,-0.17548322369895938,3.7420633140371597]}
```

Even though the proper_types: prefix is required in the shell, it won't be needed in our actual test modules, since the framework will autoimport default generators there.

Ignore the Warnings

When experimenting with generators, you may find yourself faced with a warning like this:

WARNING: Some garbage has been left in the process dictionary and the code server to allow for the returned function(s) to run normally. Please run proper:global_state_erase() when done.

Don't worry, PropEr displays this message in the shell when experimenting. Nothing will stay past the current session in your terminal, and you can usually safely ignore these.

We have the basic syntax of properties with the ?FORALL macro, a bit of an idea about what rules should be like from the previous chapter, and now we're completing the trio with a lexicon of generators that can create arbitrary data. What we need to do now is tie it all together.

Putting It All Together

To get started with writing our own properties, it may be useful to compare them with the type of tests we'd already have in place in an existing project. We'll start with a simple function, one that finds the largest element in a list. Coming up with properties isn't all easy, so beginning with regular tests can sometimes be a good idea since it can at least help us flesh out what we think the code should be doing.

Standard unit tests would probably look a bit like this, using the EUnit syntax:

```
biggest_test() ->
    ?assert(5  =:= biggest([1, 2, 3, 4, 5])),
    ?assert(8  =:= biggest([3, 8, 7, -1])),
    ?assert(-5 =:= biggest([-10, -5, -901])),
    ?assert(0  =:= biggest([0])).
```

With regular unit tests, we put together a list of assertions and hope that it will cover all cases. Here we check for lists that are presorted, lists without any specific order, single-element lists, and lists containing any positive or negative numbers. Are there any other edge cases that could exist? That's hard to say if we don't already know what they could be from experience.

With properties, we should be able to get a far better coverage of edge cases, including those we wouldn't think of by ourselves. For a property, we need to find a rule to describe the behavior of the biggest/1 function according to these examples. The obvious rule is that the function should return the biggest number of the list passed in. The problem is figuring out how to encode that rule into a property. The function is so simple and such a direct implementation of the rule that it's hard to make an encoding of the rule that is not the function itself!

Instead we'll use a second implementation of the function, and use it as a sanity check with the existing one. If both versions agree, they're both possibly right (or equally wrong, so make sure one implementation is obviously correct). Here we'll use lists:last(lists:sort(L)) as a simple way to validate the function. It's not obvious why we're using that call specifically, but we'll get to the rationale behind that in the next chapter. For now, let's focus on getting the thing working:

Erlang	code/WritingProperties/erlang/pbt/test/prop_base.erl

```
prop_biggest() ->
    ?FORALL(List, list(integer()),
        begin
            biggest(List) =:= lists:last(lists:sort(List))
        end).
```

Elixir	code/WritingProperties/elixir/pbt/test/pbt_test.exs

```
property "finds biggest element" do
  forall x <- list(integer()) do
    biggest(x) == List.last(Enum.sort(x))
  end
end
```

All properties must have a name of the form prop_Name() since the harness for PropEr in rebar3 looks at the prop_ prefix, both in the file name and the function, to know which pieces of code to run. For Elixir, propcheck just looks for the property keyword introducing the test in a regular ExUnit file.

The type generator list(integer()) is a composition of types, generating a list of integers for each iteration. We can parameterize type generators whenever it makes sense: a list can take a type as an argument, and so can a tuple, but an integer would not make sense to parameterize. The generated data is then bound to the List variable, which will be used in the property's body. The expression biggest(List) =:= lists:last(lists:sort(List)) will validate the biggest/1 function by comparing that the biggest element of the list is equivalent to the last element of a sorted list. Any expression that may evaluate to true or false can be used in the property body.

The implementation for biggest/1 is left entirely to us, but we should avoid making it use lists:sort/1 and lists:last/1 since that would nullify our test by making the code the same as the test, so if we make a mistake in one place, it's going to be in the other place as well. Here's a possible implementation:

Erlang	code/WritingProperties/erlang/pbt/test/prop_base.erl

```erlang
%%%%%%%%%%%%%%%%
%%% Helpers %%%
%%%%%%%%%%%%%%%%
biggest([Head | _Tail]) ->
    Head.
```

Elixir	code/WritingProperties/elixir/pbt/test/pbt_test.exs

```elixir
def biggest([head | _tail]) do
  head
end
```

This is obviously wrong, since the biggest element is not always going to be the first of the list. Running the tests will only confirm that:

```
$ rebar3 proper
===> Verifying dependencies...
===> Compiling pbt
===> Testing prop_base:prop_biggest()
!
Failed: After 1 test(s).
An exception was raised: error:function_clause.
```

```
① Stacktrace: [{prop_base,biggest,
②                    [[]],
                    [{file,"/.../pbt/test/prop_base.erl"},
                    {line,16}]},
                {prop_base,'-prop_biggest/0-fun-0-',1,
                    [{file,"/.../pbt/test/prop_base.erl"},
                    {line,10}]}].
③ []

Shrinking (0 time(s))
④ []
```

We get an unsurprising failure, after a single run. The PropEr output tells us about which function failed at ❶, with its arguments (as a list) at ❷. We can see the initially failing data set as generated by the framework (❸), and one simplified by the framework—a mechanism called *shrinking*—at ❹. In both cases, the empty list ([]) is displayed since it cannot be simpified any further. In short, our biggest/1 function failed when called with an empty list.

Getting the biggest entry out of an empty list is nonsensical and should reasonably fail. The use case can be ignored by forcing the property to run on nonempty lists:

Erlang	code/WritingProperties/erlang/pbt/test/prop_base.erl

```erlang
-module(prop_base).
-include_lib("proper/include/proper.hrl").

%%%%%%%%%%%%%%%%%%%%
%%% Properties %%%
%%%%%%%%%%%%%%%%%%%%
prop_biggest() ->
①    ?FORALL(List, non_empty(list(integer()))),
        begin
            biggest(List) =:= lists:last(lists:sort(List))
        end).
```

Elixir	code/WritingProperties/elixir/pbt/test/pbt_test.exs

```elixir
use ExUnit.Case
use PropCheck

property "finds biggest element" do
①  forall x <- non_empty(list(integer())) do
     biggest(x) == List.last(Enum.sort(x))
   end
end
```

The non_empty/1 generator on line ❶ wraps the generator for lists of integers so that no empty list comes out. Running the test again, we get these results:

```
$ rebar3 proper
===> Verifying dependencies...
===> Compiling pbt
===> Testing prop_base:prop_biggest()
.........!
Failed: After 10 test(s).
[-1,6,3,1]

Shrinking ...(3 time(s))
[0,1]
===>
0/1 properties passed, 1 failed
===> Failed test cases:
prop_base:prop_biggest() -> false
```

Elixir and Test Repeats

 Elixir users may have to remove the _build/propcheck.ctex file before rerunning tests to ensure fresh runs every time.

Nine tests passed. The tenth one failed. Initially, it did so with the list of numbers [-1,6,3,1]. PropEr then shrunk the list to a simpler expression that triggers the failing case: a list with two numbers, where the second one is bigger than the first one. This is legitimate input causing a legitimate failure. The code needs to be patched:

Erlang   code/WritingProperties/erlang/pbt/test/prop_base.erl

```erlang
%%%%%%%%%%%%%%%%%
%%% Helpers %%%
%%%%%%%%%%%%%%%%%
biggest([Head | Tail]) ->
    biggest(Tail, Head).

biggest([], Biggest) ->
    Biggest;
biggest([Head|Tail], Biggest) when Head > Biggest ->
    biggest(Tail, Head);
biggest([Head|Tail], Biggest) when Head < Biggest ->
    biggest(Tail, Biggest).
```

Elixir   code/WritingProperties/elixir/pbt/test/pbt_test.exs

```elixir
def biggest([head | tail]) do
  biggest(tail, head)
end
```

```elixir
defp biggest([], max) do
  max
end

defp biggest([head | tail], max) when head > max do
  biggest(tail, head)
end

defp biggest([head | tail], max) when head < max do
  biggest(tail, max)
end
```

This code iterates over the entire list while keeping note of the biggest element seen at any given point. Whenever an element is bigger than the noted element, it replaces it. At the end of the iteration, the biggest element seen is returned. With the new implementation, the previous case should be resolved:

```
$ rebar3 proper
===> Verifying dependencies...
===> Compiling pbt
===> Testing prop_base:prop_biggest()
.................!
Failed: After 18 test(s).
An exception was raised: error:function_clause.
Stacktrace: [{prop_base,biggest,
                        [[0,6,2,17],0],
                        [{file,"/.../pbt/test/prop_base.erl"},
                         {line,19}]},
              {prop_base,'-prop_biggest/0-fun-0-',1,
                        [{file,"/.../pbt/test/prop_base.erl"},
                         {line,10}]}].
[0,-4,0,6,2,17]

Shrinking ..(2 time(s))
[0,0]
===>
0/1 properties passed, 1 failed
===> Failed test cases:
  prop_base:prop_biggest() -> false
```

After eighteen runs, PropEr found a bug. The initial failing case was [0,-4,0,6,2,17]. The actual problem with that result is not necessarily obvious. Shrinking however reduces the *counterexample* (the failing case) to [0,0], and the interpretation is simpler: if a list is being analyzed and the currently largest item is equal to the one being looked at (double-check the list of arguments in the stacktrace if this is not clear!), the comparison fails.

A quick patch can address this:

Erlang   code/WritingProperties/erlang/pbt/test/prop_base.erl

```erlang
biggest([Head | Tail]) ->
    biggest(Tail, Head).

biggest([], Biggest) ->
    Biggest;
❶ biggest([Head|Tail], Biggest) when Head >= Biggest ->
    biggest(Tail, Head);
biggest([Head|Tail], Biggest) when Head < Biggest ->
    biggest(Tail, Biggest).
```

Elixir   code/WritingProperties/elixir/pbt/test/pbt_test.exs

```elixir
def biggest([head | tail]) do
  biggest(tail, head)
end

defp biggest([], max) do
  max
end
❶ defp biggest([head | tail], max) when head >= max do
  biggest(tail, head)
end

defp biggest([head | tail], max) when head < max do
  biggest(tail, max)
end
```

The > operator is changed for >= at ❶ in order to handle equality. The property finally holds:

```
$ rebar3 proper
===> Verifying dependencies...
===> Compiling pbt
===> Testing prop_base:prop_biggest()
....................................................................
...................
OK: Passed 100 test(s).
===>
1/1 properties passed
```

We're all good! We can trust our function to be alright.

Most of the development that takes place for stateless properties follows that iterative pattern: write a property you feel makes sense, then throw it against your code. Whenever there's a failure, figure out if the property itself is wrong (as when we added the non_empty() generator), or if the program itself is wrong. Modify either according to your needs.

Wrapping Up

You should now be good with knowing the basic syntax and operation of stateless properties. We've seen how the modules that contain properties tend to be structured, the syntax of a basic property, a bunch of generators to describe the data our properties will need and how to run them, and then how to debug our tests when they fail.

Writing more properties on your own should not technically be a problem, although it may prove challenging to figure out exactly what it is that makes a good property and how to come up with one. The next chapter will help by showing multiple strategies that are useful when trying to translate a rule into a property.

Exercises

Question 1

What function can you call to get a sample of a generator's data?

Solution on page 311.

Question 2

Explain what the following property could be testing or demonstrating:

Erlang	code/WritingProperties/erlang/pbt/test/prop_exercises.erl

```erlang
prop_a_sample() ->
    ?FORALL({Start,Count}, {integer(), non_neg_integer()},
        begin
            List = lists:seq(Start, Start+Count),
            Count+1 =:= length(List)
            andalso
            increments(List)
        end).

increments([Head | Tail]) -> increments(Head, Tail).

increments(_, []) -> true;
increments(N, [Head|Tail]) when Head == N+1 -> increments(Head, Tail);
increments(_, _) -> false.
```

Elixir	code/WritingProperties/elixir/pbt/test/exercises_test.exs

```elixir
property "exercise 2: a sample" do
  forall {start, count} <- {integer(), non_neg_integer()} do
    list = Enum.to_list(start..(start + count))
    count + 1 == length(list) and increments(list)
  end
end

def increments([head | tail]), do: increments(head, tail)

defp increments(_, []), do: true

defp increments(n, [head | tail]) when head == n + 1,
  do: increments(head, tail)

defp increments(_, _), do: false
```

Feel free to add output and then run it to see it execute. Do note that adding output may generate a lot of noise, so you may want to limit the number of tests for each call to make it easier to check things one bit at a time.

Solution on page 311.

## CHAPTER 3

Thinking in Properties

In the last chapter, we went over basic properties, including their syntax and generators that are available out of the box. We played with the biggest(List) function, ensuring it behaved properly. You may now have a good idea of what a property looks like and how to read it, but chances are you don't feel comfortable writing your own; it can take a long time to feel like you know how to write *effective* properties. All things considered, a big part of being good at coming up with properties is a question of experience: do it over and over again and keep trying your hand at it until it feels natural. That would usually take a long time, but we're going to try to speed things up.

Writing good properties is challenging and requires more effort than standard tests, but this chapter should provide some help. We're going to go through techniques that make the transition from using standard tests to thinking in properties feel natural. You'll become more efficient at progressing from having vague ideas of what your program should do to knowing how it should behave through well-defined properties.

We'll go over a few tips and tricks to help us figure out how to write decent enough properties in tricky situations. First, we'll try *modeling* our code, so we can skip over a lot of the challenging thinking that would otherwise be required. When that doesn't work, we'll try generalizing properties out of traditional example-based cases, which will help us determine the rules underpinning our expectations. Another approach we'll use is finding invariants so that we can ratchet up from trivial properties into a solid test suite. Finally, we'll implement symmetric properties as a kind of easy cheat code for some specific problems.

Modeling

Modeling essentially requires you to write an indirect and very simple implementation of your code—often an algorithmically inefficient one—and pit it against the real implementation. The model should be so simple that it is obviously correct. You can then optimize the real system as much as you want: as long as both implementations behave the same way, there's a good chance that the complex one is as good as the obviously correct one, but faster. So for code that does a conceptually simple thing, modeling is useful.

Let's revisit the biggest/1 function from last chapter and put it in its own module:

About the Code

 In the snippets that follow, code is labeled with both the language (Erlang and Elixir) and the file where you should put the code if you're following along.

Erlang   code/ThinkingInProperties/erlang/pbt/src/thinking.erl

```erlang
-module(thinking).
-export([biggest/1]).

biggest([Head | Tail]) ->
    biggest(Tail, Head).

biggest([], Biggest) ->
    Biggest;
biggest([Head|Tail], Biggest) when Head >= Biggest ->
    biggest(Tail, Head);
biggest([Head|Tail], Biggest) when Head < Biggest ->
    biggest(Tail, Biggest).
```

Elixir   code/ThinkingInProperties/elixir/pbt/lib/pbt.ex

```elixir
defmodule Pbt do
  def biggest([head | tail]) do
    biggest(tail, head)
  end

  defp biggest([], max) do
    max
  end

  defp biggest([head | tail], max) when head >= max do
    biggest(tail, head)
  end

  defp biggest([head | tail], max) when head < max do
    biggest(tail, max)
  end

end
```

The function iterates over the list in a single pass: the largest value seen is held in memory and replaced any time a larger one is spotted. Once the list has been fully scanned, the largest value seen so far is also the largest value of the list. That value is returned, and everything is fine.

The challenge is coming up with a good property for it. The obvious rule to encode is that the function should return the biggest number of the list passed in. The problem with this obvious rule is that it's hard to encode: the biggest/1 function is so simple and such a direct implementation of the rule that it's hard to make a property that is not going to be a copy of the function itself. Doing so would not be valuable, because we're likely to repeat the same mistakes in both places, so we might as well not test it.

In these cases, modeling is a good idea. So for this function, we need to come up with an alternative implementation that we can trust to be correct to make the property work. Here's the property for this case:

Erlang   code/ThinkingInProperties/erlang/pbt/test/prop_thinking.erl

```erlang
-module(prop_thinking).
-include_lib("proper/include/proper.hrl").

%%%%%%%%%%%%%%%%%%%%
%%% Properties %%%
%%%%%%%%%%%%%%%%%%%%

prop_biggest() ->
    ?FORALL(List, non_empty(list(integer()))),
        begin
            thinking:biggest(List) =:= model_biggest(List)
        end).
```

Elixir   code/ThinkingInProperties/elixir/pbt/test/pbt_test.exs

```elixir
property "finds biggest element" do
  forall x <- non_empty(list(integer())) do
    Pbt.biggest(x) == model_biggest(x)
  end
end
```

Most modeling approaches will look like that one. The crucial part is the model, represented by model_biggest/1. To implement the model, we can pick standard library functions to give us our alternative, slower, but so-simple-it-must-be-correct implementation:

Erlang

```erlang
model_biggest(List) ->
    lists:last(lists:sort(List)).
```

Elixir

```elixir
def model_biggest(list) do
  List.last(Enum.sort(list))
end
```

Since sorting a list orders all its elements from the smallest one to the largest one possible, picking the last element of the list should logically give us the biggest list entry. Running the property shows that it is good enough:

```
$ rebar3 proper -p prop_biggest
===> Verifying dependencies...
===> Compiling pbt
===> Testing prop_thinking:prop_biggest()
...................................................................
..................................
OK: Passed 100 test(s).
===>
1/1 properties passed
```

Chances are pretty much null that all the functions involved are buggy enough that we can't trust our test to be useful and it only passes by accident. In fact, as a general rule when modeling, we can assume that our code implementation is going to be as reliable as the model to which we compare it. That's why you should always aim to have models so simple they are obviously correct. In the case of biggest/1, it's now as trustworthy as lists:sort/1 and lists:last/1.

Modeling is also useful for integration tests of stateful systems with lots of side effects or dependencies, where "how the system does something" is complex, but "what the user perceives" is simple. Real-world libraries or systems often hide such complexities from the user to appear useful at all. Databases, for example, can do a lot of fancy operations to maintain transactional semantics, avoid loss of data, and keep good performance, but a lot of these operations can be modeled with simple in-memory data structures accessed sequentially.

Finally, there's a rare but great type of modeling that may be available, called the *oracle*. An oracle is a reference implementation, possibly coming from a different language or software package, that can therefore act as a prewritten model. The only thing required to test the system is to compare your implementation with the oracle and ensure they behave the same way.

If you can find a way to model your program, you can get pretty reliable tests that are easy to understand. You have to be careful about performance—if your so-simple-it-is-correct implementation is dead slow, so will your tests be—but models are often a good way to get started.

Generalizing Example Tests

Modeling tends to work well, as long as it is possible to write the same program multiple times, and as long as one of the implementations is so simple it is obviously correct. This is not always practical, and sometimes not possible. We need to find better properties. That's significantly harder than finding *any* property, which can already prove difficult and requires a solid understanding of the problem space. A good trick to find a property is to just start by writing a regular unit test and then abstract it away. We can take the steps that are common to coming up with all individual examples and replace them with generators.

In the previous section, we said that biggest/1 is as reliable as lists:sort/1 and lists:last/1, the two functions we used to model it in its property. Our model's correctness entirely depends on these two functions doing the right thing. To make sure they're well-behaved, we'll write some tests demonstrating they work as expected. Let's see how we can write a property for lists:last/1. This function is so simple that we can consider it to be axiomatic—just assume it's correct—and a fundamental block of the system. For this kind of function, traditional unit tests are usually a good fit since it's easy to come up with examples that should be significant. We can also transform examples into a property. After all, if we can get a property to do the work for us, we'll have thousands of examples instead of the few we'd come up with, and that's objectively better coverage.

Let's take a look at what example tests could look like for lists:last/1, so that we can generalize them into a property:

```
last_test() ->
    ?assert(-23 =:= lists:last([-23])),
    ?assert(5 =:= lists:last([1,2,3,4,5])),
    ?assert(3 =:= lists:last([5,4,3])).
```

We can write this test by hand:

1. Construct a list by picking a bunch of numbers.

   - Pick a first number.
   - Pick a second number.
   - ...
   - Pick a last number.

2. Take note of the last number in the list as the expected one.

3. Check that the value expected is the one obtained.

Since the last substep of *1.* ("Pick a last number.") is the one we really want to focus on, we can break it from the other substeps by using some clever generator usage. If we group all of the initial substeps in a list and isolate the last one, we get something like {list(number()), number()}. Here it is used in a property:

Erlang   code/ThinkingInProperties/erlang/pbt/test/prop_thinking.erl

```erlang
prop_last() ->
    %% pick a list and a last number
    ?FORALL({List, KnownLast}, {list(number()), number()},
        begin
            KnownList = List ++ [KnownLast], % known number appended to list
            KnownLast =:= lists:last(KnownList) % known last number is found
        end).
```

Elixir   code/ThinkingInProperties/elixir/pbt/test/pbt_test.exs

```elixir
property "picks the last number" do
  forall {list, known_last} <- {list(number()), number()} do
    known_list = list ++ [known_last]
    known_last == List.last(known_list)
  end
end
```

And just like that, we'll get hundreds or even millions of example cases instead of a few unit tests all done by hand. Of course, we now have to believe the ++ operator will correctly append items to a list if we want to trust this new property. We're getting pulled in deeper: is it possible to make a model out of it? Can it be turned into a simpler property, or just tested with traditional unit tests? This is ultimately a question about which parts of the system you just trust to be correct, and that is left for you to decide. It's challenging to write a lot of significant tests for very simple cases, but the next technique can help.

Invariants

Some programs and functions are complex to describe and reason about. They could be needing a ton of small parts to all work right for the whole to be correct, or we may not be able to assert their quality because it is just hard to define. For example, it's hard to say why a meal is good, but it might include criteria like: the ingredients are cooked adequately, the food is hot enough, it's not too salty, not too sweet, not too bitter, it's well-presented, the portion size is reasonable, and so on. Those factors are all easier to measure objectively and can be a good proxy for "the customer will enjoy the food." In a software system, we can identify similar conditions or facts that should always remain true. We call them *invariants*, and testing for them is a great way to get around the fact that things may just be ambiguous otherwise.

If an invariant were to be false at any time, you would know something is messed up. Seriously messed up. Here are some examples:

- A store cannot sell more items than it has in stock.

- In a binary search tree, the left child is smaller and the right child is greater than their parent's value.

- Once you insert a record in a database, you should be able to read it back and not see it as missing.

A single invariant on its own is usually not enough to show a piece of code is working as expected. But if we can come up with many invariants and small things to validate, and if they *all* always remain true, we can gain a lot more confidence in the ability of our code base to work well. Strong ropes are built from smaller threads put together. In papers or proofs about why a given data structure works, you'll find that almost all aspects of its success comes from ensuring a few invariants are respected.

For property-based testing, we can write a lot of simple properties, each representing one invariant. As we add more and more of them, we can build a strong test suite that overall demonstrates that our code is rock solid.

The lists:sort/1 function is a good example of a piece of code that could be checked with invariants. How can we identify the invariants though? We could pick the first one by saying "a sorted list has all the numbers in it ordered from smallest to largest." The problem is that this is such a complete and accurate description of the whole function that if we used it as an invariant, we'd need a complete sorting function to test it. This is circular as it boils down to saying "a proper sort function is a function that sorts properly." A test that is written the same way as the code it tests is not useful.

Instead we should try to break it down into smaller parts. Something like "each number in a sorted list is smaller than (or equal to) the one that follows." The difference is small, but important. In the first case, we declare the final state of the entire list, the intended outcome. In the latter case, we mention an invariant that should be true of any pair of elements, and not the whole output. We can do an entirely local verification without having the whole picture. Then, when we apply the property to every pair, we indirectly test for a fully ordered output:

Erlang   code/ThinkingInProperties/erlang/pbt/test/prop_thinking.erl

```erlang
prop_sort() ->
    ?FORALL(List, list(term()),
            is_ordered(lists:sort(List))).

is_ordered([A,B|T]) ->
    A =< B andalso is_ordered([B|T]);
is_ordered(_) -> % lists with fewer than 2 elements
    true.
```

Elixir   code/ThinkingInProperties/elixir/pbt/test/pbt_test.exs

```elixir
property "a sorted list has ordered pairs" do
  forall list <- list(term()) do
    is_ordered(Enum.sort(list))
  end
end

def is_ordered([a, b | t]) do
  a <= b and is_ordered([b | t])
end

# lists with fewer than 2 elements
def is_ordered(_) do
  true
end
```

Not bad. A good side effect of this approach is that the implementation is almost guaranteed to be different from the test: we only validated that some property held, and didn't transform the input at all. No modeling is involved here. As mentioned earlier though, a single invariant isn't very solid. If we'd written a sort function as follows, it would always pass:

```
sort(_) -> [].
```

We need more invariants to ensure the implementation is right. We can look for other properties that should always be true and easy to check. Here are some examples:

- The sorted and unsorted lists should both have the same size.

- Any element in the sorted list has to have its equivalent in the unsorted list (no element added).

- Any element in the unsorted list has to have its equivalent in the sorted list (no element dropped).

Let's see how these could be implemented:

Erlang   code/ThinkingInProperties/erlang/pbt/test/prop_thinking.erl

```erlang
%% @doc the sorted and unsorted list should both remain the same size
prop_same_size() ->
    ?FORALL(L, list(number()),
            length(L) =:= length(lists:sort(L))).

%% @doc any element in the sorted list has to have its equivalent in
%% the unsorted list
prop_no_added() ->
    ?FORALL(L, list(number()),
        begin
            Sorted = lists:sort(L),
            lists:all(fun(Element) -> lists:member(Element, L) end, Sorted)
        end).

%% @doc any element in the unsorted list has to have its equivalent in
%% the sorted list
prop_no_removed() ->
    ?FORALL(L, list(number()),
        begin
            Sorted = lists:sort(L),
            lists:all(fun(Element) -> lists:member(Element, Sorted) end, L)
        end).
```

Elixir   code/ThinkingInProperties/elixir/pbt/test/pbt_test.exs

```elixir
property "a sorted list keeps its size" do
  forall l <- list(number()) do
    length(l) == length(Enum.sort(l))
  end
end

property "no element added" do
  forall l <- list(number()) do
    sorted = Enum.sort(l)
    Enum.all?(sorted, fn element -> element in l end)
  end
end

property "no element deleted" do
  forall l <- list(number()) do
    sorted = Enum.sort(l)
    Enum.all?(l, fn element -> element in sorted end)
  end
end
```

That's better. Now it's harder to cheat your way through the properties, and we can trust our tests:

```
$ rebar3 proper
«build output»
===> Testing prop_sort:prop_sort()
....................................................................
............................
OK: Passed 100 test(s).
===> Testing prop_sort:prop_same_size()
....................................................................
............................
OK: Passed 100 test(s).
===> Testing prop_sort:prop_no_added()
....................................................................
............................
OK: Passed 100 test(s).
===> Testing prop_sort:prop_no_removed()
....................................................................
............................
OK: Passed 100 test(s).
===>
4/4 properties passed
```

Each of these properties is pretty simple on its own, but they make a solid suite against almost any sorting function. Another great aspect is that some invariants are easy to think about, are usually fast to validate, and are almost always going to be useful as a sanity check, no matter what. They will combine well with every other testing approach you can think of.

A small gotcha here is that our tests now depend on other functions from the lists module. This brings us back to the discussion on when to stop, since we need to trust these other functions if we want our own tests to be trustworthy. We could just call the shots and say we trust them, especially since they are given to us by the language designers. It's a calculated risk. But there's another interesting approach we could use by testing them all at once.

Symmetric Properties

From time to time, you may find it difficult to figure out which component depends on which other one to succeed. Two bits of code may perform opposite actions, such as an encoder and a decoder. You need the encoder to test the decoder, and the decoder to test the encoder. In other cases, you may have a chain of operations that could be made reversible: editing text and undoing changes, translating text from French to English to Spanish and back to French, passing a message across multiple servers until it's back to its original one, or having a character in a game walking in all directions until it makes its way back to its origin.

Whenever you have a reversible sequence of actions that you can assemble together, you can write one of the most concise types of properties: *symmetric properties*. Symmetric properties' trick is that you test all of these moving parts at once; if one action is the opposite of the other, then applying both operations should yield the initial input as its final output. You pass in some data, apply the reversible sequence of operations, and check that you get the initial data back. If it's the same, then all the parts must fit well together.

Let's say we have a piece of code that does encoding and decoding. We could write the following property for it:

```
prop_symmetric() ->
    ?FORALL(Data, list({atom(), any()}),
        Data =:= decode(encode(Data))).
```

This property demonstrates that a list of key and value pairs can go a round of encoding and decoding without changing, showing that our encoding and decoding mechanisms are stable and lossless. If you're a proponent of test-driven development's approach of "make the test pass really simply, and then refactor," then you know you'll be able to defeat this test by writing an implementation like this one:

```
encode(T) -> T.
decode(T) -> T.
```

The property will pass all the time. The problem is that while the chosen property is useful, it isn't sufficient on its own to be a good test of encoding and decoding. It checks that the encoding and decoding together don't lose any information, but we don't have anything to check that data actually gets encoded at all. An additional property of encoding could be added to the same test:

Erlang	code/ThinkingInProperties/erlang/pbt/test/prop_thinking.erl

```
prop_symmetric() ->
    ?FORALL(Data, list({atom(), any()}),
        begin
            Encoded = encode(Data), is_binary(Encoded) andalso
            Data =:= decode(Encoded)
        end).
```

```
Elixir                    code/ThinkingInProperties/elixir/pbt/test/pbt_test.exs
```

```
property "symmetric encoding/decoding" do
  forall data <- list({atom(), any()}) do
    encoded = encode(data)
    is_binary(encoded) and data == decode(encoded)
  end
end
```

The is_binary(Encoded) call forces the encoder to at least transform something. The encoder decoder may now need to look like this:

```
Erlang
```

```
%% Take a shortcut by using Erlang primitives
encode(T) -> term_to_binary(T).
decode(T) -> binary_to_term(T).
```

```
Elixir
```

```
def encode(t), do: :erlang.term_to_binary(t)
def decode(t), do: :erlang.binary_to_term(t)
```

Other properties could include ideas like "only ASCII characters are used," or "the returned binary value has proper byte alignment." Those would be invariants, which *anchor* broad generic properties with the specifics of a given implementation. Traditional tests are also a good way to anchor broad tests, and they may be simpler to come up with as well.

The invariants will show that each individual part of the chain does some things right, and none are flat-out broken. The symmetric properties will show that all the distinct parts must compose and play well together, and that overall, a large part of our implementation has to be reasonable. With both types of properties, we have some very minimalistic tests that show that a lot of stuff must be going right in our system; we get large coverage with almost no effort.

Putting It All Together

We've written a good lot of properties in this chapter covering multiple techniques, and they've been a bit all over the place. Let's put them back into the context of the full test suite so we can give them a once-over:

| Erlang | code/ThinkingInProperties/erlang/pbt/test/prop_thinking.erl |

```erlang
-module(prop_thinking).
-include_lib("proper/include/proper.hrl").

%%%%%%%%%%%%%%%%%%%%%
%%% Properties %%%
%%%%%%%%%%%%%%%%%%%%%

prop_biggest() ->
    ?FORALL(List, non_empty(list(integer())),
        begin
            thinking:biggest(List) =:= model_biggest(List)
        end).

prop_last() ->
    %% pick a list and a last number
    ?FORALL({List, KnownLast}, {list(number()), number()},
        begin
            KnownList = List ++ [KnownLast], % known number appended to list
            KnownLast =:= lists:last(KnownList) % known last number is found
        end).

prop_sort() ->
    ?FORALL(List, list(term()),
            is_ordered(lists:sort(List))).

%% @doc the sorted and unsorted list should both remain the same size
prop_same_size() ->
    ?FORALL(L, list(number()),
            length(L) =:= length(lists:sort(L))).

%% @doc any element in the sorted list has to have its equivalent in
%% the unsorted list
prop_no_added() ->
    ?FORALL(L, list(number()),
        begin
            Sorted = lists:sort(L),
            lists:all(fun(Element) -> lists:member(Element, L) end, Sorted)
        end).

%% @doc any element in the unsorted list has to have its equivalent in
%% the sorted list
prop_no_removed() ->
    ?FORALL(L, list(number()),
        begin
            Sorted = lists:sort(L),
            lists:all(fun(Element) -> lists:member(Element, Sorted) end, L)
        end).
```

```erlang
prop_symmetric() ->
    ?FORALL(Data, list({atom(), any()}),
        begin
            Encoded = encode(Data), is_binary(Encoded) andalso
            Data =:= decode(Encoded)
        end).

%%%%%%%%%%%%%%%
%%% Helpers %%%
%%%%%%%%%%%%%%%
model_biggest(List) ->
    lists:last(lists:sort(List)).

is_ordered([A,B|T]) ->
    A =< B andalso is_ordered([B|T]);
is_ordered(_) -> % lists with fewer than 2 elements
    true.

%% Take a shortcut by using Erlang primitives
encode(T) -> term_to_binary(T).
decode(T) -> binary_to_term(T).

%%%%%%%%%%%%%%%%%%
%%% Generators %%%
%%%%%%%%%%%%%%%%%%

%% nothing!
```

Elixir translation on page 325.

As you can see, the structure shown here is similar to what was introduced in *Structure of Properties*, on page 18. Because there are many properties, it's simpler to scan them all if they're all in one section. Helpers are put together, even if there's no reuse across properties for now; with most editors or IDEs, it'll be easy to jump from a property to its helpers anyway, and a familiar structure for most suites will help readability.

Interesting in the suite is prop_biggest(), which was our initial model-based property. We then added almost half a dozen other related properties, extending the model we used, to gain more confidence that it is reliable. The examples here are simple enough, and in a larger system the same approach is entirely desirable. It's hard to make one good solid property that covers everything, the same way it's hard to write one big function that does everything.

This last tip could prove helpful. Testing is like writing regular code: when the problem appears to be complex, don't try to have one big property that validates everything at once. It is often simpler to break things up and attack one chunk at a time. Have multiple property tests for each of the properties you can identify in your code. Use two or three shorter and concise properties to make the overall test suite much clearer (and faster) than a large convoluted one, especially for debugging. Also use this strategy to build a suite progressively, rather than all at once and hoping it's good enough.

Wrapping Up

In this chapter, you've seen multiple ways to come up with properties. We've been over modeling our system with a simpler or alternative implementation and checking that they both work the same, and you've seen how example tests could be generalized to the point where their creation is automated. We've also looked at how multiple small invariants can be put together to make a test more solid, and finished up with some symmetric properties. For most properties, any of these four approaches will represent a decent starting point if you're unsure how to get going.

We'll have plenty of chances to put these ideas into practice. But you'll soon see that some properties are hard to test with just the default generators: if you want to focus on a behavior for a specific class of input, then very broad generators are not the best method. In the next chapter, we'll see how to efficiently drill down into the data generation phase of properties, improving our tests with custom generators.

Exercises

Question 1

What are three types of strategies that can be used to help design properties?

Solution on page 311.

Question 2

Using prop_sort() as a source of inspiration, write some properties to show that lists:keysort/2 works properly.

Solution on page 312.

Question 3

The following property uses a model to validate that it works fine. However, the property is failing. Can you figure out if the model or the system under test is to blame? Can you fix it?

Erlang   code/ThinkingInProperties/erlang/pbt/test/prop_exercises.erl

```erlang
prop_set_union() ->
    ?FORALL({ListA, ListB}, {list(number()), list(number())},
        begin
            SetA = sets:from_list(ListA),
            SetB = sets:from_list(ListB),
            ModelUnion = lists:sort(ListA ++ ListB),
            lists:sort(sets:to_list(sets:union(SetA, SetB))) =:= ModelUnion
        end).
```

Elixir   code/ThinkingInProperties/elixir/pbt/test/exercise_test.exs

```elixir
property "set union" do
  forall {list_a, list_b} <- {list(number()), list(number())} do
    set_a = MapSet.new(list_a)
    set_b = MapSet.new(list_b)
    model_union = Enum.sort(list_a ++ list_b)

    res =
      MapSet.union(set_a, set_b)
      |> MapSet.to_list()
      |> Enum.sort()

    res == model_union
  end
end
```

Solution on page 314.

Question 4

The following property verifies that two dictionaries being merged results in each of the entries being in there only once, without conflict, by comparing each of the keys is present:

Erlang   code/ThinkingInProperties/erlang/pbt/test/prop_exercises.erl

```erlang
prop_dict_merge() ->
    ?FORALL({ListA, ListB}, {list({term(), term()}), list({term(), term()})},
        begin
            Merged = dict:merge(fun(_Key, V1, _V2) -> V1 end,
                                dict:from_list(ListA),
                                dict:from_list(ListB)),
            extract_keys(lists:sort(dict:to_list(Merged)))
            ==
            lists:usort(extract_keys(ListA ++ ListB))
        end).

extract_keys(List) -> [K || {K,_} <- List].
```

Elixir	code/ThinkingInProperties/elixir/pbt/test/pbt_test.exs

```elixir
property "merge dictionaries" do
  forall {list_a, list_b} <-
          {list({term(), term()}), list({term(), term()})} do
    merged =
      Map.merge(Map.new(list_a), Map.new(list_b), fn _k,v1,_v2 -> v1 end)

    extract_keys(Enum.sort(Map.to_list(merged))) ==
      Enum.sort(Enum.uniq(extract_keys(list_a ++ list_b)))
  end
end

def extract_keys(list), do: for({k, _} <- list, do: k)
```

Our code reviewers, however, assert that the test is not solid enough because it only superficially tests the result of merging both dictionaries. What parts of its inputs and outputs are not being validated properly, and how would you improve it?

Solution on page 314.

Question 5

Write a function that counts the number of words in a given string of text, and write a property that validates its implementation. Only consider spaces (' ') to be word separators.

Solution on page 314.

## CHAPTER 4

Custom Generators

You've now seen how to write properties, use default generators, and, by using the tips we've covered, come up with new properties. If you were to use only these tools, chances are you'd already be able to improve things quite a bit in the tests you have in your existing projects, but properties can get much more useful.

For our properties to be even more useful, we may need to get fancier. In the previous chapter, we saw how to test an encoder and a decoder with symmetric properties, but say we suspected there was a bug whenever there are more than 255 elements in a map (255 being a number that could hit the upper limits of what a *byte* can store). Would you know how to validate that your property generates any of these elements? Would you know how to generate that data at all if it weren't there already?

Put another way, the properties we've written so far have relied on fairly random generated data to act as inputs. The theory is that with enough random walks, we can eventually get into every nook and cranny of the code and find all the edge cases. But there's no guarantee that this will ever happen. In fact the opposite could be true: since the runs are limited, and given that edge cases are rare, random data could effectively be just average at finding bugs. For example, let's imagine we have a system that has a subtle bug that only gets triggered when a key gets overwritten too many times in a database. If PropEr generates sequences of random keys for our properties, chances are that few of them will be duplicates. If the keys generated are almost never duplicates, our property is unlikely to exercise overwrites at all, and therefore unlikely to ever uncover the bug. We have to differentiate between variety of data inputs and variety of operations.

In this chapter, we'll see what makes a generator tick. We'll get to play with all kinds of ways to generate the best data available for our tests: managing their size, applying arbitrary transformations on the data, preventing some values from being possible, controlling their distribution, handling recursive generators, and representing generators as symbolic calls. But first, let's take a look at evaluating the quality and fitness of our generators, to know which of these techniques we should apply.

The Limitations of Default Generators

Default generators as we have used them are critical building blocks for our properties. They cover a large potential data space, which is absolutely useful in some types of tests. The properties that could be interesting to us may however require a very narrow focus on some limited edge cases. Generators covering a large data space can be useful to discover unexpected issues and problems, but possibly not great at exploring tricky areas known to likely contain bugs in our programs.

Let's say that we're writing a list of key and value pairs to insert in a map, and we want to make sure that as long as we enter keys and values in there, all the keys will be found in the map. We may get a property that looks a bit like this:

Erlang

```erlang
prop_dupes() ->
    ?FORALL(KV, list({key(), val()}),
        begin
            M = maps:from_list(KV),
            [maps:get(K, M) || {K, _V} <- KV], % crash if K's not in map
            true
        end).
key() -> integer().
val() -> term().
```

Elixir

```elixir
property "find all keys in a map even when dupes are used" do
  forall kv <- list({key(), val()}) do
    m = Map.new(kv)
    for {k,_v} <- kv, do: Map.fetch!(m, k)
    true
  end
end

def key(), do: integer()
def val(), do: term()
```

First of all, you may have noticed that this property uses custom functions for generators; that's entirely legal. Any function can be used to wrap generators up into a higher-level, more descriptive construct, and I encourage you to do so when you can. This property works fine, but if you were to implement maps:from_list/1, you might ask yourself questions about what happens when the list is large or when keys are duplicated. How would you go about measuring that? And if the numbers are wrong, how would you go about fixing it?

To know if there's a problem, you could jump into the shell and do some sampling:

```
$ rebar3 as test shell
«build info»
1> proper_gen:sample(proper_types:list(
1>     {prop_generators:key(), prop_generators:val()}
1> )).
[{-5,-7}]
[{2,<<40,97,2,213,1:1>>},
 {5,[{{},11,0,-12,{},'\034\202g\204jÿ?»4·à'},<<104:7>>]},
 {70,<<1:1>>},
 {1,[{'h\231U',{}},{},[]]},
 {7,
  {-4.2121702104995915,
   <<225,143,31,32,72:7>>,
   -2.9483965331393125,'\216´_\205£4¢mwr\210',-1.0863023018036206,
   'ÉÏ»<\235½'}}]
«a lot more output»
```

The problem here is that it's not obvious whether things are repeated or not, or how this approach would compare to running the property 10,000 times, and it requires some programmer discipline to keep checking and analyzing these things over time as people modify and refactor code and tests. Instead, the gathering of statistics is something that should be built directly into our tests.

Gathering Statistics

While there's nothing wrong with using in-shell samples to get a quick feel for how things work, a more pragmatic approach is to display values every time we run the tests, so that we can know at a glance whether anything looks odd or out of place. There are two functions that can be used for this: collect/2 and aggregate/2.

We'll focus on collect/2 first, since it's a bit more specific and straightforward, and then expand to aggregate/2.

Collecting

The collect(Value, PropertyResult) function allows you to gather the values of one specific metric per test and build stats out of all the runs that happened for a property. It's special in that you need to use it to wrap the actual property result and add context to it:

About the Code

 In the snippets that follow, code is labeled with both the language (Erlang and Elixir) and the file where you should put the code if you're following along.

Erlang   code/CustomGenerators/erlang/pbt/test/prop_generators.erl

```erlang
prop_collect1() ->
    ?FORALL(Bin, binary(), collect(byte_size(Bin), is_binary(Bin))).
```

Elixir   code/CustomGenerators/elixir/pbt/test/generators_test.exs

---

```elixir
# make verbose for metrics
property "collect 1", [:verbose] do
  forall bin <- binary() do
    #        test              metric
    collect(is_binary(bin), byte_size(bin))
  end
end
```

The first argument is the metric from which you want to build statistics—here it's the binary's length—and the second argument is the result of the property. Under the hood, collect/2 takes both values and wraps them up in a way that lets PropEr both gather the metrics and validate the properties.

If we run the property, we see:

```
$ rebar3 proper
«build output»
===> Testing prop_generators:prop_collect1()
«build output»
OK: Passed 100 test(s).

10% 2
7% 0
7% 3
6% 1
6% 6
6% 9
6% 11
5% 7
«more statistics»
```

It works! Except that in this case, the statistics are not really convincing since we just get individual numbers with limited repetitions. If we instead group the values by a given range (by groups of 10), we get better results:

Erlang   code/CustomGenerators/erlang/pbt/test/prop_generators.erl

```
prop_collect2() ->
    ?FORALL(Bin, binary(),
            collect(to_range(10, byte_size(Bin)), is_binary(Bin))).

to_range(M, N) ->
    Base = N div M,
    {Base*M, (Base+1)*M}.
```

Elixir   code/CustomGenerators/elixir/pbt/test/generators_test.exs

```
# make verbose for metrics
property "collect 2", [:verbose] do
  forall bin <- binary() do
    #         test              metric
    collect(is_binary(bin), to_range(10, byte_size(bin)))
  end
end

def to_range(m, n) do
  base = div(n, m)
  {base * m, (base + 1) * m}
end
```

The to_range/2 function places a value M into a given bucket of size N. If you run that property, you'll get a much clearer result:

```
===> Testing prop_generators:prop_collect2()
«bunch of output»
OK: Passed 100 test(s).

56% {0,10}
27% {10,20}
13% {20,30}
3% {30,40}
1% {40,50}
===>
1/1 properties passed
```

In this case, more than 80% of generated binaries had a length between 0 and 20 bytes. If we know that our code has special handling only happening when binaries hit 1 megabyte in size, we know the current generator is not good enough.

To try it with our map encoding property to find how often duplicate keys are used, we might want to do this:

Erlang	code/CustomGenerators/erlang/pbt/test/prop_generators.erl

```erlang
prop_dupes() ->
    ?FORALL(KV, list({key(), val()}),
      begin
        M = maps:from_list(KV),
        [maps:get(K, M) || {K, _V} <- KV], % crash if K's not in map
        collect(
            {dupes, to_range(5, length(KV) - length(lists:ukeysort(1,KV)))},
            true
        )
      end).

key() -> integer().
val() -> term().
```

Elixir	code/CustomGenerators/elixir/pbt/test/generators_test.exs

```elixir
property "find all keys in a map even when dupes are used", [:verbose] do
  forall kv <- list({key(), val()}) do
    m = Map.new(kv)
    for {k,_v} <- kv, do: Map.fetch!(m, k)
    uniques =
      kv
        |> List.keysort(0)
        |> Enum.dedup_by(fn {x, _} -> x end)
    collect(true, {:dupes, to_range(5, length(kv) - length(uniques))})
  end
end

def key(), do: integer()
def val(), do: term()
```

Here, we collect the number of times keys were duplicated by taking the full list length (length(KV)) and subtracting the number of unique keys from it (lists:ukeysort(1, K)); the difference is going to be the number of duplicated keys.

Run this one and you'll get:

```
$ rebar3 proper -p prop_dupes
«build info»
===> Testing prop_generators:prop_dupes()
....................................................................
..........................
OK: Passed 100 test(s).

95% {dupes,{0,5}}
5% {dupes,{5,10}}
```

Those are not very good results. Almost no keys are duplicated. To remedy this, we can look at our default generators and see if we can do anything to help improve things.

For example, let's change the definition of key() so that we can probabilistically get better results. We'll use the oneof/1 generator for this. oneof([ListOfGenerators]) will randomly pick one of the generators within the list passed to it. It has two aliases in PropEr, named union(Types) and elements(Types), and they can all be used interchangeably.

QuickCheck Differences

In QuickCheck, oneof() will try to shrink a failing case by finding a failing element whereas elements() will try to shrink counterexamples by focusing toward the first elements of the list; PropEr does not make that distinction.

Using that one, we might rewrite key():

Erlang

```erlang
key() -> oneof([range(1,10), integer()]).
val() -> term().
```

Elixir

```elixir
def key(), do: oneof([range(1,10), integer()])
def val(), do: term()
```

With this generator, we still get the ability to generate the full range of all integers, but drastically increase the chance that some of them will be between 1 and 10. Over multiple runs, we're almost guaranteed to get repeated keys. But don't just believe it, go try it:

```
$ rebar3 proper -p prop_dupes
«build info»
===> Testing prop_generators:prop_dupes()
.........................................................
...........................
OK: Passed 100 test(s).

80% {dupes,{0,5}}
12% {dupes,{5,10}}
5% {dupes,{10,15}}
3% {dupes,{15,20}}
```

The amount of repetition is now much higher. From the same property, you get different scenarios and more interesting use cases. And any time someone runs the property or modifies it, they'll get to see the statistics to know if something looks odd.

The downside though is that collect/2 can focus on only a single value per property, not more. Instead, for cases where you need something a bit fancier, aggregate/2 is there for you.

Aggregating

Another function to gather statistics is aggregate(). aggregate() is similar to collect(), with the exception it can take a list of categories to store. To see it in action, here's some code that gathers the distribution of cards being handed to a player:

Erlang	code/CustomGenerators/erlang/pbt/test/prop_generators.erl

```erlang
prop_aggregate() ->
    Suits = [club, diamond, heart, spade],
    ?FORALL(Hand, vector(5, {oneof(Suits), choose(1,13)}),
            aggregate(Hand, true)). % `true' makes it always pass
```

Elixir	code/CustomGenerators/elixir/pbt/test/generators_test.exs

```elixir
property "aggregate", [:verbose] do
  suits = [:club, :diamond, :heart, :spade]

  forall hand <- vector(5, {oneof(suits), choose(1, 13)}) do
    # always pass
    aggregate(true, hand)
  end
end
```

This property's generator creates a hand of five cards in a list. There may be duplicate cards, since nothing keeps the generator from returning something like {spade, 1} five times. The list of cards is passed directly to aggregate/2, with no transformations. The function can use these multiple values and generate statistics for the overall set of possible cards:

```
$ rebar3 proper
«bunch of output»
OK: Passed 100 test(s).

3% {spade,11}
2% {club,1}
2% {club,8}
2% {heart,4}
2% {heart,8}
2% {heart,9}
2% {diamond,3}
«bunch of output»
```

In terms of distribution, this tells us all cards can be obtained rather uniformly. This can be done even though multiple cards are drawn at every round.

Adding Code Coverage

 Running the command as rebar3 do proper -c, cover -v will give coverage analysis to your code. For Elixir users, mix test --cover will generate a static report in the cover/ directory.

Another interesting case for aggregation is one where we might want to gather metrics on various data categories. Let's say we're analyzing generated text to see if it contains tricky characters. We may want to take the original string, and see each class of characters we get, according to some categories we define:

Erlang   code/CustomGenerators/erlang/pbt/test/prop_generators.erl

```erlang
prop_escape() ->
    ?FORALL(Str, string(),
            aggregate(classes(Str), escape(Str))).

escape(_) -> true. % we don't care about this for this example

classes(Str) ->
    L = letters(Str),
    N = numbers(Str),
    P = punctuation(Str),
    O = length(Str) - (L+N+P),
    [{letters, to_range(5,L)}, {numbers, to_range(5,N)},
     {punctuation, to_range(5,P)}, {others, to_range(5,O)}].

letters(Str) ->
    length([1 || Char <- Str,
                (Char >= $A andalso Char =< $Z) orelse
                (Char >= $a andalso Char =< $z)]).

numbers(Str) ->
    length([1 || Char <- Str, Char >= $0, Char =< $9]).

punctuation(Str) ->
    length([1 || Char <- Str, lists:member(Char, ".,;:'\"-")]).
```

Elixir   code/CustomGenerators/elixir/pbt/test/generators_test.exs

```elixir
property "fake escaping test showcasing aggregation", [:verbose] do
  forall str <- utf8() do
      aggregate(escape(str), classes(str))
  end
end
```

```
# this is a check we don't care about
defp escape(_), do: true

def classes(str) do
  l = letters(str)
  n = numbers(str)
  p = punctuation(str)
  o = String.length(str) - (l+n+p)
  [{:letters, to_range(5, l)},
   {:numbers, to_range(5, n)},
   {:punctuation, to_range(5, p)},
   {:others, to_range(5, o)}]
end

def letters(str) do
  is_letter = fn c -> (c >= ?a && c <= ?z) || (c >= ?A && c <= ?Z) end
  length(for <<c::utf8 <- str>>, is_letter.(c), do: 1)
end

def numbers(str) do
  is_num = fn c -> c >= ?0 && c <= ?9 end
  length(for <<c::utf8 <- str>>, is_num.(c), do: 1)
end

def punctuation(str) do
  is_punctuation = fn c -> c in '.,;:\'"-' end
  length(for <<c::utf8 <- str>>, is_punctuation.(c), do: 1)
end
```

Run this code, and you'll see something like this:

```
$ rebar3 proper -p prop_escape
«build info»
===> Testing prop_generators:prop_escape()
..............................................................................
...........................
OK: Passed 100 test(s).

25% {numbers,{0,5}}
25% {punctuation,{0,5}}
24% {letters,{0,5}}
10% {others,{0,5}}
5% {others,{5,10}}
4% {others,{10,15}}
2% {others,{15,20}}
2% {others,{20,25}}
1% {others,{25,30}}
0% {letters,{5,10}}
```

If our code testing for escaping was dealing with SQL, then the amount of punctuation we're throwing at it is worryingly low: most characters fit the other category and are things we may not be interested in. That's a clear sign that we need to use something fancier for string generation.

The aggregate/2 function, along with collect/2, will be critical to most of the validation for our generators, along with possibly code coverage metrics. Now that you know how to identify properties needing better generators, we can fully dive into the mechanisms that are available to help us improve them.

Basic Custom Generators

Once you discover that your data generation needs to be retargeted to better explore a problem space, plenty of constructs are available. We've seen how to use oneof(Generators) to impact our ability to get a more specific result set, but other more flexible tools exist to get even more control. In this section, we'll see the basic building blocks of writing custom generators.

Those building blocks are controlling the size and amount of generated data, applying transformation to the generators themselves, restricting and filtering out some data from your generators, and finally, playing with probabilities when none of the previous approaches work.

Resizing Generators

The first and simplest thing to do with generators is to make them grow bigger: make an integer larger, a list longer, or a string have larger codepoints. In fact, PropEr makes that happen for us on its own as the tests run. The way generator growth works is that PropEr internally uses a size parameter. Its value is usually small at first, but as tests run, the value is increased, and the data generated gains in complexity along with it. This allows the framework to start testing our systems with initially small data, and to then progressively make it more complex.

This is part of a strategy to find easy edge conditions such as 0, empty containers or strings, handling negative or positive numbers (which turn out to cover a large set of bugs) early on. Then, as each early test passes against these expected edge conditions, the framework grows the data it generates to find trickier bugs. The more tests pass in a run, the larger the data generated becomes.

It's possible that your code base is pretty solid, or that you suspect it may just fail on edge cases that only can be detected through very complex cases. It may not be worth your time to wait hundreds or thousands of tests before the data generated gets intricate enough to be interesting, so it would be good to be able to speed this up.

You can use the resize(Size, Generator) function to force a given size (a positive integer) onto a generator. In prop_collect2(), introduced in *Collecting*, on page 54, we counted the size of binaries, with the following results:

```
56% {0,10}
27% {10,20}
13% {20,30}
3% {30,40}
1% {40,50}
```

By resizing the generator to some arbitrary value, the data size can be increased:

Erlang	code/CustomGenerators/erlang/pbt/test/prop_generators.erl

```
prop_resize() ->
    ?FORALL(Bin, resize(150, binary()),  % <= resized here
            collect(to_range(10, byte_size(Bin)), is_binary(Bin))).
```

Elixir	code/CustomGenerators/elixir/pbt/test/generators_test.exs

```
property "resize", [:verbose] do
  forall bin <- resize(150, binary()) do
    collect(is_binary(bin), to_range(10, byte_size(bin)))
  end
end
```

The value 150 was chosen arbitrarily, through trial and error. Running the test again reports new statistics:

```
15% {90,100}
10% {110,120}
9% {80,90}
8% {130,140}
7% {40,50}
7% {50,60}
7% {120,130}
«more statistics»
```

The data sizes are still varied; they aren't fixed to exactly 150, but where 80% of the results were 20 bytes or smaller before, the vast majority of them now sit well above 40 bytes in size.

One caveat of using the resize function with static factors is that some of the variability of result sets may be lost. It's possible that both smaller and larger sizes would prompt interesting results, and having all of them in a single property would be useful. Another caveat is that relative sizing of various elements becomes cumbersome.

For example, the following property test's generator, to be realistic, should create shorter names than biographies, but still biographies larger than what would usually be one sentence:

```
Erlang                code/CustomGenerators/erlang/pbt/test/prop_generators.erl
```

```erlang
prop_profile1() ->
    ?FORALL(Profile, [{name, resize(10, string())},
                      {age, pos_integer()},
                      {bio, resize(350, string())}],
        begin
            NameLen = to_range(10,length(proplists:get_value(name, Profile))),
            BioLen = to_range(300,length(proplists:get_value(bio, Profile))),
            aggregate([{name, NameLen}, {bio, BioLen}], true)
        end).
```

```
Elixir                code/CustomGenerators/elixir/pbt/test/generators_test.exs
```

```elixir
property "profile 1", [:verbose] do
  forall profile <- [
          name: resize(10, utf8()),
          age: pos_integer(),
          bio: resize(350, utf8())
        ] do
    name_len = to_range(10, String.length(profile[:name]))
    bio_len = to_range(300, String.length(profile[:bio]))
    aggregate(true, name: name_len, bio: bio_len)
  end
end
```

Because size requirements vary between elements of the generator—part of it should be smaller than another one—multiple resize/2 function calls must be made and kept synchronized so that the data ratio is respected. But because we used static sizes, we've lost PropEr's helpful tendency to try very large or very small values. The only way we could get it back would be by manually modifying all those resize calls to increase or decrease their values in unison. That's annoying.

To avoid having to micromanage all these calls to make sure everything is preserved, you can instead use the ?SIZED(VarName, Expression) macro, which introduces the variable VarName into the scope of Expression, bound to the internal *size* value for the current execution. This size value changes with every test, so what we do with the macro is change its scale, rather than replacing it wholesale. Here's the same property using it:

```
Erlang                code/CustomGenerators/erlang/pbt/test/prop_generators.erl
```

```erlang
prop_profile2() ->
    ?FORALL(Profile, [{name, string()},
                      {age, pos_integer()},
                      {bio, ?SIZED(Size, resize(Size*35, string()))}],
```

```
        begin
            NameLen = to_range(10,length(proplists:get_value(name, Profile))),
            BioLen = to_range(300,length(proplists:get_value(bio, Profile))),
            aggregate([{name, NameLen}, {bio, BioLen}], true)
        end).
```

Elixir   code/CustomGenerators/elixir/pbt/test/generators_test.exs

```
property "profile 2", [:verbose] do
  forall profile <- [
          name: utf8(),
          age: pos_integer(),
          bio: sized(s, resize(s * 35, utf8()))
        ] do
    name_len = to_range(10, String.length(profile[:name]))
    bio_len = to_range(300, String.length(profile[:bio]))
    aggregate(true, name: name_len, bio: bio_len)
  end
end
```

In this property, the bio string is specified to be thirty-five times larger than the current size, which is implicitly the size value for name and age values. Doing this allows us to scale both the name and the biography relative to each other without imposing an anchor in terms of absolute size to the framework. This, in turn, provides some additional flexibility for the framework to do what it wants:

```
$ rebar3 proper -m prop_generators -p prop_profile1,prop_profile2
===> Testing prop_generators:prop_profile1()
«test output»

45% {name,{0,10}}
40% {bio,{0,300}}
10% {bio,{300,600}}
5% {name,{10,20}}

===> Testing prop_generators:prop_profile2()
«test output»

32% {name,{0,10}}
28% {bio,{0,300}}
12% {bio,{300,600}}
10% {name,{10,20}}
7% {name,{20,30}}
4% {bio,{600,900}}
3% {bio,{900,1200}}
1% {bio,{1200,1500}}
1% {name,{30,40}}
```

As you can see, with the value obtained through the ?SIZED/2 macro applied relatively to a single generator with resize/2, PropEr is able to generate a much wider range of sizes, while we get to preserve the difference in ratio between names and biographies' lengths.

We could even combine approaches to get more variability, but over larger basic sizes if we wanted to. We could for example use an expression like ?SIZED(Size, resize(min(100,Size)*35, string())) to ensure a minimal size without imposing a ceiling on the value. We can see the beginning of our ability to tune each generator individually to our needs.

Transforming Generators

In the course of writing generators, one of the patterns you'll encounter is the need to generate data types that can't be described with the basic Erlang data structures that default generators support. For example, you may want to generate a first-in-first-out queue of key/value pairs, using the queue[1] module. Just using tuples and lists won't be enough to enforce the internal constraints of the data structure. In some cases, the data structure may be *opaque* (meaning you can't or shouldn't peek at how it's built, just stick to the interface the module exposes), and then you're plain out of luck. To solve this problem, PropEr exposes macros that let you apply arbitrary transformations to data while generating it.

To illustrate the issue, let's take a look at the queue module. If we wanted to have a queue of keys and values stored as tuples, we couldn't safely create it out of default generators without digging inside the implementation and understanding how all the data is handled internally. Instead what we'd need to do is write a property similar to this:

Erlang   code/CustomGenerators/erlang/pbt/test/prop_generators.erl

```
prop_queue_naive() ->
    ?FORALL(List, list({term(), term()}),
        begin
            Queue = queue:from_list(List),
            queue:is_queue(Queue)
        end).
```

Elixir   code/CustomGenerators/elixir/pbt/test/generators_test.exs

```
property "naive queue generation" do
  forall list <- list({term(), term()}) do
    q = :queue.from_list(list)
    :queue.is_queue(q)
  end
end
```

---

1.   http://erlang.org/doc/man/queue.html

Because we can only use queue:from_list/1 on an actual list—and therefore not from within the generator—we call it within the property. The problem with this approach is that even though we want a queue, we generate a list of tuples. Once in the property, we must then convert the list to an actual queue data structure. This splits up the generation of the data type and the conversion between the generator and the property. Any property requiring a queue is stuck using the generator, and then manually adding bits that should belong in it to the property. Even worse, if you wanted to generate a list of queues, the majority of the generators would have to live inside the property rather than within the generators themselves. That's bad abstraction.

A better approach would be to use the ?LET(InstanceOfType, TypeGenerator, Transform) macro to apply a transformation to the generated data itself. The macro takes the TypeGenerator and binds it to the InstanceOfType variable. That variable can then be used in the Transform expression as if it were fully evaluated. The evaluation of the final generator is still deferred until later though, which is important because it lets us transform it without preventing it from being composable with others generators. In other words, ?LET lets you accumulate function calls to run on the generator whenever it will be evaluated.

Here's the same queue generator, but with the ?LET/3 macro:

Erlang	code/CustomGenerators/erlang/pbt/test/prop_generators.erl

```erlang
prop_queue_nicer() ->
    ?FORALL(Q, queue(),
            queue:is_queue(Q)).

queue() ->
    ?LET(List, list({term(), term()}),
         queue:from_list(List)).
```

Elixir	code/CustomGenerators/elixir/pbt/test/generators_test.exs

```elixir
property "queue with let macro" do
  forall q <- queue() do
    :queue.is_queue(q)
  end
end

def queue() do
  let list <- list({term(), term()}) do
    :queue.from_list(list)
  end
end
```

With this form, there is no more bleeding of parts of generators into properties themselves. The composable aspect also means that a list of generators would be as simple as calling list(queue()). A custom generator of this kind has all the same capabilities as any built-in one.

This covers the need to *transform* a piece of data into another one. Another related piece of functionality you may find yourself needing is preventing some data from being generated altogether, rather than a transformation. How can we prevent a generator from generating data?

Imposing Restrictions

A common trait to all default generators is that they're pretty broad in the data they generate, and from time to time, we'll want to exclude specific counterexamples (the technical word for "input causing a property to fail"). In fact, we already needed to do that when we used the non_empty() generator to remove empty lists or binaries from the generated data set. Such a filter generator can be implemented with the ?SUCHTHAT(InstanceOfType, TypeGenerator, BooleanExp) macro.

The macro works in a similar manner as ?LET/3: the TypeGenerator is bound to InstanceOfType, which can then be used in BooleanExp. One distinction is that BooleanExp needs to be a boolean expression, returning true or false. If the value is true, the data generated is kept and allowed to go through. If the value is false, the data is prevented from being passed to the test; instead, PropEr will try to generate a new piece of data that hopefully satisfies the filter. The non_empty() filter can in fact be implemented as:

Erlang

```erlang
non_empty(ListOrBinGenerator) ->
    ?SUCHTHAT(L, ListOrBinGenerator, L =/= [] andalso L =/= <<>>).
```

Elixir

```elixir
def non_empty(list_type) do
  such_that l <- list_type, when: l != [] and l != <<>>
end
```

Quite simply, if the data generated is an empty list or an empty binary, the generator must try again. Maps or queues are not impacted by this filter, but you could write your own constraints as well:

Erlang

```erlang
non_empty_map(Gen) ->
    ?SUCHTHAT(G, Gen, G =/= #{}).
```

Elixir

```elixir
def non_empty_map(gen) do
  such_that g <- gen, when: g != %{}
end
```

Filtering Too Hard

There is a limit to the number of times PropEr will retry building a generator; after too many failed attempts, it will give up with an error message such as Error: Couldn't produce an instance that satisfies all strict constraints after 50 tries.

Similarly, generating a list of even or uneven numbers could be done by using ?SUCHTHAT() macros:

Erlang

```erlang
even() -> ?SUCHTHAT(N, integer(), N rem 2 =:= 0).
uneven() -> ?SUCHTHAT(N, integer(), N rem 2 =/= 0).
```

Elixir

```elixir
def even(), do: such_that n <- integer(), when: rem(n, 2) == 0
def uneven(), do: such_that n <- integer(), when: rem(n, 2) != 0
```

But in this specific case it may be faster to use a transform to get there by using the ?LET() macro instead of filtering with ?SUCHTHAT():

Erlang

```erlang
even() -> ?LET(N, integer(), N*2).
uneven() -> ?LET(N, integer(), N*2 + 1).
```

Elixir

```elixir
def even(), do: let n <- integer(), do: n * 2
def uneven(), do: let n <- integer(), do: n * 2 + 1
```

Since these transforms can generate correct data on the first try every time, they will be more efficient than using ?SUCHTHAT. Whenever you use a filter, try to see if you could be reworking a restriction into a transformation. Think probabilistically: will you need to filter out a tiny portion of the generator's possible space? A filter's perfect. If you're going to filter out a significant chunk of the potential data, then a transformation may pay for itself in speed.

Another thing to note is that not just guard expressions are accepted in ?SUCHTHAT macros. For example, the following generator looks for ISO Latin1[2] strings by using the io_lib:printable_latin1_list/1 function,[3] which will let us restrict down the range of string():

```
latin1_string() ->
    ?SUCHTHAT(S, string(), io_lib:printable_latin1_list(S)).
```

A similar one for unicode—ensuring nothing goes out of range—would be:

```
unicode_string() ->
    ?SUCHTHAT(S, string(), io_lib:printable_unicode_list(S)).
```

With transforms, filters, and resizes, we can get pretty far in terms of retargeting our generators to do what we want. The latin1 generator shows something interesting though. The default string() generator has a large search space, and therefore filtering out the unwanted data can be expensive. On the other hand, most unicode characters can't be represented within latin1, and transforming the generated strings themselves would also be expensive: how would you map emojis to latin1 characters?

Unicode Generation

 If you need valid Unicode strings, it is simpler to use utf8() as a base generator. It will return a properly encoded UTF-8 binary. If you need strings, you can then use a ?LET macro to turn it back with unicode:characters_to_list/1. By default, Elixir's PropCheck only has utf8() exported.

We can't get what we want (and have it done efficiently) with transforms and filters alone, and for this specific issue, resizing wouldn't be of much help either. Instead, we'll have to build our own generators while controlling probabilities to make them do what we want.

Changing Probabilities

The last fundamental building block that really gives us control over data generation is having the ability to tweak the probabilities of how data is generated. By default, the generators introduced in *Default Generators*, on page 22 are either going to generate data in a large potential space, like string(), number(), or binary(), or in a rather narrow scope, such as boolean() or range(X,Y).

---

2.   https://en.wikipedia.org/wiki/ISO/IEC_8859-1

3.   http://erlang.org/doc/man/io_lib.html#printable_latin1_list-1

Using ?LET() lets us transform *all* of that data, and ?SUCHTHAT() lets us remove *some* of it, but it's hard to get something in between. When you truly need a custom solution, probabilistic generators can help.

We've seen oneof(ListOfGenerators) already, which helped us gain more repeatable keys in the following generator:

```
key() -> oneof([range(1,10), integer()]).
```

This shows how two distinct generators can be used together to help build and steer things in the direction we want. The oneof(Types) generator is simple and useful, but the most interesting one is frequency(), which allows you to control and choose the probability of each generator it contains.

Let's take strings as an example, since they were already causing us problems. Just using string() tended to yield a lot of control characters, codepoints that were pretty much anything, and very little in terms of the latin1 or ASCII characters we English readers are used to. And let's not even think about words or sentences. This can be remediated with frequency/1:

Erlang	code/CustomGenerators/erlang/pbt/test/prop_generators.erl

```
text_like() ->
    list(frequency([{80, range($a, $z)},        % letters
                    {10, $\s},                  % whitespace
                    {1,  $\n},                  % linebreak
                    {1,  oneof([$., $-, $!, $?, $,])}, % punctuation
                    {1,  range($0, $9)}         % numbers
                   ])).
```

Elixir	code/CustomGenerators/elixir/pbt/test/generators_test.exs

```
def text_like() do
  let l <-
      list(
        frequency([
          {80, range(?a, ?z)},
          {10, ?\s},
          {1, ?\n},
          {1, oneof([?., ?-, ?!, ??, ?,])},
          {1, range(?0, ?9)}
        ])
      ) do
    to_string(l)
  end
end
```

Using it gives us this:

```
1> proper_gen:pick(proper_types:string()).
{ok,[35,15,0,12,2,3,3,1,10,25]}
2> proper_gen:pick(prop_generators:text_like()).
{ok,"rdnpw hxwd"}
3> proper_gen:pick(proper_types:resize(79, prop_generators:text_like())).
{ok,"vyb hhceqai  m f ejibfiracplkcn gqfvmmbspbt\nn.qbbzwmd"}
```

This generator produces something a lot closer to realistic text than what is obtained through string(). It's no Shakespeare yet, and may look more like a Scrabble rack, but with more monkeys hitting the keys randomly, we may get there. In any case, by tweaking the frequency values, specific characters can see their probability raised or lowered as required to properly exercise a property.

This will ensure that a parser for comma-separated values (CSV)[4] could get a higher frequency of quotation marks, commas, and line breaks to find more parsing-related corner cases, whereas a generator for XML would want to focus on < and > characters, for example.

Using frequency() or oneof() with other custom generators therefore lets you choose and mix and match all kinds of techniques to get as flexible as you need. If you need a list of "mostly sorted data," then you could make a generator like this one:

Erlang	code/CustomGenerators/erlang/pbt/test/prop_generators.erl

```erlang
mostly_sorted() ->
    ?LET(Lists,
        list(frequency([
            {5, sorted_list()},
            {1, list()}
        ])),
        lists:append(Lists)).

sorted_list() ->
    ?LET(L, list(), lists:sort(L)).
```

Elixir	code/CustomGenerators/elixir/pbt/test/generators_test.exs

```elixir
def mostly_sorted() do
  gen = list(
    frequency([
      {5, sorted_list()},
      {1, list()}
    ])
  )
  let lists <- gen, do: Enum.concat(lists)
end
```

---

4. https://en.wikipedia.org/wiki/Comma-separated_values

```
def sorted_list() do
  let l <- list(), do: Enum.sort(l)
end
```

This would give you a bunch of sublists that may or may not be sorted, all concatenated into a big list and would have been much harder to do with just ?LET(), ?SUCHTHAT(), and ?SIZED().

But even though probabilistic generators are nicer than just default ones, for cases like CSV or XML, more structure would make sense; just random tokens thrown around won't necessarily lead to much, so we'll need more advanced techniques.

Fancy Custom Generators

You can get pretty far with just the basic techniques, but whenever they can't bring you up to where you want your generators to be, you'll have to look into more advanced techniques. But even then, the advanced techniques will still make use of the basic ones, so don't worry, they'll remain useful.

In this section, we'll focus on how we can make use of the basic techniques and put them in a fancier context through writing our own recursive generators, with some need for laziness. We'll then finish it up by introducing symbolic calls, which help make complex generators more understandable once properties fail.

Recursive Generators

Whenever a piece of data can be represented by a repetitive or well-ordered structure, or when a step-by-step approach can be used to create the data, recursion is our friend. We'll see how generator recursion works, and even how it can compose with probabilistic generation, although we'll find some pitfalls there.

Let's say we have a robot, and want to give it directions. We might want to test things such as whether it can go through a room without hitting obstacles, whether it can cover all areas, and so on, but first we need to be able to create and plan an itinerary for it. Let's say our robot works on a grid with coordinates, and can go left, right, up, or down. A simple generator might look like:

Erlang

```
path() -> list(oneof([left, right, up, down])).
```

Elixir

```
def path(), do: list(oneof([:left, :right, :up, :down]))
```

And it would be fine. If we wanted to eliminate things like "going left then right" or "going up then down" where moves cancel each other, a ?LET() would probably be fine as well: just scan the list, and every time two opposite directions are taken, drop them from the list. But what if we wanted to generate a path such that the robot never crosses a part of its path it has already covered? Doing so with a ?SUCHTHAT might not be superefficient, and it might also be hard to do with a ?LET(). But it's kind of easy to do with recursion.

Tracking if we've been somewhere before would require us to internally track coordinates with {X,Y} values:

- Our robot always starts at {0,0}
- Going left means subtracting 1 from the X value: {-1,0}
- Going right means adding 1 to the X value: {+1,0}
- Going up means adding 1 to the Y value: {0,+1}
- Going down means subtracting 1 from the Y value: {0,-1}

All we need to do then is track coordinates in a map; if a value exists in the map, we finish. Also, to put an upper bound on the path length, we'll use a low-probability event of terminating right away.

Our generator for this might look like this one:

Erlang   code/CustomGenerators/erlang/pbt/test/prop_generators.erl

```
path() ->
    % Current, Acc, VisitedMap      ToIgnore
    path({0,0}, [], #{{0,0} => seen}, []).

path(_Current, Acc, _Seen, [_,_,_,_]) -> %% all directions tried
    Acc; % we give up
path(Current, Acc, Seen, Ignore) ->
    frequency([
        {1, Acc}, % probabilistic stop
        {15, increase_path(Current, Acc, Seen, Ignore)}
    ]).
```

Elixir   code/CustomGenerators/elixir/pbt/test/generators_test.exs

```
def path() do
  path({0,0}, [], %{{0,0} => :seen}, [])
end
```

```
def path(_current, acc, _seen, [_,_,_,_]) do
  acc
end
def path(current, acc, seen, ignore) do
  frequency([
    {1, acc},
    {15, increase_path(current, acc, seen, ignore)}
  ])
end
```

So this is an interesting bit of code. The first function is a wrapper, where path() calls out to a recursive path/4 function. That function takes the current coordinate ({X,Y}), the current path it has built (a list of the form [up, down, left, ...]), the map of visited coordinates, and a list of directions to ignore. These directions are those that have been attempted recently and that resulted in a conflict. If the list contains all four of them, then we know there's no way to go that won't result in a repeated run, and so we give up.

The second function clause uses frequency/1 to ensure that once in a while, we stop. This will prevent a case where we'd just go forward forever and never finish generating data. In the vast majority of cases (with a 15-to-1 probability), we'll try and lengthen the path. The function that does this is defined as follows:

Erlang	code/CustomGenerators/erlang/pbt/test/prop_generators.erl

```erlang
increase_path(Current, Acc, Seen, Ignore) ->
    DirectionGen = oneof([left, right, up, down] -- Ignore),
    ?LET(Direction, DirectionGen,
      begin
        NewPos = move(Direction, Current),
        case Seen of
            #{NewPos := _} -> % exists
                path(Current, Acc, Seen, [Direction|Ignore]); % retry
            _ ->
                path(NewPos, [Direction|Acc], Seen#{NewPos => seen}, [])
        end
      end).

move(left, {X,Y}) -> {X-1,Y};
move(right, {X,Y}) -> {X+1,Y};
move(up, {X,Y}) -> {X,Y+1};
move(down, {X,Y}) -> {X,Y-1}.
```

Elixir	code/CustomGenerators/elixir/pbt/test/generators_test.exs

```elixir
def increase_path(current, acc, seen, ignore) do
  let direction <- oneof([:left, :right, :up, :down] -- ignore) do
    new_pos = move(direction, current)
```

```
    case seen do
      %{^new_pos => _} ->
        path(current, acc, seen, [direction|ignore])
      _ ->
        path(new_pos, [direction|acc], Map.put(seen, new_pos, :seen), [])
    end
  end
end

def move(:left, {x, y}), do: {x-1, y}
def move(:right, {x, y}), do: {x+1, y}
def move(:up, {x, y}), do: {x, y+1}
def move(:down, {x, y}), do: {x, y-1}
```

Let's decompose this one. First, we have a call to oneof([left, right, up, down] -- Ignore). This generator tries to pick a random direction that has not been chosen yet. By default, this Ignore list is [], which means all directions are attempted. The tricky bit is that this call to oneof() returns a generator, not an actual value; PropEr will take care of changing the generator into a value.

If we want to use the value of that generator within the current generator, the ?LET() macro lets us do that. Remember that ?LET() chains up operations to be run once PropEr *actualizes* generators into data, so writing the function as above lets us use the result (Direction) from the generator (DirectionGen) within the macro's transfomed expression (begin ... end).

Within that expression, we apply the position by calling move/2 on the current one, and look it up in the Seen map. If it is found there, it means this direction crosses a path we've taken before, so we retry while ignoring it. If the position has not been visited before, we call path/4 again with the new data.

If you try to run this generator in the shell, it might take a very long time to return, and with some other generators that only probabilistically stop, it may never return. The more branches, the costlier. That's because of the order of evaluation in Erlang. To evaluate frequency(), which is a regular function, its arguments need to be expanded. Since the arguments to frequency() include the generator itself, the generator must be called first, and the process loops deeper and deeper, until memory runs out.

For those specific cases, PropEr provides a ?LAZY() macro, which allows you to defer the evaluation of an expression until it is required by the generator. This fixes things:

Erlang	code/CustomGenerators/erlang/pbt/test/prop_generators.erl

```
path(_Current, Acc, _Seen, [_,_,_,_]) -> %% all directions tried
    Acc; % we give up
```

```
path(Current, Acc, Seen, Ignore) ->
    frequency([
        {1, Acc}, % probabilistic stop
        {15, ?LAZY(increase_path(Current, Acc, Seen, Ignore))}
    ]).
```

Elixir	code/CustomGenerators/elixir/pbt/test/generators_test.exs

```elixir
def path(_current, acc, _seen, [_,_,_,_]) do
  acc
end
def path(current, acc, seen, ignore) do
  frequency([
    {1, acc},
    {15, lazy(increase_path(current, acc, seen, ignore))}
  ])
end
```

This macro lets us defer the evaluation of its contents until they are needed, which means that we can now safely use it within alternative clauses. Now the generator should run:

```
$ rebar3 as test shell
«build info»
1> proper_gen:pick(prop_generators:path()).
{ok,[down,right,down,left,left]}
2> proper_gen:sample(prop_generators:path()).
[right,down,right,up,up,right,up,left]
[]
[down,right,down,left,left,left,left,down,down,left,up,up,left,
 up,left,up,left,up,left,left,up,right,right,right,down,right,
 right,up,up,right,down,down,right,down,down,right,up,up,right,
 right,right,right,down,right,up,right]
[right,right,right,up,right,right,down,left,down]
[left,up,right,up,left,up,up,up]
[down,right,down,left,left,down,down,down,right,down,left,left,
 down,left,up,up,up,right,up,left,left,up,right,up,left,left,up,
 right,up,right,right,down,down,right,up,up,right]
[down,left,down,down,right]
[left,left,down]
[up,left,up,right,right,down,right,right,up,right,right,up,left,
 up,up,right,down,right,down]
[]
[left,left,up,left,down,down,right,down]
ok
```

That's good, but there's a small problem. The caveat with this approach is that probabilities for recursion can mean one of two things:

1. Because the probabilities are fixed, the size of the created data structure will generally be unchanging and always average to a ratio in line with the defined probabilities. (Here, 15-to-1 probabilities means we may have paths roughly 15 steps long on average.)

2. Because there are probabilities at all, there is a lingering chance some data structures will be enormous, possibly large enough to crash our program.

Each of these is undesirable on its own, but we may end up with tests that get both. In some cases, the potential variation for very large or very small structures will be desirable, but not always. We can improve the generator by forcing it to be more deterministic in its size by writing recursive functions that are much more similar to what we usually write in regular Erlang or Elixir code:

Erlang   code/CustomGenerators/erlang/pbt/test/prop_generators.erl

```erlang
path(0, _Current, Acc, _Seen, _Ignore) -> % directions limit
    Acc; % max depth reached
path(_Max, _Current, Acc, _Seen, [_,_,_,_]) -> % all directions tried
    Acc; % we give up
path(Max, Current, Acc, Seen, Ignore) ->
    increase_path(Max, Current, Acc, Seen, Ignore).

increase_path(Max, Current, Acc, Seen, Ignore) ->
    DirectionGen = oneof([left, right, up, down] -- Ignore),
    ?LET(Direction, DirectionGen,
      begin
        NewPos = move(Direction, Current),
        case Seen of
            #{NewPos := _} -> % exists
                path(Max, Current, Acc, Seen, [Direction|Ignore]); % retry
            _ ->
                path(Max-1, NewPos, [Direction|Acc],
                    Seen#{NewPos => seen}, [])
        end
      end).
```

Elixir   code/CustomGenerators/elixir/pbt/test/generators_test.exs

```elixir
def path(0, _current, acc, _seen, _ignore) do
  acc
end
def path(_max, _current, acc, _seen, [_,_,_,_]) do
  acc
end
```

```
def path(max, current, acc, seen, ignore) do
    increase_path(max, current, acc, seen, ignore)
end

def increase_path(max, current, acc, seen, ignore) do
  let direction <- oneof([:left, :right, :up, :down] -- ignore) do
    new_pos = move(direction, current)
    case seen do
      %{^new_pos => _} ->
        path(max, current, acc, seen, [direction|ignore])
      _ ->
        path(
          max-1,
          new_pos,
          [direction|acc],
          Map.put(seen, new_pos, :seen),
          []
        )
    end
  end
end
```

All we've done here is add a counter (Max) to each function clause, which halts the execution when it reaches 0. You'll see that this is pretty much how you'd write any recursive function to generate a list of a known length in Erlang or Elixir. In fact, because we have only distinct function clauses with no frequency() usage anymore, the ?LAZY() macro is no longer necessary.

All we need to add is a wrapper to seed the size parameter. That's where the ?SIZED macro can be of use:

Erlang   code/CustomGenerators/erlang/pbt/test/prop_generators.erl

```
path() ->
    ?SIZED(Size,
           %  Max, Current, Acc,  VisitedMap      ToIgnore
           path(Size, {0,0}, [], #{{0,0} => seen}, [])).
```

Elixir   code/CustomGenerators/elixir/pbt/test/generators_test.exs

```
def path() do
  sized(
    size,
    path(size, {0,0}, [], %{{0,0} => :seen}, [])
  )
end
```

And just like that, we have pretty good recursion with a great way to dynamically resize recursive data structures. The Size parameter will grow along with test execution, and if you want it to grow faster than what PropEr gives, just multiply it. This will give us much more interesting path variations than probabilistic generators.

```
$ rebar3 as test shell
«build info»
1> proper_gen:sample(prop_generators:path()).
[down,down,down,down,down,left,left,down,down,down]
[down,left,left,down,left,down,left,down,left,up,left]
[down,down,down,right,right,up,left,up,up,up,right,down]
[down,left,down,left,down,down,left,down,left,up,up,right,up]
[down,right,right,right,down,left,left,down,left,up,left,up,left,up]
[down,right,up,right,up,up,left,left,left,up,left,left,up,left,down]
[right,right,up,up,left,left,left,up,up,right,up,up,up,up,right,down]
[down,left,down,right,right,up,right,right,down,right,right,right,down,
 down,left,left,left]
[left,left,down,left,left,up,left,up,left,down,left,left,down,right,down,
 right,up,right]
[down,left,left,up,right,up,up,up,up,up,left,left,left,up,right,right,up,
 right,right]
[down,right,right,up,left,up,right,up,up,right,up,left,up,left,down,down,
 down,left,left,left]
ok
```

For Elixir users, the commands are a bit trickier:

```
$ MIX_ENV=test iex -S mix
iex(1)> ExUnit.start()
iex(2)> c "test/generators_test.exs" # compiles the test script
iex(3)> :proper_check.sample(PbtGenerators.path()) # generates samples
«output»
```

In comparison to the previous version's samples, this one has a path length capped and guided by size, meaning the framework can do a better job at scaling the list size up and down and the generator will never end up in an infinite loop. This also prevents us from getting a fixed ratio of empty lists. (If there's a 5% chance to stop at any iteration, you should expect around 5% of empty lists as well.) If you're interested in testing the diversity of paths, the latest approach is probably both faster and likelier to play well with PropEr.

The same approach can be used to generate any recursive structure: trees of a depth proportional to the size (or with as many elements as the size), grammar rules encoding more complex variations, or even sequences of transitions in a state machine, which would require many nested and mutually recursive generators.

You may also be interested to use this technique to build side-effectful generators, such as those populating ETS tables or even writing files to disk, but those would be a bit more problematic to debug since we can't easily see how they reached their end state.

Symbolic Calls

Some of the data structures or state that we need to generate for tests can be opaque and difficult to decipher. Think of debugging a binary protocol by looking at the individual bytes once the whole thing is encoded, or creating a process and sending it a bunch of messages to prime its state. The output of a failing property will be a lot of hard-to-read bits and bytes, or a term like <0.213.0>, which frankly don't help a whole lot no matter how much shrinking you may apply to them. The solution to this problem is a special category of generators built from *symbolic calls*.

A symbolic call is just a special notation for function calls so that they can be represented as data in generators. Rather than executing the operation straight away, the calls are built up as a data structure. Once the generator materializes, they get executed at once. The notation for them is {call, Module, Function, ArgumentList}—a format supported by QuickCheck and Triq as well as PropEr. Another format, {$call, Module, Function, ArgumentList} (named *automated symbolic call*), is similar, but a bit friendlier in practice:

Function Call	Symbolic Call	Automated Symbolic Call (PropEr only)
sets:new()	{call, sets, new, []}	{'$call', sets, new, []}
queue:join(Q1, Q2)	{call, queue, join, [Q1, Q2]}	{'$call', queue, join, [Q1, Q2]}
lists:sort([1,2,3])	{call, lists, sort, [[1,2,3]]}	{'$call', lists, sort, [[1,2,3]]}
local(Arg) (if exported)	{call, ?MODULE, local, [Arg]}	{'$call', ?MODULE, local, [Arg]}

Using either format of symbolic calls can make things simpler when looking at shrunken results. Let's try with the Erlang dict data structure, which can be opaque if you don't know how it's implemented. This example will also show the difference between symbolic calls and automated symbolic calls.

Erlang	code/CustomGenerators/erlang/pbt/test/prop_generators.erl

```erlang
dict_gen() ->
    ?LET(X, list({integer(),integer()}), dict:from_list(X)).

dict_symb() ->
    ?SIZED(Size, dict_symb(Size, {call, dict, new, []})).

dict_symb(0, Dict) ->
    Dict;
```

```
dict_symb(N, Dict) ->
    dict_symb(N-1, {call, dict, store, [integer(), integer(), Dict]}).

dict_autosymb() ->
    ?SIZED(Size, dict_autosymb(Size, {'$call', dict, new, []})).

dict_autosymb(0, Dict) ->
    Dict;
dict_autosymb(N, Dict) ->
    dict_autosymb(N-1, {'$call', dict, store, [integer(), integer(), Dict]}).
```

| Elixir | code/CustomGenerators/elixir/pbt/test/generators_test.exs |

```elixir
def dict_gen() do
  let(x <- list({integer(), integer()}), do: :dict.from_list(x))
end

def dict_symb(),
  do: sized(size, dict_symb(size, {:call, :dict, :new, []}))

def dict_symb(0, dict), do: dict

def dict_symb(n, dict) do
  dict_symb(n - 1, {:call, :dict, :store, [integer(), integer(), dict]})
end

def dict_autosymb() do
  sized(size, dict_autosymb(size, {:"$call", :dict, :new, []}))
end

def dict_autosymb(0, dict), do: dict

def dict_autosymb(n, dict) do
  dict_autosymb(
    n - 1,
    {:"$call", :dict, :store, [integer(), integer(), dict]}
  )
end
```

This specifies three generators: one with the normal function calls, one with
symbolic calls, and one with automated symbolic calls. Here are three matching
properties that will pretty much always fail:

| Erlang | code/CustomGenerators/erlang/pbt/test/prop_generators.erl |

```erlang
prop_dict_gen() ->
    ?FORALL(D, dict_gen(), dict:size(D) < 5).

prop_dict_symb() ->
    ?FORALL(DSymb, dict_symb(), dict:size(eval(DSymb)) < 5).

prop_dict_autosymb() ->
    ?FORALL(D, dict_autosymb(), dict:size(D) < 5).
```

```
Elixir                    code/CustomGenerators/elixir/pbt/test/generators_test.exs
```

```elixir
property "dict generator" do
  forall d <- dict_gen() do
    :dict.size(d) < 5
  end
end

property "symbolic generator" do
  forall d <- dict_symb() do
    # propcheck does not automatically handle eval() calls
    :proper_gen.eval(:dict.size(d)) < 5
  end
end

property "automated symbolic generator" do
  forall d <- dict_autosymb() do
    :dict.size(d) < 5
  end
end
```

See how the symbolic call form has to call eval(SymbolicGenerator) to use the code within the property. This is a downside where the implementation details of the generator leak into the property. The automated symbolic call by comparison is automatically evaluated by PropEr before being passed to the property. Let's see how they fail:

```
===> Testing prop_generators:prop_dict_gen()
..............!
Failed: After 16 test(s).
{dict,5,16,16,8,80,48,{[],[],[],[],[],[],[],[],[],[],[],
 [],[],[],[],[]},{{[],[[3|-6]],[],[],[],[[-1|-5]],
[[-14|10],[2|3]],[[5|1]],[],[],[],[],[],[],[],[]}}}
«more output»
===> Testing prop_generators:prop_dict_symb()
.............!
Failed: After 15 test(s).
{call,dict,store,[-6,8,
  {call,dict,store,[46,-13,
    {call,dict,store,[2,-2,
      {call,dict,store,[22,-2,
        {call,dict,store,[-12,-2,
          {call,dict,new,[]}]}]}]}]}]}
«more output»
===> Testing prop_generators:prop_dict_autosymb()
...........!
Failed: After 13 test(s).
{'$call',dict,store,[7,2,
  {'$call',dict,store,[-1,2,
    {'$call',dict,store,[1,18,
```

```
    {'$call',dict,store,[-9,0,
      {'$call',dict,store,[-10,3,
        {'$call',dict,new,[]}]}]}]}]}]}
```
《more output》

As you can see, the first property (prop_dict_gen()) returns a weird data structure. That one is a bit hard to debug since it's hard to see what inputs we can give a dictionary to yield that result. Both forms of symbolic calls let us see the keys and values inserted to yield a failing dictionary.

With the help of symbolic calls, generated terms that are too obscure (whether through their complex size or because side effects hide the way the state was obtained) can be made simpler to debug. Even if we were to use a generator to configure a remote server into a given state, symbolic calls would let us know which sequence of calls may have led to a failure.

Wrapping Up

You now have all the tools you need to make the fanciest of all generators. You're ready to make some that have a wide-spectrum approach to fuzz your systems, down to accurate ones to exercise specific invariants your code should respect. All of these methods can be mixed together. Nothing keeps you from using symbolic calls created through complex recursive generators that filter with ?SUCHTHAT and transform with ?LET, with some terms created probabilistically with a dynamic size.

Going overboard is not the best idea though. It's not because you have a fancy set of hammers that you have to crush all the nails with them. We have strategies to come up with properties and to build generators, but you still need to find strategies to make proper use of properties within a project. The next chapter will cover responsible testing, how to know when enough is enough, or where a little property-testing magic can go a long way.

Exercises

Question 1

Which functions can be used to check the distribution of generated entries in a test run?

Solution on page 316.

Question 2

Which macro can be used to apply regular Erlang or Elixir functions to a generator to modify it?

Solution on page 316.

Question 3

When and why would you use the ?LAZY macro?

Solution on page 316.

Question 4

The following probabilistic generator creates trees that are not necessarily balanced:

Erlang   code/CustomGenerators/erlang/pbt/test/prop_exercises.erl

---

```erlang
%% The tree generates a data type that represents the following types:
-type tree() :: tree(term()).
-type tree(T) :: {node,
                  Value :: T,
                  Left  :: tree(T) | undefined,
                  Right :: tree(T) | undefined}.

tree() ->
    tree(term()).

tree(Type) ->
    frequency([
        {1, {node, Type, tree(Type), undefined}},
        {1, {node, Type, undefined, tree(Type)}},
        {5, {node, Type, tree(Type), tree(Type)}}
    ]).
```

Elixir   code/CustomGenerators/elixir/pbt/test/exercises_test.exs

---

```elixir
def tree(), do: tree(term())

def tree(type) do
  frequency([
    {1, {:node, type, tree(type), nil}},
    {1, {:node, type, nil, tree(Type)}},
    {5, {:node, type, tree(type), tree(type)}}
  ])
end
```

Make sure it can consistently terminate and generate trees of an interesting size. Using the ?SIZED macro may be an advantage for better complexity scaling.

Solution on page 316.

Question 5

The following generators allow you to generate stamps of the format {Hour, Minute, Second}:

Erlang	code/CustomGenerators/erlang/pbt/test/prop_exercises.erl

```erlang
stamp() -> {hour(), min(), sec()}.
hour() -> choose(0,23).
min()   -> choose(0,59).
sec()   -> choose(0,59).
```

Elixir	code/CustomGenerators/elixir/pbt/test/exercises_test.exs

```elixir
def stamp(), do: {hour(), min(), sec()}
def hour(), do: choose(0, 23)
def min(), do: choose(0, 59)
def sec(), do: choose(0, 59)
```

The following are pairs of modified or restricted timestamps. Compare their implementations, and explain which of each pair is the most appropriate.

Erlang	code/CustomGenerators/erlang/pbt/test/prop_exercises.erl

```erlang
%% Return hours in the morning
am_stamp1() ->
    ?SUCHTHAT({H,_,_}, stamp(), H < 12).
am_stamp2() ->
    ?LET({H,M,S}, stamp(), {H rem 12, M, S}).

%% Return two ordered timestamps
stamps1() ->
    ?SUCHTHAT({S1, S2}, {stamp(), stamp()}, S1 =< S2).
stamps2() ->
    ?LET({S1, S2}, {stamp(), stamp()}, {min(S1,S2), max(S1,S2)}).

%% Return any time that does not overlap standup meetings
no_standup1() ->
    ?SUCHTHAT({H,M,_}, stamp(), H =/= 9 orelse M > 10).
no_standup2() ->
    ?LET({H,M,S}, stamp(),
        case H of
            9 when M =< 10 -> {8, M, S};
            _ -> {H,M,S}
        end).
```

Elixir   code/CustomGenerators/elixir/pbt/test/exercises_test.exs

---

```elixir
# returning hours in the morning
def am_stamp1() do
  such_that({h, _, _} <- stamp(), when: h < 12)
end

def am_stamp2() do
  let({h, m, s} <- stamp(), do: {rem(h, 12), m, s})
end

# Return two ordered timestamps
def stamps1() do
  such_that({s1, s2} <- {stamp(), stamp()}, when: s1 <= s2)
end

def stamps2() do
  let({s1, s2} <- {stamp(), stamp()}, do: {min(s1, s2), max(s1, s2)})
end

# Return any time that does not overlap standup meetings
def no_standup1() do
  such_that({h, m, _} <- stamp(), when: h != 9 or m > 10)
end

def no_standup2() do
  let {h, m, s} <- stamp() do
    case h do
      9 when m <= 10 -> {8, m, s}
      _ -> {h, m, s}
    end
  end
end
```

Solution on page 318.

Question 6

Write a symbolic generator that creates a file containing various bytes. When a property fails, the user should be able to see the failing output without having to peek inside files.

You may need wrappers for file:open/2 and file:write/2 to ensure easier composability of these functions. Here's an example of those:

Erlang   code/CustomGenerators/erlang/pbt/test/prop_exercises.erl

---

```erlang
file_open(Name, Opts) ->
    {ok, Fd} = file:open(Name, Opts),
    %% ensure the file is refreshed on each test run
    file:truncate(Fd),
    Fd.
```

```
file_write(Fd, Data) ->
    ok = file:write(Fd, Data),
    Fd.
```

Elixir	code/CustomGenerators/elixir/pbt/test/exercises_test.exs

```elixir
def file_open(name, opts) do
  {:ok, fd} = File.open(name, opts)
  # ensure the file is refreshed on each run
  :file.truncate(fd)
  fd
end

def file_write(fd, data) do
  IO.write(fd, data)
  fd
end
```

Solution on page 319.

Part II

Stateless Properties in Practice

Let's get practical. We'll see how properties can be used in actual projects, and we'll also cover some more advanced topics in here.

## CHAPTER 5

Responsible Testing

A common sight in a team that just started learning property-based testing is that almost all the new tests written are properties, even when it doesn't really make sense to do so. The pendulum swings too far and too fast, and the project suffers for it. In this chapter, we'll see multiple example situations where property tests may or may not be appropriate, how they can be enhanced through careful addition of traditional tests in a regular project or other external tool like Dialyzer, or where they may be just plain inappropriate. We'll move from knowing *how* properties work—you can write generators, measure their efficiency, and come up with properties through various strategies—to having a good feel of *when* properties work best.

We'll take a practical project based on the birthday greeting kata.[1] This exercise asks us to organize unit tests for a little application in a manner such that as few tests as possible will need to be modified or trashed when implementation details or requirements change. It's an exercise usually meant for object-oriented languages, but since we're using Elixir and Erlang here, we'll also see how to approach the design in a functional manner.

The exercise will contain parts having to do with data storage, text parsing, data manipulation, and templating. We will *only focus on unit tests*, and we'll leave more side-effectful integration and system tests to later chapters such as Chapter 9, *Stateful Properties*, on page 201 and Chapter 10, *Case Study: Bookstore*, on page 233. For now, we'll see how to choose between traditional example-based unit tests and property tests, how they can be used together to complement each other, and we'll get a feel for figuring out how to add properties to our workflow in a project started from scratch.

---

1. http://matteo.vaccari.name/blog/archives/154

The Specification

We're going to write a program that will first load a set of employee records from a flat file and then send a greeting email to each employee whose birthday is today. In our example, the flat file we receive contains employee records and looks a bit like a *comma-separated values* (CSV)[2] file. We're given this sample:

```
last_name, first_name, date_of_birth, email
Doe, John, 1982/10/08, john.doe@foobar.com
Ann, Mary, 1975/09/11, mary.ann@foobar.com
```

The email sent on an employee's birthday should contain text like

> Subject: Happy birthday!

> Happy birthday, dear John!

On its own, this is straightforward. The challenge comes from the additional constraints given:

- The tests written should be *unit tests*, meaning none of the tests should talk to a database, touch the filesystem, interact with the network, or toy with the environment (config). Tests that do any of these are qualified as integration tests and are out of scope. This actually takes restraint to do!

- The CSV format won't be kept forever. Eventually, a database or web service should be used to fetch the employee records, and similarly for the email sending. The tests should be written to require as few modifications as possible whenever these implementation details change.

Let's see how we can approach the design of this system, one step at a time.

Thinking About Program Structure

The single most helpful thing we can do to make our testing experience easier is to design a system that is inherently testable. To do this well, thinking in terms of what are the observable effects we want to test against is crucial. In object-oriented code, the traditional approach asks us to limit ourselves to specific objects and to observe their behavior and side effects carefully. To prevent the test scope from being too large, mocking[3] and dependency injection[4] represent a good way to wall things off.

---

2. https://en.wikipedia.org/wiki/Comma-separated_values
3. https://en.wikipedia.org/wiki/Mock_object
4. https://en.wikipedia.org/wiki/Dependency_injection

In the case of Erlang and Elixir, these practices can and will make sense when testing specific actors, although this may bring us closer to integration testing. For most cases though, since we're doing functional programming, the lesson taught by pure languages like Haskell is that side effects can be grouped together at one end of the system, and we can keep the rest of the code as pure as possible. Haskell enforces that mechanism, but nothing prevents us from doing it by hand here. Let's see how we could classify the different actions in our program:

Side-Effectful	Functional
Reading a flat file	Converting CSV data to employee records
Finding today's date	Searching for employees based on a date
Sending an email	Formatting an email as a string

Things are a bit clearer now. Everything on the left column will go in integration tests (not covered in this chapter), and everything on the right column can go in unit tests and is in scope. In fact, if we use this classification to design the entire system, we can have something fairly easy to test, as shown in the following figure:

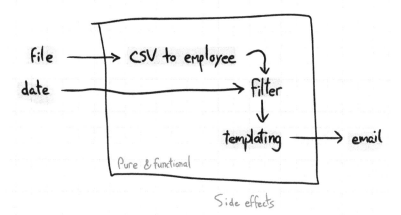

Everything in the box should be pure and functional, everything outside of it will provide side effects. Some main() function will have the responsibility of tying both universes together. With this approach, the program becomes a sequence of transformations carried over known (but configurable) bits of data. This structure isn't cast in stone, but should be a fairly good guideline that ensures strict decoupling of components, easy testing, and simple refactoring.

With this top-level view in place, we can start working on specific components that can then be integrated after the fact. Here are the building blocks to be written:

1. CSV parsing of terms into maps

2. Filtering of objects based on date or time (If the program used a SQL database or a service to handle search, we wouldn't have to write this.)

3. Putting the filtering and CSV parsing together into an employee module providing a well-isolated interface

4. Templating of the email and subject to be sent, based on the employee data

Although sending emails and reading from disk are side-effectful items that are out of scope, we'll add a fifth step where we tie up all the parts together with a top-level module (exposing the main() function mentioned earlier). For this, we can use a simple escript project format, which lets us run simple programs easily:

```
$ rebar3 new escript bday
===> Writing bday/src/bday.erl
===> Writing bday/src/bday.app.src
===> Writing bday/rebar.config
===> Writing bday/.gitignore
===> Writing bday/LICENSE
===> Writing bday/README.md
```

And then edit the configuration to add PropEr to the project:

About the Code

In the snippets that follow, code is labeled with both the language (Erlang and Elixir) and the file where you should put the code if you're following along.

Erlang   code/ResponsibleTesting/erlang/bday/rebar.config

```
%% the plugin itself
{project_plugins, [rebar3_proper]}.

{escript_incl_apps, [bday]}.
{escript_main_app, bday}.
{escript_name, bday}.

%% The PropEr dependency is still required to compile the test cases,
%% but only as a test dependency
{profiles,
    [{test, [
        {erl_opts, [nowarn_export_all]},
        {deps, [proper]}
    ]}
]}.
```

Given Elixir has mix run -e Mod.function as a command that can run an arbitrary function, a regular project can be used there instead. Just make sure to re-configure the mix file in it the same way we've done in *Elixir*, on page 12:

```
$ mix new bday
* creating README.md
* creating .gitignore
* creating mix.exs
* creating config
* creating config/config.exs
«more build output»
```

Include the proper mix file modifications:

Elixir	code/ResponsibleTesting/elixir/bday/mix.exs

```
# Run "mix help deps" to learn about dependencies.
defp deps do
  [
    {:propcheck, "~> 1.1", only: [:test, :dev]}
  ]
end
```

With this in place, we can start working on individual functional parts.

CSV Parsing

The first part of the program we'll work on is handling CSV conversion. No specific order is better than another in this case, and starting with CSV instead of filtering or email rendering is entirely arbitrary. In this section, we'll explore how to come up with the right type of properties for encoding and decoding CSV, and how to get decent generators for that task. We'll also see how regular example-based unit tests can be used to strengthen our properties, and see how each fares compared to the other.

CSV is a loose format that nobody really implements the same way. It's really a big mess, even though RFC 4180[5] tries to provide a simple specification:

- Each record is on a separate line, separated by *CRLF* (a \r followed by a \n).

- The last record of the file may or may not have a CRLF after it. (It is optional.)

- The first line of the file may be a header line, ended with a CRLF. In this case, the problem description includes a header, which will be assumed to always be there.

---

5. https://tools.ietf.org/html/rfc4180

- Commas go between fields of a record.

- Any spaces are considered to be part of the record. (The example in the problem description doesn't respect that, as it adds a space after each comma even though it's clearly not part of the record.)

- Double quotes (") can be used to wrap a given field.

- Fields that contain line breaks (CRLF), double quotes, or commas must be wrapped in double quotes.

- All records in a document contain the same number of fields.

- A double quote within a double-quoted field can be escaped by preceding it with another double quote ("a""b" means a"b).

- Field values or header names can be empty.

- Valid characters for records include only

```
! #$%&'()*+-./0123456789:;<=>?@ABCDEFGHIJKLMNOPQRSTUVWXYZ[\\]^_`
abcdefghijklmnopqrstuvwxyz{|}~
```

Which means the official CSV specs won't let us have employees whose names don't fit that pattern, but if you want, you can always extend the tests later and improve things. For now though, we'll implement this specification, and as far as our program is concerned, whatever we find in the CSV file will be treated as correct.

For example, if a row contains a, b, c, we'll consider the three values to be "a", " b", and " c" with the leading spaces, and patch them up in our program, rather than modifying the CSV parser we'll write. We'll do this because, in the long run, it'll be simpler to reason about our system if all independent components are well-defined reusable units, and we instead only need to reason about adapters to glue them together. Having business-specific code and workarounds injected through all layers of the code base is usually a good way to write unmaintainable systems.

Out of the approaches we've seen in Chapter 3, *Thinking in Properties*, on page 33, we could try the following:

- Modeling—make a simpler less efficient version of CSV parsing and compare it to the real one.

- Generalizing example tests—a standard unit test would be dumping data, then reading it, and making sure it matches expectations; we need to generalize this so one property can be equivalent to all examples.

- Invariants—find a set of rules that put together represent CSV operations well enough.

- Symmetric properties—serialize and unserialize the data, ensuring results are the same.

The latter technique is the most interesting one for parsers and serializers, since we need encoded data to validate decoding, and that decoding is required to make sure encoding works well. Both sides will need to agree and be tested together no matter what. Plugging both into a single property tends to be ideal. All we need after that is to *anchor* the property with either a few traditional unit tests or simpler properties to make sure expectations are met.

Let's start by writing tests first, so we can think of properties before writing the code. Since we'll do an encoding/decoding sequence, generating Erlang terms that are encodable in CSV should be the first step. CSV contains rows of text records separated by commas. We'll start by writing generators for the text records themselves, and assemble them later. We'll currently stay with the simplest CSV encoding possible: everything is a string. How to handle integers, dates, and so on, tends to be application-specific.

Because CSV is a text-based format, it contains some escapable sequences, which turn out to always be problematic no matter what format you're handling. In CSV, as we've seen in the specification, escape sequences are done through wrapping strings in double quotes ("), with some special cases for escaping double quotes themselves. For now, let's not worry about it, besides making sure the case is well-represented in our data generators:

Erlang	code/ResponsibleTesting/erlang/bday/test/prop_csv.erl

```erlang
field() -> oneof([unquoted_text(), quotable_text()]).

unquoted_text() -> list(elements(textdata())).

quotable_text() -> list(elements([$\r, $\n, $", $,] ++ textdata())).

textdata() ->
    "ABCDEFGHIJKLMNOPQRSTUVWXYZabcdefghijklmnopqrstuvwxyz0123456789"
    ":;<=>?@ !#$%&'()*+-./[\\]^_`{|}~".
```

Elixir	code/ResponsibleTesting/elixir/bday/test/csv_test.exs

```elixir
def field() do
  oneof([unquoted_text(), quotable_text()])
end
```

```
# using charlists for the easy generation
def unquoted_text() do
  let chars <- list(elements(textdata())) do
    to_string(chars)
  end
end

def quotable_text() do
  let chars <- list(elements('\r\n",' ++ textdata())) do
    to_string(chars)
  end
end

def textdata() do
  'ABCDEFGHIJKLMNOPQRSTUVWXYZabcdefghijklmnopqrstuvwxyz0123456789' ++
    ':;<=>?@ !#$%&\'()*+-./[\\]^_`{|}~'
end
```

The field() generator depends on two other generators: unquoted_text() and quotable_text(). The former will be used to generate Erlang data that will require no known escape sequence in it once converted, whereas the latter will be used to generate sequences that may possibly require escaping (the four escapable characters are only present in this one). Both generators rely on textdata(), which contains all the valid characters allowed by the specification.

You'll note that we've put an Erlang string for textdata() with alphanumeric characters coming first, and that we pass it to list(elements()). This approach will randomly pick characters from textdata() to build a string, but what's interesting is what will happen when one of our tests fail. Because elements() shrinks toward the first elements of the list we pass to it, PropEr will try to generate counterexamples that are more easily human-readable when possible by limiting the number of special characters they contain. Rather than generating {#$%a~, it might try to generate ABFe#c once a test fails.

We can now put these records together. A CSV file will have two types of rows: a header on the first line, and then data entries in the following lines. In any CSV document, we expect the number of columns to be the same on all of the rows:

Erlang	code/ResponsibleTesting/erlang/bday/test/prop_csv.erl

```
header(Size) -> vector(Size, name()).

record(Size) -> vector(Size, field()).

name() -> field().
```

```elixir
def header(size) do
  vector(size, name())
end

def record(size) do
  vector(size, field())
end

def name() do
  field()
end
```

Those generators basically generate the same types of strings for both headers and rows, with a known fixed length as an argument. name() is defined as field() because they have the same requirements specification-wise, but it's useful to give each generator a name according to its purpose: if we end up modifying or changing requirements on one of them, we can do so with minimal changes. We can then assemble all of that jolly stuff together into one list of maps that contain all the data we need:

```erlang
csv_source() ->
    ?LET(Size, pos_integer(),
        ?LET(Keys, header(Size),
            list(entry(Size, Keys)))).

entry(Size, Keys) ->
    ?LET(Vals, record(Size),
        maps:from_list(lists:zip(Keys, Vals))).
```

```elixir
def csv_source() do
  let size <- pos_integer() do
    let keys <- header(size) do
      list(entry(size, keys))
    end
  end
end

def entry(size, keys) do
  let vals <- record(size) do
    Map.new(Enum.zip(keys, vals))
  end
end
```

The csv_source() generator picks up a Size value that represents how many entries will be in each row. By putting it in a ?LET macro, we make sure that whatever the expression that uses Size is, it uses a discrete value, and not the generator itself. This will allow us to use Size multiple times safely with always the same value in the second ?LET macro. That second macro generates one set of headers (the keys of every map), and then uses them to create a list of entries.

The entries themselves are specified by the entry/2 generator, which creates a list of record values, and pairs them up with the keys from csv_source() into a map. This generates values such as these:

```
$ rebar3 as test shell
«build output»
1> proper_gen:pick(prop_csv:csv_source()).
{ok,[#{[] => "z","&_f" => "t,:S","cH^*M" => "{6Z#"},
     #{[] => "kS3>","&_f" => "/","cH^*M" => "eK"},
     #{[] => "~","&_f" => [],"cH^*M" => "Bk#?X7h"}]}
2> proper_gen:pick(prop_csv:csv_source()).
{ok,[#{"D" => "\nQNUO","D4D" => "!E$0; )KL",
       "R\r~P{qC-" => "4L(Q4-N9","T6FAGuhf" => "wSP4jONE3Q"},
     #{"D" => "!Y7H\rQ?I7\r","D4D" => [],
       "R\r~P{qC-" => "}66W2I9+?R","T6FAGuhf" => "pF8/C"},
     #{"D" => [],"D4D" => "?'_6","R\r~P{qC-" => "j|Q",
       "T6FAGuhf" => "f$s7=sFx2>"},
     #{"D" => "e;hol\njn!2","D4D" => ".8B{k|+|}",
       "R\r~P{qC-" => "V","T6FAGuhf" => "a\"/J\rfE#$"},
«more maps»
```

As you can see, all the maps for a given batch share the same keys, but have varying values. Those are ready to be encoded and passed to our property:

Erlang   code/ResponsibleTesting/erlang/bday/test/prop_csv.erl

```
prop_roundtrip() ->
    ?FORALL(Maps, csv_source(),
            Maps =:= bday_csv:decode(bday_csv:encode(Maps))).
```

Elixir   code/ResponsibleTesting/elixir/bday/test/csv_test.exs

```
property "roundtrip encoding/decoding" do
  forall maps <- csv_source() do
    maps == Csv.decode(Csv.encode(maps))
  end
end
```

Running it at this point would be an instant failure since we haven't written the code to go with it. Since this chapter is about tests far more than how to implement a CSV parser, we'll go over the latter rather quickly. Here's an implementation that takes about a hundred lines:

Erlang	code/ResponsibleTesting/erlang/bday/src/bday_csv.erl

```erlang
-module(bday_csv).
-export([encode/1, decode/1]).

%% @doc Take a list of maps with the same keys and transform them
%% into a string that is valid CSV, with a header.
-spec encode([map()]) -> string().
encode([]) -> "";
encode(Maps) ->
    Keys = lists:join(",", [escape(Name) || Name <- maps:keys(hd(Maps))]),
    Vals = [lists:join(",", [escape(Field) || Field <- maps:values(Map)])
            || Map <- Maps],
    lists:flatten([Keys, "\r\n", lists:join("\r\n", Vals)]).

%% @doc Take a string that represents a valid CSV data dump
%% and turn it into a list of maps with the header entries as keys
-spec decode(string()) -> list(map()).
decode("") -> [];
decode(CSV) ->
    {Headers, Rest} = decode_header(CSV, []),
    Rows = decode_rows(Rest),
    [maps:from_list(lists:zip(Headers, Row)) || Row <- Rows].
```

First, there's the public interface with two functions: encode/1 and decode/1. The functions are fairly straightforward, delegating the more complex operations to private helper functions. Let's start by looking at those helping with encoding:

```erlang
%%%%%%%%%%%%%%%%
%%% PRIVATE %%%
%%%%%%%%%%%%%%%%

%% @private return a possibly escaped (if necessary) field or name
-spec escape(string()) -> string().
escape(Field) ->
    case escapable(Field) of
        true -> "\"" ++ do_escape(Field) ++ "\"";
        false -> Field
    end.

%% @private checks whether a string for a field or name needs escaping
-spec escapable(string()) -> boolean().
escapable(String) ->
    lists:any(fun(Char) -> lists:member(Char, [$",$,,$\r,$\n]) end, String).
```

```erlang
%% @private replace escapable characters (only `"') in CSV.
%% The surrounding double-quotes are not added; caller must add them.
-spec do_escape(string()) -> string().
do_escape([]) -> [];
do_escape([$"|Str]) -> [$", $" | do_escape(Str)];
do_escape([Char|Rest]) -> [Char | do_escape(Rest)].
```

If a string is judged to need escaping (according to escapable/1), then the string is wrapped in double quotes (") and all double quotes inside of it are escaped with another double quote. With this, encoding is covered. Next there's decoding's private functions:

```erlang
%% @private Decode the entire header line, returning all names in order
-spec decode_header(string(), [string()]) -> {[string()], string()}.
decode_header(String, Acc) ->
    case decode_name(String) of
        {ok, Name, Rest} -> decode_header(Rest, [Name | Acc]);
        {done, Name, Rest} -> {[Name | Acc], Rest}
    end.

%% @private Decode all rows into a list.
-spec decode_rows(string()) -> [[string()]].
decode_rows(String) ->
    case decode_row(String, []) of
        {Row, ""} -> [Row];
        {Row, Rest} -> [Row | decode_rows(Rest)]
    end.

%% @private Decode an entire row, with all values in order
-spec decode_row(string(), [string()]) -> {[string()], string()}.
decode_row(String, Acc) ->
    case decode_field(String) of
        {ok, Field, Rest} -> decode_row(Rest, [Field | Acc]);
        {done, Field, Rest} -> {[Field | Acc], Rest}
    end.

%% @private Decode a name; redirects to decoding quoted or unquoted text
-spec decode_name(string()) -> {ok|done, string(), string()}.
decode_name([$" | Rest]) -> decode_quoted(Rest);
decode_name(String) -> decode_unquoted(String).

%% @private Decode a field; redirects to decoding quoted or unquoted text
-spec decode_field(string()) -> {ok|done, string(), string()}.
decode_field([$" | Rest]) -> decode_quoted(Rest);
decode_field(String) -> decode_unquoted(String).
```

Decoding is done by fetching headers, then fetching all rows. A header line is parsed by reading each column name one at a time, and a row is parsed by reading each field one at a time. At the end you can see that both fields and names are actually implemented as quoted or unquoted strings:

```
%% @private Decode a quoted string
-spec decode_quoted(string()) -> {ok|done, string(), string()}.
decode_quoted(String) -> decode_quoted(String, []).

%% @private Decode a quoted string
-spec decode_quoted(string(), [char()]) -> {ok|done, string(), string()}.
decode_quoted([$"], Acc) -> {done, lists:reverse(Acc), ""};
decode_quoted([$",$\r,$\n | Rest], Acc) -> {done, lists:reverse(Acc), Rest};
decode_quoted([$",$, | Rest], Acc) -> {ok, lists:reverse(Acc), Rest};
decode_quoted([$",$" | Rest], Acc) -> decode_quoted(Rest, [$" | Acc]);
decode_quoted([Char | Rest], Acc) -> decode_quoted(Rest, [Char | Acc]).

%% @private Decode an unquoted string
-spec decode_unquoted(string()) -> {ok|done, string(), string()}.
decode_unquoted(String) -> decode_unquoted(String, []).

%% @private Decode an unquoted string
-spec decode_unquoted(string(), [char()]) -> {ok|done, string(), string()}.
decode_unquoted([], Acc) -> {done, lists:reverse(Acc), ""};
decode_unquoted([$\r,$\n | Rest], Acc) -> {done, lists:reverse(Acc), Rest};
decode_unquoted([$, | Rest], Acc) -> {ok, lists:reverse(Acc), Rest};
decode_unquoted([Char | Rest], Acc) -> decode_unquoted(Rest, [Char | Acc]).
```

Elixir translation on page 326.

Both functions to read quoted or unquoted strings mostly work the same, except quoted ones have specific rules about unescaping content baked in. And with this, our CSV handling is complete.

The code was developed against the properties by running the tests multiple times and refining the implementation iteratively. For brevity, we'll skip all the failed attempts that did some dirty odd parsing, except for one failing implementation that's particularly interesting since it had a failure against the following input:

```
\r\na
```

This is technically a valid CSV file with a single column, for which the empty name "" is chosen (commas only split values, so a single \r\n means a 0-length string as a value on that line), and with a single value "a". The expected output from decoding this is [#{"" ⇒ "a"}]. The first version of the parser had no way to cope with such cases, since I couldn't imagine them either. The parser shown previously is handling such cases, but the digging and rewriting has been skipped for brevity.

If you run the property over the previous (correct) implementation, you'll find it still fails on this tricky test:

```
bday_csv:encode([#{""=>""},#{""=>""}]) => "\r\n\r\n"
bday_csv:decode("\r\n\r\n")            => [#{"" => ""}]
```

This is an ambiguity embedded directly in the CSV specification. Because a trailing \r\n is acceptable, it is impossible to know whether there is an empty trailing line or not in the case of one-column data sets. Above one column, at least one comma (,) is going to be on the line. At one column, there is no way to know.

Under fifty lines of tests were enough to discover inconsistencies in RFC 4180 itself, inconsistencies that can't be reconciled or fixed in our program. Instead, we'll have to relax the property, making sure we don't cover that case by changing csv_source() and adding +1 to every Size value we generate. That way, we shift the range for columns from 1..N to 2..(N+1), ensuring we always have two or more columns in generated data.

Erlang   code/ResponsibleTesting/erlang/bday/test/prop_csv.erl

```erlang
csv_source() ->
    ?LET(Size, pos_integer(),
        ?LET(Keys, header(Size+1),
            list(entry(Size+1, Keys)))).
```

Elixir   code/ResponsibleTesting/elixir/bday/test/csv_test.exs

```elixir
def csv_source() do
  let size <- pos_integer() do
    let keys <- header(size + 1) do
      list(entry(size + 1, keys))
    end
  end
end
```

After this change, the property works fine. For good measure, we should add a unit test representing the known unavoidable bug to the same test suite, documenting known behavior:

Erlang   code/ResponsibleTesting/erlang/bday/test/prop_csv.erl

```erlang
-module(prop_csv).
-include_lib("proper/include/proper.hrl").
-include_lib("eunit/include/eunit.hrl").
-compile(export_all).

«existing code»

%%%%%%%%%%%%%%
%%% EUnit %%%
%%%%%%%%%%%%%%

%% @doc One-column CSV files are inherently ambiguous due to
%% trailing CRLF in RFC 4180. This bug is expected
```

```
one_column_bug_test() ->
    ?assertEqual("\r\n\r\n", bday_csv:encode([#{""=>""},#{""=>""}])),
    ?assertEqual([#{"" => ""}], bday_csv:decode("\r\n\r\n")).
```

Elixir	code/ResponsibleTesting/elixir/bday/test/csv_test.exs

```
## Unit Tests ##
test "one column CSV files are inherently ambiguous" do
  assert "\r\n\r\n" == Csv.encode([%{"" => ""}, %{"" => ""}])
  assert [%{"" => ""}] == Csv.decode("\r\n\r\n")
end
```

The Erlang suite can be run with rebar3 eunit as well as rebar3 proper. Using prop_ as a prefix to both the module and properties lets the proper plugin detect what it needs. For EUnit, the _test suffix for functions lets it do the proper detection. If you also wanted to use the common test framework in Erlang, the _SUITE suffix should be added to the module.

There is a last gotcha implicit to the implementation of our CSV parser: since it uses maps, duplicate column names are not tolerated. Since our CSV files have to be used to represent a database, it is probably a fine assumption to make about the data set that column names are all unique. All in all, we're probably good ignoring duplicate columns and single-column CSV files since it's unlikely database tables would be that way either, but it's not fully CSV-compliant. This gotcha was discovered by adding good old samples from the RFC into the EUnit test suite:

Erlang	code/ResponsibleTesting/erlang/bday/test/prop_csv.erl

```
rfc_record_per_line_test() ->
    ?assertEqual([#{"aaa" => "zzz", "bbb" => "yyy", "ccc" => "xxx"}],
                 bday_csv:decode("aaa,bbb,ccc\r\nzzz,yyy,xxx\r\n")).

rfc_optional_trailing_crlf_test() ->
    ?assertEqual([#{"aaa" => "zzz", "bbb" => "yyy", "ccc" => "xxx"}],
                 bday_csv:decode("aaa,bbb,ccc\r\nzzz,yyy,xxx")).

rfc_double_quote_test() ->
    ?assertEqual([#{"aaa" => "zzz", "bbb" => "yyy", "ccc" => "xxx"}],
                 bday_csv:decode("\"aaa\",\"bbb\",\"ccc\"\r\nzzz,yyy,xxx")).

rfc_crlf_escape_test() ->
    ?assertEqual([#{"aaa" => "zzz", "b\r\nbb" => "yyy", "ccc" => "xxx"}],
                 bday_csv:decode("\"aaa\",\"b\r\nbb\",\"ccc\"\r\nzzz,yyy,xxx")).

rfc_double_quote_escape_test() ->
    %% Since we decided headers are mandatory, this test adds a line
    %% with empty values (CLRF,,) to the example from the RFC.
    ?assertEqual([#{"aaa" => "", "b\"bb" => "", "ccc" => ""}],
                 bday_csv:decode("\"aaa\",\"b\"\"bb\",\"ccc\"\r\n,,")).
```

```erlang
%% @doc this counterexample is taken literally from the RFC and cannot
%% work with the current implementation because maps have no dupe keys
dupe_keys_unsupported_test() ->
    CSV = "field_name,field_name,field_name\r\n"
          "aaa,bbb,ccc\r\n"
          "zzz,yyy,xxx\r\n",
    [Map1,Map2] = bday_csv:decode(CSV),
    ?assertEqual(1, length(maps:keys(Map1))),
    ?assertEqual(1, length(maps:keys(Map2))),
    ?assertMatch(#{"field_name" := _}, Map1),
    ?assertMatch(#{"field_name" := _}, Map2).
```

Elixir translation on page 328.

The last test was impossible to cover with the current property implementation, so doing it by hand in an example case still proved worthwhile. In the end, ignoring comments and blank lines, twenty-seven lines of example tests let us find one gotcha about our code and validate specific cases against the RFC, and nineteen lines of property-based tests that let us exercise our code to the point we found inconsistencies in the RFC itself (which is not too representative of the real world).[6] That's impressive.

All in all, this combination of example-based unit tests and properties is a good match. The properties can find very obtuse problems that require complex searches into the problem space, both in breadth and in depth. On the other hand, they can be written in a way that they're general enough that some basic details could be overlooked. In this case, the property exercised encoding and decoding exceedingly well, but didn't do it infallibly—we programmers are good at making mistakes no matter the situation, and example tests could also catch some things. They're great when acting as *anchors*, an additional safety net making sure our properties are not drifting away on their own.

Another similar good use of unit tests are to store *regressions*, specific tricky bugs that need to be explicitly called out or validated frequently. PropEr with Erlang and Elixir both contain options to store and track regressions automatically if you want them to. Otherwise, example tests are as good of a place as any to store that information.

With the CSV handling in place, we can now focus on filtering employee records.

Filtering Records

We have a module to convert CSV to maps, and we know that we'll need employee records and a way to filter them to move the project forward. We

---

6.　http://tburette.github.io/blog/2014/05/25/so-you-want-to-write-your-own-CSV-code/

could start by defining the records' specific fields, but since we know they'll be implemented using maps, and that maps are a fairly dynamic data structure, then nothing prevents us from jumping directly to the filtering step.

In this section, we'll see a case where even though the problem space is large, we can explore it *better* with example tests than with properties. The reason for this is that the type of data we can get is very regular and easy to enumerate, such that a brute force strategy pretty much guarantees a more exhaustive and reliable testing approach than a probabilistic one with properties. Properties are not *always* the best way to go about tests, and this is true in the next case. By filtering employee maps based on dates, we'll see that even when they're not the best tool, properties can still be a useful source of inspiration to come up with examples as well.

In most implementations that rely on an external component to filter and sort records, the functionality would be provided at the interface level: in a SQL query or as arguments to an API for example. So it wouldn't require tests at the unit level at all, and maybe just integration tests, if any. Filtering itself is straightforward: just use a standard library function like lists:filter/2 and pass in the date with which we want to filter. What's trickier is ensuring that the predicate passed to the function is correct.

Since the birthday search is based on 366 possible dates to verify, it could be reasonable to just run all of them through an exhaustive search. But in practice, we need to consider leap years, multiple matching employees, and so on. For example, to run an exhaustive search, we would need a list of 366 employees (or 732, or even 1,098 to ensure more than one employee per day), each with their own birthday. We would then need to run the program for every day of every year starting in 2018 (year of this writing) until 2118, making sure that each employee is greeted once per year on the same day as that employee's birthday.

That gives slightly more than one million runs to cover the whole foreseeable future. We can try a sample run to estimate how long that would take, to see if it's worth doing. Let's get an approximation by running a filter function as many times as we'd need to cover around a hundred years with 1,098 employees:

```
1> L = lists:duplicate(366*3, #{name => "a", bday => {1,2,3}}),
1> timer:tc(fun() ->
1>    [lists:filter(fun(X) -> false end, L) || _ <- lists:seq(1,100*366)], ok
1> end).
{17801551,ok}
```

Around eighteen seconds. Not super fast, but not insufferable. The run could be faster by checking only twenty years, which takes under three seconds.

That may be good enough to warrant bypassing unit tests and property-based testing altogether. Brute force it is! We'll inspire ourselves from the principles we use when coming up with properties, but do so outside of any property-based testing framework. The general approach to write our tests will be similar, except that we'll replace generators with fully deterministic data sets that cover all cases.

Oh yes, and then there are leap years to handle. There's a well-known formula for which year will be a leap year, with Erlang implementing it in the calendar:is_leap_year/1 function (working on years greater than 0):

```erlang
-spec is_leap_year(non_neg_integer()) -> boolean().
is_leap_year(Year) when Year rem 4 =:= 0, Year rem 100 > 0 -> true;
is_leap_year(Year) when Year rem 400 =:= 0 -> true;
is_leap_year(_) -> false.
```

By using such a function, we can hand roll a full exhaustive property test. Rather than using a ?FORALL macro, we will write some code to generate exhaustive data (as opposed to PropEr generators, which are unpredictable) and then manually validate every call in a lists:foreach/2 call:

Erlang	code/ResponsibleTesting/erlang/bday/test/bday_filter_tests.erl

```erlang
-module(bday_filter_tests).
-include_lib("eunit/include/eunit.hrl").

%% Property
bday_filter_test() ->
    Years = generate_years_data(2018,2038),
    People = generate_people_for_year(3),
    lists:foreach(fun(YearData) ->
        Birthdays = find_birthdays_for_year(People, YearData),
        every_birthday_once(People, Birthdays),
        on_right_date(People, Birthdays)
    end, Years).

find_birthdays_for_year(_, []) -> [];
find_birthdays_for_year(People, [Day|Year]) ->
    Found = bday_filter:birthday(People, Day), % <= function being tested
    [{Day, Found} | find_birthdays_for_year(People, Year)].
```

Elixir	code/ResponsibleTesting/elixir/bday/test/filter_test.exs

```elixir
defmodule FilterTest do
  use ExUnit.Case
  alias Bday.Filter, as: Filter
```

```
test "property-style filtering test" do
  years = generate_years_data(2018, 2038)
  people = generate_people_for_year(3)

  for yeardata <- years do
    birthdays = find_birthdays_for_year(people, yeardata)
    every_birthday_once(people, birthdays)
    on_right_date(people, birthdays)
  end
end

defp find_birthdays_for_year(_, []), do: []

defp find_birthdays_for_year(people, [day | year]) do
  found = Filter.birthday(people, day) # <- function being tested
  [{day, found} | find_birthdays_for_year(people, year)]
end
```

The data being generated is stored in Years, for the ability to generate all dates in a year, and People, which contains all the employees in a company. The search itself is run for each date of a year by the function find_birthdays_for_year/2, which just calls our actual implementation under test, bday_filter:birthday(People, Day). The result is then passed to two assertions, every_birthday_once/2 and on_right_date/2. Let's start by digging into the generators, so that we can see what data the rest of the tests will use.

The first generator is for years, which really just iterates through all possible days and assembles a list of all dates:

Erlang	code/ResponsibleTesting/erlang/bday/test/bday_filter_tests.erl

```
%% Generators
generate_years_data(End, End) ->
    [];
generate_years_data(Start, End) ->
    [generate_year_data(Start) | generate_years_data(Start+1, End)].

generate_year_data(Year) ->
    DaysInFeb = case calendar:is_leap_year(Year) of
        true -> 29;
        false -> 28
    end,
    month(Year,1,31) ++ month(Year,2,DaysInFeb) ++ month(Year,3,31) ++
    month(Year,4,30) ++ month(Year,5,31) ++ month(Year,6,30) ++
    month(Year,7,31) ++ month(Year,8,31) ++ month(Year,9,30) ++
    month(Year,10,31) ++ month(Year,11,30) ++ month(Year,12,31).

month(Y,M,1) -> [{Y,M,1}];
month(Y,M,N) -> [{Y,M,N} | month(Y,M,N-1)].
```

Elixir	code/ResponsibleTesting/elixir/bday/test/filter_test.exs

```elixir
# Generators
defp generate_years_data(stop, stop), do: []

defp generate_years_data(start, stop) do
  [generate_year_data(start) | generate_years_data(start + 1, stop)]
end

defp generate_year_data(year) do
  {:ok, date} = Date.new(year, 1, 1)

  days_in_feb =
    case Date.leap_year?(date) do
      true -> 29
      false -> 28
    end

  month(year, 1, 31) ++
    month(year, 2, days_in_feb) ++
    month(year, 3, 31) ++
    month(year, 4, 30) ++
    month(year, 5, 31) ++
    month(year, 6, 30) ++
    month(year, 7, 31) ++
    month(year, 8, 31) ++
    month(year, 9, 30) ++
    month(year, 10, 31) ++ month(year, 11, 30) ++ month(year, 12, 31)
end

defp month(y, m, 1) do
  {:ok, date} = Date.new(y, m, 1)
  [date]
end

defp month(y, m, n) do
  {:ok, date} = Date.new(y, m, n)
  [date | month(y, m, n - 1)]
end
```

There's the little special case for leap years adding a twenty-ninth day to February, but that's about it.

Now, for generating people, things are a bit trickier. The first thing we'll use is a *seed year*, which just contains all possible days and months—a leap year, such as 2016, is required—and then use it to create employee records. By using the dates as a seed for employee creation, we simply ensure that we'll get one employee per date. If we need more than one employee per date, we just need to run the function more than once. This is precisely what the generate_people_for_year(N) function does:

Erlang   code/ResponsibleTesting/erlang/bday/test/bday_filter_tests.erl

```erlang
generate_people_for_year(N) ->
    YearSeed = generate_year_data(2016), % leap year so all days are covered
    lists:append([people_for_year(YearSeed) || _ <- lists:seq(1,N)]).

people_for_year(Year) ->
    [person_for_date(Date) || Date <- Year].

person_for_date({_, M, D}) ->
    #{"name" => make_ref(),
      "date_of_birth" => {rand:uniform(100)+1900,M,D}}.
```

Elixir   code/ResponsibleTesting/elixir/bday/test/filter_test.exs

```elixir
defp generate_people_for_year(n) do
  # leap year so all days are covered
  year_seed = generate_year_data(2016)
  Enum.flat_map(1..n, fn _ -> people_for_year(year_seed) end)
end

defp people_for_year(year) do
  for date <- year do
    person_for_date(date)
  end
end

defp person_for_date(%Date{month: m, day: d} = date) do
  case Date.new(:rand.uniform(100) + 1900, m, d) do
    {:error, :invalid_date} ->
      person_for_date(date)

    {:ok, date} ->
      %{"name" => make_ref(), "date_of_birth" => date}
  end
end
```

You can see that people_for_year is just an iterator that will create one person
for each date, and person_for_date/1 will generate a unique name (an Erlang *reference*), and pick a random birth year from 1901 to 2000. It doesn't really
matter if the fake data we generate tells us someone is born on February 29
of a non–leap year since we're searching by the month and day of the *current
year*, and the birth year is ignored. In Elixir, this case is handled explicitly
since the date struct requires correct dates.

So that's for the generation. Let's get back to our assertions, our manual
replacement for rules for properties. We are testing two rules:

1. Every birthday is found exactly once. (Nobody is left behind nor found too often.)

2. Every birthday is found on the right date. (Don't write a system that cheats by telling everyone "happy birthday" on January 1st.)

These can be implemented using regular EUnit assertion macros, which cause a failure if the condition is false and will succeed by not crashing otherwise. The function every_birthday_once(People, Birthdays) takes in a list of all employees (People) and all birthdays found through filtering (Birthdays), builds a list of how many birthdays were not found or found more than once, and asserts that both lists are empty—because they've been found exactly once:

Erlang	code/ResponsibleTesting/erlang/bday/test/bday_filter_tests.erl

```erlang
%% Assertions
every_birthday_once(People, Birthdays) ->
    Found = lists:sort(lists:append([Found || {_, Found} <- Birthdays])),
    NotFound = People -- Found,
    FoundManyTimes = Found -- lists:usort(Found), % usort drops dupes
    ?assertEqual([], NotFound),
    ?assertEqual([], FoundManyTimes).

on_right_date(_People, Birthdays) ->
    [?assertEqual({M,D}, {PM,PD})
     || {{Y,M,D}, Found} <- Birthdays,
        #{"date_of_birth" := {_,PM,PD}} <- Found].
```

Elixir	code/ResponsibleTesting/elixir/bday/test/filter_test.exs

```elixir
defp every_birthday_once(people, birthdays) do
  found =
    birthdays
    |> Enum.flat_map(fn {_, found} -> found end)
    |> Enum.sort()

  not_found = people -- found
  found_many_times = found -- Enum.uniq(found)
  assert [] == not_found
  assert [] == found_many_times
end

defp on_right_date(_people, birthdays) do
  for {date, found} <- birthdays do
    for %{"date_of_birth" => dob} <- found do
      assert {date.month, date.day} == {dob.month, dob.day}
    end
  end
end
```

The assertion in on_right_date/2 checks that an employee's birthday (PM and PD for the month and day respectively) lands on the right month and day used for the search.

If you run the test, it will unsurprisingly fail since bday_filter:birthday/2 is currently undefined. Let's write a first implementation:

Erlang   code/ResponsibleTesting/erlang/bday/src/bday_filter.erl

```erlang
-module(bday_filter).
-export([birthday/2]).

birthday(People, {_Year, Month, Day}) ->
    lists:filter(
      fun(#{"date_of_birth" := {_,M,D}}) -> {Month,Day} == {M,D} end,
      People
    ).
```

Elixir   code/ResponsibleTesting/elixir/bday/lib/filter.ex

```elixir
def birthday(people, %Date{month: month, day: day}) do
  Enum.filter(
    people,
    fn %{"date_of_birth" => %Date{month: m, day: d}} ->
      {month, day} == {m, d}
    end
  )
end
```

The implementation is straightforward, using lists:filter/2 to check for the right month and date. Running it fails in a fun way:

```
$ rebar3 eunit
«build and test output»
Failures:

  1) bday_filter_tests:bday_filter_test/0: module 'bday_filter_tests'
     Failure/Error: ?assertEqual([], NotFound)
       expected: []
            got: [#{"date_of_birth" => {1940,2,29},
                    "name" => #Ref<0.1413896841.873201667.109143>},
                  #{"date_of_birth" => {1917,2,29},
                    "name" => #Ref<0.1413896841.873201667.109509>},
                  #{"date_of_birth" => {1972,2,29},
                    "name" => #Ref<0.1413896841.873201667.109875>}]
     %% lists.erl:1338:in `lists:foreach/2`
«more output»
```

So the ?assertEqual([], NotFound) assertion fails, which tells us that we have birthdays that haven't been found while they should have been. We don't have shrinking since we're writing our own properties without a framework, but by looking at the dates, we can figure out that something failed when looking up birthdays related to February 29. It's pretty certain that the problem with our filter function is that folks with their birthdays on leap days will be ignored on non–leap years.

We can patch this up by making sure that if we hit February 28 on a non–leap year, we should also look for people whose birthday would be on the 29th:

Erlang   code/ResponsibleTesting/erlang/bday/src/bday_filter.erl

```erlang
-module(bday_filter).
-export([birthday/2]).

birthday(People, {Year, 2, 28}) ->
    case calendar:is_leap_year(Year) of
        true -> filter_dob(People, 2, 28);
        false -> filter_dob(People, 2, 28) ++ filter_dob(People, 2, 29)
    end;
birthday(People, {_Year, Month, Day}) ->
    filter_dob(People, Month, Day).

filter_dob(People, Month, Day) ->
    lists:filter(
      fun(#{"date_of_birth" := {_,M,D}}) -> {Month,Day} == {M,D} end,
      People
    ).
```

Elixir   code/ResponsibleTesting/elixir/bday/lib/filter.ex

```elixir
defmodule Bday.Filter do
  def birthday(people, date = %Date{month: 2, day: 28}) do
    case Date.leap_year?(date) do
      true -> filter_dob(people, 2, 28)
      false -> filter_dob(people, 2, 28) ++ filter_dob(people, 2, 29)
    end
  end

  def birthday(people, %Date{month: m, day: d}) do
    filter_dob(people, m, d)
  end

  defp filter_dob(people, month, day) do
    Enum.filter(
      people,
      fn %{"date_of_birth" => %Date{month: m, day: d}} ->
        {month, day} == {m, d}
      end
    )
  end
end
```

Run the EUnit tests again and you should see another failing case:

```
$ rebar3 eunit
«build and test output»
Failures:

  1) bday_filter_tests:bday_filter_test/0: module 'bday_filter_tests'
     Failure/Error: ?assertEqual({2,28}, { PM , PD })
       expected: {2,28}
            got: {2,29}
     %% lists.erl:1338:in `lists:foreach/2`
«more output»
```

The test is now off. Since people whose birthday is on February 29 are greeted on the 28th in non–leap years, the on_right_date/2 assertion gets tripped: the 29th is clearly not the 28th. The test is wrong here, and it needs patching—the same kind of deal we get with regular property testing—by relaxing the assertion. We'll adjust it so the test accepts people being greeted on the wrong day when their birthday falls on an invalid date for the given search year:

Erlang	code/ResponsibleTesting/erlang/bday/test/bday_filter_tests.erl

```erlang
on_right_date(_People, Birthdays) ->
    [calendar:valid_date({Y,PM,PD}) andalso ?assertEqual({M,D}, {PM,PD})
     || {{Y,M,D}, Found} <- Birthdays,
        #{"date_of_birth" := {_,PM,PD}} <- Found].
```

Elixir	code/ResponsibleTesting/elixir/bday/test/filter_test.exs

```elixir
defp on_right_date(_people, birthdays) do
  for {date, found} <- birthdays do
    for %{"date_of_birth" => dob} <- found do
      case Date.new(date.year, dob.month, dob.day) do
        {:error, :invalid_date} -> :skip
        _ -> assert {date.month, date.day} == {dob.month, dob.day}
      end
    end
  end
end
```

The reason for picking calendar:valid_date/1 over checking leap years explicitly is that it lets us avoid reusing the same implementation between the function being tested and the test itself. It has a better chance of catching us making mistakes than duplicating the logic around would.

Now running the EUnit suite yields:

```
$ rebar3 eunit
===> Verifying dependencies...
===> Compiling bday
```

```
===> Performing EUnit tests...
........

Top 8 slowest tests (1.403 seconds, 88.3% of total time):
  bday_filter_tests:bday_filter_test/0: module 'bday_filter_tests'
    1.403 seconds
  prop_csv:rfc_double_quote_test/0
    0.000 seconds
  prop_csv:rfc_record_per_line_test/0
    0.000 seconds
«more output»

Finished in 1.589 seconds
8 tests, 0 failures
```

Not too bad! Under one and a half seconds for an exhaustive property-like test of the next twenty years of operation. While it's technically not property-based testing, the results are more trustworthy in this case since we're going over all possibilities rather than some random selected ones. We just get to debug things ourselves since there's no shrinking.

The lesson here is that even though property tests can be very exciting, it's always good to look for alternative ways to test things that might be more effective. In this case, when the various states or possible inputs are limited, exhaustive testing is an interesting way to do better than a property would.

Now that we have CSV handling and employee filtering, what we're missing is the actual employee module to tie both parts together.

Employee Module

The employee module is where we'll bridge the parsing of records with filtering and searching through employees. Proper isolation of concerns should make it possible for both types of users, those who create and those who consume employee data, to do everything they need without knowing about the requirements of the other.

In this section we'll tackle the requirements, then work on the CSV adapter, and finally tie up the internal usage of employee records. This will let us go through a critial-but-annoying part of the system—the plumbing, full of pesky business rules—and see how we can use properties to validate them.

Setting Requirements

Our challenge here is to come up with an internal data representation that can easily be converted to CSV, while also allowing us to use employee entries the way we would handle any other Erlang data structure. Of course, we'll want to test this with properties. Let's start with the transformations from what the CSV parser hands to us:

```
last_name, first_name, date_of_birth, email
Doe, John, 1982/10/08, john.doe@foobar.com
Ann, Mary, 1975/09/11, mary.ann@foobar.com
```

We can notice a couple of issues in the document format:

- The fields are messy and have extra leading spaces.
- The dates are in "YYYY/MM/DD" format, whereas Erlang works on {Year,Month,Day} tuples and Elixir uses a *Date struct*.

The transformation requires additional processing after the conversion from CSV, which could usually be done or handled by a framework or adapter. For example, most PostgreSQL connection libraries will convert the internal data type for dates and time to Erlang's {{Year,Month,Day}, {H,Min,Sec}} tuple format without much of a problem. In the case of CSV, the specification is really lax and as such it's our responsibility to convert from a string to the appropriate type, along with some additional validation.

We'll define the following functionality:

- An accessor for each field (last_name/1, first_name/1, date_of_birth/1, email/1)
- A function to search employees by birthday
- A from_csv/1 function that takes a CSV string and returns a cleaned-up set of maps representing individual employees. Erlang's opaque types[7] will let us use Dialyzer to ensure that nobody looks at the internal employee data set other than as a thoroughly abstract piece of data. This will allow us to change data representations later, moving from CSV to a SQL-based iterator transparently, for example. Remember that we're aiming for long term flexibility, not the simplest thing that can work.

This should encapsulate all of our requirements without a problem.

Adapting CSV Data

Since we have already tested CSV conversion itself, what we need to do is take the output from the parser and hammer it into shape. For our tests, this means that we won't have to work with generating CSV data, but with generating the data that needs cleaning up. Let's start with the leading spaces. We know all the fields required, and we know that all of them but the first will be messy, so a property about that only needs to ensure that once handled, no fields start with whitespace:

---

7. http://erlang.org/doc/reference_manual/typespec.html#id80458

Erlang	code/ResponsibleTesting/erlang/bday/test/prop_bday_employee.erl

```erlang
-module(prop_bday_employee).
-include_lib("proper/include/proper.hrl").

%%%%%%%%%%%%%%%%%%%%
%%% Properties %%%
%%%%%%%%%%%%%%%%%%%%
prop_fix_csv_leading_space() ->
    ?FORALL(Map, raw_employee_map(),
        begin
            Emp = bday_employee:adapt_csv_result(Map),
            Strs = [X || X <- maps:keys(Emp) ++ maps:values(Emp), is_list(X)],
            lists:all(fun(String) -> hd(String) =/= $\s end, Strs)
        end).
```

Elixir	code/ResponsibleTesting/elixir/bday/test/employee_test.exs

```elixir
property "check that leading space is fixed" do
  forall map <- raw_employee_map() do
    emp = Employee.adapt_csv_result_shim(map)
    strs = Enum.filter(Map.keys(emp) ++ Map.values(emp), &is_binary/1)
    Enum.all?(strs, fn s -> String.first(s) != " " end)
  end
end
```

As you can see, we rely on the yet undefined raw_employee_map() generator, call the adapting function (which will be private), and then check that the first character is not a space in any key or value. Let's see how to implement the generator. The first trick there is that instead of generating a map with the map() generator provided by PropEr, we'll build one from a proplist. The issue with the default generator as supported at the time of this writing is that it takes types for keys and values, and doesn't let us set specific values easily. A proplist and a ?LET macro will do just fine:

Erlang	code/ResponsibleTesting/erlang/bday/test/prop_bday_employee.erl

```erlang
%%%%%%%%%%%%%%%%%%%%
%%% Generators %%%
%%%%%%%%%%%%%%%%%%%%
raw_employee_map() ->
    %% PropEr's native map type does not allow pre-defined static
    %% keys (just `map(T1, T2)') so we convert from a proplist
    ?LET(PropList,
        [{"last_name", prop_csv:field()}, % 1st col has no leading space
         {" first_name", whitespaced_text()},
         {" date_of_birth", text_date()},
         {" email", whitespaced_text()}],
        maps:from_list(PropList)).
```

```
whitespaced_text() ->
    ?LET(Txt, prop_csv:field(), " " ++ Txt).

text_date() ->
    %% leading space and leading 0s for months and days; since we're
    %% checking string formats, it doesn't matter if dates are invalid
    ?LET({Y,M,D}, {choose(1900,2020), choose(1,12), choose(1,31)},
        lists:flatten(io_lib:format(" ~w/~2..0w/~2..0w", [Y,M,D]))).
```

Elixir   code/ResponsibleTesting/elixir/bday/test/employee_test.exs

```
defp raw_employee_map() do
  let proplist <- [
        {"last_name", CsvTest.field()},
        {" first_name", whitespaced_text()},
        {" date_of_birth", text_date()},
        {" email", whitespaced_text()}
      ] do
    Map.new(proplist)
  end
end

defp whitespaced_text() do
  let(txt <- CsvTest.field(), do: " " <> txt)
end

defp text_date() do
  rawdate = {choose(1900, 2020), choose(1, 12), choose(1, 31)}
  # only generate valid dates
  date =
    such_that(
      {y, m, d} <- rawdate,
      when: {:error, :invalid_date} != Date.new(y, m, d)
    )
  let {y, m, d} <- date do
    IO.chardata_to_string(:io_lib.format(" ~w/~2..0w/~2..0w", [y, m, d]))
  end
end
```

You can also see that we reuse the previously defined prop_csv:field() generator we defined when writing the CSV parser; no reason to reinvent that one. All we do is add an unconditional leading whitespace in front of it. We also write a generator for the arbitrary date format provided for us in the file sample, which will need to be properly cleaned up as well.

Running this property will fail because the bday_employee:adapt_csv_result/1 function doesn't exist. Since it's not going to be in our interface, though, we shouldn't export it in usual circumstances. With traditional example tests, people would colocate their EUnit test within the bday_employee module. A nicer trick to keep our tests separate from the production code is to use a conditional macro based on the TEST profile to only export the function while writing tests:

Erlang	code/ResponsibleTesting/erlang/bday/src/bday_employee.erl

```erlang
-module(bday_employee).

%% CSV exports
-export([from_csv/1]).

-ifdef(TEST).
-export([adapt_csv_result/1]).
-endif.
```

Elixir	code/ResponsibleTesting/elixir/bday/lib/employee.ex

```elixir
if Mix.env() == :test do
  def adapt_csv_result_shim(map), do: adapt_csv_result(map)
end
```

Then we can start focusing on implementing the CSV conversion itself. We'll use a special approach by wrapping all our conversions into a {raw, ...} tuple, hidden behind an opaque type. We'll see why soon, but for now, just trust that this will buy us a lot of flexibility for future changes.

Erlang	code/ResponsibleTesting/erlang/bday/src/bday_employee.erl

```erlang
-opaque employee() :: #{string() := term()}.
-opaque handle() :: {raw, [employee()]}.
-export_type([handle/0, employee/0]).

-spec from_csv(string()) -> handle().
from_csv(String) ->
    {raw, [adapt_csv_result(Map) || Map <- bday_csv:decode(String)]}.
```

Elixir	code/ResponsibleTesting/elixir/bday/lib/employee.ex

```elixir
@opaque employee() :: %{required(String.t()) => term()}
@opaque handle() :: {:raw, [employee()]}
def from_csv(string) do
  {:raw,
   for map <- Bday.Csv.decode(string) do
     adapt_csv_result(map)
   end}
end
```

Then skip it for brevity we're actually testing:

```
Erlang                  code/ResponsibleTesting/erlang/bday/src/bday_employee.erl
```

```erlang
-spec adapt_csv_result(map()) -> employee().
adapt_csv_result(Map) ->
    maps:fold(fun(K,V,NewMap) -> NewMap#{trim(K) => trim(V)} end,
              #{}, Map).

trim(Str) -> string:trim(Str, leading, " ").
```

```
Elixir                   code/ResponsibleTesting/elixir/bday/lib/employee.ex
```

```elixir
defp adapt_csv_result(map) do
  for {k, v} <- map, into: %{} do
    {trim(k), trim(v)}
  end
end

defp trim(str), do: String.trim_leading(str, " ")
```

Let's run the tests to see how this goes:

```
$ rebar3 proper -m prop_bday_employee
===> Verifying dependencies...
===> Compiling bday
===> Testing prop_bday_employee:prop_fix_csv_leading_space()
!
Failed: After 1 test(s).
An exception was raised: error:badarg.
Stacktrace: [{erlang,hd,[[]],[]},
             {prop_bday_employee,'-prop_fix_csv_leading_space/0-fun-1-',1,
                 [{file,
                      "«absolute path»/bday/test/prop_bday_employee.erl"},
                  {line,13}]},
             {lists,all,2,[{file,"lists.erl"},{line,1213}]}].
«more output»
```

So the error here is when the function hd([]) is called; of course we can't check what the first character of a string is if it's empty. In fact, we could argue that empty strings should be replaced by the atom undefined, or :nil in Elixir.

Making that change will implicitly fix the test at the same time, since it already filters out nonstring results with is_list(X) in the property. (We could add a test to check for undefined values, but we'll skip it for brevity.)

Erlang   code/ResponsibleTesting/erlang/bday/src/bday_employee.erl

```erlang
-spec adapt_csv_result(map()) -> employee().
adapt_csv_result(Map) ->
    maps:fold(fun(K,V,NewMap) -> NewMap#{trim(K) => maybe_null(trim(V))} end,
              #{}, Map).

trim(Str) -> string:trim(Str, leading, " ").

maybe_null("") -> undefined;
maybe_null(Str) -> Str.
```

Elixir   code/ResponsibleTesting/elixir/bday/lib/employee.ex

```elixir
defp adapt_csv_result(map) do
  for {k, v} <- map, into: %{} do
    {trim(k), maybe_null(trim(v))}
  end
end

defp trim(str), do: String.trim_leading(str, " ")

defp maybe_null(""), do: nil
defp maybe_null(str), do: str
```

Run the property again and you'll see that it passes. The next requirement is to convert known date columns (such as "date_of_birth") into the internal Erlang date format. We'll check this one with a new property, rather than adding complexity to the previous one:

Erlang   code/ResponsibleTesting/erlang/bday/test/prop_bday_employee.erl

```erlang
prop_fix_csv_date_of_birth() ->
    ?FORALL(Map, raw_employee_map(),
        case bday_employee:adapt_csv_result(Map) of
            #{"date_of_birth" := {Y,M,D}} ->
                is_integer(Y) and is_integer(M) and is_integer(D);
            _ ->
                false
        end).
```

Elixir   code/ResponsibleTesting/elixir/bday/test/employee_test.exs

```elixir
property "check that the date is formatted right" do
  forall map <- raw_employee_map() do
```

```
      case Employee.adapt_csv_result_shim(map) do
        %{"date_of_birth" => %Date{}} ->
          true
        _ ->
          false
      end
    end
end
```

The generator sequence is identical to prop_fix_csv_leading_whitespace(), but rather than looking at strings, we make sure that the date format is valid. To make it pass, we must implement the matching code in the bday_employee module by patching the adapt_csv_result/1 function:

Erlang   code/ResponsibleTesting/erlang/bday/src/bday_employee.erl

```erlang
-spec adapt_csv_result(map()) -> employee().
adapt_csv_result(Map) ->
    NewMap = maps:fold(
        fun(K,V,NewMap) -> NewMap#{trim(K) => maybe_null(trim(V))} end,
        #{},
        Map
    ),
    DoB = maps:get("date_of_birth", NewMap), % crash if key missing
    NewMap#{"date_of_birth" => parse_date(DoB)}.

trim(Str) -> string:trim(Str, leading, " ").

maybe_null("") -> undefined;
maybe_null(Str) -> Str.

parse_date(Str) ->
    [Y,M,D] = [list_to_integer(X) || X <- string:lexemes(Str, "/")],
    {Y,M,D}.
```

Elixir   code/ResponsibleTesting/elixir/bday/lib/employee.ex

```elixir
defp adapt_csv_result(map) do
  map =
    for {k, v} <- map, into: %{} do
      {trim(k), maybe_null(trim(v))}
    end

  dob = Map.fetch!(map, "date_of_birth")
  %{map | "date_of_birth" => parse_date(dob)}
end
```

```
defp trim(str), do: String.trim_leading(str, " ")

defp maybe_null(""), do: nil
defp maybe_null(str), do: str

defp parse_date(str) do
  [y, m, d] = Enum.map(String.split(str, "/"), &String.to_integer(&1))
  {:ok, date} = Date.new(y, m, d)
  date
end
```

Run the properties and everything should pass:

```
$ rebar3 proper -m prop_bday_employee
===> Verifying dependencies...
===> Compiling bday
===> Testing prop_bday_employee:prop_fix_csv_leading_space()
....................................................................
......................
OK: Passed 100 test(s).
===> Testing prop_bday_employee:prop_fix_csv_date_of_birth()
....................................................................
......................
OK: Passed 100 test(s).
===>
2/2 properties passed
```

Good! We've covered the entire CSV correction and integration. We now just have to put the accessor functions in place.

Using Employees

Because the employee module ties together the data conversion functionality with the search itself, it turns out to be the perfect place for us to hide implementation details about the data storage layer. If we do things right, the bits that rely on the data to do something useful get isolated from how the data is obtained. This is not necessarily that big of a deal for tests, but it's a critical part of future-proofing our system design.

Start with data accessors, which should be trivial and simple enough they don't require testing. We just have to add them to bday_employee and export:

Erlang	code/ResponsibleTesting/erlang/bday/src/bday_employee.erl

```
-export([from_csv/1, last_name/1, first_name/1, date_of_birth/1, email/1]).

«existing code»

-spec last_name(employee()) -> string() | undefined.
last_name(#{"last_name" := Name}) -> Name.
```

```
-spec first_name(employee()) -> string() | undefined.
first_name(#{"first_name" := Name}) -> Name.

-spec date_of_birth(employee()) -> calendar:date().
date_of_birth(#{"date_of_birth" := DoB}) -> DoB.

-spec email(employee()) -> string().
email(#{"email" := Email}) -> Email.
```

Elixir	code/ResponsibleTesting/elixir/bday/lib/employee.ex

```
@spec last_name(employee()) :: String.t() | nil
def last_name(%{"last_name" => name}), do: name

@spec first_name(employee()) :: String.t() | nil
def first_name(%{"first_name" => name}), do: name

@spec date_of_birth(employee()) :: Date.t()
def date_of_birth(%{"date_of_birth" => dob}), do: dob

@spec email(employee()) :: String.t()
def email(%{"email" => email}), do: email
```

Now our users can truly ignore the underlying map implementation.

You may have noticed that all these accessors just take a direct employee() type value as an argument (a map), but from_csv(String) returned a value of type handle() ({raw, [employee()]}). The question is, How are we going to transition from one to the other? The answer is that this opaque handle() type is a way to represent an abstract resource that can be substituted at a later point.

For example, if at a later date we were to replace the CSV-backed employee storage with a database, we may change the definition of handle() from {raw, [employee()]} to {db, Config, Connection, SQLQuery}. This data structure could then be built and modified lazily, and only be materialized with real data by executing a final query. A similar functionality backed by a microservice could be using a handle of the form {service, URI, ExtraData}, and so on. All that's needed is a function to actualize the result set into a discrete list of maps users are free to poke into:

Erlang	code/ResponsibleTesting/erlang/bday/src/bday_employee.erl

```
-spec fetch(handle()) -> [employee()].
fetch({raw, Maps}) -> Maps.
```

Elixir	code/ResponsibleTesting/elixir/bday/lib/employee.ex

```
@spec fetch(handle()) :: [employee()]
def fetch({:raw, maps}), do: maps
```

Export this function by adding -export([fetch/1]). with other export attributes. In the current implementation, the {raw, ...} format just lets us do everything locally with the same interface. With this in mind, we can now represent every call that could be a remote query or action through this format. For example, we can implement the filter_birthday/3 call as:

Erlang   code/ResponsibleTesting/erlang/bday/src/bday_employee.erl

```erlang
-spec filter_birthday(handle(), calendar:date()) -> handle().
filter_birthday({raw, Employees}, Date) ->
    {raw, bday_filter:birthday(Employees, Date)}.
```

Elixir   code/ResponsibleTesting/elixir/bday/lib/employee.ex

```elixir
@spec filter_birthday(handle(), Date.t()) :: handle()
def filter_birthday({:raw, employees}, date) do
  {:raw, Bday.Filter.birthday(employees, date)}
end
```

That whole mechanism is a bit complex, so let's write a property that shows how this should all be used together:

Erlang   code/ResponsibleTesting/erlang/bday/test/prop_bday_employee.erl

```erlang
prop_handle_access() ->
    ?FORALL(Maps, non_empty(list(raw_employee_map())),
        begin
            CSV = bday_csv:encode(Maps),
            Handle = bday_employee:from_csv(CSV),
            Partial = bday_employee:filter_birthday(Handle, date()),
            ListFull = bday_employee:fetch(Handle),
            true = is_list(bday_employee:fetch(Partial)),
            %% Check for no crash
            _ = [{bday_employee:first_name(X),
                  bday_employee:last_name(X),
                  bday_employee:email(X),
                  bday_employee:date_of_birth(X)} || X <- ListFull],
            true
        end).
```

Elixir   code/ResponsibleTesting/elixir/bday/test/employee_test.exs

```elixir
property "check access through the handle" do
  forall maps <- non_empty(list(raw_employee_map())) do
    handle =
      maps
      |> Csv.encode()
      |> Employee.from_csv()
```

```
    partial = Employee.filter_birthday(handle, ~D[1900-01-01])
    list = Employee.fetch(partial)
    # check for absence of crash
    for x <- list do
      Employee.first_name(x)
      Employee.last_name(x)
      Employee.email(x)
      Employee.date_of_birth(x)
    end

    true
  end
end
```

You can see that we first generate all the employee maps, encode them with our CSV encoder, and then extract them with bday_employee:from_csv/1, which creates an opaque handle. This opaque handle is then passed to bday_employee:filter_birthday/2 along with the result of date() (an Erlang built-in function returning today's date). If you're a purist for unit testing, feel free to replace date() with any hardcoded date, possibly one from the existing employee set. That filter returns a new handle, and we can only get a list of employees once bday_employee:fetch/1 is called. Then we just look to make sure everything works without crashing, and that's the whole property.

What's interesting with this program structure is that if you were to use, say, Ecto from Elixir, raw SQL queries, or any other ORM, the only thing you'd need to change *as a caller* is how the initial fetch for data is done. Use something like bday_employee:from_sql(...) or bday_employee:from_cache(...) instead of bday_employee:from_csv(...) and then the rest of the changes can be hidden within the module itself. This is generally a good sign that we've prevented leaky abstractions: swapping the implementation of the backing structure altogether doesn't really break the interface we've chosen for consumers.

We can run the full suite and have a look at the coverage statistics:

```
$ rebar3 do eunit -c, proper -c, cover -v
«build information»
===> Performing EUnit tests...
........
«timing output»
8 tests, 0 failures
«PropEr output»
===>
4/4 properties passed
«build information»
===> Performing cover analysis...
```

```
|-----------------------|------------|
|                module |   coverage |
|-----------------------|------------|
|              bday_csv  |       100% |
|         bday_employee  |       100% |
|           bday_filter  |       100% |
|-----------------------|------------|
|                 total  |       100% |
|-----------------------|------------|
```

That kind of vanity metrics feels good! Perfect is not a sign that there are no bugs, but it's probably still looking better than if we'd found out all our properties only exercised 20% of the code.

We have most of the functional components of our system in place now. All we need is to take the employees we are looking for and create the emails we'll want to send.

Templating

Our last task before tying it all up is templating. This will be a simple section with limited tests, but we'll still manage with properties. The requirement is straightforward. Send an email whose content is just Happy birthday, dear $first_name!. The function should take one employee term and that's it. Since the focus is on unit tests and we won't send actual emails, only templating needs coverage for now. Let's start by writing a property in a standalone suite:

Erlang   code/ResponsibleTesting/erlang/bday/test/prop_bday_mail_tpl.erl

```erlang
-module(prop_bday_mail_tpl).
-include_lib("proper/include/proper.hrl").

prop_template_email() ->
    ?FORALL(Employee, employee_map(),
            nomatch =/= string:find(bday_mail_tpl:body(Employee),
                                    maps:get("first_name", Employee))
    ).

employee_map() ->
    %% Convert from a proplist to have specific keys in a map
    ?LET(PropList,
        [{"last_name", non_empty(prop_csv:field())},
         {"first_name", non_empty(prop_csv:field())},
         {"date_of_birth", {choose(1900,2020),choose(1,12),choose(1,31)}},
         {"email", non_empty(prop_csv:field())}],
        maps:from_list(PropList)).
```

Elixir   code/ResponsibleTesting/elixir/bday/test/mail_tpl_test.exs

```elixir
defmodule MailTplTest do
  use ExUnit.Case
  use PropCheck
  alias Bday.MailTpl, as: MailTpl

  property "email template has first name" do
    forall employee <- employee_map() do
      String.contains?(
        MailTpl.body(employee),
        Map.fetch!(employee, "first_name")
      )
    end
  end

  defp employee_map() do
    let proplist <- [
          {"last_name", non_empty(CsvTest.field())},
          {"first_name", non_empty(CsvTest.field())},
          {"date_of_birth", date()},
          {"email", non_empty(CsvTest.field())}
        ] do
      Enum.reduce(proplist, %{}, fn {k, v}, m -> Map.put(m, k, v) end)
    end
  end

  defp date() do
    rawdate = {choose(1900, 2020), choose(1, 12), choose(1, 31)}
    # only generate valid dates
    date =
      such_that(
        {y, m, d} <- rawdate,
        when: {:error, :invalid_date} != Date.new(y, m, d)
      )

    let {y, m, d} <- date do
      {:ok, val} = Date.new(y, m, d)
      val
    end
  end
end
```

The string:find/2 function looks for a given string within another one and returns it if found, or nomatch if missing. One gotcha is that some fields are defined as nullable in the employee module (they may return undefined). The initial specification did not mention if it were possible or not for them to be missing, but since the sample of two entries all had fields, we'll assume that so will our production data, and our generators reflect that fact.

With the following implementation, the test should pass every time:

Erlang   code/ResponsibleTesting/erlang/bday/src/bday_mail_tpl.erl

```erlang
-module(bday_mail_tpl).
-export([body/1]).

-spec body(bday_employee:employee()) -> string().
body(Employee) ->
    lists:flatten(io_lib:format("Happy birthday, dear ~s!",
                                [bday_employee:first_name(Employee)])).
```

Elixir   code/ResponsibleTesting/elixir/bday/lib/mail_tpl.ex

```elixir
defmodule Bday.MailTpl do
  def body(employee) do
    name = Bday.Employee.first_name(employee)
    "Happy birthday, dear #{name}!"
  end
```

A trivially correct convenience function that extracts all that is needed for an email to be sent (address, subject, body) can be added to provide further decoupling:

Erlang   code/ResponsibleTesting/erlang/bday/src/bday_mail_tpl.erl

```erlang
-export([full/1]). % add this export near the top of the file

-spec full(bday_employee:employee()) -> {[string()], string(), string()}.
full(Employee) ->
    {[bday_employee:email(Employee)],
     "Happy birthday!",
     body(Employee)}.
```

Elixir   code/ResponsibleTesting/elixir/bday/lib/mail_tpl.ex

```elixir
def full(employee) do
  {[Bday.Employee.email(employee)], "Happy birthday!", body(employee)}
end
```

The email address is put in a list since email clients typically allow more than one entry in the To: field.

And with this in place, the last individual component of the system is done. All we have to do is assemble everything.

Plumbing It All Together

It's now time to take these well-tested bits, and integrate them. Fortunately for us, integration is not a concern for this chapter (we care about *unit* tests), so we can just throw everything together quickly and consider our job done:

Erlang   code/ResponsibleTesting/erlang/bday/src/bday.erl

```
-module(bday).
-export([main/1]).

main([Path]) ->
    {ok, Data} = file:read_file(Path),
    Handle = bday_employee:from_csv(binary_to_list(Data)),
    Query = bday_employee:filter_birthday(Handle, date()), % date = local time
    BdaySet = bday_employee:fetch(Query),
    Mails = [bday_mail_tpl:full(Employee) || Employee <- BdaySet],
    [send_email(To, Topic, Body) || {To, Topic, Body} <- Mails].

send_email(To, _, _) ->
    io:format("sent birthday email to ~p~n", [To]).
```

Elixir   code/ResponsibleTesting/elixir/bday/lib/bday.ex

```
defmodule Bday do
  def run(path) do
    set =
      path
      |> File.read!()
      |> Bday.Employee.from_csv()
      |> Bday.Employee.filter_birthday(DateTime.to_date(DateTime.utc_now()))
      |> Bday.Employee.fetch()

    for employee <- set do
      employee
      |> Bday.MailTpl.full()
      |> send_email()
    end

    :ok
  end

  defp send_email({to, _topic, _body}) do
    IO.puts("sent birthday email to #{to}")
  end
end
```

The email client is not implemented since it is also out of scope for now (and is left as an exercise to the reader, to steal a frustrating quote from academia). For now we'll stick with a simple io:format/2 call to stand in for the actual email client handling and call it a day. We just need to package the program to be run. Erlang lets you do this by calling rebar3 escriptize, generating a stand-alone script. If you're using Elixir, call mix run -e 'Bday.run("db.csv")' instead:

```
$ rebar3 escriptize
===> Verifying dependencies...
===> Compiling bday
===> Building escript...
```

The script is generated in the _build/default/bin directory. The program can now be run, as long as the sample CSV file has full CRLF line terminations:

ResponsibleTesting/erlang/bday/priv/db.csv
```
last_name, first_name, date_of_birth, email
Doe, John, 1982/10/08, john.doe@foobar.com
Ann, Mary, 1975/09/11, mary.ann@foobar.com
Robert, Joe, 2002/03/18, born.today@example.com
```

Don't forget to ensure one of the employees in the sample database has their birthday *today* for the program to output anything:

```
$ _build/default/bin/bday priv/db.csv
sent birthday email to ["born.today@example.com"]
```

And it works! All in all, we can now say that coverage is good, critical units are tested, and changing implementations for our data layer will have limited effects in the testing code base.

We can pat ourselves on the back for a job well done.

Wrapping Up

When it comes to writing properties, you're now in a pretty good place. You should feel better about balancing properties with regular example-based unit tests, as we've seen for regression cases. Using example tests as an anchoring mechanism to backstop your properties can help make them a lot more trustworthy. In some cases, just exhaustively enumerating the whole data set is a possibility, letting you cover more than what properties would in the first place.

Your experience gained writing properties against a well-specified program is sure to prove useful, but property-based testing has another face entirely. We can use properties to explore the design of our program itself, rather than just testing a well-specified one. In the next chapter, we'll do just that, by using them in properties-driven development.

## CHAPTER 6

Properties-Driven Development

If you're reading this book, it's because programming is kind of difficult. Difficult enough that we need fancy tools to make sure our programs are doing the right thing. But while programming is hard, even harder is figuring out *what our programs should be doing* in the first place, especially when we find all kinds of fun corner cases. There are plenty of tools available to help here, and for software developers, test-driven development (TDD) is one of the most frequently used approaches. TDD forces you to position yourself first as a user of the program rather than an implementer. Before writing any new feature, we first need to write a failing test exercising the feature, and then write the code to make it pass. All program improvements are a series of small iterations built on well-understood foundations.

This kind of approach can be interesting in the context of property-based testing: before writing a program, we'll want to think about what it should do. Unsurprisingly, we'll want to encode these assumptions as rules for properties. Then, we'll run our program against them as we go. What happens next is a series of increasing failures, where we have to figure out if it's the program that is wrong, or our understanding of what it should do in the first place that needs to change.

In this chapter, we'll go through a properties-driven approach and explore techniques related to positive tests (validate what the program does) and negative ones (test what the program can't handle). We'll also push generators further than we've done before, which will be a good exercise on its own. We'll do all of that by developing a short program inspired by the *Back to the Checkout* code kata,[1] where we implement a pricing system for a supermarket.

---

1. http://codekata.com/kata/kata09-back-to-the-checkout/

The Specification

Although it'd be great to have a well-defined specification, we'll work from a more realistic starting point by keeping things vague. We'll write a system that's given a bunch of items that have been scanned. We have to look up the price of these items and calculate the total amount to charge. A fun bit to add is that some items in groups give an instant rebate: you may get two articles for the price of one, or specific amounts like five bags of chips for $7.

In fact, the code kata gives the following table:

Item	Unit Price	Special Price
A	50	3 for 130
B	30	2 for 45
C	20	
D	15	

The checkout function should accept items in any order, so ["B","A","B"] would give the 2-for-45 rebate for the Bs being bought. The only call that needs to be exposed is checkout:total(ListOfItemsBought, UnitPrices, SpecialPrices) → Price.

That's it. The requirements are vague, but we can extract the following list of things to tackle:

- Items are identified by unique names (nonempty strings).

- The list of items has no set length (though it appears nonempty), and the items it contains are in no specific order.

- The unit prices appear to be integers. (Not a bad idea, since floating point numbers lose precision; we can assume values are written in cents, for example.)

- The special prices are triggered only once the right number of items of the proper type can match a given special.

- All items have a unit price.

- It is not mandatory for a given item to have a special price.

The rest is seemingly undefined or underspecified, so the assumptions we bake into the program about the rest could be tricky and bug prone.

Aside from these requirements, see if you can come up with a few properties. Here are two possibilities:

- Without any special prices defined, the total is just the sum of all of the items' prices.

- With a known count for each item, the total comes from two parts added together.

  1. The special price multipled by the number of times it can be applied to a given set of items

  2. The remainder (not evenly divisible by the special's required number of items), which is added on top of the special prices

Since we're interested in discovering and improving the design of the program through properties, we can start by implementing the first two properties we've come up with, and then writing the code to make them pass. This will bring us to a point where the basic program does what we want. Then, we'll see how properties can be used in *negative tests*, checking that the program does what we want, but also deals with things we don't want to happen.

Before we get going, though, don't forget to set up a new project as we did in prior chapters such as Foundations on page 10—call rebar3 new lib checkout for Erlang, mix new checkout for Elixir, and then add PropEr to dependencies.

Writing the First Test

The first property doesn't have to be fancy. In fact, it's better if it's simple. Start with something trivial-looking that represents how we want to use the program. Then, our job as developers is to make sure we can write code that matches our expectations, or to change them. Of our two properties, the simplest one concerns counting sums without caring about specials.

You'll want to avoid a property definition such as sum(ItemList, PriceList) =:= checkout:total(ItemList, PriceList, []) since that would risk making the test similar to the implementation. A good approach to try here is generalizing regular example-based tests. Let's imagine a few cases:

```
20 = checkout:total(["A","B","A"], [{"A",5},{"B",10}], []),
20 = checkout:total(["A","B","A"], [{"A",5},{"B",10},{"C",100}], []),
115 = checkout:total(["F","B","C"], [{"F",5},{"B",10},{"C",100}], []),
«and so on»
```

That's actually tricky to generalize. It's possible that to come up with examples you just make a list of items, assign them prices, pick items from the list, and then sum them up yourself. Even if it's not really straightforward, you can build on that. The base step to respect here looks something like this:

```
ExpectedPrice = checkout:total(ChosenItems, PriceList, [])
```

If we write a generator that gives us all known values for these variables, we *can* use the steps the same way we'd do it with examples. The generator will literally generate test cases so we don't have to. So let's get a property that looks like this:

About the Code

 In the snippets that follow, code is labeled with both the language (Erlang and Elixir) and the file where you should put the code if you're following along.

Erlang
code/PropertiesDrivenDevelopment/erlang/checkout/test/prop_checkout.erl

---

```erlang
-module(prop_checkout).
-include_lib("proper/include/proper.hrl").
-compile(export_all).

%%%%%%%%%%%%%%%%%%%
%%% Properties %%%
%%%%%%%%%%%%%%%%%%%
prop_no_special1() ->
    ?FORALL({ItemList, ExpectedPrice, PriceList}, item_price_list(),
            ExpectedPrice =:= checkout:total(ItemList, PriceList, [])).
```

Elixir
code/PropertiesDrivenDevelopment/elixir/checkout/test/checkout_test.exs

---

```elixir
defmodule CheckoutTest do
  use ExUnit.Case
  use PropCheck

  ## Properties
  property "sums without specials" do
    forall {item_list, expected_price, price_list} <- item_price_list() do
      expected_price == Checkout.total(item_list, price_list, [])
    end
  end
end
```

The generator for the property will need to generate the three expected arguments: a list of items bought by the customer (ItemList), the expected price of those items (ExpectedPrice), and then the list of items with their prices as expected by the register itself (PriceList).

Since the price list is required to generate the item list and expected prices, the generator will need to come in layers with ?LET macros:

Erlang

```erlang
%%%%%%%%%%%%%%%%%%%%%
%%% Generators %%%
%%%%%%%%%%%%%%%%%%%%%
item_price_list() ->
    ?LET(PriceList, price_list(),
         ?LET({ItemList, ExpectedPrice}, item_list(PriceList),
              {ItemList, ExpectedPrice, PriceList})).
```

Elixir

```elixir
## Generators
defp item_price_list() do
  let price_list <- price_list() do
    let {item_list, expected_price} <- item_list(price_list) do
      {item_list, expected_price, price_list}
    end
  end
end
```

The price list itself is a list of tuples of the form [{ItemName, Price}]. The ?LET macro actualizes the list into one value that won't change for the rest of the generator. This means that the item_list/1 generator can then use PriceList as the actual Erlang data structure rather than the abstract intermediary format PropEr uses. But first, let's implement the price_list/0 generator:

Erlang

```erlang
%% generate a list of {ItemName, Price} to configure the checkout
price_list() ->
    ?LET(PriceList, non_empty(list({non_empty(string()), integer()})),
         lists:ukeysort(1, PriceList)). % remove duplicates
```

Elixir

```elixir
defp price_list() do
  let price_list <- non_empty(list({non_empty(utf8()), integer()})) do
    sorted = Enum.sort(price_list)
    Enum.dedup_by(sorted, fn {x, _} -> x end)
  end
end
```

Here, price_list/0 generates all the tuples as mentioned earlier, each with an integer for the price. To avoid duplicate item options, such has having the same hotdogs at two distinct prices within the same list, we use lists:ukeysort(KeyPos, List). That function will remove all list items that share the same key as any item that has already been seen, ensuring we have only unique entries.

Now, with a sleight of hand, we'll use the PriceList as a seed for item_list/1, which should return a complete selection of items along with their expected price:

Erlang

```erlang
%% set up recursive generator for the purchased item list along with
%% its expected price, based off the price list.
item_list(PriceList) ->
    ?SIZED(Size, item_list(Size, PriceList, {[], 0})).

item_list(0, _, Acc) -> Acc;
item_list(N, PriceList, {ItemAcc, PriceAcc}) ->
    ?LET({Item, Price}, elements(PriceList),
        item_list(N-1, PriceList, {[Item|ItemAcc], Price+PriceAcc})).
```

Elixir

```elixir
defp item_list(price_list) do
  sized(size, item_list(size, price_list, {[], 0}))
end

defp item_list(0, _, acc), do: acc

defp item_list(n, price_list, {item_acc, price_acc}) do
  let {item, price} <- elements(price_list) do
    item_list(n - 1, price_list, {[item | item_acc], price + price_acc})
  end
end
```

For the tests to pass, we'll have to write the implementation code itself. Let's start with a minimal case that should easily work:

Erlang
code/PropertiesDrivenDevelopment/erlang/checkout/src/checkout.erl

```erlang
-module(checkout).

-export([total/3]).

-type item() :: string().
-type price() :: integer().

-spec total([item()], [{item(), price()}], any()) -> price().
total(ItemList, PriceList, _Specials) ->
    lists:sum([proplists:get_value(Item, PriceList) || Item <- ItemList]).
```

Elixir
code/PropertiesDrivenDevelopment/elixir/checkout/lib/checkout.ex

```elixir
def total(item_list, price_list, _specials) do
  Enum.sum(
    for item <- item_list do
      elem(List.keyfind(price_list, item, 0), 1)
    end
  )
end
```

Run the property and you'll see that it does work.

Now that we have a working property, the next step we should take is to validate how effective it is. This is a bit tedious, but it ensures that the hundred or so tests we run for the property are actually different. We can do this in a straightforward manner using the collect/2 function:

Erlang
code/PropertiesDrivenDevelopment/erlang/checkout/test/prop_checkout.erl

```erlang
prop_no_special2() ->
    ?FORALL({ItemList, ExpectedPrice, PriceList}, item_price_list(),
            collect(
              bucket(length(ItemList), 10),
              ExpectedPrice =:= checkout:total(ItemList, PriceList, [])
            )).

%%%%%%%%%%%%%%%%
%%% Helpers %%%
%%%%%%%%%%%%%%%%
bucket(N, Unit) ->
    (N div Unit) * Unit.
```

Elixir
code/PropertiesDrivenDevelopment/elixir/checkout/test/checkout_test.exs

```elixir
property "sums without specials (but with metrics)", [:verbose] do
  forall {item_list, expected_price, price_list} <- item_price_list() do
    (expected_price == Checkout.total(item_list, price_list, []))
    |> collect(bucket(length(item_list), 10))
  end
end

## Helpers
defp bucket(n, unit) do
  div(n, unit) * unit
end
```

Running this property will then reveal metrics:

```
27% 0
27% 10
20% 20
20% 30
6% 40
```

This appears reasonable. Lists of zero to forty items being bought probably covers most cases. Alternatively running the call with collect(lists:usort(ItemList), <Property>) shows good results as well, meaning that the variety of items being bought also seems reasonable.

With the regular case (without specials) being taken care of, we're good to start implementing specials. That one will be a bit trickier though.

Testing Specials

Alright, before moving further, let's reevaluate our TODO list:

- ~~Items are identified by unique names (nonempty strings).~~

- ~~The list of items has no set length (though it appears nonempty), and the items it contains are in no specific order.~~

- ~~The unit prices appear to be integers. (Not a bad idea, since floating point numbers lose precision; we can assume values are written in cents, for example.)~~

- The special prices are triggered only once the right number of items of the proper type can match a given special.

- ~~All items have a unit price.~~

- ~~It is not mandatory for a given item to have a special price.~~

That's decent coverage in terms of features and requirements we extracted, with few lines of tests! It may not feel like we've accomplished much for now, but most features are okay as per our spec. The specials are the one thing left to handle.

Rather than modifying the existing property—a property that does a fine job of checking nonspecial prices—we'll add a new one to check specials. The separation will help narrow down problems when they happen. If the property for basic prices always works, then we know that failures in the more complex one handling specials as well will likely relate to bugs in specials-handling. Here's the new property:

```
Erlang
code/PropertiesDrivenDevelopment/erlang/checkout/test/prop_checkout.erl
```

```erlang
prop_special() ->
    ?FORALL({ItemList, ExpectedPrice, PriceList, SpecialList},
            item_price_special(),
        ExpectedPrice =:= checkout:total(ItemList, PriceList, SpecialList)).
```

```
Elixir
code/PropertiesDrivenDevelopment/elixir/checkout/test/checkout_test.exs
```

```elixir
property "sums including specials" do
  forall {items, expected_price, prices, specials}
        <- item_price_special() do
    expected_price == Checkout.total(items, prices, specials)
  end
end
```

This property is similar to the one we wrote earlier, except that we now expect a fourth term out of the generator, which is a list of special prices (SpecialList). The easiest way to go about this would be to just come up with a static list of specials and then couple it with the previous property's generator, but that wouldn't necessarily exercise the code as well as fully dynamic lists, so let's try to do that instead.

Planning the Generator

So first things first; we'll need the basic list of items and prices. For that, we can reuse the price_list() generator, which gives us a fully dynamic list. Then, if we want the specials list to be effective, we should probably build it off the items in the price list. That can be done by wrapping the call to price_list() in a ?LET macro so that other generators can see it as a static value:

```erlang
?LET(PriceList, price_list(),
    «rest of the generator»).
```

The challenge, really, will be to generate the list of items to buy, while maintaining a proper expected price (ExpectedPrice). Let's say we were to reuse the item_list/1 generator from earlier here. If the checkout counter sells three donuts for the price of two, but the generator creates a list of four donuts without expecting a special, then our test will be wrong. If you were to patch things up by still using the generator and figuring out the specials from the generated list, then chances are the generator code would be as complex as the actual program's code. That's a bad testing approach, since it makes it hard to trust our tests.

The way to go about it is to shift your perspective. Look at the problem from a different direction and you'll see the trick—it's probably the sneakiest and cleverest one in the entire book; it's a decent example of the creative thinking sometimes required to write good generators.

Here it goes. Instead of building the list one item at a time and figuring out if or when specials apply, we can try to break it up by separately generating both types of sequences: items that *never* amount to a special, and items that *always* amount to a special. If these types of sequences are well-generated and distinct, then they can be used independently or as one big list, and always remain consistent!

So we can have two generators. On the one hand, we have a list where all the items of each type are in a quantity smaller than required for the special price. We can sum up their prices to give us one part of the expected price. Then on the other side, we have a generator where all the items in a list are in a quantity that is an even multiple of the quantity required for a special. For that list, the expected price is the sum of all specials we triggered. We can then merge both lists, add both expected prices, and end up with a list that covers all kinds of cases possible in a totally predictable manner.

Let's step through this with our example where three donuts are being sold at the price of two. If we have a list with eight donuts in it, we'd expect the the special to be applied twice, with two remaining donuts being sold at full price. So let's see how this would work with our two planned generators. First we generate a list of two donuts—below the special number—and track their expected price with the nonspecial value. Then we generate a list of six donuts (twice the special quantity) with their expected price based off the special value. Then, we merge both lists together and sum up their expected prices, and end up with the same eight donuts and the correct expected price.

This should work fine. So the generator should have this kind of flow:

The symbol ++ stands for list concatenation, and + is regular addition. Let's build it step by step.

Writing the Generator

First, we'll want to isolate the PriceList value to be standing alone and reusable by all generators:

```
item_price_special() ->
    %% first LET: freeze the PriceList
    ?LET(PriceList, price_list(),
        «rest of the generator»).
```

We can then fill it in by generating a SpecialList that will contain the specials definition:

```
item_price_special() ->
    %% first LET: freeze the PriceList
    ?LET(PriceList, price_list(),
        %% second LET: freeze the SpecialList
        ?LET(SpecialList, special_list(PriceList),
            «rest of the generator»)).
```

Okay, that part was still straightforward. The special_list/1 generator is not written yet, but we can do that later. Let's finish the current generator first. For the next level, we have to generate the two sets of prices, the regular ones and the special ones, which can each have their own dedicated generator:

```
item_price_special() ->
    %% first LET: freeze the PriceList
    ?LET(PriceList, price_list(),
        %% second LET: freeze the SpecialList
        ?LET(SpecialList, special_list(PriceList),
            %% third LET: Regular + Special items and prices
            ?LET({{RegularItems, RegularExpected},
                  {SpecialItems, SpecialExpected}},
                 {regular_gen(PriceList, SpecialList),
                  special_gen(PriceList, SpecialList)},
                 «rest of the generator»))).
```

You'll notice that both of the two new (and yet undefined) generators have the PriceList and SpecialList passed in. From within the generators, those will look like regular Erlang terms.

All we have left to do is merge the lists and sum up the prices:

Erlang
code/PropertiesDrivenDevelopment/erlang/checkout/test/prop_checkout.erl

```erlang
item_price_special() ->
    %% first LET: freeze the PriceList
    ?LET(PriceList, price_list(),
        %% second LET: freeze the SpecialList
        ?LET(SpecialList, special_list(PriceList),
            %% third LET: Regular + Special items and prices
            ?LET({{RegularItems, RegularExpected},
                  {SpecialItems, SpecialExpected}},
                 {regular_gen(PriceList, SpecialList),
                  special_gen(PriceList, SpecialList)},
                 %% And merge + return initial lists:
                 {shuffle(RegularItems ++ SpecialItems),
                  RegularExpected + SpecialExpected,
                  PriceList, SpecialList}))).

shuffle(L) ->
    %% Shuffle the list by adding a random number first,
    %% then sorting on it, and then removing it
    Shuffled = lists:sort([{rand:uniform(), X} || X <- L]),
    [X || {_, X} <- Shuffled].
```

Elixir
code/PropertiesDrivenDevelopment/elixir/checkout/test/checkout_test.exs

```elixir
defp item_price_special() do
  # first let: freeze the price list
  let price_list <- price_list() do
    # second let: freeze the list of specials
    let special_list <- special_list(price_list) do
      # third let: regular + special items and prices
      let {{regular_items, regular_expected},
           {special_items, special_expected}} <-
            {regular_gen(price_list, special_list),
             special_gen(price_list, special_list)} do
        # and merge + return initial lists:
        {Enum.shuffle(regular_items ++ special_items),
          regular_expected + special_expected, price_list, special_list}
      end
    end
  end
end
```

Whew! That's the whole thing. The list shuffling is added to make sure the final result is truly unpredictable. You'll rarely see generators this complex, but it's good to try your hand at it and see what can be done. Sadly, we can't use this yet, because we still need to define the special list generators, and then both the regular and special list generators.

Generating the List of Specials

We'll start with the list of specials, since it's conceptually simpler and a prerequisite of other generators. The method here is to first extract the list of all item names from the price list, and then create a matching table of specials:

Erlang

```erlang
%% Generates specials in a list of the form
%% [{Name, Count, SpecialPrice}]
special_list(PriceList) ->
    Items = [Name || {Name, _} <- PriceList],
    ?LET(Specials, list({elements(Items), choose(2,5), integer()}),
        lists:ukeysort(1, Specials)). % no dupes
```

Elixir

```elixir
defp special_list(price_list) do
  items = for {name, _} <- price_list, do: name

  let specials <- list({elements(items), choose(2, 5), integer()}) do
    sorted = Enum.sort(specials)
    Enum.dedup_by(sorted, fn {x, _, _} -> x end)
  end
end
```

The generated list of specials contains the name of the item, how many of them are required for the special to apply, and then the price for the whole group. The specials are generated from randomly selected entries from the item list—with the duplicates removed—so that there is always a matching nonspecial item to any special one. Note that it is possible for the special price to be higher than the nonspecial price with this generator.

Generating the List of Regular Items

The list of items *never* being on special is a bit tricky to generate. We have to make it so we generate zero or more items, as long as the maximal value is below any specials for it:

Erlang

```erlang
%% Generates lists of regular items, at a price below the special value.
regular_gen(PriceList, SpecialList) ->
    regular_gen(PriceList, SpecialList, [], 0).
```

```erlang
regular_gen([], _, Items, Price) ->
    {Items, Price};
regular_gen([{Item, Cost}|PriceList], SpecialList, Items, Price) ->
    CountGen = case lists:keyfind(Item, 1, SpecialList) of
        {_, Limit, _} -> choose(0, Limit-1); % has special; set max amount
        _ -> non_neg_integer()               % no special; generate at will
    end,
    %% Use the conditional generator to generate items
    ?LET(Count, CountGen,
        regular_gen(PriceList, SpecialList,
                    ?LET(V, vector(Count, Item), V ++ Items),
                    Cost*Count + Price)).
```

Elixir

```elixir
defp regular_gen(price_list, special_list) do
  regular_gen(price_list, special_list, [], 0)
end

defp regular_gen([], _, list, price), do: {list, price}

defp regular_gen([{item, cost} | prices], specials, items, price) do
  count_gen =
    case List.keyfind(specials, item, 0) do
      {_, limit, _} -> choose(0, limit - 1)
      _ -> non_neg_integer()
    end

  let count <- count_gen do
    regular_gen(
      prices,
      specials,
      let(v <- vector(count, item), do: v ++ items),
      cost * count + price
    )
  end
end
```

First, at ❶, we just wrap the generator to start with a null expected price. The clause at ❷ contains the recursive function's base case; whenever all items in the list have been iterated over, the full list and expected price are returned.

Now for the fun part, the last clause. The first thing to do is look up whether the item from PriceList can be found in SpecialList, then the count required to trigger the special is used as an upper bound to generation. Otherwise, any nonnegative integer is fine. Using a lower bound of 0—explicitly with choose/2 and implicitly with non_neg_integer/0—we make it possible that not all items will be included.

You'll note that in both branches of the case ... of expression, a generator is directly returned, and bound to the variable CountGen at ❸. This generator has no value yet, and is still just an abstract piece of data waiting to be processed by PropEr. This is why we actualize it in a ?LET macro at ❹, after which we can use it multiple times with a single fixed value.

Then at ❺, the count is used to generate a list of fixed size (using vector/2), being added to the accumulated items, with the expected price calculated at ❻. The generator is then called recursively until the full list of items has been used.

This gives us a full generator of items that won't be in sufficient amounts to trigger a single special offer. We are free to implement the specials next.

Generating the List of Items on Special

The specials generator is a bit simpler by comparison, although it uses a similar recursive approach:

Erlang

```erlang
special_gen(_, SpecialList) ->
    %% actually do not need the item list
    special_gen(SpecialList, [], 0).

special_gen([], Items, Price) ->
    {Items, Price};
special_gen([{Item, Count, Cost} | SpecialList], Items, Price) ->
    %% Generate sequences of items equal to the special, based on a
    %% multiplier. If we have a need for 3 items for a special, we can
    %% generate 0, 3, 6, 9, ... of such items at once
    ?LET(Multiplier, non_neg_integer(),
         special_gen(SpecialList,
                     ?LET(V, vector(Count * Multiplier, Item), V ++ Items),
                     Cost * Multiplier + Price)).
```

Elixir

```elixir
defp special_gen(_, special_list) do
  special_gen(special_list, [], 0)
end

defp special_gen([], items, price), do: {items, price}

defp special_gen([{item, count, cost} | specials], items, price) do
  let multiplier <- non_neg_integer() do
    special_gen(
      specials,
      let(v <- vector(count * multiplier, item), do: v ++ items),
      cost * multiplier + price
    )
  end
end
```

The only conceptual difference takes place after ❶. Because a special being applied requires a specific number of items (Count), any multiple of that number is going to be fair. If we need three bagels to get a rebate, then lists of zero, three, six, or nine bagels are all equally good here.

With this, we finally have everything we need to run the property and make it work!

Implementing Specials

So we have a more complex generator for specials, and a basic checkout implementation that doesn't consider specials at all. We have everything we need to get started on implementing specials. Our first step should be making sure our test actually fails eventually, as a sanity check to know it's good at detecting bad cases:

```
$ rebar3 proper
«build information and other properties»
===> Testing prop_checkout:prop_special()
......!
Failed: After 7 test(s).
{[[0],[6,1],[0],[0],[6,1],[6,1],[6,1],[0],[6,1],[6,1],[0],[6,1],[6,1],[6,1],
[6,1],[6,1],[6,1],[6,1],[6,1],[0],[6,1],[6,1],[6,1],[0],[6,1],[0],[0],[6,1],
[6,1],[6,1],[6,1],[0],[0],[0],[6,1],[6,1],[0]],20,[{[0],-2},{[6,1],1}],
[{[0],2,3},{[6,1],5,0}]}

Shrinking .........(10 time(s))
{[[0],[0]],1,[{[0],0}],[{[0],2,1}]}
===>
2/3 properties passed, 1 failed
===> Failed test cases:
  prop_checkout:prop_special() -> false
```

The original counterexample is pretty much incomprehensible, but the shrunken one is simpler. The term {[[0],[0]],1,[{[0],0}],[{[0],2,1}]}, can be imagined to stand for {[A, A], 1, [{A,0}], [{A,2,1}]} if [0] is substituted with A—basically any list with a special being triggered causes a test failure. This is good, since that's exactly what we want to see tested.

With our test shown to catch failures, we can start implementing the feature.

A simple method is to count how many of each item is in the list. Account for the specials first, reducing the count every time the specials apply, and then run over the list of items that are not on sale. At a high level, it should look like this:

Erlang
code/PropertiesDrivenDevelopment/erlang/checkout/src/checkout.erl

```erlang
-module(checkout).

-export([total/3]).

-type item() :: string().
-type price() :: integer().
-type special() :: {item(), pos_integer(), price()}.

-spec total([item()], [{item(), price()}], [special()]) -> price().
total(ItemList, PriceList, Specials) ->
    Counts = count_seen(ItemList),
    {CountsLeft, Prices} = apply_specials(Counts, Specials),
    Prices + apply_regular(CountsLeft, PriceList).
```

Elixir
code/PropertiesDrivenDevelopment/elixir/checkout/lib/checkout.ex

```elixir
def total(item_list, price_list, specials) do
  counts = count_seen(item_list)
  {counts_left, prices} = apply_specials(counts, specials)
  prices + apply_regular(counts_left, price_list)
end
```

Here, count_seen/1 should create a list of each item and how many times it is seen. We then pass that data to apply_specials/2, which returns a tuple with two elements: the number of items not processed as part of a special on the left, and the summed-up prices of all specials on the right. Finally, we take that sum, and add it to the cost of the rest of the items, as defined by apply_regular/2.

This method is kind of the opposite approach from the test; instead of generating both lists and mashing them together, this splits them up to get the final count.

Let's look at the helper functions, first with count_seen/2:

Erlang

```erlang
-spec count_seen([item()]) -> [{item(), pos_integer()}].
count_seen(ItemList) ->
    Count = fun(X) -> X+1 end,
    maps:to_list(
      lists:foldl(fun(Item, M) -> maps:update_with(Item, Count, 1, M) end,
                  maps:new(), ItemList)
    ).
```

Elixir

```elixir
defp count_seen(item_list) do
  count = fn x -> x + 1 end

  Map.to_list(
    Enum.reduce(item_list, Map.new(), fn item, m ->
      Map.update(m, item, 1, count)
    end)
  )
end
```

A Count function is defined and passed to maps:update_with/4, which allows us to increment a counter associated with each item's name as we iterate over ItemList. The map is then turned to a list for convenience.

The next function to write is apply_specials/2, which is a little bit trickier:

Erlang

```erlang
-spec apply_specials([{item(), pos_integer()}], [special()]) ->
    {[{item(), pos_integer()}], price()}.
apply_specials(Items, Specials) ->
    lists:mapfoldl(fun({Name, Count}, Price) ->
        case lists:keyfind(Name, 1, Specials) of
            false -> % not found
                {{Name, Count}, Price};
            {_, Needed, Value} ->
                {{Name, Count rem Needed},
                 Value * (Count div Needed) + Price}
        end
    end, 0, Items).
```

❶
❷
❸

Elixir

```elixir
defp apply_specials(items, specials) do
  Enum.map_reduce(items, 0, fn {name, count}, price ->
    case List.keyfind(specials, name, 0) do
      nil ->
        {{name, count}, price}

      {_, needed, value} ->
        {{name, rem(count, needed)},
         value * div(count, needed) + price}
    end
  end)
end
```

❹
❷
❸

The core component here is the lists:mapfoldl/3 function, which both applies a map operation and a fold operation over a list in a single pass. The map operation consists of applying a function to every value of the list and building a new list from them, and has its result stored on the left-hand side of every returned tuple. It is used to build a list of the form [{Name, Count},...], consisting of the items left to be processed once the specials' prices have been processed. The fold operation consists of looking at every element of the list and combining them into one accumulator, with its result stored on the right-hand side of every returned tuple. It's used here to sum up all of the specials prices that apply into a single total value.

The line at ❶ shows an item for which there are no specials: both the item count and the seen price remain unchanged. By comparison, the code at ❷ shows a matching item with its count reduced by how many times a special matches, and the code at ❸ increments the total price as expected.

The only function left is the one to apply the nonspecial prices, and it is fortunately straightforward:

Erlang

```erlang
-spec apply_regular([{item(), integer()}], [{item(), price()}]) -> price().
apply_regular(Items, PriceList) ->
    lists:sum([Count * proplists:get_value(Name, PriceList)
                || {Name, Count} <- Items]).
```

Elixir

```elixir
defp apply_regular(items, price_list) do
  Enum.sum(
    for {name, count} <- items do
      {_, price} = List.keyfind(price_list, name, 0)
      count * price
    end
  )
end
```

With this in place, we can give our test suite a spin, and even get some coverage metrics:

```
$ rebar3 do proper -c, cover -v
«build information and other properties»
===> Testing prop_checkout:prop_special()
...........................................................................
......................
OK: Passed 100 test(s).
===>
3/3 properties passed
```

```
===> Performing cover analysis...
|-------------------------|-----------|
|                  module |  coverage |
|-------------------------|-----------|
|                checkout |      100% |
|-------------------------|-----------|
|                   total |      100% |
|-------------------------|-----------|
```

That's good!

Order of Failures

 Property tests are probabilistic. If you are following along, you may find different issues (or the same issues in a different order) than those in this text. This is normal, and rerunning the property a few times may yield different errors each time, or sometimes none at all.

If you get an unexpected failure, you can skip ahead and see if we'll cover it later; chances are that we will.

If we look at our list, we are now feature-complete.

- ~~Items are identified by unique names (nonempty strings).~~

- ~~The list of items has no set length (though it appears nonempty), and the items it contains are in no specific order.~~

- ~~The unit prices appear to be integers. (Not a bad idea, since floating point numbers lose precision; we can assume values are written in cents, for example.)~~

- ~~The special prices are triggered only once the right number of items of the proper type can match a given special.~~

- ~~All items have a unit price.~~

- ~~It is not mandatory for a given item to have a special price.~~

And the 100% code coverage sure makes it sound like we can trust everything here. But can we really? Negative testing is an additional safety check we can use.

Negative Testing

An interesting aspect of the code and tests we have written so far is that the list of items being bought is generated through the list of supported items. By designing the test case from the price list, there is a lack of tests looking for unexpected use cases. Our tests are positive, happy-path tests, validating that everything is right and good things happen. Negative tests, by comparison, try to specifically exercise underspecified scenarios to find what happens in less happy paths.

Our current properties are good; we don't want to modify them or make them more complex. Instead, we'll write a few broad properties that test more general properties of the code and see if the requirements we had in the first place are actually consistent. On their own, broad (and often vague) properties are not too useful, but as a supplement or anchor to specific ones, they start to shine. And the broader the properties, the lower chances are that we'll be searching *only* for expected problems, as is usually done with traditional tests.

Broad Properties

Let's start with a very, very broad property: the checkout:total/3 function should return an integer and not crash:

```
Erlang
code/PropertiesDrivenDevelopment/erlang/checkout/test/prop_checkout.erl
```

```erlang
prop_expected_result() ->
    ?FORALL({ItemList, PriceList, SpecialList}, lax_lists(),
        try checkout:total(ItemList, PriceList, SpecialList) of
            N when is_integer(N) -> true
        catch
            _:_ -> false
        end).
```

```
Elixir
code/PropertiesDrivenDevelopment/elixir/checkout/test/checkout_test.exs
```

```elixir
property "negative testing for expected results" do
  forall {items, prices, specials} <- lax_lists() do
    try do
      is_integer(Checkout.total(items, prices, specials))
    rescue
      _ ->
        false
    end
  end
end
```

This introduces a new generator, lax_lists(), defined as broadly as possible at first:

Erlang

```erlang
lax_lists() ->
    {list(string()),                           % item list
     list({string(), integer()}),             % price list
     list({string(), integer(), integer()})}. % specials list
```

Elixir

```elixir
defp lax_lists() do
  {list(utf8()),
   list({utf8(), integer()}),
   list({utf8(), integer(), integer()})}
end
```

That kind of property, based on the types of inputs and outputs, is usually the kind of stuff where a type system could catch most errors. If you have any type analysis available (as we do in Erlang and Elixir with Dialyzer), it's best to leave those kinds of issues to it. In fact, we do this here by using integer() as a generator rather than number()—it's no use sending it wrongly typed data when another tool will catch the error. But even if type analysis can find plenty of issues, not all interesting errors will be found there. Case in point, running the property finds this:

```
«commands to run the property»
===> Testing prop_checkout:prop_expected_result()
.!
Failed: After 2 test(s).
{[[]],[],[]}

Shrinking (0 time(s))
{[[]],[],[]}
```

The PropEr representation of strings is lacking, but if a single item (with name "" shown as []) is used, then the lookups fail. The price of an unknown item can't be used in the calculation, and the function bails out. All items being bought must also be within the price list, something rather hard to encode in a type system if the set of items is not known at compile-time.

This type of error is fine, but maybe we could give a clearer exception. We could raise a descriptive error instead, alerting the caller to the true nature of the problem. Let's first make the new exception acceptable to our property:

Erlang

```erlang
prop_expected_result() ->
    ?FORALL({ItemList, PriceList, SpecialList}, lax_lists(),
```

```erlang
try checkout:total(ItemList, PriceList, SpecialList) of
    N when is_integer(N) -> true
catch
    error:{unknown_item, _} -> true;
    _:_ -> false
end).
```

Elixir

```elixir
property "negative testing for expected results" do
  forall {items, prices, specials} <- lax_lists() do
    try do
      is_integer(Checkout.total(items, prices, specials))
    rescue
      e in [RuntimeError] ->
        String.starts_with?(e.message, "unknown item:")
      _ ->
        false
    end
  end
end
```

And attach a similar patch that adds validation:

Erlang
code/PropertiesDrivenDevelopment/erlang/checkout/src/checkout.erl

```erlang
-spec apply_regular([{item(), integer()}], [{item(), price()}]) -> price().
apply_regular(Items, PriceList) ->
    lists:sum([Count * cost_of_item(Name, PriceList)
               || {Name, Count} <- Items]).

cost_of_item(Name, PriceList) ->
    case proplists:get_value(Name, PriceList) of
        undefined -> error({unknown_item, Name});
        Price -> Price
    end.
```

Elixir
code/PropertiesDrivenDevelopment/elixir/checkout/lib/checkout.ex

```elixir
defp apply_regular(items, price_list) do
  Enum.sum(
    for {name, count} <- items do
      count * cost_of_item(price_list, name)
    end
  )
end
```

```
defp cost_of_item(price_list, name) do
  case List.keyfind(price_list, name, 0) do
    nil -> raise RuntimeError, message: "unknown item: #{name}"
    {_, price} -> price
  end
end
```

Go and run the properties, and you'll find the bug fixed. In fact, nothing else is revealed by the property. Before calling victory and considering our code bug-free, though, we want to make sure we actually did our negative property testing right.

Calibrating Negative Properties

The easiest and best tools you have to check whether a property is good is always going to be gathering statistics. Let's take a look again at prop_expected_result(). This time, we'll look into the type of end result we get. Right now, the poperty has two valid cases: one where the list of items is all valid, and one where at least some item is missing from the price list and would fail. Let's see what kind of split we get by using collect/2:

```
prop_expected_result() ->
    ?FORALL({ItemList, PriceList, SpecialList}, lax_lists(),
        collect(
          item_list_type(ItemList, PriceList),
          try checkout:total(ItemList, PriceList, SpecialList) of
              N when is_integer(N) -> true
          catch
              error:{unknown_item, _} -> true;
              _:_ -> false
          end)).

item_list_type(Items, Prices) ->
    case lists:all(fun(X) -> has_price(X, Prices) end, Items) of
        true -> valid;
        false -> prices_missing
    end.

has_price(Item, ItemList) ->
    proplists:get_value(Item, ItemList) =/= undefined.
```

Run this and check the stats:

```
«other properties»
===> Testing prop_checkout:prop_expected_result()
....................................................................
......................
OK: Passed 100 test(s).

91% prices_missing
9% valid
```

Chances are you'll get something equally lopsided when trying it. The vast majority of all failing test cases only exercise the one failing case we have identified, the one where an item isn't in the price list.

Our negative property is depressing. If we represent the test space to explore with a spectrum—where one end contains tests about the happiest of all paths where everything goes according to plan, and the other end contains tests about the terrible cases where all input is garbage and nothing works—we get something that looks a bit like this:

```
[Perfect happy case] <-a---------------b------c-> [nothing works]
```

Our current positive properties are probably sitting around point a right now—pretty much everything we pass them is ideal—and our negative property is around c, choking on predictable garbage over 90% of the time. We've got very little coverage on the gradient in between, where things are neither perfect nor wrong. To fix this, we will have to drag our negative properties somewhere closer to b.

One common trick to do this is to take our very lax generator and make it a bit stricter. We can do that with a kind of hybrid approach where we not only generate entirely random items, but also purposefully put in repeating predictible items:

Erlang
code/PropertiesDrivenDevelopment/erlang/checkout/test/prop_checkout.erl

```erlang
lax_lists() ->
    KnownItems = ["A", "B", "C"],
    MaybeKnownItemGen = elements(KnownItems ++ [string()]),
    {list(MaybeKnownItemGen),                           % item list
     list({MaybeKnownItemGen, integer()}),              % price list
     list({MaybeKnownItemGen, integer(), integer()})}.  % specials list
```

Elixir
code/PropertiesDrivenDevelopment/elixir/checkout/test/checkout_test.exs

```elixir
defp lax_lists() do
  known_items = ["A", "B", "C"]
  maybe_known_item_gen = elements(known_items ++ [utf8()])

  {list(maybe_known_item_gen), list({maybe_known_item_gen, integer()}),
   list({maybe_known_item_gen, integer(), integer()})}
end
```

Try the prop_expected_result() property once again and check the results:

```
$ rebar3 proper
«build info and other properties»
===> Testing prop_checkout:prop_expected_result()
.........!
Failed: After 10 test(s).
{[[44,0,2,0],[66],[65],[1,3,6,5]],[{[6,6,0],-7}],[{[65],0,-1},
 {[66],3,8},{[2],-3,0},{[67],12,0}]}

Shrinking ......(6 time(s))
{[[65]],[],[{[65],0,0}]}
```

A new interesting bug is triggered whenever a list of specials requires exactly zero items to work. This is, in fact, due to a division by zero when calculating totals. It's a bit surprising that none of our other properties ever encountered that case through all their random walks, but at least it's caught in one of them. Fixing it will require validating the specials—first the property, and then the code:

Erlang

```erlang
prop_expected_result() ->
    ?FORALL({ItemList, PriceList, SpecialList}, lax_lists(),
        try checkout:total(ItemList, PriceList, SpecialList) of
            N when is_integer(N) -> true
        catch
            error:{unknown_item, _} -> true;
            error:invalid_special_list -> true;
            _:_ -> false
        end).
```

Elixir

```elixir
property "negative testing for expected results" do
  forall {items, prices, specials} <- lax_lists() do
    try do
      is_integer(Checkout.total(items, prices, specials))
    rescue
      e in [RuntimeError] ->
        e.message == "invalid list of specials" ||
          String.starts_with?(e.message, "unknown item:")

      _ ->
        false
    end
  end
end
```

This handles the invalid specials list. Now for the actual code:

Erlang
code/PropertiesDrivenDevelopment/erlang/checkout/src/checkout.erl

```erlang
-module(checkout).

-export([valid_special_list/1, total/3]).

-type item() :: string().
-type price() :: integer().
-type special() :: {item(), pos_integer(), price()}.

-spec valid_special_list([special()]) -> boolean().
valid_special_list(List) ->
    lists:all(fun({_,X,_}) -> X =/= 0 end, List).

-spec total([item()], [{item(), price()}], [special()]) -> price().
total(ItemList, PriceList, Specials) ->
    valid_special_list(Specials) orelse error(invalid_special_list),
    Counts = count_seen(ItemList),
    {CountsLeft, Prices} = apply_specials(Counts, Specials),
    Prices + apply_regular(CountsLeft, PriceList).
```

Elixir
code/PropertiesDrivenDevelopment/elixir/checkout/lib/checkout.ex

```elixir
def valid_special_list(list) do
  Enum.all?(list, fn {_, x, _} -> x != 0 end)
end

def total(item_list, price_list, specials) do
  if not valid_special_list(specials) do
    raise RuntimeError, message: "invalid list of specials"
  end

  counts = count_seen(item_list)
  {counts_left, prices} = apply_specials(counts, specials)
  prices + apply_regular(counts_left, price_list)
end
```

The new function is valid_special_list/1, which checks that all list terms have 3-tuples and that the middle value is not a 0. This is something Dialyzer could already handle in your code, but it wouldn't necessarily detect if the data were coming from a database. Then at ❶, we integrate the function into the regular workflow.

This patches the test up. How do we know we've covered everything with our negative tests now? We don't. We could try to play with metrics again to see what we could improve, but there's another approach that can work well: relaxing constraints further.

Relaxing Constraints

While metrics are always a good thing to keep an eye on, another very interesting way to improve our negative tests and explore the program's problem space is to play with constraints, and relax them with existing generators. Let's revisit our TODO list. The items in *italics* are properties or assumptions we made about the system that we may want to play with:

- Items are identified by *unique names* (nonempty strings).

- The list of items has no set length (though it appears nonempty), and the items it contains are in no specific order.

- The *unit prices appear to be integers*. (Not a bad idea, since floating point numbers lose precision; we can assume values are written in cents, for example.)

- The special prices are triggered only once the right number of items of the proper type can match a given special.

- All *items have a unit price.*

- It is not mandatory for a given item to have a special price.

The way we relax constraints is usually through simple code modifications. Check your working code into source control, and do most of the changes right in place. Modify a bunch of generators, making them less strict so they trigger some unexpected case. Find out why that happened, revert the change, and then either add a unit test or a property test to validate the bug before fixing it.

Then we can rinse and repeat, gradually weeding out more and more bugs from our code.

Let's start with the first one, checking what happens when item names are not unique in the price list, which we can do by changing the last line of the price_list() generator:

```
%% generate a list of {ItemName, Price} to configure the checkout
price_list() ->
    ?LET(PriceList, non_empty(list({non_empty(string()), integer()})),
        lists:keysort(1, PriceList)). % allow duplicates
```

Here we replaced lists:ukeysort/2 with lists:keysort/2, keeping similar semantics but without removing duplicates. Run the properties again and you should see a failure:

```
«build information»
===> Testing prop_checkout:prop_no_special1()
.....................!
Failed: After 25 test(s).
{[[4],[4],[7,9,9,4,1,3,5,12,9],[4],[4],[4],[4],[4],[5,3,3]],-13,
[{[2,2,53,3,1,0,29,3,0],4},{[4],-4},{[4],1},{[5,3,3],-3},{[5,5,3,8,40],0},
{[6,0],-7},{[7,9,9,4,1,3,5,12,9],-2},{[12,3,5,14,16,2,4],-5}]}

Shrinking .........(10 time(s))
{[[4],[4],[4],[4],[4],[4],[4],[4],[4]],1,[{[4],0},{[4],1}]}
«other properties»
3/4 properties passed, 1 failed
===> Failed test cases:
  prop_checkout:prop_no_special1() -> false
```

Unsurprisingly, it appears that whenever a list of prices contains two identical items ([4] with both a price of 0 and 1), our system gets confused and dies. We don't support duplicates in the price list, and our generator implementation aligned itself with that fact. We baked the uniqueness assumption into our model but didn't necessarily expose that to our users, nor did we test for it explicitly. This could lead to problems. For example, someone might send malformed price lists, only to then open a support ticket once they discover the prices are wrong at checkout, and they'd be right to do so. It would in fact be nicer to let users know if the item list they submitted is valid without needing to buy anything through the checkout.

Let's revert the generator change, and add a property to copy that behavior:

Erlang
code/PropertiesDrivenDevelopment/erlang/checkout/test/prop_checkout.erl

```erlang
prop_dupe_list_invalid() ->
    ?FORALL(PriceList, dupe_list(),
        false =:= checkout:valid_price_list(PriceList)).

dupe_list() ->
    ?LET(Items, non_empty(list(string())),
        vector(length(Items)+1, {elements(Items), integer()})).
```

Elixir
code/PropertiesDrivenDevelopment/elixir/checkout/test/checkout_test.exs

```elixir
property "list of items with duplicates" do
  forall price_list <- dupe_list() do
    false == Checkout.valid_price_list(price_list)
  end
end
```

```
defp dupe_list() do
  let items <- non_empty(list(utf8())) do
    vector(length(items) + 1, {elements(items), integer()})
  end
end
```

The dupe_list() generator works by generating a random list of item names, and then using it to generate the price list. By asking for more price list entries than there are item names—that's what using vector(length(Items)+1, ...) accomplishes—we're guaranteeing duplicate entries.

You'll note that the property does not check against the checkout:total/3 function, but against a valid_special call that we'll add to the implementation module, matching what we did earlier for the specials list validation:

Erlang
code/PropertiesDrivenDevelopment/erlang/checkout/src/checkout.erl

```
-export([valid_price_list/1, valid_special_list/1, total/3]).

-spec valid_price_list([{item(), price()}]) -> boolean().
valid_price_list(List) ->
    length(List) =:= length(lists:ukeysort(1, List)).
```

Elixir
code/PropertiesDrivenDevelopment/elixir/checkout/lib/checkout.ex

```
def valid_price_list(list) do
  sorted = Enum.sort(list)
  length(list) == length(Enum.dedup_by(sorted, fn {x, _} -> x end))
end
```

And as with the earlier case, we should also wire it into the total/3 call, just to be thorough, at ❶ in the following code:

Erlang

```
-spec total([item()], [{item(), price()}], [special()]) -> price().
total(ItemList, PriceList, Specials) ->
    valid_price_list(PriceList) orelse error(invalid_price_list),
    valid_special_list(Specials) orelse error(invalid_special_list),
    Counts = count_seen(ItemList),
    {CountsLeft, Prices} = apply_specials(Counts, Specials),
    Prices + apply_regular(CountsLeft, PriceList).
```

Elixir

```elixir
def total(item_list, price_list, specials) do
  if not valid_price_list(price_list) do
    raise RuntimeError, message: "invalid list of prices"
  end

  if not valid_special_list(specials) do
    raise RuntimeError, message: "invalid list of specials"
  end

  counts = count_seen(item_list)
  {counts_left, prices} = apply_specials(counts, specials)
  prices + apply_regular(counts_left, price_list)
end
```

Run the tests again and see what happens:

```
«build information»
===> Testing prop_checkout:prop_expected_result()
........!
Failed: After 9 test(s).
{[[67],[8],[2,3,1]],[{[67],-2},{[67],-1}],[{[67],-3,3}]}

Shrinking .......(7 time(s))
{[],[{[67],0},{[67],0}],[]}
«other properties»
4/5 properties passed, 1 failed
===> Failed test cases:
  prop_checkout:prop_expected_result() -> false
```

Our prop_expected_result() property fails again, this time because of the new exception we added. It turns out that this property would sometimes generate the right kind of inputs to trigger that case, but it didn't know the business rules well enough to recognize it as invalid.

Fuzzing vs. Properties

This perfectly highlights the distinction between fuzzing—generating garbage input to see if the program fails—compared to property-based testing, where we check that the program behaves the right way given all kinds of inputs. Both scanning largely with negative tests and relaxing constraints find interesting but distinct results.

We can fix the failing test by adding a specific exception handler for the one failing case:

```
Erlang
code/PropertiesDrivenDevelopment/erlang/checkout/test/prop_checkout.erl
```

```erlang
prop_expected_result() ->
    ?FORALL({ItemList, PriceList, SpecialList}, lax_lists(),
        try checkout:total(ItemList, PriceList, SpecialList) of
            N when is_integer(N) -> true
        catch
            error:{unknown_item, _} -> true;
            error:invalid_price_list -> true;
            error:invalid_special_list -> true;
            _:_ -> false
        end).
```

```
Elixir
code/PropertiesDrivenDevelopment/elixir/checkout/test/checkout_test.exs
```

```elixir
property "negative testing for expected results" do
  forall {items, prices, specials} <- lax_lists() do
    try do
      is_integer(Checkout.total(items, prices, specials))
    rescue
      e in [RuntimeError] ->
        e.message == "invalid list of prices" ||
          e.message == "invalid list of specials" ||
          String.starts_with?(e.message, "unknown item:")

      _ ->
        false
    end
  end
end
```

And while we're at it, add a property to deal with duplicates in the specials list:

```
Erlang
code/PropertiesDrivenDevelopment/erlang/checkout/test/prop_checkout.erl
```

```erlang
prop_dupe_specials_invalid() ->
    ?FORALL(SpecialList, dupe_special_list(),
        false =:= checkout:valid_special_list(SpecialList)).

dupe_special_list() ->
    ?LET(Items, non_empty(list(string())),
        vector(length(Items)+1, {elements(Items), integer(), integer()})).
```

```
Elixir
code/PropertiesDrivenDevelopment/elixir/checkout/test/checkout_test.exs
```

```
property "list of items with specials" do
  forall special_list <- dupe_special_list() do
    false == Checkout.valid_special_list(special_list)
  end
end

defp dupe_special_list() do
  let items <- non_empty(list(utf8())) do
    vector(length(items) + 1, {elements(items), integer(), integer()})
  end
end
```

Include the matching code to fix things:

```
Erlang
code/PropertiesDrivenDevelopment/erlang/checkout/src/checkout.erl
```

```
-spec valid_special_list([special()]) -> boolean().
valid_special_list(List) ->
    lists:all(fun({_,X,_}) -> X =/= 0 end, List) andalso
    length(List) =:= length(lists:ukeysort(1, List)).
```

```
Elixir
code/PropertiesDrivenDevelopment/elixir/checkout/lib/checkout.ex
```

```
def valid_special_list(list) do
  sorted = Enum.sort(list)

  Enum.all?(list, fn {_, x, _} -> x != 0 end) &&
    length(list) == length(Enum.dedup_by(sorted, fn {x, _, _} -> x end))
end
```

Run the properties and you'll see that they all pass. You could still dig for more bugs; here, we found three bugs by relaxing only one of the properties, and relaxing more them would likely find more interesting bugs:

- Not handling unit prices for some items (or specials) creates unexpected crashes; more interestingly, replacing integers with numbers (specifically floats) yields multiple failures because the current implementation uses rem and div, two integer-specific operators.

- Using negative numbers for prices would technically mean we credit people rather than charging them to walk away with items, and currently we don't validate for that.

- Passing in nonnumeric values in the price list or specials list is considered valid by the code but can't logically work.

Given how vague the specification was, we probably would have to discuss these discoveries with stakeholders to figure out what is acceptable or not before the code hits production. A strict interpretation of the specification will mean our current implementation is sufficient. A lax one will cause explosions for multiple cases that may or may not be preposterous.

Of course, in a statically typed language (or in the case of Erlang and Elixir, with Dialyzer's type analysis), a strict interpretation of the spec is the only one accepted. The potential bugs we could discover through relaxing the properties above do not even register as a possibility with type analysis, and the current state of affairs is very likely acceptable.

In general, when strict assumptions are made and are enforced by manual checks, the compiler, and/or static code analysis, then the program shouldn't get into unexpected states. It may be inflexible and frustrating for the user, but it'll be less likely to go wrong—at least not on the bugs that may be preventable through type analysis.

Wrapping Up

Through properties-driven development, we've extrapolated properties from a vague spec, testing our happy paths in a test-first approach. Code coverage, while a useful metric to show code is tested, isn't great to assess test quality. Instead, you've seen how negative testing in a fuzzing-inspired approach can help, as well as how playing with properties by relaxing constraints can uncover all kinds of bugs and underspecifications that could prove problematic.

We've done all this while going through the most complex generators this book contains. You should now have a pretty good idea of what can and can't be done well with stateless properties. Most of your unit testing needs should now be covered, in fact. Go ahead and try a bunch of that stuff in your own projects. As you get trickier and trickier generators, you may find them hard to debug. If so, the next chapter should have you covered, as it discusses *Shrinking*.

## CHAPTER 7

Shrinking

A critical component of property-based testing is shrinking—the mechanism by which a property-based testing framework can be told how to simplify failure cases enough to let us figure out exactly what the minimal reproducible case is. While finding complex obtuse cases is worthwhile, being able to reduce failing inputs (data generated) to a simple counterexample truly is the killer feature here. But there are some cases where what PropEr does isn't what we need. Either it can't shrink large data structures well enough to be understandable, or it's not shrinking them the way we want it to. In this chapter we'll see two ways to handle things: the ?SHRINK and the LETSHRINK macros, which let us give the framework hints about what to do.

But first, we have to see how shrinking works at a high level. In general you can think of shrinking as the framework attempting to bring the data generator closer to its own zero point, and successfully doing so as long as the property fails. A zero for a generator is somewhat arbitrary, but if you play with the default generators a bit by calling proper_gen:sampleshrink/1 on them in the shell, you may notice the following:

- A number tends to shrink from floating point values toward integers, and integers tend to shrink toward the number 0 (floating point numbers themselves shrink toward 0.0).

- Binaries tend to shrink from things full of bytes toward the empty binary (<<>>).

- Lists tend to shrink toward the empty list.

- elements([A,B,C]) will shrink toward the value A.

In short, data structures that contain other data tend to empty themselves, and other values try to find a neutral point. The nice aspect of this is that as custom generators are built from other generators, the shrinking is inherited, and a custom generator may get its own shrinking for free: a map full of people records made of strings and numbers will see the strings get shorter and simpler, the numbers will get closer to zero, and the map will get fewer and fewer elements, until only the components essential to trigger a failure are left.

But for some data types, there is no good zero point: a vector of length 15 will always have length 15, and same with a tuple. Similarly, larger recursive data structures that have been defined by the user may not have obvious ways to shrink (such as probabilistic ones), or may require shrinking toward values other than the default for a generator. Examples of special shrinking points are things such as a chessboard, which is at its neutral point not when it's empty but when it's full, with all its pieces in their initial positions. Similarly, in chemistry, pH[1] has a neutral value of 7. In a database, an interesting boundary position is usually triggered when records reach 4 kilobytes—a common minimal page size[2] for computer memory.

For such cases, even if they are relatively rare, the ?SHRINK macro might be what you need.

Re-centering with ?SHRINK

?SHRINK is conceptually the simplest of the two macros that can be used to impact shrinking. It is best used to pick a custom zero point toward which PropEr will try to shrink data. You can do this mainly by giving the framework a normal generator for normal cases, and then suggesting it uses other simpler generators whenever an error is discovered.

The macro takes the form ?SHRINK(DefaultGenerator, [AlternativeGenerators]) in Erlang, and shrink(default_generator, [alternative_generators]) in Elixir. The DefaultGenerator will be used for all passing tests. Once a property fails, however, ?SHRINK lets us tell PropEr that any of the alternative generators in the list are interesting ways to get simpler relevant data. We can give *hints* about how the framework should search for failures, basically. And if the alternative generators are not fruitful, so be it, the shrinking will continue in other ways until no progress can be made.

To make things practical, if we're generating timestamps or dates, we may be interested in including years from 0 to 9999 to make sure we cover all kinds of weird cases. But if you know that the underlying implementation of your

---

1. https://en.wikipedia.org/wiki/PH
2. https://en.wikipedia.org/wiki/Page_(computer_memory)#Multiple_page_sizes

system uses Unix timestamps, then you should consider that its epoch (starting time) is on January 1, 1970. Since January 1, 1970, is the underlying system's zero value, picking 1970 as a shrinking target makes more sense than the literal year 0 (particularly since year zero is not necessarily a valid concept[3] in the first place).

Let's take a look at the following set of generators used to create strings of the form "1997-08-04T12:02:18-05:00", in accordance with the ISO 8601[4] standard. This set of generators will center its shrinking efforts toward January 1, 1970. Let's start with the overall structure, and see what we can do with years:

About the Code

 In the snippets that follow, code is labeled with both the language (Erlang and Elixir) and the file where you should put the code if you're following along.

Erlang   code/Shrinking/erlang/pbt/test/prop_shrink.erl

```erlang
-module(prop_shrink).
-include_lib("proper/include/proper.hrl").
-compile([export_all, {no_auto_import,[date/0]}, {no_auto_import,[time/0]}]).

strdatetime() ->
    ?LET(DateTime, datetime(), to_str(DateTime)).

datetime() ->
    {date(), time(), timezone()}.

date() ->
    ?SUCHTHAT({Y,M,D}, {year(), month(), day()},
              calendar:valid_date(Y,M,D)).

year() ->
    ?SHRINK(range(0, 9999), [range(1970, 2000), range(1900, 2100)]).
```

Elixir   code/Shrinking/elixir/pbt/test/pbt_test.exs

```elixir
def strdatetime() do
  let(date_time <- datetime(), do: to_str(date_time))
end

def datetime() do
  {date(), time(), timezone()}
end
```

---

3. https://en.wikipedia.org/wiki/Year_zero
4. https://en.wikipedia.org/wiki/ISO_8601

```
def strdatetime() do
  let(date_time <- datetime(), do: to_str(date_time))
end

def datetime() do
  {date(), time(), timezone()}
end
```

As you can see, we have our first generator functions to call the ?SHRINK macro. The year() generator at ❶ uses range(0,9999) as its default generator. This covers all thousand or so years we are interested in. The alternative generators for the macro are range(1970,2000) and range(1900,2100), which means that if some generated year causes a property to fail, rather than trying years such as 73 or 8763, PropEr will try years closer to the epoch, like 1988 or 2040. ?SHRINK lets us narrow PropEr's search space down significantly to get relevant results faster.

Let's look at the rest of the generators:

Erlang	code/Shrinking/erlang/pbt/test/prop_shrink.erl

```
month() ->
    range(1, 12).

day() ->
    range(1, 31).

time() ->
    {range(0, 24), range(0, 59), range(0, 60)}.

timezone() ->
    {elements(['+', '-']),
     ?SHRINK(range(0, 99), [range(0, 14), 0]),
     ?SHRINK(range(0, 99), [0, 15, 30, 45])}.

%% Helper to convert the internal format to a string
to_str({{Y,M,D}, {H,Mi,S}, {Sign,Ho,Mo}}) ->
    FormatStr = "~4..0b-~2..0b-~2..0bT-2..0b:~2..0b:~2..0b~s~2..0b:~2..0b",
    lists:flatten(io_lib:format(FormatStr, [Y,M,D,H,Mi,S,Sign,Ho,Mo])).
```

Elixir	code/Shrinking/elixir/pbt/test/pbt_test.exs

```
def month(), do: range(1, 12)

def day(), do: range(1, 31)

def time(), do: {range(0, 24), range(0, 59), range(0, 60)}

def timezone() do
  {elements([:+, :-]), shrink(range(0, 99), [range(0, 14), 0]),
    shrink(range(0, 99), [0, 15, 30, 45])}
end
```

```
def to_str({{y, m, d}, {h, mi, s}, {sign, ho, mo}}) do
  format_str = "~4..0b-~2..0b-~2..0bT~2..0b:~2..0b:~2..0b~s~2..0b:~2..0b"

  :io_lib.format(format_str, [y, m, d, h, mi, s, sign, ho, mo])
  |> to_string()
end
```

One thing you should note is that the standard is somewhat lax and allows (or rather, doesn't forbid) the notation of a timezone that is +99:76, lagging about four days behind standard time, even if that is nonsensical from a human perspective.

Similarly, our timezone() generator will look for values between 0 and 99, but in any failure case, will try to settle between 0 and 14 when possible, which are ranges that we humans find more reasonable. Similarly, the minutes offsets will try to match currently standard offsets of 0, 15, 30, or 45 minutes.

And as you can see, generators that use ?SHRINK can be used like any other; the macro adds some metadata to the underlying structure representing a generator, so they remain entirely composable. From anybody else's point of view, it's a generator like any other.

Oh, and do note that seconds go up to 60, due to leap seconds.[5]

You can see shrinking in action by calling proper_gen:sampleshrink/1 in the shell, and PropEr will generate sequences of more and more aggressive shrinks:

```
1> proper_gen:sampleshrink(prop_shrink:strdatetime()).
"1757-06-26T02:36:60-64:38"
"1995-06-26T02:36:60-64:38"
"1970-06-26T02:36:60-64:38"
"1970-01-26T02:36:60-64:38"
"1970-01-01T02:36:60-64:38"
"1970-01-01T00:36:60-64:38"
"1970-01-01T00:00:60-64:38"
"1970-01-01T00:00:00-64:38"
"1970-01-01T00:00:00+64:38"
"1970-01-01T00:00:00+09:38"
"1970-01-01T00:00:00+00:38"
"1970-01-01T00:00:00+00:00"
ok
```

Elixir's equivalent to proper_gen:sample_shrink/1 is PropCheck.sample_shrink(PbtTest.strdatetime()), which provides the same functionality but with a more idiomatic format.

_____

5. https://en.wikipedia.org/wiki/Leap_second

In practice, shrinking will be done less linearly than this. A given attempt at shrinking that fails to create another failing case won't be used. That means that if a test failed on every month of July, the shrinking would end up looking like "1970-07-01T00:00:00+00:00".

That is as complex as ?SHRINK gets. For a lot of cases, you may find yourself using other generators like element([A,B,C,...,Z]), which will do something kind of equivalent by shrinking toward A rather than Z. When element/1 no longer suffices, then ?SHRINK becomes interesting. The one thing that it won't necessarily help with is huge chunks of data that are hard to reduce to smaller counterexamples. That is where ?LETSHRINK shines.

Dividing with ?LETSHRINK

As you use PropEr, you may find yourself stuck with generators creating huge data structures that take a long time to shrink and often don't give very interesting results back. This often happens when some very low-probability failure is triggered, meaning that the framework had to generate a lot of data to find it, and has limited chances of shrinking things in a significant manner.

Whenever that happens, the ?LETSHRINK([Pattern, ...], [Generator, ...], Expression) is what you need. In practice, we use the generator like this:

Erlang

```
?LETSHRINK([A,B,C], [list(number()), list(number()), list(number())],
           A ++ B ++ C)
```

Elixir

```
let_shrink([
    a <- list(number()),
    b <- list(number()),
    c <- list(number())
]) do
    a ++ b ++ c
end
```

The macro looks a lot like a regular ?LET macro, but with a few constraints: the first two arguments must always be lists, and the third argument is an operation where all list elements get combined into one. Here, A, B, and C are three lists filled with integers, and A ++ B ++ C is just a bigger list of integers. The important part is that any of A, B or C can be used by the program instead of A ++ B ++ C.

The reason for that is that once a property fails and PropEr tries to shrink the data set, it will instead pick just one of A, B, or C *without applying the transformation* and return that directly. ?LETSHRINK is particularly appropriate for recursive structures, data made through branching, and all kinds of pieces of data that are generated by smashing others together and applying transformations, since taking a part of it is a legitimate way to get a simpler version.

Basically, we're giving PropEr a way to divide the data up to isolate a failing subset more efficiently.

The most common form of ?LETSHRINK is the one you'd use on tree data structures. For a binary tree generator of size N, we'd write something like this:

Erlang	code/Shrinking/erlang/pbt/test/prop_shrink.erl

```erlang
tree(N) when N =< 1 ->
    {leaf, number()};
tree(N) ->
    PerBranch = N div 2,
    {branch, tree(PerBranch), tree(PerBranch)}.
```

Elixir	code/Shrinking/elixir/pbt/test/pbt_test.exs

```elixir
def tree(n) when n <= 1 do
  {:leaf, number()}
end

def tree(n) do
  per_branch = div(n, 2)
  {:branch, tree(per_branch), tree(per_branch)}
end
```

If you run sampleshrink/1 on it, you'll find out that the elements within the tree shrink, but the tree itself stays the same size:

```erlang
1> proper_gen:sampleshrink(prop_shrink:tree(4)).
{branch,{branch,{leaf,13},{leaf,0.6154862580810709}},
        {branch,{leaf,8},{leaf,-3}}}
{branch,{branch,{leaf,0},{leaf,0.6154862580810709}},
        {branch,{leaf,8},{leaf,-3}}}
{branch,{branch,{leaf,0},{leaf,-6}},{branch,{leaf,8},{leaf,-3}}}
{branch,{branch,{leaf,0},{leaf,0}},{branch,{leaf,8},{leaf,-3}}}
{branch,{branch,{leaf,0},{leaf,0}},{branch,{leaf,0},{leaf,-3}}}
{branch,{branch,{leaf,0},{leaf,0}},{branch,{leaf,0},{leaf,0}}}
```

Each of the trees in the sample contains exactly four entries: all the integers tend toward zero, but the structure itself has a fixed size. The obvious way to get the tree to shrink is through parameterizing it with the Size variable obtained from the ?SIZED(Var, Exp) macro. But if the failure requires internal tree elements to remain large while the tree structure itself is small, then the chances are fewer that shrinking by size only would work well.

Instead, if we use ?LETSHRINK, we can get a more shrink-friendly version:

Erlang	code/Shrinking/erlang/pbt/test/prop_shrink.erl

```erlang
tree_shrink(N) when N =< 1 ->
    {leaf, number()};
tree_shrink(N) ->
    PerBranch = N div 2,
    ?LETSHRINK([L, R], [tree_shrink(PerBranch), tree_shrink(PerBranch)],
               {branch, L, R}).
```

Elixir	code/Shrinking/elixir/pbt/test/pbt_test.exs

```elixir
def tree_shrink(n) when n <= 1 do
  {:leaf, number()}
end

def tree_shrink(n) do
  per_branch = div(n, 2)

  let_shrink([
    left <- tree_shrink(per_branch),
    right <- tree_shrink(per_branch)
  ]) do
    {:branch, left, right}
  end
end
```

The leaf clause is left unchanged, but the inner-node (branch) clause is modified. Instead of generating {branch, Left, Right} right away, we generate both the left and right side in a list within ?LETSHRINK. In the third argument, we assemble both parts within the branch tuple. Effectively, we take exactly the same approach, but with the macro as a layer of indirection.

This is a small change, but it has a large impact. We can now start from larger trees to initially find bugs, without losing clarity when getting good counterexamples:

```
2> proper_gen:sampleshrink(prop_shrink:tree_shrink(16)).
{branch,{branch,{branch,{branch,{leaf,28},{leaf,-0.039220389013186946}},
                {branch,{leaf,3.9013940456284684},{leaf,-3}}},
        {branch,{branch,{leaf,14.576812882147989},{leaf,-16}},
                {branch,{leaf,-2.0345272435474966},
                        {leaf,-8.151564195158691}}}},
```

```
        {branch,{branch,{branch,{leaf,-12},{leaf,-85}},
                        {branch,{leaf,16.829645166380576},{leaf,-1}}},
               {branch,{branch,{leaf,1},{leaf,5.058669843388856}},
                        {branch,{leaf,7},{leaf,2}}}}}
{branch,{branch,{branch,{leaf,28},{leaf,-0.039220389013186946}},
                {branch,{leaf,3.9013940456284684},{leaf,-3}}},
        {branch,{branch,{leaf,14.576812882147989},{leaf,-16}},
               {branch,{leaf,-2.0345272435474966},
                        {leaf,-8.151564195158691}}}}
{branch,{branch,{leaf,28},{leaf,-0.039220389013186946}},
       {branch,{leaf,3.9013940456284684},{leaf,-3}}}
{branch,{leaf,28},{leaf,-0.039220389013186946}}
{leaf,28}
{leaf,0}
```

Rather than a constant tree size, each shrink subsequently makes the tree smaller (if the property still fails). If you pay close attention, you'll also notice that the values within the tree are initially *not modified*. So if the tree size is at play, the tree will remain large by failing to shrink that way, telling PropEr to instead try with its contents. If the bug is due to contents before structure and the size doesn't matter, we'll know rapidly as well. We're giving a good search stategy to the framework here by telling it how the recursive aspects of our generators work.

In general, for a framework like PropEr or Quickcheck, adding shrinking instructions isn't something that needs to be done as part of writing the generator the first time around. Instead, it's something that will be worth doing once a confusing counterexample is found and the minimal counterexample given by the framework is not understandable on its own.

As with other property-based testing debugging practices, improving generators will likely be iterative and a bit explorative. We can improve the generator, its shrinking, the test cases, and our understanding of the program itself as we discover the hidden properties embedded in the code that was written.

Wrapping Up

We've covered what is pretty much an optimization when we have large counterexamples that PropEr doesn't necessarily know how to handle. By using the ?SHRINK macro, you can let it know how to retarget shrinking toward more meaningful neutral values for a given generator. You've also seen that with ?LETSHRINK, we can give PropEr tips on how to divide up a data structure to find problems with more ease.

With shrinking under your belt, you now have pretty much all of the tools you'll need to handle stateless property tests. In fact, we're almost done with stateless properties. Right now, the only thing left to see is a brand new PropEr feature called *Targeted Property-Based Testing*, which at this point will just be a bonus for some amazing flexibility in property testing.

Exercises

Question 1

What are the two macros used for shrinking and what do their arguments stand for?

Solution on page 320.

Question 2

What are the differences between the ?LETSHRINK macro and the ?LET macro?

Solution on page 320.

Question 3

In the following property, a list of servings for a meal is generated. If any serving contains dairy, the property fails:

Erlang	code/Shrinking/erlang/pbt/test/prop_shrink.erl

```erlang
prop_too_much_dairy() ->
    ?FORALL(Food, meal(), dairy_count(Food) =:= 0).

dairy_count(L) ->
    length([X || X <- L, is_dairy(X)]).

is_dairy(cheesesticks) -> true;
is_dairy(lasagna) -> true;
is_dairy(icecream) -> true;
is_dairy(milk) -> true;
is_dairy(_) -> false.
```

Elixir	code/Shrinking/elixir/pbt/test/pbt_test.exs

```elixir
defmodule PbtTest do
  use ExUnit.Case
  use PropCheck

  property "dairy" do
    forall food <- meal() do
      dairy_count(food) == 0
    end
  end
```

```
defmodule PbtTest do
  use ExUnit.Case
  use PropCheck

  property "dairy" do
    forall food <- meal() do
      dairy_count(food) == 0
    end
  end
end
```

The generator looks like this:

Erlang	code/Shrinking/erlang/pbt/test/prop_shrink.erl

```
meal() ->
    ?LETSHRINK([Appetizer, Drink, Entree, Dessert],
               [elements([soup, salad, cheesesticks]),
                elements([coffee, tea, milk, water, juice]),
                elements([lasagna, tofu, steak]),
                elements([cake, chocolate, icecream])],
               [Appetizer, Drink, Entree, Dessert]).
```

Elixir	code/Shrinking/elixir/pbt/test/pbt_test.exs

```
def meal() do
  let_shrink([
    appetizer <- elements([:soup, :salad, :cheesesticks]),
    drink <- elements([:coffee, :tea, :milk, :water, :juice]),
    entree <- elements([:lasagna, :tofu, :steak]),
    dessert <- elements([:cake, :chocolate, :icecream])
  ]) do
    [appetizer, drink, entree, dessert]
  end
end
```

But whenever the test case fails, we instead get a result set that always contains the four courses. Fix the ?LETSHRINK usage in the generator so that data can be appropriately shrunk.

Solution on page 320.

Question 4

In *Writing the Generator*, on page 143, the following generator was introduced to create lists of items with expected prices and specials:

Erlang

```erlang
item_price_special() ->
    %% first LET: freeze the PriceList
    ?LET(PriceList, price_list(),
        %% second LET: freeze the SpecialList
        ?LET(SpecialList, special_list(PriceList),
            %% third LET: Regular + Special items and prices
            ?LET({{RegularItems, RegularExpected},
                  {SpecialItems, SpecialExpected}},
                 {regular_gen(PriceList, SpecialList),
                  special_gen(PriceList, SpecialList)},
                 %% And merge + return initial lists:
                 {shuffle(RegularItems ++ SpecialItems),
                  RegularExpected + SpecialExpected,
                  PriceList, SpecialList}))).

shuffle(L) ->
    %% Shuffle the list by adding a random number first,
    %% then sorting on it, and then removing it
    Shuffled = lists:sort([{rand:uniform(), X} || X <- L]),
    [X || {_, X} <- Shuffled].
```

Elixir

```elixir
defp item_price_special() do
  # first let: freeze the price list
  let price_list <- price_list() do
    # second let: freeze the list of specials
    let special_list <- special_list(price_list) do
      # third let: regular + special items and prices
      let {{regular_items, regular_expected},
           {special_items, special_expected}} <-
           {regular_gen(price_list, special_list),
            special_gen(price_list, special_list)} do
        # and merge + return initial lists:
        {Enum.shuffle(regular_items ++ special_items),
         regular_expected + special_expected, price_list, special_list}
      end
    end
  end
end
```

This generator merges two types of data: those without a special, and those with a special. The two types are joined together into one larger item list with prices, which can then be passed to the property.

Modify the generator so that both types of pricing can shrink independently.

Solution on page 321.

## CHAPTER 8

Targeted Properties

So far, the properties we have written have been rather tightly coupled with generators, since by needing to write specific properties, we tend to need specific generators. More general generators tend to be more useful when we do broader scanning rather than intricate validation, and so we rarely can have just one generator that can do it all.

This is necessary because we need to control randomness to some extent. In this chapter, you'll learn about targeted properties, which are straight up witchcraft. They let you use generic generators and from within the property specialize them so they generate data more relevant to the property. You can use them for simple stuff like "make the numbers in the list bigger," but also for weirder ideas such as "ensure the generated data results in more processes running in the VM" or "a compressed file should be as large as possible."

In this chapter, we'll cover what targeted properties look like, how they work (and where they break down), and how to customize them, and then you can try some examples to put it all in practice.

Targeted Properties and Elixir

 Targeted Properties are so new in PropEr that the Elixir wrapper for it (PropCheck) has not yet had the time to replicate the functionality at the time of writing.

This chapter's code will be provided only in Erlang

Understanding Targeted Properties

Regular properties work by using generators to create random data for each iteration of a test, running some checks, and then seeing if it works for all inputs. Inputs for each iteration are mostly independent—the framework scales the size element of generation between each one—and if you want the data generated to be diverse and relevant, you have to use metrics to tweak the generator by hand.

By comparison, targeted properties operate with a different principle: each iteration of a property can be used to influence later iterations' data generation. Even better, the property itself can give feedback to PropEr telling it whether things are headed in the right direction.

This is a bit abstract, so let's make things practical.

What They Look Like

In appearances, targeted properties are fairly similar to regular properties. Instead of using the ?FORALL(Pattern, Generator, Property) macro, you just have to use the ?FORALL_TARGETED(Pattern, Generator, Property) macro in PropEr v1.3.0 or later.

Let's try them. First we'll write a simple path generator that we can use to create sequences of directions:

About the Code

In the snippets that follow, code is labeled with both the language (Erlang) and the file where you should put the code if you're following along.

Erlang   code/TargetedProperties/erlang/target/test/prop_target.erl

```erlang
-module(prop_target).
-include_lib("proper/include/proper.hrl").
-compile(export_all).

path() -> list(oneof([left, right, up, down])).
```

It's going to be pretty random, going in any direction. Let's write a property with the new macro, one that should always pass:

```erlang
prop_path() ->
    ?FORALL_TARGETED(P, path(),
        begin
            {X,Y} = lists:foldl(fun move/2, {0,0}, P),
            io:format("~p",[{X,Y}]),
            true
        end).

move(left, {X,Y}) -> {X-1,Y};
move(right, {X,Y}) -> {X+1,Y};
move(up, {X,Y}) -> {X,Y+1};
move(down, {X,Y}) -> {X,Y-1}.
```

The move/2 function just enacts each movement on a {X,Y} coordinate system, where -X goes to the left, +X to the right. Similarly, -Y is to the bottom, and +Y is to the top. By applying it over every direction, we can get a general feeling for all the travel done by a path. The path [left, top, left, top] should return {-2,2}, and a path such as [top,down,left,right] would come back to {0,0}.

If you run this property, you'll see that most of the paths tend to average to the {0,0} coordinates:

```
$ rebar3 proper -p prop_path
[{0,-1}.{0,0}.{0,-1}.{1,-2}.{0,1}.{0,-1}.{0,-2}.{0,-1}.{1,-1}.{-1,-1}.
 {0,0}.{1,1}.{-2,1}.{0,-1}.{0,-2}.{0,-1}.{1,-2}.{-1,-1}.{-1,-1}.
 {0,-1}.{0,-1}.{0,-1}.{1,-1}.{1,0}.{0,-1}.{1,0}.{0,-1}.{0,0}.
 «more output»
 {1,-2}.{0,-1}.{1,-1}.{0,-1}.].
OK: Passed 1 test(s).
===>
1/1 properties passed
```

This means that we mostly have an equal distribution between all runs. You'll notice two things about this output. Instead of just being ..... for each test, we have [..........] (if we remove the {X,Y} output). You'll also notice that instead of saying it ran one hundred tests as the usual default, it ran way more than that—one thousand tests to be exact—but only reported one.

Targeted properties have a slightly different interface. You can control the number of iterations in a test either with the -s or --search_steps argument.

To show what targeted properties can do, we'll give some feedback to PropEr about what we'd like the data to look like. You can do this by calling either the ?MAXIMIZE(Num) or ?MINIMIZE(Num) macros from within the property. The argument must be a numeric value that can gradually be increased or decreased—not just a thing that goes "0 or 1"—to let PropEr know it's doing the right thing.

With our paths, we can try to head toward the bottom left by maximizing X-Y: the higher the value X and the lower the value Y, the higher the maximized value:

```
prop_path(opts) -> [{search_steps, 100}]. % otherwise this runs 1000 times!
prop_path() ->
    ?FORALL_TARGETED(P, path(),
        begin
            {X,Y} = lists:foldl(fun move/2, {0,0}, P),
            io:format("~p",[{X,Y}]),
            ?MAXIMIZE(X-Y),
            true
        end).
```

> ## Rebar3 PropEr Meta-Functions
>
> The rebar3 plugin for PropEr lets you specify optional callbacks to define a documen-
> tation line to be output in case of failure and to override the general options being
> set in rebar.config or from the command line:
>
> ```
> -module(prop_demo).
> -include_lib("proper/include/proper.hrl").
> %% NOT auto-exported by PropEr, we must do it ourselves.
> %% Alternatively use -compile(export_all).
> -export([prop_demo/1]).
>
> prop_demo(doc) ->
>     %% Docs are shown when the test property fails
>     "only properties that return `true' are seen as passing";
> prop_demo(opts) ->
>     %% Override CLI and rebar.config option for `numtests' only
>     [{numtests, 500}].
>
> prop_demo() -> % auto-exported by Proper
>     ?FORALL(_N, integer(), false). % always fail
> ```
>
> When run, the prop_demo/0 property will always run 500 times (if it doesn't fail), and
> on failure, properties' doc values are displayed:
>
> ```
> ===> Failed test cases:
> prop_demo:prop_demo() -> false (only properties that return `true' are
> seen as passing)
> ```

Run it to see the new results you get instead:

```
$ rebar3 proper -p prop_path
===> Testing prop_target:prop_path()
[{0,0}.{0,-1}.{0,-1}.{-1,0}.{1,-1}.{1,-2}.{2,-2}.{2,-2}.{2,1}.{-3,-1}.
 «more output»
 {11,-11}.{10,-13}.{14,-13}.{11,-12}.{13,-7}.{9,-19}.{12,-13}.{10,-14}.].
OK: Passed 1 test(s).
```

And just like that, we can use what is essentially a set of default generators
and get tailor-made results for our properties.

Before pushing things any further, let's take a look at how this works under
the hood.

How They Work

Understanding the mechanism under which targeted properties operate will
help you make the right choice about how to use them, and will also help
with customizing strategies to help PropEr maximize or minimize values. It's
good to know how things work rather than just feeling they are magic.

Historically, researchers tried a few mechanisms when first developing targeted properties,[1] but the most flexible one turned out to be *simulated annealing.*[2] Simulated annealing is a kind of complex method to probabilistically find good approximations of the possible maximal value of a function.

Let's say you're looking for the best way to optimize data throughput for some packet-based communication. You have to juggle factors such as packet size, path cost, latency, bandwidth, and so on. There are multiple things that can impact the end result, but you worry about one principal metric: how many bytes per second can make it through.

All the solutions and parameters can be represented something like this:

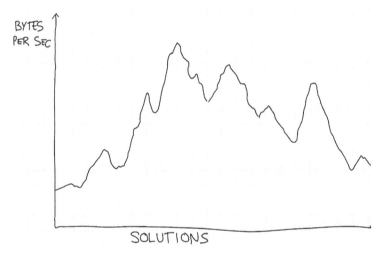

There's one optimal solution, but trying all possibilities has a prohibitive cost. You could point at random and hope to get something good, or try something like hill climbing,[3] which greedily tries to just pick the best obvious improvement repeatedly. The problem with an approach like that is that it's impossible to know if you're stuck in a *local maxima*, meaning a point that right now looks best but there's no guarantee it actually is the best. This results in searches looking like the top figure on page 184.

Initial experiments for targeted properties exposed this hill climbing mechanism. Experiments however showed that targeted properties using simulated annealing had great results. Rather than always picking the best option for the next improved solution (called *next neighbor*), simulated annealing uses

---

1. http://proper.softlab.ntua.gr/papers/issta2017.pdf
2. https://en.wikipedia.org/wiki/Simulated_annealing
3. https://en.wikipedia.org/wiki/Hill_climbing

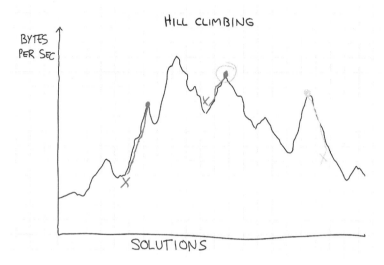

a statistical method where, from time to time, it will decide to switch to a worse next neighbor.

The acceptance criteria is done through statistical analysis and a parameter called *temperature*. At the beginning of the search, temperature is high and the algorithm is ready to accept a lot of worse neighbors. But as time goes, temperature is decreased and the search starts being more conservative. This will lead to a search ready to scan a lot more of the global solution space, looking a bit like this:

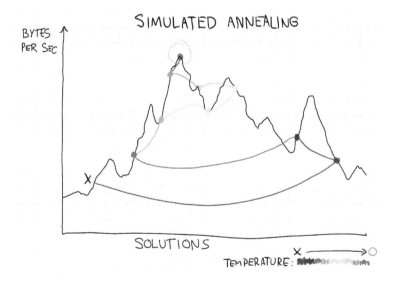

Each potential solution (or neighbor) chosen by the algorithm is a dot on the diagram. While there's no guarantee that an optimal solution will be found, chances are that simulated annealing will find very good and close to optimal solutions. But this may rely on two things: a good ability to measure and impact the value to maximize or minimize, and a good neighbor selection.

Out of the box, PropEr's targeted properties provide rather decent neighbor selection mechanisms, which you might not need to tweak at all. But as we'll see later in this chapter, providing a simple custom neighbor selection can do wonders to guide the algorithm.

Limitations

Important to note is that targeted properties do *not* allow all the same facilities as you'd get with regular properties. They don't work well with recursive generators, whether you use ?LAZY or not. Using that combination may yield infinite loops. You'll want to stick with rather straightforward combinations of default generators in those cases.

They also don't allow gathering of statistics and metrics using collect/2 and aggregate/2, so any validation and accounting you want to do about your targeted properties, you'll need to do by hand, through regular output and other side effects.

At the time of writing, these limitations are due to an implementation detail of targeted properties. Targeted properties are in fact a special variation of a feature called *search macros*. There are two of them:

- ?EXISTS(Var, Generator, Expression)—the arguments are similar to those in ?FORALL. However this macro will succeed as soon as Expression returns true once, and will otherwise fail if it is allowed to run all of its executions while only returning false.

- ?NOT_EXISTS(Var, Generator, Expression)—the opposite of ?EXISTS; it only succeeds if all executions run to completion while returning false.

Search macros allow you to add further search and validation to an existing property by embedding them inside the property. For example, if you're a company doing video streaming or IoT data reporting, you may want to test a client that has multiple possible endpoints to contact based on arbitrary failures. In such a case, you may not just want a property that always passes, but one that just eventually works. It doesn't matter if it fails fifty times, as long as at some point it does pass once.

So we could, for example, illustrate the retry logic we just described with the following pseudocode:

```
prop_retry() ->
    ?FORALL({Data, Config}, {term(), environment_generator()},
      begin
        cause_some_server_failures(Config),
        ?EXISTS(IP, pick_server(Config),
            is_successful(request(IP, Data)))
      end).
```

In this pseudocode, it doesn't matter if all but one of the servers fail, as long as eventually the right server is picked and things pass.

Targeted properties were initially added to these search macros before being generalized with the ?FORALL_TARGETED mechanism. In fact, FORALL_TARGETED(Pattern, Generator, Property) is implemented roughly as ?NOT_EXISTS(Pattern, Generator, not(Property)).

Regardless of their limitations, targeted properties can prove to be very interesting and useful. Let's see how exactly they can help you out.

Targeted Properties in Practice

The targeted properties you've seen so far are pretty representative of the whole thing. Aside from respecting their limitations (no recursive generators nor stats), not much changes. The path example from early in the chapter was easy for simulated annealing to handle, so in this section, we'll explore a slightly trickier case: forcing trees to be more or less balanced or skewed, and how to best optimize that.

A binary tree[4] is generally simple to keep balanced when using random data; if the data's randomness is uniform (or follows a standard distribution), chances are that you'll get numbers that will naturally distribute themselves on both sides of the tree. But let's validate that.

We'll start by writing a simple set of tree functions: one to build a binary search tree, and one to check its balance or skew (how many more nodes are on the left side than the right side). We'll build the tree through insertion, and add a convenience function to turn a list into a tree:

Erlang	code/TargetedProperties/erlang/target/test/prop_target.erl

```
to_tree(L) ->
    lists:foldl(fun insert/2, undefined, L).
```

---

4. https://en.wikipedia.org/wiki/Binary_tree

```
insert(N, {node, N, L, R}) -> {node, N, L, R};
insert(N, {node, M, L, R}) when N < M -> {node, M, insert(N, L), R};
insert(N, {node, M, L, R}) when N > M -> {node, M, L, insert(N, R)};
insert(N, {leaf, N}) -> {leaf, N};
insert(N, {leaf, M}) when N < M -> {node, N, undefined, {leaf, M}};
insert(N, {leaf, M}) when N > M -> {node, N, {leaf, M}, undefined};
insert(N, undefined) -> {leaf, N}.
```

This is a fairly standard tree. A single lone element is denoted with the {leaf, Element} tuple. An inner node (one that contains branches) has the structure {node, Element, LeftChild, RightChild}. An inner node with a child missing has this child replaced with the value undefined:

```
1> Tree = prop_target:to_tree([1,4,2,3,7,5]).
{node,4,
     {node,2,{leaf,1},{leaf,3}},
     {node,5,undefined,{leaf,7}}}
```

We'll use the following functions to check the balance of the binary tree by counting how many inner nodes are on the left and the right of the current one, and then apply this recursively:

```
sides({node, _, Left, Right}) ->
    {LL, LR} = sides(Left),
    {RL, RR} = sides(Right),
    {count_inner(Left)+LL+LR, count_inner(Right)+RL+RR};
sides(_) ->
    {0,0}.

count_inner({node, _, _, _}) -> 1;
count_inner(_) -> 0.
```

You can then use this as follows:

```
2> prop_target:sides(Tree).
{1,1}
3> Tree2 = prop_target:to_tree([1,2,3,4,5,6,7,8]).
{node,2,
     {leaf,1},
     {node,4,
          {leaf,3},
          {node,6,{leaf,5},{node,8,{leaf,7},undefined}}}}
4> prop_target:sides(Tree2).
{0,3}
```

So the sides function can be used to verify how balanced an arbitrary tree is.

Let's see it at work with a regular property, first by writing its generator, and then just outputting the balance results directly:

```erlang
tree() ->
    ?LET(L, non_empty(list(integer())), to_tree(L)).

prop_tree_regular(opts) -> [{numtests, 1000}].
prop_tree_regular() ->
    ?FORALL(T, tree(),
        begin
            Weight = sides(T),
            io:format(" ~p", [Weight]),
            true
        end).
```

This should be familiar as a property. We're asking for 1,000 iterations, because targeted properties default to that value, and it will be easier to compare end results if as many iterations are given to all of our experiments. Run this one to see the overall balance:

```
$ rebar3 proper -p prop_tree_regular
«monstrous amounts of output»
{3,18}. {0,4}. {5,3}. {8,14}. {2,11}. {2,8}. {17,2}. {0,12}. {0,0}. {0,2}.
{4,0}. {0,0}. {14,6}. {4,6}. {7,16}. {4,11}. {17,6}. {13,1}. {11,5}.
{3,0}. {0,16}. {0,6}. {4,6}.
OK: Passed 1000 test(s).
```

So on average this shows a reasonable amount of balance. There's one very slanted tree with sixteen nodes on the right side and zero on the left, but it's possible that the heavy left-side subtree is balanced on its own; our sides/1 function is not perfect, but it's a decent enough proxy of balancedness.

Let's say that we have a suspicion bugs may hide in how extremely slanted trees are handled. We'd want to generate very left-heavy trees. Doing so with a generator would be fairly tricky: the position of an element within a tree is not only dependent on its value but also its order of insertion with regard to all other elements. Fortunately, targeted properties make this easy. All we have to do is find a numeric value to maximize or minimize.

Since we have the balancedness proxy given by sides/1 returning {NumNodesLeft, NumNodesRight}, we can optimize for a left-heavy tree by picking NumNodesLeft - NumNodesRight—the larger the value on the left and the smaller the value on the right, the better:

```erlang
prop_tree() ->
    ?FORALL_TARGETED(T, tree(),
        begin
            {Left, Right} = Weight = sides(T),
            io:format(" ~p", [Weight]),
            ?MAXIMIZE(Left-Right),
            true
        end).
```

Compare that tree with the previous one and, aside from the substitution of ?FORALL with ?FORALL_TARGETED along with the ?MAXIMIZE macro, nothing has changed. Run the property though, and you'll notice a few things:

```
$ rebar3 proper -p prop_tree
[«monstrous amounts of output»
 {58,0}. {37,21}. {32,28}. {58,0}. {62,0}. {61,0}. {60,0}. {31,25}.
 {58,0}. {27,35}. {32,29}. {61,0}. {55,0}. {55,1}. {34,27}. {57,0}.
 {58,0}. {33,27}. {56,0}. {54,0}. {35,25}. {32,24}. {31,30}. {58,1}.
 {55,0}. {34,27}. {55,2}.].
```

You'll see first that it's noticeably slower. This is because simulated annealing has a cost, which is higher than the cost of regular generators. You'll also notice that the search will do multiple runs where the tree appears balanced, and then successively unbalances itself (as we asked for).

Those results are pretty good, and we got them almost for free. This makes targeted properties a *fantastic* tool for exploratory properties and also for when you want to keep generators simple while still being able to tailor your data to your properties.

But you'll inevitably find cases where, on its own, targeted properties don't give you as good of a result as you'd like. Simulated annealing can't do everything on its own, so we'll need a mechanism to help it.

Writing Neighbor Functions

A core part of simulated annealing is effective neighbor selection. The neighbor is basically the next arbitrary modification to apply to the data to advance the search. In a graph trying to find the shortest path between all nodes, it might be to pick paths to swap. In a tree, it might be to remove or add a node. In a pathfinding exercise it may be to add one or five steps.

To submit your own neighbor function, you must use the ?USERNF(Generator, Next) macro. The Generator value is the same generator pattern you'd usually give to ?FORALL_TARGETED. The Next argument is where you pass in the function used to create the next value. The overall patterns looks like this:

```
prop_example() ->
    ?FORALL_TARGETED(Var, ?USERNF(list(integer()), next_list()),
        some_check(Var).

next_list() ->
    fun(PreviousValue, {Depth, CurrentTemperature}) ->
        ?LET(Val, some_generator(),
            modify(Val, PreviousValue))
    end.
```

The tricky stuff is all within the next_list() function. This is a function with no arguments that must return an anonymous function. That anonymous function itself takes two arguments: the previously generated term on which we are searching (PreviousValue), and then temperature parameters. Depth is a positive integer representing how deep the generator is nested (to scale the temperature accordingly if desired), and CurrentTemperature is any number, representing the current temperature.

Let's try it with our tree property:

```
prop_tree_neighbor() ->
    ?FORALL_TARGETED(T, ?USERNF(tree(), next_tree()),
        begin
            {Left, Right} = Weight = sides(T),
            io:format(" ~p", [Weight]),
            ?MAXIMIZE(Left-Right),
            true
        end).
```

The macro specifies the neighbor function, and the neighbor function takes the previous tree and just inserts one additional element in it. At runtime, PropEr will first call the generator (tree()) to get the initial piece of data, to later pass it on to next_tree()'s inner function, which looks like this:

```
next_tree() ->
    fun(OldTree, {_,T}) ->
        ?LET(N, integer(), insert(trunc(N*T*100), OldTree))
    end.
```

That could be enough on its own. Do note that the number inserted in the tree is first scaled according to the temperature. The temperature is usually a floating point value from 0.0 to 1.0 and so it's used as a multiplicative percentage (T*100). The final result is retransformed into an integer with trunc/1 and then inserted.

Run the property and you'll suddenly see it go much deeper than before:

```
$ rebar3 proper -p prop_tree_neighbor
[«monstrous amounts of output»
 {192,0}. {192,0}. {192,0}. {193,0}. {193,0}. {193,0}. {193,0}. {193,0}.
 {193,0}. {193,0}. {193,0}. {193,0}. {194,0}. {194,0}. {194,0}. {195,0}.
 {195,0}. {195,0}. {195,0}. {195,0}. {195,0}. {195,0}. {195,0}. {195,0}.
 {196,0}. {196,0}. {196,0}. {196,0}. {196,0}. {196,0}. {196,0}.].
```

This is giving us extremely skewed trees, and improves drastically on what other properties gave.

Considering Temperature

When it comes to simulated annealing, some people will advise against using temperature as part of your neighbor selection: temperature guides the selection of acceptable solutions first and foremost, and using it may interfere with that selection.

However, you'll come across problem spaces where you know that as you go forward, you'll need a lot more variability early on than later on. Knowing that a higher temperature correlates with a higher variation of acceptable solutions means that you can scale the neighborhood search space accordingly. Play with the parameters and see what you get. For the tree examples here, using the temperature made the search almost fifty times more effective than not using it.

You may wonder when you should use a neighbor function or not, and what it entails to have custom ones. At this point, it's not obvious what would be better or worse; you have to rely on trial and error. Let's at least get some tips and tricks to help make decisions.

Variations and Search

You'll notice, if you look at all the output generated by a single property of this kind with a simple neighbor function, that they are *all* a variation of the initially generated data. This is no surprise, considering we used the same initial seed data for all runs and just kept refining it. So while each test iteration is more likely than the previous one to have the desired shape you want, overall they're also more likely to show very little variation from one test instance to the next. That last point is one of the big attractions to property-based testing, so it definitely hurts not to have a good neighbor function.

At the same time, a custom neighbor function can help the search a lot. In fact, it is able to more effectively search because there are fewer random variations past a certain point in time. So how can we balance both?

Should you make more chaotic neighbor functions? First of all, a good rule of thumb is to stick with the default neighbor functions when you can—they are reasonably implemented and give decent results. If you're not getting the results you want, check if you can pick a better metric to maximize or minimize.

If you can't work around it and you end up writing a neighbor search function, then sit down and look at the quality of the results. See if they have enough variations to be able to uncover tricky bugs. If you're not excited by the prospect of doing that analysis by hand, an easy workaround is to use search macros to do your work for you.

Using the tree properties as an example, you could instead change the previous search approach to the following:

```
%% This one takes long because it does 100 rounds for ?FORALL
%% and 1000 rounds for ?NOT_EXISTS; this gives 100,000 executions!
prop_tree_search() ->
    ?FORALL(L, list(integer()),
        ?NOT_EXISTS(T,
            ?USERNF(
                ?LET(X, L, to_tree(X)), % trick to wrap the generator
                next_tree()             % same neighbor function
            ),
            begin
                {Left, Right} = sides(T),
                ?MAXIMIZE(Left-Right),
                false % using `false' for NOT_EXISTS to pass
            end)).
```

We use the ?LET(X, L, to_tree(X)) trick here because ?USERNF must accept a generator as a first argument, and the list L is not a generator by the time we reach the internal nested search. By wrapping L in ?LET, we take the initial list as is, but return the necessary generator structure for the framework to work.

Since the search function will reuse and improve on a previous iteration every time, it's not a big deal that the first list passed to the search is immutable; each successive iteration of ?NOT_EXISTS will improve the search, and each iteration of ?FORALL will bring in modifications to improve the test case's diversity of inputs. So instead of making a very high-quality neighbor function that generates better *and* diverse trees on each run, our search function will only care about providing a good search.

Because the search will run once per property iteration, this does mean that the test will run for much longer (100,000 iterations instead of 1,000), but you'll be trading off the time and complexity of writing a neighbor function with the time it takes to wait for the result. It'll take longer, but you'll have both a good search and diverse test cases overall. Of course, if you can stick to default search functions, you'll get both speed and quality.

Run the nested property to see what we get:

```
$ rebar3 proper -p prop_tree_search
[...............«a few hundred more runs».].[............
«monstrous amounts of output»
........].
```

```
OK: Passed 100 test(s).
===>
1/1 properties passed
```

And just like that, you can cheat a bit to get variation while still getting easy neighborhood functions. It's a clever trick if you don't need your tests to be particularly fast and do need a custom search mechanism.

Thinking Outside the Box

The examples we've seen so far can be impressive, but they mostly aimed to directly impact the way data was generated. Targeted properties can help in much more creative ways, but it tends to require approaching problems differently from most other types of testing. For this section, we'll use targeted properties to weed out a bug we suspect might lie in a quicksort function.

If you're familiar with quicksort, you know it's a fast sorting algorithm—especially in imperative languages where in-place sorting can be done to save on memory. It's also one of the most often used algorithms when demonstrating list comprehensions. The official Erlang documentation gives an example looking like this:

Erlang	code/TargetedProperties/erlang/target/test/prop_target.erl

```
sort([]) -> [];
sort([Pivot|T]) ->
    sort([ X || X <- T, X < Pivot])
    ++ [Pivot] ++
    sort([ X || X <- T, X >= Pivot]).
```

It's a very simple implementation that works rather well, but there's a reason why the Erlang standard library instead uses a mergesort[5] implementation. Quicksort has notoriously bad behavior when bad pivots or repeated elements are present[6]: it starts to use quadratically more time on every sorted element. Mergesort, by comparison, doesn't suffer from that behavior.

We'll devise an experiment to see whether the quicksort implementation proposed by Erlang is safe or not, to see how applying targeted properties can find really interesting stuff in our programs.

---

5. https://en.wikipedia.org/wiki/Mergesort
6. https://en.wikipedia.org/wiki/Quicksort#Implementation_issues

Establishing a Baseline

To find a case that is exponential in time, we'll need to set up properties that measure how long sorting a list takes. We'll maximize for *running time*; the longer the function takes to run, the better. It's hard to imagine this would be easy to tweak in a manually written custom generator, especially if you don't really know what to look for. Targeted properties can do a good job there, but we'll first want to establish a baseline for the experiment, to show whether they can really help us.

Let's start with a regular property:

```
prop_quicksort_time_regular(opts) -> [{numtests, 1000}].
prop_quicksort_time_regular() ->
    ?FORALL(L, ?SUCHTHAT(L, list(integer()), length(L) < 100000),
        begin
            T0 = erlang:monotonic_time(millisecond),
            sort(L),
            T1 = erlang:monotonic_time(millisecond),
            T1-T0 < 5000
        end).
```

The property checks that no single iteration takes more than five seconds. If you try to run it, you'll see that the sum of all runs for the property takes under five seconds:

```
$ rebar3 proper -p prop_quicksort_time_regular
«large amounts of output»
OK: Passed 1000 test(s).
===>
1/1 properties passed
```

So clearly basic properties won't cut it. Let's establish another comparison point: will mergesort survive our experiment? Here's a similar targeted property using lists:sort/1, which implements mergesort:

```
prop_mergesort_time() ->
    ?FORALL_TARGETED(L, ?SUCHTHAT(L, list(integer()), length(L) < 100000),
        begin
            T0 = erlang:monotonic_time(millisecond),
            lists:sort(L),
            T1 = erlang:monotonic_time(millisecond),
            ?MAXIMIZE(T1-T0),
            T1-T0 < 5000
        end).
```

We've added a max length to the list of 100,000 elements, because it would probably be very easy to find nasty cases that take more than five seconds when they contain a billion elements. Since we're looking for some exponential time, it should not, in theory, take that many elements to trigger it.

Running it takes quite a bit longer, mostly because of simulated annealing's overhead and maximizing for time taken, which will naturally seek much larger lists:

```
$ rebar3 proper -p prop_mergesort_time
[«large amounts of output»]
OK: Passed 1000 test(s).
===>
1/1 properties passed
```

Now if you run that code on an old computer from the 90s, chances are the test would fail, but on any laptop from the 2010s or later, it should pass.

We're now ready to see if the default quicksort can do a good job.

Targeting the Quicksort

The targeted property we'll use to find exponential cases is pretty much the same as the mergesort one:

```
prop_quicksort_time(opts) -> [noshrink].
prop_quicksort_time() ->
    ?FORALL_TARGETED(L, ?SUCHTHAT(L, list(integer()), length(L) < 100000),
        begin
            T0 = erlang:monotonic_time(millisecond),
            sort(L),
            T1 = erlang:monotonic_time(millisecond),
            ?MAXIMIZE(T1-T0),
            T1-T0 < 5000
        end).
```

You will notice a meta-function that disables shrinking. If the execution takes over five seconds, we have our answer and don't necessarily want PropEr to spend hours trying to make a simpler case. If it accidentally finds worse ones, it'll take forever.

Run the test, and you'll see how incredible targeted properties can be:

```
$ rebar3 proper -p prop_quicksort_time
«build output»
==> Testing prop_target:prop_quicksort_time()
[............................................................
.............................................................
.........................................................!]!
Failed: After 1 test(s).
[1,-1,-12,0,-1,0,1,3,0,1,1,1,-1,-8«horrifying amounts of output»]
```

```
===>
0/1 properties passed, 1 failed
===> Failed test cases:
prop_target:prop_quicksort_time() -> false
```

In fewer than 250 iterations, PropEr has managed to find inputs that on their own were sufficient to make the time taken by the sort function explode. That's amazing.

We can try fixing the sort function by simply picking a random pivot and preventing ourselves from resorting all entries equal to the pivot:

```
sort_fixed([]) -> [];
sort_fixed(L) ->
    N = rand:uniform(length(L)),
    Pivot = lists:nth(N, L),
    sort_fixed([X || X <- L, X < Pivot])
    ++ [X || X <- L, X == Pivot] ++
    sort_fixed([X || X <- L, X > Pivot]).
```

At a glance, this function is going to be slower. It calls a pseudorandom number generator, which is work the previous function didn't have to do, but it also iterates over each dataset five times instead of two:

1. To get the length of the list

2. To pick a random element (will average to half the list)

3. To find the elements smaller than the pivot

4. To find elements equal to the pivot

5. To find elements greater than the pivot

So without knowing about the edge cases that take very long that we found earlier, it would look like a pretty bad way to implement the function. But let's change the property to use this function and let our experiment do the talking instead:

```
prop_quicksort_time_fixed(opts) -> [noshrink].
prop_quicksort_time_fixed() ->
    ?FORALL_TARGETED(L, ?SUCHTHAT(L, list(integer()), length(L) < 100000),
        begin
            T0 = erlang:monotonic_time(millisecond),
            sort_fixed(L),
            T1 = erlang:monotonic_time(millisecond),
            ?MAXIMIZE(T1-T0),
            T1-T0 < 5000
        end).
```

This just subsitutes sort/1 for sort_fixed/1. Yet, when running the test, the result is entirely different:

```
$ rebar3 proper -p prop_quicksort_time_fixed
[«large amounts of output»]
OK: Passed 1 test(s).
===>
1/1 properties passed
```

And just like that, our sorting function falls into the same ballpark as our mergesort did.

In terms of thinking outside the box, people have attempted other interesting approaches, with interesting results: what if you maximized code coverage, memory usage, lock contention, or erroneous log lines? There might just be some amazing stuff to find.

Wrapping Up

Targeted properties are still very new, and few people have had the opportunity to put them in practice in real world projects at the time of this writing. In this chapter, we've covered what targeted properties look like and explored how they work, including simulated annealing.

You've seen how to write a neighbor selection function, although how to write a good one is still not extremely obvious. But to help with that, we have seen how targeted properties used with search macros (EXISTS and NOT_EXISTS) within regular properties can make up for some less-than-ideal neighbor functions. The ability to nest searches this way also explained some of the more annoying weaknesses of targeted properties—the inability to gather metrics and use complex generators.

Still, as we've seen in this chapter, it's a very promising improvement to PropEr. It promises to allow some impressive searches that would usually be very difficult if not downright impossible to do with regular tests, and even with regular properties. We're not yet done with the impressive material though, as the next part of the book introduces mechanisms for stateful properties.

Part III

Stateful Properties

Now we're cooking. Property-based testing becomes really amazing once you deal with testing complex interactions with stateful systems, and this part of the book will show you everything you need to be comfortable with these advanced features.

## CHAPTER 9

Stateful Properties

Most of the amazing stories of property-based testing—those that make you go *holy crap I need to get in on this*—involve large and complex stateful systems where tricky bugs are found with a relatively tiny test. Those usually turn out to be stateful properties.

Stateful property tests are particularly useful when "what the code should do"—what the user perceives—is simple, but "how the code does it"—how it is implemented—is complex. A large number of integration and system tests fit this description, and stateful property-based testing will become one of the most interesting tools to have in your toolbox since it can exercise major parts of your systems with little code.

Stateful property tests are a nonformal variation on model checking,[1] something a bit fancier than the modeling approach we used in stateless properties. The core concept is that you must define a (mostly) predictable model of the system, and then use PropEr to generate a series of commands that represent operations that can be applied to the system. PropEr then runs these operations on both the model and the actual system, and compares the two. If they agree, the test passes; if they disagree, it fails.

This chapter will cover the basic structure of properties, and expand on how exactly PropEr executes them. This will be critical to understanding how to write your own stateful properties, which we'll explore by testing a cache implementation. As a bonus, we'll see how stateful properties can be used to find concurrency bugs. We'll have to start with a bit of theory first, to prevent some major confusion.

1.　https://en.wikipedia.org/wiki/Model_checking

Laying Out Stateful Properties

Stateful properties all have a few parts in common, with a bit more scaffolding than we had in stateless ones. It's important to keep these parts in mind, because they'll be interacting with each other for all test executions. These are the three major components:

- A model, which represents what the system should do at a high level.

- A generator for commands, which represent the execution flow of the program.

- An actual system, which is validated against our model.

The Model

A core part of a stateful property is the model. It represents a simple and straightforward version of what our actual system should be doing. By ensuring that the real system behaves like the model does, we show that our programs are most likely correct. The model itself is made of two important parts:

1. A data structure that represents the expected state of the system—the data it should contain and that you'd expect to be able to get from it.

2. A function that transforms the model's state based on commands that could be applied to the system (named next_state).

This sounds a bit tricky, but an example should help. Let's say we have a web service where we can upload files, which get to be replicated in multiple datacenters. A lot of complex operations are taking place, and a command like upload_file(Name, Contents) involves the network, various computers, and a bunch of protocols with multiple data representations. Things can go wrong in lots of places.

Our model, by comparison, could have its data structure (the first important part) be a map of the form #{Name => Contents} that represents what files the service should know about. The next_state function that transforms the model state (the second important bit) would just be a function that adds a (Name, Contents) pair to the map based on the command, something like next_state(Map, [Name, Contents]) -> Map#{Name => Contents}.

That's it. We have a very simple abstract representation of what the system should do, and that's a model!

The Commands

The next core part is a bunch of commands that can be generated by the framework. These represent operations that can be run against the actual system. Their generation has two components:

1. A list of potential *symbolic calls*, with generators defining their arguments

2. A series of functions that defines whether a given symbolic call would make sense to apply according to the current model state

The first point is rather simple. We've seen symbolic calls in Custom Generators on page 80. They are tuples that represent function calls of the form {call, Module, Function, [Arg1, Arg2, ..., ArgN]}. All the arguments can use regular PropEr generators, and the function calls map to actual system calls. So in our example file upload, we may have something like {call, actual_system, upload_file, [Name, Contents]}.

The second point is interesting. The functions that validate if a call is acceptable in a sequence are called *preconditions*, and they define invariants that should hold true in the system for the current test. For example, it's possible that an ATM only exposes functionality to deposit money if a debit card is inserted; a precondition of depositing money would therefore be that a valid debit card is currently in the ATM. You can think of preconditions as the stateful properties' equivalent to ?SUCHTHAT macros in stateless properties.

The Validation

Finally, we have the validation of the system against the model. This is done through *postconditions*, which are invariants that should hold true after a given operation has been applied. They're how we check that things are right.

For example, if our model's state for an ATM says a user with the PIN 1984 has inserted their card, and that the last operation against the real system was the user typing in the password 2421, then the postcondition would validate that the actual system properly returns a failure to log in. Such postcondition validation can be done by checking global invariants that are expected to always be true, but also frequently takes place by comparing the system's output with the expected result based on the model state. In this example, we did the latter: it doesn't matter what the actual system stores as a PIN or how it stores it. We just want it to return what our model says it should.

We'll get to put that into practice soon, but for now, in a nutshell, remember these points:

- We need a model, which is comprised of some data (the state) that gets modified by a next_state function.

- We need a lot of symbolic calls that represent operations that can be applied to the real system, and which can be constrained with preconditions.

- We need to ensure that the results from the actual system match those we would expect from our model, which is done through postconditions.

With this in mind, we can go figure out how PropEr is going to line all of those things up.

How Stateful Properties Run

PropEr divides the execution of a stateful test in two phases, one abstract and one real. The abstract phase is used to create a test scenario, and is executed without any code from your actual system running. Its whole objective is to take the model and command generation callbacks, and call these to build out the sequence of calls that will later be applied to the system.

Put visually, it looks like this:

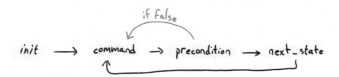

Note the lack of postcondition or calls to the actual system. In the abstract mode, a command generator creates a symbolic call with its arguments based on an initial model state. PropEr then applies the preconditions to that command to know if it would be valid. If the validation fails, PropEr tries again with a new generated command. Once a suitable command is found, we can move forward. The next_state function takes the command and the current state, and has to return a new state data structure. Then the whole process is repeated over and over, until PropEr decides it has enough commands.

Once this is done, we're left with a valid and legitimate sequence of commands, with all its expected state transitions. Our model is ready.

With our model in hand, PropEr can start applying the commands to the real system, and our postconditions can check that things all remain valid as shown in figure on page 205.

The execution is repeated, except that now, at every step of the way, PropEr also runs the commands against the real system. The preconditions are still

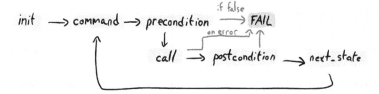

reevaluated to ensure consistency so that if a generated precondition that used to work suddenly fails, the entire test also fails. The next symbolic call in the list is executed, with its result stored. The postcondition is then evaluated, and if it succeeds, the state transition for the command is applied to the state and the next command can be processed.

In case of a failure, shrinking is done by modifying the command sequence as required, mostly by removing operations and seeing if things still work. Preconditions will be used by the framework to make sure that the various attempts are valid.

So with all of this theory, we can start putting it all in practice, and seeing what the implementation looks like.

Writing Properties

In earlier chapters, you've seen that stateless properties all follow a pretty similar structure. The layout of code around files may vary from project to project, but overall, most test suites do share a separation between properties, generators, and helper functions. When it comes to stateful properties, there is far less of a standard: some people put properties in one file, models in another one, with helper functions and wrappers around the actual system in a third module. Other developers prefer to have everything in one spot.

In this book, we'll stick to having the properties and the model in one file. As with basic properties, we can make use of the rebar3 plugin's templating facilities to get the file we need within any standard Erlang project. Call the following within an existing project:

```
$ rebar3 new proper_statem base
===> Writing test/prop_base.erl
```

The generated file contains the prop_base module, a test suite that is divided in two sections: one section for the stateful property we'll want to execute, and one for the model, which is a mix of callbacks and generators. Let's start by looking at the property:

Erlang

```erlang
-module(prop_base).
-include_lib("proper/include/proper.hrl").

%% Model Callbacks
-export([command/1, initial_state/0, next_state/3,
         precondition/2, postcondition/3]).

%%%%%%%%%%%%%%%%%%%%%
%%% PROPERTIES %%%
%%%%%%%%%%%%%%%%%%%%%
prop_test() ->
    ?FORALL(Cmds, commands(?MODULE),
            begin
                actual_system:start_link(),
                {History, State, Result} = run_commands(?MODULE, Cmds),
                actual_system:stop(),
                ?WHENFAIL(io:format("History: ~p\nState: ~p\nResult: ~p\n",
                                    [History,State,Result]),
                          aggregate(command_names(Cmds), Result =:= ok))
            end).
```

Elixir

```elixir
defmodule PbtTest do
  use ExUnit.Case
  use PropCheck
  use PropCheck.StateM # <-- this is a new one to use

  property "stateful property" do
    forall cmds <- commands(__MODULE__) do
      ActualSystem.start_link()
      {history, state, result} = run_commands(__MODULE__, cmds)
      ActualSystem.stop()

      (result == :ok)
      |> aggregate(command_names(cmds))
      |> when_fail(
        IO.puts("""
        History: #{inspect(history)}
        State: #{inspect(state)}
        Result: #{inspect(result)}
        """)
      )
    end
  end
end
```

This looks similar to standard properties, but with a few differences. We do have a bunch of model callbacks to export, but that's expected. The change starts in the property itself. First, the generator is the commands/1 function at

❶. This is a generator automatically imported by PropEr, which calls the model functions to create the command sequence that will be used. This includes the symbolic execution only.

The commands will then be run against the real system (❸), which is where the real execution (with validation of postconditions) takes place.

At points ❷ and ❹, we have functions having to do with the setup and tear-down of tests. PropEr provides no specific place or construct to do this for each iteration, so it has to be done inline within the property.

Setting Up and Tearing Down Tests

While PropEr offers no special mechanism to let you set up and tear down some state before specific iterations of a test, it does allow you to set things up before all iterations of a given property.

This can be done with the ?SETUP macro, of the form:

```erlang
prop_example() ->
    ?SETUP(fun() ->
        %% setup phase as any code running within the macro
        OptionalData = do_setup(),
        %% teardown phase as a no-argument function returned
        %% by the setup function
        fun() -> do_teardown(OptionalData) end
    end,
    ?FORALL(«property»)
).
```

Multiple macros of this kind can be nested together. But do remember: the setup will be run only once for all iterations for any given property. If you want to run something equivalent for each individual iteration, it has to be done inline.

The rest works as usual. Let's take a look at the callbacks now:

```erlang
Erlang

%%%%%%%%%%%%%
%%% MODEL %%%
%%%%%%%%%%%%%
%% @doc Initial model value at system start. Should be deterministic.
initial_state() ->
    #{}.

%% @doc List of possible commands to run against the system
command(_State) ->
    oneof([
        {call, actual_system, some_call, [term(), term()]}
    ]).
```

```erlang
%% @doc Determines whether a command should be valid under the
%% current state.
precondition(_State, {call, _Mod, _Fun, _Args}) ->
    true.

%% @doc Given the state `State' *prior* to the call
%% `{call, Mod, Fun, Args}', determine whether the result
%% `Res' (coming from the actual system) makes sense.
postcondition(_State, {call, _Mod, _Fun, _Args}, _Res) ->
    true.

%% @doc Assuming the postcondition for a call was true, update the model
%% accordingly for the test to proceed.
next_state(State, _Res, {call, _Mod, _Fun, _Args}) ->
    NewState = State,
    NewState.
```

Elixir

```elixir
  # Initial model value at system start. Should be deterministic.
  def initial_state() do
    %{}
  end

  # List of possible commands to run against the system
  def command(_state) do
    oneof([
      {:call, ActualSystem, :some_call, [term(), term()]}}
    ])
  end

  # Determines whether a command should be valid under the current state
  def precondition(_state, {:call, _mod, _fun, _args}) do
    true
  end

  # Given that state prior to the call `{:call, mod, fun, args}`,
  # determine whether the result (res) coming from the actual system
  # makes sense according to the model
  def postcondition(_state, {:call, _mod, _fun, _args}, _res) do
    true
  end

  # Assuming the postcondition for a call was true, update the model
  # accordingly for the test to proceed
  def next_state(state, _res, {:call, _mod, _fun, _args}) do
    newstate = state
    newstate
  end
end
```

Every model must have an initial state. The initial_state() callback (❶) lets you pick it. The state has to be deterministic, always the same. If the initial state is unpredictable, then there'll be no way to know whether shrinking can be effective or not. The program exploration comes from various commands being applied, not the initial state.

The commands themselves are generated through the command/1 callback at ❷. Do note that the model's State is available and can be used to generate commands and their arguments—such as trying to read an entry that is already existing within the model. In fact, the State variable can even be used to generate context-specific commands. For example, you could decide that when the state is empty, only commands about initializing it can run and no other. This can help with generating valid command chains faster and boost the speed of your model quite a bit.

Preconditions (defined at ❸) can be used to constrain whenever a command is acceptable or not: you could decide to limit their frequency, or that "inserting a new entry" doesn't work if the entry is already in the State variable. Much like the ?SUCHTHAT macro, too much filtering in preconditions can tend to slow down the model generation as the framework has to try building more commands to find something that works.

You might be asking why use preconditions when matching within command/1 should be faster and has access to the same data. The reason is that preconditions are used when shrinking as well as generating, and basically help ensure that whatever the framework tries to do with the command sequence remains valid. Whatever matching rule or constraint you put in command/1 must be duplicated in precondition/2 (or live *only* in the latter) for shrinking to work best.

Postconditions are where the validation takes place. The _Res variable declared at ❹ contains the result of a command being applied to the actual system, with the model's State variable containing the state *before* the call was made to the system and the _Args passed to the system. This gives us all the ingredients to check everything: given the model state and the function called, does the actual return value match what we think it should be?

The last callback is next_state/3 (❺). This one is a bit tricky because it accepts a _Res value *even during symbolic execution, where no result exists* to put in _Res. As such you can't easily use the return value for any transformations or comparisons (a workaround exists with symbolic calls, but it's not all that obvious). Instead, it's easier to pretend next_state/3 is only run during symbolic execution: assume that _Res contains opaque placeholders, and only use its value to blindly update your model's state, without the ability to look at what it contains and reveals about the running system.

The two execution flows are important to keep in mind: since the calls to preconditions, commands, and state transitions are executed both when generating commands and when running the actual system, side effects should be avoided in the model. And any value coming from the actual system that gets transferred to the model should be treated as an opaque blob that can't be inspected, matched against, or used in a function call that aims to transform it.

The abstract phase has to pass some of these values in to make them available to the model, but since the actual system isn't running, it can't provide the data. PropEr instead passes in abstract placeholders. These don't look like the actual expected data; they can be of an entirely different type than what you expect, which is why the data must be treated as opaque.

The Model Decides

 This is very abstract for now, but the core concept to keep in mind is that the model is the source of authority that leads the test execution, not the system; the system is being tested and is not in the driver's seat.

That's a lot of theory, but it'll really make things simpler when it comes to putting it in practice. Not being aware of the execution model makes for a difficult learning experience. Feel free to come back to the diagrams and descriptions as often as you need them, until it becomes natural. You might need them a bit in the following example, which uses stateful testing with a cache process.

Testing a Basic Concurrent Cache

To use stateful tests, we'll first need a stateful system to validate. In this section, we'll use a cache implemented as an OTP gen_server. A common optimization pattern in Erlang is to use an ETS table for reads, and to make the writes sequential through calls to the gen_server, which ensures they're safe. This creates a bit of contention on the write operations, so instead, we'll try to write a cache that *only* uses ETS for all operations, and the gen_server's job is just to keep the ETS table alive. The simple conceptual model—a cache handling data like a key-value store—along with an implementation dangerously accessing ETS tables concurrently makes this is a great candidate to demonstrate stateful property tests. We'll see the cache implementation, and then how to approach modeling it to find potential bugs it may hide.

Our cache will have a simple set of requirements:

- Values can be read by searching for their key.

- The cache can be emptied on demand.

- The cache can be configured with a maximum number of items to hold in memory.

- Once the maximal size is reached, the oldest written value is replaced.

- If an item is overwritten, even with a changed value, the cache entry remains in the same position.

Those are a bit unconventional: most caches care about evicting entries that were not *accessed* for a long time, whereas ours focuses on writes, and does not even care about updates in its eviction policy. But that is fine because we want to show how to model that cache, not necessarily how to write a good one, so we will stick with these requirements that are friendlier to a succint implementation.

Implementing the Cache

In general, stateful tests are often used during integration tests. So you'll likely use stateful properties later in a project's lifetime, and will likely write tests after the program has been written. We'll respect this by writing the cache implementation itself first, then we'll put the system in place and add tests after the fact.

We'll start with a standard gen_server set of callbacks and public exports:

About the Code

In the snippets that follow, code is labeled with both the language (Erlang and Elixir) and the file where you should put the code if you're following along.

Erlang   code/StatefulProperties/erlang/pbt/src/cache.erl

```erlang
-module(cache).
-export([start_link/1, stop/0, cache/2, find/1, flush/0]).
-behaviour(gen_server).
-export([init/1, handle_call/3, handle_cast/2, handle_info/2]).

start_link(N) ->
    gen_server:start_link({local, ?MODULE}, ?MODULE, N, []).

stop() ->
    gen_server:stop(?MODULE).
```

Elixir	code/StatefulProperties/elixir/pbt/lib/cache.ex

```elixir
defmodule Cache do
  use GenServer

  def start_link(n) do
    GenServer.start_link(__MODULE__, n, name: __MODULE__)
  end

  def stop() do
    GenServer.stop(__MODULE__)
  end
```

The process will be unique to the entire node by virtue of having the {local, ?MODULE} name. Since all operations will be done in an ETS table, we can read from the cache using the table directly, assuming the table is named cache. We'll give the table's records a structure of the form {Index, {Key, Val}}, where Index ranges from 1 to the max value allowed, basically forcing the table to be used like a big 1-indexed array. Whenever we write to the table, we increment the Index value before doing so, wrapping around to the first entry whenever we fill the array.

Unfortunately, this does mean we'll need to scan the table on every read operation, but optimizing is not the point here. Here's how the table is initialized:

Erlang	code/StatefulProperties/erlang/pbt/src/cache.erl

```erlang
init(N) ->
    ets:new(cache, [public, named_table]),
    ets:insert(cache, {count, 0, N}),
    {ok, nostate}.

handle_call(_Call, _From, State) -> {noreply, State}.

handle_cast(_Cast, State) -> {noreply, State}.

handle_info(_Msg, State) -> {noreply, State}.
```

Elixir	code/StatefulProperties/elixir/pbt/lib/cache.ex

```elixir
def init(n) do
  :ets.new(:cache, [:public, :named_table])
  :ets.insert(:cache, {:count, 0, n})
  {:ok, :nostate}
end

def handle_call(_call, _from, state), do: {:noreply, state}

def handle_cast(_cast, state), do: {:noreply, state}

def handle_info(_msg, state), do: {:noreply, state}
```

You'll see a magic record {count, 0, Max} inserted in the table. That's basically our index-tracking mechanism. Each writer will be able to increment it before writing its own data, ensuring the index is always moving forward. You'll also note that the gen_server callbacks are otherwise empty, since we don't need them. Let's see how reads work:

Erlang	code/StatefulProperties/erlang/pbt/src/cache.erl

```erlang
find(Key) ->
    case ets:match(cache, {'_', {Key, '$1'}}) of
        [[Val]] -> {ok, Val};
        [] -> {error, not_found}
    end.
```

Elixir	code/StatefulProperties/elixir/pbt/lib/cache.ex

```elixir
def find(key) do
  case :ets.match(:cache, {:_, {key, :"$1"}}) do
    [[val]] -> {:ok, val}
    [] -> {:error, :not_found}
  end
end
```

Here the ets:match/2 pattern basically means "ignore the index" ('_'), "match the key we want" (Key), and "return the value" ('$1'). The documentation for ets:match/2[2] contains more details if you need further explanations.

Writing to the cache is a bit more complex:

Erlang	code/StatefulProperties/erlang/pbt/src/cache.erl

```erlang
cache(Key, Val) ->
    case ets:match(cache, {'$1', {Key, '_'}}) of % find dupes
①      [[N]] ->
            ets:insert(cache, {N,{Key,Val}}); % overwrite dupe
        [] ->
            case ets:lookup(cache, count) of % insert new
②              [{count,Max,Max}] ->
                    ets:insert(cache, [{1,{Key,Val}}, {count,1,Max}]);
③              [{count,Current,Max}] ->
                    ets:insert(cache, [{Current+1,{Key,Val}},
                                       {count,Current+1,Max}])
            end
    end.
```

---

2.   http://erlang.org/doc/man/ets.html#match-2

Elixir   code/StatefulProperties/elixir/pbt/lib/cache.ex

```
def cache(key, val) do
  case :ets.match(:cache, {:"$1", {key, :_}}) do
❶    [[n]] ->
      :ets.insert(:cache, {n, {key, val}})

    [] ->
      case :ets.lookup(:cache, :count) do
❷        [{:count, max, max}] ->
          :ets.insert(:cache, [{1, {key, val}}, {:count, 1, max}])

❸        [{:count, current, max}] ->
          :ets.insert(:cache, [
            {current + 1, {key, val}},
            {:count, current + 1, max}
          ])
      end
  end
end
```

We have three cases considered here:

1. When the value to insert matches a key that already exists (at ❶), we just overwrite.

2. When the value is inserted in a regular case (at ❸), we insert it after having incremented the index.

3. When we reach the max point of the index (at ❷), we reset the index and start writing from the start, wrapping the cache around.

That's all a bit convoluted—and probably feels risky when thinking of concurrent code execution—but let's keep going with the last function, the one to flush the cache:

Erlang   code/StatefulProperties/erlang/pbt/src/cache.erl

```
flush() ->
    [{count,_,Max}] = ets:lookup(cache, count),
    ets:delete_all_objects(cache),
    ets:insert(cache, {count, 0, Max}).
```

Elixir   code/StatefulProperties/elixir/pbt/lib/cache.ex

```
def flush() do
  [{:count, _, max}] = :ets.lookup(:cache, :count)
  :ets.delete_all_objects(:cache)
  :ets.insert(:cache, {:count, 0, max})
end
```

This empties the cache table and resets the {count, CurrentIndex, Max} entry.

You can play with the code in the shell a bit if you want to see if it works; otherwise we'll get started right away with the stateful property tests.

Writing the Tests

With the cache complete, we can write tests for it that will show whether it works correctly. As we've seen earlier, stateful properties are executed in two big phases: a symbolic one to generate the command set, and a real one, where the commands are run against the real system for validation purposes.

We're going to follow the same pattern here, and we'll start with a focus on the symbolic execution by setting up the model before adding validation rules, and then running the property to see if it seems sound.

Building the Model

The first step in coming up with a good stateful model is to think like an operator, someone in charge of running or debugging your code in production. If people are to operate and run your code, they have to be able to understand what to expect out of it. Whatever expectations they form as operators turn out to be a *mental model*: they play the operations in their heads and make guesses as to what data or behavior they'll get back out of the system. Whenever their mental model is wrong ("the system doesn't do what I think it should"), you get a bug report or a production incident.

If you can figure out how you'd explain how the system works to an operator in a way that is both realistic and simple, you've given them a reliable mental model to work with. That mental model is something we can try to encode as a property.

Interestingly, if a good way to come up with a model is to try to figure out how you'd explain your component to a human operator having to run it in production, the opposite is true as well: if you have to explain your system to someone, the model you used in your tests could be a good starting point. If your tests are complex, convoluted, and hard to explain, then know that your testing experience is likely to match their operational experience as well.

Since our cache works a bit like a big array where old entries are evicted to make place for new ones, we can use any data structure or implementation with first-in-first-out (FIFO) semantics as a model, and it should be accurate. We'll use all of proper_statem's callbacks to write our simpler FIFO structure to show whether the real cache works or not. Let's set this up:

Erlang	code/StatefulProperties/erlang/pbt/test/prop_cache.erl

```erlang
-module(prop_cache).
-include_lib("proper/include/proper.hrl").
-behaviour(proper_statem).
-export([command/1, initial_state/0, next_state/3,
         precondition/2, postcondition/3]).

-define(CACHE_SIZE, 10).

prop_test() ->
    ?FORALL(Cmds, commands(?MODULE),
        begin
            cache:start_link(?CACHE_SIZE),
            {History, State, Result} = run_commands(?MODULE, Cmds),
            cache:stop(),
            ?WHENFAIL(io:format("History: ~p\nState: ~p\nResult: ~p\n",
                                [History,State,Result]),
                      aggregate(command_names(Cmds), Result =:= ok))
        end).
```

Elixir	code/StatefulProperties/elixir/pbt/test/cache_test.exs

```elixir
defmodule CacheTest do
  use ExUnit.Case
  use PropCheck
  use PropCheck.StateM
  doctest Cache
  @moduletag timeout: :infinity

  @cache_size 10

  property "stateful property", [:verbose] do
    forall cmds <- commands(__MODULE__) do
      Cache.start_link(@cache_size)
      {history, state, result} = run_commands(__MODULE__, cmds)
      Cache.stop()

      (result == :ok)
      |> aggregate(command_names(cmds))
      |> when_fail(
        IO.puts("""
        History: #{inspect(history)}
        State: #{inspect(state)}
        Result: #{inspect(result)}
        """)
      )
    end
  end
end
```

We've used an arbitrary ?CACHE_SIZE value for the sake of simplicity. We could have used a generator for more thorough testing, but we'll get the basics of stateful testing without that. Important to note is that the setup and teardown functions (cache:start_link/1 and cache:stop/0) run as part of the property, every time. Had we used the ?SETUP macro instead, we'd have needed to only call cache:flush() after every run to ensure it's always empty, but the current form is just a bit longer, and it provides few enough setup and teardown requirements that it'll do fine for our example.

For our model's state, we'll try to use as little data as possible, carrying only what's strictly necessary to validate everything:

Erlang	code/StatefulProperties/erlang/pbt/test/prop_cache.erl

```erlang
-record(state, {max=?CACHE_SIZE, count=0, entries=[]}).

%% Initial model value at system start. Should be deterministic.
initial_state() ->
    #state{}.
```

Elixir	code/StatefulProperties/elixir/pbt/test/cache_test.exs

```elixir
defmodule State do
  @cache_size 10
  defstruct max: @cache_size, count: 0, entries: []
end

def initial_state(), do: %State{}
```

We'll use a list to contain the model's data, along with a count of how many entries seen. The list will contain {Key,Value} pairs, and the counter will know when to drop pairs from the list—as simple as it can be.

The command generation is straightforward as well. We put emphasis on writes for the tests by using the frequency/1 generator:

Erlang	code/StatefulProperties/erlang/pbt/test/prop_cache.erl

```erlang
command(_State) ->
    frequency([
        {1, {call, cache, find, [key()]}},
        {3, {call, cache, cache, [key(), val()]}},
        {1, {call, cache, flush, []}}
    ]).
```

Elixir	code/StatefulProperties/elixir/pbt/test/cache_test.exs

```elixir
def command(_state) do
  frequency([
    {1, {:call, Cache, :find, [key()]}},
    {3, {:call, Cache, :cache, [key(), val()]}},
    {1, {:call, Cache, :flush, []}}
  ])
end
```

We can then use the precondition to add constraints, such as preventing calls to empty the cache when it's already empty:

Erlang	code/StatefulProperties/erlang/pbt/test/prop_cache.erl

```erlang
%% Picks whether a command should be valid under the current state.
precondition(#state{count=0}, {call, cache, flush, []}) ->
    false; % don't flush an empty cache for no reason
precondition(#state{}, {call, _Mod, _Fun, _Args}) ->
    true.
```

Elixir	code/StatefulProperties/elixir/pbt/test/cache_test.exs

```elixir
def precondition(%State{count: 0}, {:call, Cache, :flush, []}) do
  false
end

def precondition(%State{}, {:call, _mod, _fun, _args}) do
  true
end
```

You can define the generators for key() and val() as such:

Erlang	code/StatefulProperties/erlang/pbt/test/prop_cache.erl

```erlang
key() ->
    oneof([range(1,?CACHE_SIZE), % reusable keys, raising chance of dupes
           integer()]).         % random keys

val() ->
    integer().
```

Elixir	code/StatefulProperties/elixir/pbt/test/cache_test.exs

```elixir
def key() do
  oneof([range(1, @cache_size), integer()])
end

def val() do
  integer()
end
```

The generator for keys is designed to allow some keys to be repeated multiple times: by using a restricted set of keys (with the range/2 generator) along with an unrestricted integer(), we ensure some keys will be reused, which forces our property to exercise any code related to key reuse or matching, but without losing the ability to fuzz the system with occasionally unexpected new keys.

The next_state callback completes command generation by allowing the model to stay up-to-date with what the system state should be:

Erlang	code/StatefulProperties/erlang/pbt/test/prop_cache.erl

```erlang
%% Assuming the postcondition for a call was true, update the model
%% accordingly for the test to proceed.
next_state(State, _, {call, cache, flush, _}) ->
    State#state{count=0, entries=[]};
next_state(S=#state{entries=L, count=N, max=M}, _Res,
           {call, cache, cache, [K, V]}) ->
    case lists:keyfind(K, 1, L) of
        false when N =:= M -> S#state{entries = tl(L) ++ [{K,V}]};
        false when N < M -> S#state{entries = L ++ [{K,V}], count=N+1};
        {K,_} -> S#state{entries = lists:keyreplace(K,1,L,{K,V})}
    end;
next_state(State, _Res, {call, _Mod, _Fun, _Args}) ->
    State.
```

Elixir	code/StatefulProperties/elixir/pbt/test/cache_test.exs

```elixir
# Assuming the postcondition for a call was true, update the model
# accordingly for the test to proceed
def next_state(state, _res, {:call, Cache, :flush, _}) do
  %{state | count: 0, entries: []}
end

def next_state(
      s = %State{entries: l, count: n, max: m},
      _res,
      {:call, Cache, :cache, [k, v]}
    ) do
  case List.keyfind(l, k, 0) do
    nil when n == m ->
      %{s | entries: tl(l) ++ [{k, v}]}

    nil when n < m ->
      %{s | entries: l ++ [{k, v}], count: n + 1}

    {^k, _} ->
      %{s | entries: List.keyreplace(l, k, 0, {k, v})}
  end
end
```

```
def next_state(state, _res, {:call, _mod, _fun, _args}) do
  state
end
```

The first clause says that whenever we flush the cache, we must empty the model by dropping all its entries and returning the count to 0. The second clause is about adding items to the cache. There are three cases identified. First, at ❶ is a clause entered when the FIFO list is full. Whenever that happens, we drop the oldest element of the list by calling tl(L) and then add the new entry at the end. The case just after that, at ❷, deals with a cache that still has space and so it just adds the term at the end of the list and increments the counter. The last branch (❸) replaces an existing entry wherever it was in the list.

Finally, the last function clause tells us that any other call (like lookups) have no impact on the model state; it remains unchanged.

With this in place, commands can be generated. If you stub out postcondition/3 (write it as something like postcondition(_, _, _) -> true.) and try it in the shell, you can see the kinds of commands PropEr generates:

```
$ rebar3 as test shell
«build output»
1> proper_gen:sample(proper_statem:commands(prop_cache)).
[{set,{var,1},{call,cache,cache,[3,63]}},
 {set,{var,2},{call,cache,find,[2]}},
 {set,{var,3},{call,cache,find,[5]}}]
[{set,{var,1},{call,cache,cache,[2,-1]}},
 {set,{var,2},{call,cache,flush,[]}},
 {set,{var,3},{call,cache,cache,[9,-9]}},
 {set,{var,4},{call,cache,cache,[3,1]}},
 {set,{var,5},{call,cache,cache,[8,18]}},
 {set,{var,6},{call,cache,cache,[-14,6]}},
 {set,{var,7},{call,cache,cache,[8,-12]}}]
«more runs»
[{set,{var,1},{call,cache,cache,[-4,-1]}},
 {set,{var,2},{call,cache,flush,[]}},
 {set,{var,3},{call,cache,cache,[3,2]}},
 {set,{var,4},{call,cache,cache,[-25,-43]}},
 {set,{var,5},{call,cache,cache,[3,3]}},
 {set,{var,6},{call,cache,find,[3]}}]
```

Don't worry about the format it has ({set, VarNum, Call}) since that's something PropEr deals with internally. Just know that you can see the sequence of calls it would run, and in what order. The run_commands/2 function provided by PropEr and used in our property will deal with the rest. Now let's see how we can validate the actual system.

Validating the System

When dealing with a cache like this, we expect all writes to always succeed. So the only operation we can really use to validate the system is find/1. By observing the results we get when reading values, we can see if they match those the model predicts we'd return based on the write sequences we applied. If the key we're looking up is in the model state, then the actual system better return the value we expect, and return nothing when it's not there.

This is rather straightforward to implement:

Erlang	code/StatefulProperties/erlang/pbt/test/prop_cache.erl

```erlang
%% Given the state `State' *prior* to the call `{call, Mod, Fun, Args}',
%% determine whether the result `Res' (coming from the actual system)
%% makes sense.
postcondition(#state{entries=L}, {call, cache, find, [Key]}, Res) ->
    case lists:keyfind(Key, 1, L) of
        false      -> Res =:= {error, not_found};
        {Key, Val} -> Res =:= {ok, Val}
    end;
postcondition(_State, {call, _Mod, _Fun, _Args}, _Res) ->
    true.
```

Elixir	code/StatefulProperties/elixir/pbt/test/cache_test.exs

```elixir
# Given that state prior to the call `{:call, mod, fun, args}`,
# determine whether the result (res) coming from the actual system
# makes sense according to the model
def postcondition(%State{entries: l}, {:call, _, :find, [key]}, res) do
  case List.keyfind(l, key, 0) do
    nil ->
      res == {:error, :not_found}

    {^key, val} ->
      res == {:ok, val}
  end
end

def postcondition(_state, {:call, _mod, _fun, _args}, _res) do
  true
end
```

The lookup is done on the model's state (the L list), and based on this expected value, we compare the result Res from the actual system. Only if they agree do we say the operation is valid.

Go ahead and run the property:

```
$ rebar3 proper -n 1000
《build information》
===> Testing prop_cache:prop_test()
.................................................《more tests》
OK: Passed 1000 test(s).

63% {cache,cache,2}
21% {cache,find,1}
14% {cache,flush,0}
```

This looks decent enough. In a real project, we may want to repeat the steps we've taken in earlier chapters: measure whether the operations executed are those we really want. Are the reads numerous enough? Are we only reading nonexisting keys? Do we ever have a read after a flush to validate that it worked? And so on. You know how to do this by now, so let's just do a simple sanity check to make sure our property works fine by injecting a bug and seeing if it picks up on it.

Replace the init/1 function with this one:

```
init(N) ->
    ets:new(cache, [public, named_table]),
    ets:insert(cache, {count, 0, N-1}),
    {ok, nostate}.
```

This simply makes sure that the maximum cache size is one less than what is asked for, which means we should start dropping entries earlier than expected by the model. Run the property a bunch of times and you should eventually trigger a failure like:

```
$ rebar3 proper -n 10000
《build information》
===> Testing prop_cache:prop_test()
.....《more tests》.....!
Failed: After 747 test(s).
```
① `[{set,{var,1},{call,cache,find,[8]}},[...]]`
```
History: [{{state,10,0,[]},{error,not_found}},
         《more history》]
State: {state,10,10, 《cache model list》}
Result: {postcondition,false}
```

② `Shrinking ......(6 time(s))`
③ `[{set,{var,5},{call,cache,cache,[10,36]}},《more commands》,`
```
  {set,{var,18},{call,cache,find,[10]}}]
```
④ `History: [{{state,10,0,[]},true},`
```
         {{state,10,1,[{10,36}]},true},
         {{state,10,2,[{10,36},{-19,-6}]},true},
         {{state,10,3,[{10,36},{-19,-6},{12,5}]},true},
         《more history》
```

```
        {{state,10,10,[{10,36},{-19,-6},{12,5},{9,26},{-4,-30},{-75,17},
                    {13,-22},{42,5},{31,55},{197,18}]},
            {error,not_found}}]
State: {state,10,10, [{10,36},{-19,-6},{12,5},
                    {9,26},{-4,-30},{-75,17},{13,-22},
                    {42,5},{31,55},{197,18}]}
Result: {postcondition,false}
```

This is very noisy output, with a lot of data. Let's go through and figure it out. First, at ❶, we get the initial failing case. It can be huge with a high number of operations, so when possible, we ignore that one. Instead you should move past the shrinking step (at ❷), so that we get a simpler minimal counterexample.

The shortened output, based on the ?WHENFAIL macro we have in our property, is divided in four categories: the failing list of commands, the state and call history, the final state, and the failing result. ❸ shows the final set of commands that caused the failure as output by PropEr. It's all on one line and a bit hard to read. You can cross-reference this set of commands with the history, starting at ❹. The history section tracks the progression of all of our model's states. The {state, 10, N, List} format is the underlying representation of the record #state{max=10, count=N, entries=List}, followed with the result of the command that caused it. The history starts at the initial state, so there should be one more entry in there than there are commands.

Checking the sequence of commands against the history will prove helpful in most cases, but it requires quite careful attention to detail. To help a bit, the final model state is output at ❺, and the last line contains the error for the failure—usually just false, unless you make your postcondition fails with something more descriptive.

In this case, data shows that the last call to find(10) had the system return {error, not_found} whereas the model contains a tuple {10,36} in its state list, meaning that we expected that key to be found. The pair is the first one of the list (the next to be dropped!), and the shrinking also managed to drop all commands it could until the counter hit the value 10, which is also a clue. With all of that data, identifying the bug and fixing it is hopefully doable.

In this case we know what the error is, but it's nice to see that our test picks it up, albeit with many iterations. Perhaps improving the test by altering generators to get longer sequences or more repeated reads would prove useful.

This is pretty neat. Anything we can model, we can likely test with this kind of property. If the actual system used geodistributed databases with complex protocols instead of just ETS tables, the same model could be used to validate it, since the expectations it fulfills are the same—albeit with more tolerance to local datacenter outages. That's pretty amazing stuff.

One thing this property doesn't do, however, is find concurrency errors that could happen with our ETS usage. Our model is purely sequential, but we decided to use ETS specifically for concurrency. The good news is that PropEr gives us one more tool just for that.

Testing Parallel Executions

One of the most interesting features of stateful tests with PropEr is the ability to take the models we write for sequential ones and automatically turn them into parallel tests that have a decent chance at finding concurrency bugs in your code at nearly no cost. It requires just a few minor changes to the property, and the rest is done for you.

The way it works is conceptually simple. The framework first takes the existing command generation mechanism, and then builds a sequence—something like the following, in abstract terms:

```
A -> B -> C -> D -> E -> F -> G
```

It next picks a common root of operations. Here for example, A -> B is shared by all operations that follow them both. PropEr will take the remaining chain (C -> D -> E -> F -> G) and split it up in concurrent timelines based on some fancypants analysis (your preconditions will help drive this process), giving something like this:

```
        , -> C -> E -> G
A -> B
        ' -> D -> F
```

This new sequence will be represented as a tuple of the form {SequentialRoot, [LeftBranch, RightBranch]}. PropEr will run the common sequential root, and then run both alternative branches in parallel in an attempt to cause bugs to surface. It will check the model for any possible interleaving that matches what the actual system returns. If nothing works and the postconditions fail no matter what, then there's a bug.

The only changes required will be in the generator and command used to run the tests, and some adjustments to the ?WHENFAIL macro:

Erlang	code/StatefulProperties/erlang/pbt/test/prop_cache.erl

```erlang
prop_parallel() ->
    ?FORALL(Cmds, parallel_commands(?MODULE),
        begin
```

```
            cache:start_link(?CACHE_SIZE),
            {History, State, Result} = run_parallel_commands(?MODULE, Cmds),
            cache:stop(),
            ?WHENFAIL(io:format("=======~n"
                                "Failing command sequence:~n~p~n"
                                "At state: ~p~n"
                                "=======~n"
                                "Result: ~p~n"
                                "History: ~p~n",
                                [Cmds,State,Result,History]),
                    aggregate(command_names(Cmds), Result =:= ok))
      end).
```

Elixir	code/StatefulProperties/elixir/pbt/test/cache_test.exs

```elixir
property "parallel stateful property", numtests: 10000 do
  forall cmds <- parallel_commands(__MODULE__) do
    Cache.start_link(@cache_size)
    {history, state, result} = run_parallel_commands(__MODULE__, cmds)
    Cache.stop()

    (result == :ok)
    |> aggregate(command_names(cmds))
    |> when_fail(
      IO.puts("""
      =======
      Failing command sequence
      #{inspect(cmds)}
      At state: #{inspect(state)}
      =======
      Result: #{inspect(result)}
      History: #{inspect(history)}
      """)
    )
  end
end
```

As you can see here, we replaced commands/1 with parallel_commands/1, and run_commands/2 with run_parallel_commands/2. Our model remains exactly the same. If you run this test, it will likely pass even with thousands of runs:

```
$ rebar3 proper
«build info and other test runs»
===> Testing prop_cache:prop_parallel()
...............f...............................................f........
........................
OK: Passed 100 test(s).

65% {cache,cache,2}
19% {cache,find,1}
14% {cache,flush,0}
```

Here, each f stands for a nonparallelizable command generation that failed
and had to be retried. PropEr tried to make parallel branches of the command,
but couldn't do it without breaking some precondition. This lets you know if
it's hard to make good parallel executions or not for your property.

Unfortunately for us, the Erlang scheduler is rather predictable, and making
it test random interleavings is not really obvious nor something we can control.
This means that if it doesn't fail right away, it will need more luck finding
bugs, which means more executions. Only after an ungodly number of iterations might it find something in this cache, if at all:

```
$ rebar3 proper -p prop_parallel -n 10000
«build info and other test runs»
===> Testing prop_cache:prop_parallel()
«lots of dots»
Failed: After 3850 test(s).
An exception was raised:
    error:{'EXIT',{{case_clause,[[-27],[3]]},[{cache,find,«stacktrace»]
Stacktrace: [«stacktrace»].
«huge command dump»
Shrinking ......(6 time(s))
{[[{set,{var,2},{call,cache,find,[-4]}},{set,{var,3},{call,cache,cache,
[7,22]}},{set,{var,4},{call,cache,cache,[2,3]}}],[[{set,{var,5},{call,cache,
cache,[9,15]}},{set,{var,6},{call,cache,find,[2]}},{set,{var,7},{call,cache,
cache,[2,14]}},{set,{var,8},{call,cache,cache,[-1,2]}},{set,{var,12},{call,
cache,find,[4]}}],[{set,{var,11},{call,cache,flush,[]}},{set,{var,14},{call,
cache,cache,[2,-27]}}]]]}
===>
1/2 properties passed, 1 failed
===> Failed test cases:
prop_cache:prop_parallel() -> false
```

Ouch. We'll get back to this one a bit later, because first we should talk about
why it took so many tests to find the bug. As mentioned earlier, the Erlang
scheduler is quite predictable even if it isn't deterministic. The best you can
do to help from the outside is pass some flags to the Erlang VM that will force
it to preempt processes more often, even if that has no guarantee of finding
anything. You can do this through the +T0 to +T9 emulator flags, which allow
you to play with timing values such as how long a process takes to spawn,
the amount of work it can do before being scheduled out, or the perceived
cost of IO operations. Those are intended for testing only and can be enabled
by setting them like this: ERL_ZARGS="+T4" rebar3 proper -n 10000.

This is unlikely to help much with our cache since there's not that much
work going on for it (but in larger systems it may prove useful). Instead, we
can go the manual way and tell Erlang when to deschedule processes by

peppering calls to erlang:yield() around the places in code that seem worrisome. This will tend to generate errors fast:

```
Erlang                        code/StatefulProperties/erlang/pbt/src/cache.erl

cache(Key, Val) ->
    case ets:match(cache, {'$1', {Key, '_'}}) of % find dupes
        [[N]] ->
            ets:insert(cache, {N,{Key,Val}}); % overwrite dupe
        [] ->
            erlang:yield(),
            case ets:lookup(cache, count) of % insert new
                [{count,Max,Max}] ->
                    ets:insert(cache, [{1,{Key,Val}}, {count,1,Max}]);
                [{count,Current,Max}] ->
                    ets:insert(cache, [{Current+1,{Key,Val}},
                                       {count,Current+1,Max}])
            end
    end.

flush() ->
    [{count,_,Max}] = ets:lookup(cache, count),
    ets:delete_all_objects(cache),
    erlang:yield(),
    ets:insert(cache, {count, 0, Max}).
```

```
Elixir                        code/StatefulProperties/elixir/pbt/lib/cache.ex

def cache(key, val) do
  case :ets.match(:cache, {:'$1', {key, :'_'}}) do
    [[n]] ->
      :ets.insert(:cache, {n,{key,val}})
    [] ->
      :erlang.yield()
      case :ets.lookup(:cache, :count) do
        [{:count,max,max}] ->
          :ets.insert(:cache, [{1,{key,val}}, {:count,1,max}])
        [{:count,current,max}] ->
          :ets.insert(:cache, [{current+1, {key,val}},
                               {:count,current+1,max}])
      end
  end
end

def flush() do
  [{:count,_,max}] = :ets.lookup(:cache, :count)
  :ets.delete_all_objects(:cache)
  :erlang.yield()
  :ets.insert(:cache, {:count, 0, max})
end
```

Here we've added calls to erlang:yield/0 at ❶ and ❷. These calls basically tell the Erlang VM: "once you reach this point, deschedule my process and run another one if you can." Since they are placed in suspect code—the places where various reads and writes take place on a shared resource—PropEr finds issues almost instantly:

```
$ rebar3 proper -n 10000 -p prop_parallel
===> Testing prop_cache:prop_parallel()
..!
Failed: After 3 test(s).
An exception was raised:
    error:{'EXIT',{{case_clause,[[1],[2]]},[{cache,cache,2,[«stacktrace»
Stacktrace: «stacktrace»
{[],[[{set,{var,1},{call,cache,find,[0]}},«commands»

Shrinking ....(4 time(s))
{[],[[{set,{var,2},{call,cache,cache,[0,2]}}],
     [{set,{var,5},{call,cache,cache,[0,1]}}]]]}
```

And just like that, in merely three runs, it found conflicts between two cache write operations. The most basic functionality of our cache is not safe for concurrency. Put in a graphical form, this is what breaks:

```
     ,-> cache(0,2)
[] --+
     '-> cache(0,1)
```

With the error being a case_clause in cache:cache/2 as per the exception, we know the bug to be in here:

```
cache(Key, Val) ->
    case ets:match(cache, {'$1', {Key, '_'}}) of % find dupes
        [[N]] ->
            ets:insert(cache, {N,{Key,Val}}); % overwrite dupe
        [] ->
            «insertion code»
    end.
```

Whenever two insertions happen concurrently, there's a slight chance that our two writes check for an existing key before either of them is written, and that both of them increment the counter one after the other, causing two records to exist: {0,{Key,Val1}} and {1,{Key,Val2}}. We have two items in the cache sharing the same key, but with two distinct values. Unless the model is wrong (it isn't in this case), that's our bug.

Alternative Tools

If finding concurrency bugs is a big concern for you, a QuickCheck license may be worthwhile since it comes with PULSE, a user-level scheduler that you can use to augment concurrency in the VM to weed out these bugs in property tests.

Otherwise, look into tools like Concuerror (at concuerror.com), which aims to focus solely on concurrency bugs in Erlang. In fact, it can be used as a full formal proof that some execution paths are not going to be sensitive to concurrency bugs.

Fixing the bug requires changing our approach fundamentally, by making sure all destructive updates to the cache are done in a mutually exclusive manner. We could do this with locks, but an easier fix is to move write operations within the process that owns the table so that it will force all destructive updates to be sequential:

Erlang   code/StatefulProperties/erlang/pbt/src/cache.erl

```erlang
-module(cache).

-export([start_link/1, stop/0, cache/2, find/1, flush/0]).
-behaviour(gen_server).
-export([init/1, handle_call/3, handle_cast/2, handle_info/2]).

start_link(N) ->
    gen_server:start_link({local, ?MODULE}, ?MODULE, N, []).

stop() ->
    gen_server:stop(?MODULE).

find(Key) ->
    case ets:match(cache, {'_', {Key, '$1'}}) of
        [[Val]] -> {ok, Val};
        [] -> {error, not_found}
    end.

cache(Key, Val) ->
    gen_server:call(?MODULE, {cache, Key, Val}).

flush() ->
    gen_server:call(?MODULE, flush).

%%%%%%%%%%%%%%%%
%%% Private %%%
%%%%%%%%%%%%%%%%
init(N) ->
    ets:new(cache, [public, named_table]),
    ets:insert(cache, {count, 0, N}),
    {ok, nostate}.
```

```
handle_call({cache, Key, Val}, _From, State) ->
    case ets:match(cache, {'$1', {Key, '_'}}) of % find dupes
        [[N]] ->
            ets:insert(cache, {N,{Key,Val}}); % overwrite dupe
        [] ->
            erlang:yield(),
            case ets:lookup(cache, count) of % insert new
                [{count,Max,Max}] ->
                    ets:insert(cache, [{1,{Key,Val}}, {count,1,Max}]);
                [{count,Current,Max}] ->
                    ets:insert(cache, [{Current+1,{Key,Val}},
                                       {count,Current+1,Max}])
            end
    end,
    {reply, ok, State};
handle_call(flush, _From, State) ->
    [{count,_,Max}] = ets:lookup(cache, count),
    ets:delete_all_objects(cache),
    erlang:yield(),
    ets:insert(cache, {count, 0, Max}),
    {reply, ok, State}.

handle_cast(_Cast, State) -> {noreply, State}.

handle_info(_Msg, State) -> {noreply, State}.
```

Elixir translation on page 329.

Now you can re-run the property and see that it always works:

```
$ rebar3 proper -p prop_parallel -n 10000
.......f......................................f...«more tests»
OK: Passed 10000 test(s).

63% {cache,cache,2}
21% {cache,find,1}
15% {cache,flush,0}
```

You can then take out the erlang:yield() calls from the code before committing it, and be more confident that the cache works well.

Wrapping Up

This chapter has shown you the basics of stateful property testing, based on a single simple model. We've been through the two phases of the test: the symbolic one, where the model is used to generate a sequence of commands that represents what the system should do, and the real one, where the symbolic sequence of commands is applied to the real system, and the results compared with what the model expects.

We've put these concepts in practice through a cache server modeled as a first-in-first-out list and showed that the model seems to hold fine under sequential operations. You've then seen how PropEr can take that same exact model and create a parallel version of it that could, with some amount of help, find concurrency bugs in our cache program.

You've seen the base mechanism of how stateful properties work, but truth be told, the cache example we used resulted in a rather simple model. In the next chapter, we'll experiment with a more complex stateful system based on SQL queries, with varying amounts of determinism. We'll move past the basics of stateful properties and explore more advanced techniques to handle the complexity of modeling large systems for integration tests.

Exercises

Question 1

Which callbacks for stateful tests belong in which execution phases?

Solution on page 323.

Question 2

Pattern matching on the model state can be used to direct the generation of commands based on the current context, but preconditions are still required. Why are commands alone not sufficient and why do preconditions need to be used?

Solution on page 323.

Question 3

A file shows the three ways to initialize a stateful property test:

```erlang
Erlang

prop_test1() ->
    ?FORALL(Cmds, commands(?MODULE),
        begin
            actual_system:start_link(),
            {_History, _State, Result} = run_commands(?MODULE, Cmds),
            actual_system:stop(),
            Result =:= ok
        end).
prop_test2() ->
    ?SETUP(fun() ->
        actual_system:start_link(),
        fun() -> actual_system:stop() end
    end,
```

```
        ?FORALL(Cmds, commands(?MODULE),
          begin
              {_History, _State, Result} = run_commands(?MODULE, Cmds),
              Result =:= ok
          end)
    end).
prop_test3() ->
    actual_system:start_link(),
    ?FORALL(Cmds, commands(?MODULE),
        begin
            {_History, _State, Result} = run_commands(?MODULE, Cmds),
            Result =:= ok
        end),
    actual_system:stop().
```

Elixir

```
property "first example" do
    forall cmds <- commands(__MODULE__) do
        ActualSystem.start_link()
        {_history, _state, result} = run_commands(__MODULE__, cmds)
        ActualSystem.stop()
        result == :ok
    end
end

# The second example cannot be translated in Elixir since PropCheck
# Does not support the setup macro at the time of this writing --
# instead, you may use ExUnit's own setup macro as a workaround

property "third example" do
    ActualSystem.start_link()
    forall cmds <- commands(__MODULE__) do
        {_history, _state, result} = run_commands(__MODULE__, cmds)
        result == :ok
    end
    ActualSystem.stop()
end
```

What will happen to the actual system in every one of them?

Solution on page 323.

Question 4

What is the caveat of using the Res value—the result from the actual system—in the next_state/3 callback? Is there a scenario where it is absolutely useful to use it?

Solution on page 324.

## CHAPTER 10

Case Study: Bookstore

One of the things that make stateful properties really impressive is that once you understand them well enough to test a basic Erlang or Elixir component, you also understand them well enough to test almost anything, including systems not related to Erlang nor Elixir at all. The modeling and testing approaches mostly remain the same no matter how the actual system is implemented; only the calls reaching out to it end up changing.

In this chapter, we'll see how to do this with a more complex system—an Erlang bookstore implementation that uses a PostgreSQL back end, with SQL queries and network connections as part of the code to be tested. Even with all these moving pieces, we'll still be able to test it all using either Erlang or Elixir.

Since real-world systems contain more moving parts, they'll have a far larger portfolio of errors and weird behaviors to detect and to debug. We'll keep on using stateful properties, but we may have to adjust our strategy a bit to make our life easier.

We'll start by setting up the system we're going to test. For the testing, we'll first write generators that map to the types we expect to see in the system, and then we'll start throwing our stateful tests from a very broad position ("Does the system even boot?"), slowly narrowing it down ("Can it run random queries?"), until we close up with far more deterministic and rigorous tests ("Does the system behave the way I expect it to?"). This will let you get familiar with a bunch of techniques to write effective properties and how to debug them.

Introducing the Application

Like many other system tests, we'll start with a prewritten system, and mainly focus on testing it. The base system will use a few open source libraries, mostly around interacting with a database.

For Elixir Readers

If you're following along with Elixir, the dependencies of the Erlang application won't be replaced by their equivalents from the Elixir ecosystem: we'll stick with the Erlang ones. Since the various integration bugs our test suites could find may differ based on the libraries used, you'll be able to follow along the text more easily by reusing the same components as those used in the base Erlang implementation, even if the final implementation may look less idiomatic than if it had all been written in Elixir.

The first big dependency for this chapter is going to be an install of PostgreSQL, at version 9.6 or above. (While things may work with an older version, this chapter's material wasn't tested with anything prior to 9.6.) We'll assume that you have it on your system. If you don't, you'll find instructions in Appendix 3, *Installing PostgreSQL*, on page 343. With PostgreSQL installed, you're ready to set up the application.

Project Setup

To get started in Erlang, use a standard OTP application template from rebar3 to start a new project (call `rebar3 new app name=bookstore`), and then edit the `rebar3.config` file to look like this:

About the Code

In the snippets that follow, code is labeled with both the language (Erlang and Elixir) and the file where you should put the code if you're following along.

Erlang   code/Bookstore/erlang/bookstore/rebar.config

```erlang
{project_plugins, [rebar3_proper]}.

%% Set up a standalone script to set up the DB
{escript_name, "bookstore_init"}.
{escript_emu_args, "%%! -escript main bookstore_init\n"}.

{deps, [
    eql,
    {pgsql, "26.0.1"}
]}.

{profiles, [
  {test, [
    {erl_opts, [nowarn_export_all]},
    {deps, [{proper, "1.3.0"}]}
  ]}
]}.
```

```
%% auto-boot the app when calling `rebar3 shell'
{shell, [{apps, [bookstore]}]}.
```

This sets up a standard project with the PropEr dependencies, but also includes some configuration values related to an escript[1] we will use to initialize the database.

With this in place, you'll want to modify the file at src/bookstore.app.src to contain the following:

Erlang	code/Bookstore/erlang/bookstore/src/bookstore.app.src

```
{application, bookstore,
 [{description, "Handling books and book accessories"},
  {vsn, "0.1.0"},
  {registered, []},
  {mod, { bookstore_app, []}},
  {applications, [kernel, stdlib, eql, pgsql]},
  {env,[
      {pg, [
          {user, "ferd"}, % replace with your own $USER
          {password, ""},
          {database, "bookstore_db"}, % as specified by bookstore_init.erl
          {host, "127.0.0.1"},
          {port, 5432},
          {ssl, false} % not for tests!
      ]}
  ]},
  {modules, []}
 ]}.
```

This adds all dependencies and applications variables (in the env tuple) required to make things work. You can put the information relating to your user, password, and port for the database here.

Elixir users may prefer to use the following commands and configuration instead, for an equivalent experience. First create a new project (mix new bookstore) and set the following mix.exs file, which sets up the same environment variables and escript setup:

Elixir	code/Bookstore/elixir/bookstore/mix.exs

```
defmodule Bookstore.MixProject do
  use Mix.Project
```

---

1. http://erlang.org/doc/man/escript.html

```elixir
def project do
  [
    app: :bookstore,
    version: "0.1.0",
    elixir: "~> 1.6",
    elixirc_paths: elixirc_paths(Mix.env),
    start_permanent: Mix.env() == :prod,
    deps: deps(),
    escript: escript_config()
  ]
end

defp elixirc_paths(:test), do: ["lib","test/"]
defp elixirc_paths(_), do: ["lib"]

# Run "mix help compile.app" to learn about applications.
def application do
  [
    extra_applications: [:logger],
    mod: {Bookstore.App, []},
    env: [
      pg: [
        # Single quotes are important
        user: 'ferd', # replace with your own $USER
        password: '',
        database: 'bookstore_db', # as specified by bookstore_init.ex
        host: '127.0.0.1',
        port: 5432,
        ssl: false # not for tests!
      ]
    ]
  ]
end

# Run "mix help deps" to learn about dependencies.
defp deps do
  [
    {:eql, "~> 0.1.2", manager: :rebar3},
    {:pgsql, "~> 26.0"},
    {:propcheck, "~> 1.1", only: [:test, :dev]}
  ]
end

defp escript_config do
  [main_module: Bookstore.Init, app: nil]
end
end
```

Do take the time to set the right user for your PostgreSQL installation.

These configuration files show the PropEr plugin being used, an escript being generated (to set up the database), and dependencies on pgsql, a database client, and eql, a library used to access SQL queries stored on disk by name within the BEAM VM.

We can now add the first code file for the project, the initialization script that sets up the database:

Erlang	code/Bookstore/erlang/bookstore/src/bookstore_init.erl

```erlang
-module(bookstore_init).
-export([main/1]).

main(_) ->
    %% See: https://www.postgresql.org/docs/9.6/static/server-start.html
    ok = filelib:ensure_dir("postgres/data/.init-here"),
    io:format("initializing database structure...~n"),
    cmd("initdb -D postgres/data"),
    io:format("starting postgres instance...~n"),

    %% On windows this is synchronous and never returns until done
    StartCmd = "pg_ctl -D postgres/data -l logfile start",
    case os:type() of
        {win32, _} -> spawn(fun() -> cmd(StartCmd) end);
        {unix, _} -> cmd(StartCmd)
    end,
    timer:sleep(5000), % wait and pray!

    io:format("setting up 'bookstore_db' database...~n"),
    cmd("psql -h localhost -d template1 -c "
        "\"CREATE DATABASE bookstore_db;\""),
    io:format("OK.~n"),
    init:stop().

cmd(Str) -> io:format("~s~n", [os:cmd(Str)]).
```

Elixir translation on page 331.

All this script does is call PostgreSQL tools for the initial set up in a portable manner. Rebar3 users can call the script as follows:

```
$ rebar3 escritpize
«building the project»
$ _build/default/bin/bookstore_init
initializing database structure...
«DB build output»
starting postgres instance...
setting up 'bookstore_db' database...
CREATE DATABASE

OK.
```

Or you can just call escript <path/to/file> and get the same result. Elixir users will instead run this:

```
$ mix deps.get
《fetching dependencies》
$ mix escript.build
《building the project》
$ ./bookstore
initializing database structure...
《DB build output》
```

With that in place, we can start looking at the actual application code.

Application Code

The application starts a standard supervisor without children:

Erlang	code/Bookstore/erlang/bookstore/src/bookstore_app.erl

```erlang
-module(bookstore_app).
-behaviour(application).

%% Application callbacks
-export([start/2, stop/1]).

start(_StartType, _StartArgs) ->
    bookstore_sup:start_link().

stop(_State) ->
    ok.
```

Elixir	code/Bookstore/elixir/bookstore/lib/bookstore/app.ex

```elixir
defmodule Bookstore.App do
  use Application

  def start(_type, _args) do
    Bookstore.Sup.start_link()
  end

  def stop(_state) do
    :ok
  end
end
```

And for the supervisor itself, we have this:

Erlang	code/Bookstore/erlang/bookstore/src/bookstore_sup.erl

```erlang
-module(bookstore_sup).
-behaviour(supervisor).
```

```
-export([start_link/0]).
-export([init/1]).

start_link() ->
    supervisor:start_link({local, ?MODULE}, ?MODULE, []).

init([]) ->
    bookstore_db:load_queries(),
    {ok, {{one_for_all, 0, 1}, []}}.
```

Elixir	code/Bookstore/elixir/bookstore/lib/bookstore/sup.ex

```
defmodule Bookstore.Sup do
  use Supervisor

  def start_link() do
    Supervisor.start_link(__MODULE__, [], name: __MODULE__)
  end

  def init([]) do
    Bookstore.DB.load_queries()
    Supervisor.init([], strategy: :one_for_one)
  end
end
```

Note that bookstore_db:load_queries() gets called. This function is not yet defined
(we'll get there in a minute). Its role, though, will be to find all the SQL queries
within a file we'll define in priv/queries.sql, and which are labeled by name in
comments (-- :<name>):

Bookstore/erlang/bookstore/priv/queries.sql
```
-- Setup the table for the book database
-- :setup_table_books
CREATE TABLE books (
  isbn varchar(20) PRIMARY KEY,
  title varchar(256) NOT NULL,
  author varchar(256) NOT NULL,
  owned smallint DEFAULT 0,
  available smallint DEFAULT 0
);

-- Clean up the table
-- :teardown_table_books
DROP TABLE books;

-- Add a book
-- :add_book
INSERT INTO books (isbn, title, author, owned, available)
       VALUES     ($1,  $2,    $3,     $4,    $5        );
```

```
-- Add a copy of an existing book
-- :add_copy
UPDATE books SET
  owned = owned + 1,
  available = available + 1
WHERE isbn = $1;

-- Borrow a copy of a book
-- :borrow_copy
UPDATE books SET available = available - 1 WHERE isbn = $1 AND available > 0;

-- Return a copy of a book
-- :return_copy
UPDATE books SET available = available + 1 WHERE isbn = $1;

-- Find books
-- :find_by_author
SELECT * FROM books WHERE author LIKE $1;
-- :find_by_isbn
SELECT * FROM books WHERE isbn = $1;
-- :find_by_title
SELECT * FROM books WHERE title LIKE $1;
```

Those represent all possible operations our system can do with the database. Each query supports a format amenable to *parameterized queries*,[2] which lets us securely replace each $1, $2 and other variables with actual values without having to escape them.

Elixir users can put the same queries.sql file in a priv/ directory in the root of the project as well for a similar result.

To make use of the queries, we'll write a module called bookstore_db, which will export wrappers around each operation:

Erlang   code/Bookstore/erlang/bookstore/src/bookstore_db.erl

```erlang
-module(bookstore_db).
-export([load_queries/0, setup/0, teardown/0,
         add_book/3, add_book/5, add_copy/1, borrow_copy/1, return_copy/1,
         find_book_by_author/1, find_book_by_isbn/1, find_book_by_title/1]).

%% @doc Create the database table required for the bookstore
setup() ->
    run_query(setup_table_books, []).

%% @doc Delete the database table required for the bookstore
teardown() ->
    run_query(teardown_table_books, []).
```

---

2.   https://www.postgresql.org/docs/9.6/static/protocol-overview.html#PROTOCOL-QUERY-CONCEPTS

```
%% @doc Add a new book to the inventory, with no copies of it.
add_book(ISBN, Title, Author) ->
    add_book(ISBN, Title, Author, 0, 0).

%% @doc Add a new book to the inventory, with a pre-set number of owned
%% and available copies.
add_book(ISBN, Title, Author, Owned, Avail) ->
    BinTitle = iolist_to_binary(Title),
    BinAuthor = iolist_to_binary(Author),
    case run_query(add_book, [ISBN, BinTitle, BinAuthor, Owned, Avail) of
        {{insert,0,1},[]} -> ok;
        {error, Reason} -> {error, Reason};
        Other -> {error, Other}
    end.

%% @doc Add a copy of a book to the bookstore's inventory
add_copy(ISBN) ->
    handle_single_update(run_query(add_copy, [ISBN])).

%% @doc Borrow a copy of a book; reduces the count of available
%% copies by one. Who borrowed the book is not tracked at this
%% moment and is left as an exercise to the reader.
borrow_copy(ISBN) ->
    handle_single_update(run_query(borrow_copy, [ISBN])).

%% @doc Return a book copy, making it available again.
return_copy(ISBN) ->
    handle_single_update(run_query(return_copy, [ISBN])).

%% @doc Search all books written by a given author. The matching is loose
%% and so searching for `Hawk' will return copies of books written
%% by `Stephen Hawking' (if such copies are in the system)
find_book_by_author(Author) ->
    handle_select(
        run_query(find_by_author, [iolist_to_binary(["%",Author,"%"])])
    ).

%% @doc Find books under a given ISBN.
find_book_by_isbn(ISBN) ->
    handle_select(run_query(find_by_isbn, [ISBN])).

%% @doc Find books with a given title. The matching us loose and searching
%% for `Test' may return `PropEr Testing'.
find_book_by_title(Title) ->
    handle_select(
        run_query(find_by_title, [iolist_to_binary(["%",Title,"%"])])
    ).
```

Elixir translation on page 332.

This module acts as a *model* by abstracting away the implementation from the data we want to obtain. It becomes rather cheap to change storage layers, whether they'll be using SQL, a microservice, or just raw files on disk. Each function has its own doc line explaining what it does. You'll find that all of them depend on a run_query/2 function, which accepts the query name and its arguments. Before showing its implementation, let's first take a look at how queries are loaded and made available:

Erlang   code/Bookstore/erlang/bookstore/src/bookstore_db.erl

```erlang
load_queries() ->
    ets:new(bookstore_sql, [named_table, public, {read_concurrency, true}]),
    SQLFile = filename:join(code:priv_dir(bookstore), "queries.sql"),
    {ok, Queries} = eql:compile(SQLFile),
    ets:insert(bookstore_sql, Queries),
    ok.

query(Name) ->
    case ets:lookup(bookstore_sql, Name) of
        [] -> {query_not_found, Name};
        [{_, Query}] -> Query
    end.
```

Elixir   code/Bookstore/elixir/bookstore/lib/bookstore/db.ex

```elixir
def load_queries() do
  :ets.new(
    :bookstore_sql,
    [:named_table, :public, {:read_concurrency, true}]
  )
  sql_file = Path.join(:code.priv_dir(:bookstore), "queries.sql")
  {:ok, queries} = :eql.compile(sql_file)
  :ets.insert(:bookstore_sql, queries)
  :ok
end

defp query(name) do
  case :ets.lookup(:bookstore_sql, name) do
    [] -> {:query_not_found, name}
    [{_, query}] -> query
  end
end
```

The first function creates an ETS table,[3] reads the queries from disk with eql:compile/1, and stores them in there. That function is called once, by bookstore_sup, which therefore owns the ETS table. The query/1 function can then be used by the module to fetch the right query from the ETS cache.

This is exactly what run_query/2 ends up doing. Here's how it's implemented:

Erlang   code/Bookstore/erlang/bookstore/src/bookstore_db.erl

```erlang
%% @doc Run a query with a given set of arguments. This function
%% automatically wraps the whole operation with a connection to
%% a database.
run_query(Name, Args) ->
    with_connection(fun(Conn) -> run_query(Name, Args, Conn) end).

%% @doc Run a query with a given set of arguments, within the scope
%% of a specific PostgreSQL connection. For example, this allows to run
%% multiple queries within a single connection, or within larger
%% transactions.
run_query(Name, Args, Conn) ->
    pgsql_connection:extended_query(query(Name), Args, Conn).

%% @doc Takes a function, and runs it with a connection to a PostgreSQL
%% database connection as an argument. Closes the connection after
%% the call, and returns its result.
with_connection(Fun) ->
    %% A pool call could be hidden and wrapped here, rather than
    %% always grabbing a new connection
    {ok, Conn} = connect(),
    Res = Fun(Conn),
    close(Conn),
    Res.

%% @doc open up a new connection to a PostgreSQL database from
%% the application configuration
connect() -> connect(application:get_env(bookstore, pg, [])).

%% @doc open up a new connection to a PostgreSQL database with
%% explicit configuration parameters.
connect(Args) ->
    try pgsql_connection:open(Args) of
        {pgsql_connection, _} = Conn -> {ok, Conn}
    catch
        throw:Error -> {error, Error}
    end.

%% @doc end a connection
close(Conn) -> pgsql_connection:close(Conn).
```

Elixir translation on page 334.

This lets you simply execute the parameterized queries, and encapsulate the connection mechanisms and logic behind utility functions. While it currently uses a new connection for every request, it would be relatively simple to use a connection pool instead, for example.

Another set of functions you may have noticed being called are the following, which wrap the SQL results and reformats them into a more useful format for our module:

Erlang   code/Bookstore/erlang/bookstore/src/bookstore_db.erl

```erlang
handle_select({{select, _}, List}) -> {ok, List};
handle_select(Error) -> Error.

handle_single_update({{update,1}, _}) -> ok;
handle_single_update({error, Reason}) -> {error, Reason};
handle_single_update(Other) -> {error, Other}.
```

Elixir   code/Bookstore/elixir/bookstore/lib/bookstore/db.ex

```elixir
defp handle_select({{:select, _}, list}), do: {:ok, list}
defp handle_select(error), do: error

defp handle_single_update({{:update, 1}, _}), do: :ok
defp handle_single_update({:error, reason}), do: {:error, reason}
defp handle_single_update(other), do: {:error, other}
```

This is all that we need for our application to work at a basic level, and more than enough for us to test:

```
$ rebar3 shell
«build output»
===> Booted eql
===> Booted pgsql
===> Booted bookstore
1> bookstore_db:setup().
{{create,table},[]}
2> bookstore_db:add_book(
2>    "978-0-7546-7834-2", "Behind Human Error", "David D Woods"
2> ).
ok
3> bookstore_db:find_book_by_author("Woods").
{ok,[{<<"978-0-7546-7834-2">>,<<"Behind Human Error">>,
      <<"David D. Woods">>,0,0}]}
4> bookstore_db:borrow_copy(<<"978-0-7546-7834-2">>).
{error,{{update,0},[]}}
5> bookstore_db:add_copy(<<"978-0-7546-7834-2">>).
ok
6> bookstore_db:borrow_copy(<<"978-0-7546-7834-2">>).
ok
7> bookstore_db:borrow_copy(<<"978-0-7546-7834-2">>).
{error,{{update,0},[]}}
8> bookstore_db:teardown().
{{drop,table},[]}
```

Some of the output could be made nicer, but this is good enough for our purposes. The system seems to work well enough for us to start testing with stateful properties, bit by bit. We'll start with broad sequential tests, but first, let's write some generators that will remain useful for everything we do.

Writing Generators

When you've got a fairly large stateful system to validate, a good strategy to get you going is to start by figuring out what data the system should accept—what is valid and invalid. This is useful because it sets some baseline for expectations on which to build and can hint at useful paths or strategies moving forward.

We've got a basic idea about the shape of data based on our database schema. Let's start a property test module and begin with the title and author generators:

Erlang	code/Bookstore/erlang/bookstore/test/prop_bookstore.erl

```erlang
-module(prop_bookstore).
-include_lib("proper/include/proper.hrl").
-compile(export_all).

title() ->
    ?LET(S, string(), elements([S, unicode:characters_to_binary(S)])).

author() ->
    ?LET(S, string(), elements([S, unicode:characters_to_binary(S)])).
```

Elixir	code/Bookstore/elixir/bookstore/test/bookstore_test.exs

```elixir
defmodule BookstoreTest do
  use ExUnit.Case
  use PropCheck
  use PropCheck.StateM
  doctest Bookstore

  def title() do
    let s <- utf8() do
      elements([s, String.to_charlist(s)])
    end
  end

  def author() do
    let s <- utf8() do
      elements([s, String.to_charlist(s)])
    end
  end
  «...»
end
```

Since this is Erlang (or Elixir), and given that the virtual machine has no dedicated string types, both generators will create either lists of characters (string()) or binaries of the same text encoded as UTF-8. This will let us check out whether the entire stack can support both types.

The next generator is for ISBNs. *ISBN* stands for the *International Standard Book Number,*[4] a series of ten or thirteen digits that uniquely identify every book published.

We don't really care about their format too much for this text and will assume some other part of the system would test, validate, and normalize them. Instead, we'll use a more random generator that will let us focus on state transitions for the stateful model. The generator looks like this:

Erlang	code/Bookstore/erlang/bookstore/test/prop_bookstore.erl

```erlang
isbn() ->
    ?LET(ISBN,
        [oneof(["978","979"]),
         ?LET(X, range(0,9999), integer_to_list(X)),
         ?LET(X, range(0,9999), integer_to_list(X)),
         ?LET(X, range(0,999), integer_to_list(X)),
         frequency([{10, range($0,$9)}, {1, "X"}])],
        iolist_to_binary(lists:join("-", ISBN))).
```

Elixir	code/Bookstore/elixir/bookstore/test/bookstore_test.exs

```elixir
def isbn() do
  let isbn <- [
        oneof(['978', '979']),
        let(x <- range(0, 9999), do: to_charlist(x)),
        let(x <- range(0, 9999), do: to_charlist(x)),
        let(x <- range(0, 999), do: to_charlist(x)),
        frequency([{10, [range(?0, ?9)]}, {1, 'X'}])
      ] do
    to_string(Enum.join(isbn, "-"))
  end
end
```

You can see the kind of identifiers this generates in the shell:

```
$ rebar3 as test shell
≪build output≫
1> proper_gen:sample(prop_bookstore:isbn()).
<<"978-1507-2709-357-1">>
<<"978-1347-142-554-X">>
<<"979-9363-9561-334-0">>
<<"979-531-2666-141-X">>
<<"978-8024-8930-890-9">>
<<"979-245-64-445-5">>
```

---

4. https://en.wikipedia.org/wiki/Isbn

```
<<"978-3938-5049-65-3">>
<<"979-9883-2469-411-1">>
<<"978-208-3140-344-0">>
<<"979-8351-3610-508-6">>
<<"979-4012-3820-833-X">>
```

We now have generators for authors, titles, and the ISBNs. The only other values we'll need for our tests are going to be counters for books, which are just integers. We're good to get started with the initial stateful property.

Broad Stateful Testing

We'll start with a very wide scanning of the system to make sure the basic stuff works. This will check for simple API misunderstandings, errors that type analysis couldn't reveal, or issues with configuration or the basic test setup.

Let's first add the actual property declaration to our module:

Erlang	code/Bookstore/erlang/bookstore/test/prop_bookstore.erl

```erlang
-module(prop_bookstore).
-include_lib("proper/include/proper.hrl").
-compile(export_all).

prop_test() ->
    ?SETUP(fun() ->
        {ok, Apps} = application:ensure_all_started(bookstore),
        fun() -> [application:stop(App) || App <- Apps], ok end
      end,
      ?FORALL(Cmds, commands(?MODULE),
        begin
            bookstore_db:setup(),
            {History, State, Result} = run_commands(?MODULE, Cmds),
            bookstore_db:teardown(),
            ?WHENFAIL(io:format("History: ~p\nState: ~p\nResult: ~p\n",
                        [History, State, Result]),
                    aggregate(command_names(Cmds), Result =:= ok))
        end)
    ).
```

Elixir	code/Bookstore/elixir/bookstore/test/bookstore_test.exs

```elixir
defmodule BookstoreTest do
  use ExUnit.Case
  use PropCheck
  use PropCheck.StateM
  doctest Bookstore
```

```
property "bookstore stateful operations", [:verbose] do
  forall cmds <- commands(__MODULE__) do
    # No setup macro in PropCheck yet, do it all inline
    {:ok, apps} = Application.ensure_all_started(:bookstore)
    Bookstore.DB.setup()
    {history, state, result} = run_commands(__MODULE__, cmds)
    Bookstore.DB.teardown()
    for app <- apps, do: Application.stop(app)

    (result == :ok)
    |> aggregate(command_names(cmds))
    |> when_fail(
      IO.puts("""
      History: #{inspect(history)}
      State: #{inspect(state)}
      Result: #{inspect(result)}
      """)
    )
  end
end
```

As you can see, we make use of the ?SETUP macro to boot the bookstore OTP application once for all the tests, making sure that all libraries and dependencies are in place, and then call the bookstore:setup/0 and bookstore:teardown/0 functions on each iteration to get rid of the database table and its state between each test so that the execution is clean.

We can start on the model. To keep with the spirit of broad testing, let's do nothing but call the functions:

Erlang	code/Bookstore/erlang/bookstore/test/prop_bookstore.erl

```
%% Initial model value at system start. Should be deterministic.
initial_state() -> #{}.

command(_State) ->
    oneof([
        {call, bookstore_db, add_book, [isbn(), title(), author(), 1, 1]},
        {call, bookstore_db, add_copy, [isbn()]},
        {call, bookstore_db, borrow_copy, [isbn()]},
        {call, bookstore_db, return_copy, [isbn()]},
        {call, bookstore_db, find_book_by_author, [author()]}, % or part
        {call, bookstore_db, find_book_by_title, [title()]}, % or title part
        {call, bookstore_db, find_book_by_isbn, [isbn()]}
    ]).

%% Picks whether a command should be valid under the current state.
precondition(_State, {call, _Mod, _Fun, _Args}) ->
    true.
```

```
%% Given the state `State' *prior* to the call `{call, Mod, Fun, Args}',
%% determine whether the result `Res' (coming from the actual system)
%% makes sense.
postcondition(_State, {call, _Mod, _Fun, _Args}, _Res) ->
    true.

%% Assuming the postcondition for a call was true, update the model
%% accordingly for the test to proceed.
next_state(State, _Res, {call, _Mod, _Fun, _Args}) ->
    NewState = State,
    NewState.
```

Elixir	code/Bookstore/elixir/bookstore/test/bookstore_test.exs

```elixir
# initial model value at system start. Should be deterministic.
def initial_state(), do: %{}

def command(_state) do
  oneof([
    {:call, Bookstore.DB, :add_book, [isbn(), title(), author(), 1, 1]},
    {:call, Bookstore.DB, :add_copy, [isbn()]},
    {:call, Bookstore.DB, :borrow_copy, [isbn()]},
    {:call, Bookstore.DB, :return_copy, [isbn()]},
    {:call, Bookstore.DB, :find_book_by_author, [author()]}, # or part
    {:call, Bookstore.DB, :find_book_by_title, [title()]}, # or part
    {:call, Bookstore.DB, :find_book_by_isbn, [isbn()]}
  ])
end

# Picks whether a command should be valid under the current state.
def precondition(_state, {:call, _mod, _fun, _args}) do
  true
end

# Given the state *prior* to the call {:call, mod, fun, args},
# determine whether the result (coming from the actual system)
# makes sense.
def postcondition(_state, {:call, _mod, _fun, _args}, _res) do
  true
end

# Assuming the postcondition for a call was true, update the model
# accordingly for the test to proceed
def next_state(state, _res, {:call, _mod, _fun, _args}) do
  new_state = state
  new_state
end
```

The command/1 function is the only significant one, with the rest untouched from the rebar3 template. You can run this property to see how things go:

```
$ rebar3 proper
===> Verifying dependencies...
===> Compiling bookstore
===> Testing prop_bookstore:prop_test()
.....................................................!
Failed: After 65 test(s).
«failure output»
Shrinking ....(4 time(s))
[{set,{var,11},{call,bookstore_db,find_book_by_author,[
 [6,13,3,1,15,23,5,115,30,0,3,523,0,27]]}}]
History: []
State: #{}
Result: {exception,error,badarg,
            [{erlang,iolist_to_binary,
                [["%",[6,13,3,1,15,23,5,115,30,0,3,523,0,27],"%"]],
                []},
             {bookstore_db,find_book_by_author,1,
                [{file, «path»/src/bookstore_db.erl},
                 {line,49}]},
«stacktrace»
```

So at some point in our code, an author name is getting converted from an
iolist data type into a binary, but in this specific case, it fails. It's interesting to
note that the iolist that causes problems hasn't been shrunk down to a simpler
string: are the 0s what cause issues, the length, or something else? We don't
necessarily know, because stateful properties primarily focus on finding tricky
state transitions over plain tricky data inputs, which are rather the specialty
of stateless properties. We'll see later in this chapter how shrinking works for
stateful properties, which will explain this kind of behavior.

Erlang and Unicode

Erlang's Unicode situation is complex, with multiple formats of strings:

- Lists of bytes and binaries mixed together; they are assumed to be latin1 text
  and named *iolists*

- Lists of unicode codepoints (0..16#10ffff), to be converted to a specific UTF encoding
  by whatever driver handles the output

- A binary piece of data representing text in any of UTF-8, UTF-16, or UTF-32
  encodings

- Lists of unicode codepoints and UTF-encoded binaries mixed together, referred
  to as *chardata*; they are the unicode-aware version of iolists

All unicode-aware types can be converted and handled by the unicode module, and
unicode string algorithms are implemented starting in OTP 20 in the string module.

To make things simple and to save us the time of writing a stateless property to find the bad input, the problem in the counterexample above is the value 523. The iolist_to_binary/1 function converts bytes (0..255) from a list format to a binary format, but doesn't care for string encoding. The number 523 represents the character ȋ (*Latin small letter i with inverted breve*) in Unicode. The function we need here, specifically for Unicode support, is unicode:characters_to_binary/1.

By changing the database queries to always convert all forms of input to utf8-encoded binaries, the bug should go away. Let's start with the book addition:

Erlang	code/Bookstore/erlang/bookstore/src/bookstore_db.erl

```erlang
%% @doc Add a new book to the inventory, with no copies of it.
add_book(ISBN, Title, Author) ->
    add_book(ISBN, Title, Author, 0, 0).

%% @doc Add a new book to the inventory, with a pre-set number of owned
%% and available copies.
add_book(ISBN, Title, Author, Owned, Avail) ->
    BinTitle = unicode:characters_to_binary(Title),
    BinAuthor = unicode:characters_to_binary(Author),
    case run_query(add_book, [ISBN, BinTitle, BinAuthor, Owned, Avail]) of
        {{insert,0,1},[]} -> ok;
        {error, Reason} -> {error, Reason};
        Other -> {error, Other}
    end.
```

Elixir	code/Bookstore/elixir/bookstore/lib/bookstore/db.ex

```elixir
@doc """
Add a new book to the inventory, with no copies of it
"""
def add_book(isbn, title, author) do
  add_book(isbn, title, author, 0, 0)
end

@doc """
Add a new book to the inventory, with a pre-set number of
owned and available copies
"""
def add_book(isbn, title, author, owned, avail) do
  bin_title = IO.chardata_to_string(title)
  bin_author = IO.chardata_to_string(author)

  case run_query(:add_book, [isbn, bin_title, bin_author, owned, avail]) do
    {{:insert, 0, 1}, []} -> :ok
    {:error, reason} -> {:error, reason}
    other -> {:error, other}
  end
end
```

And then the lookup functions can be adjusted as well:

Erlang   code/Bookstore/erlang/bookstore/src/bookstore_db.erl

```erlang
%% @doc Search all books written by a given author. The matching is loose
%% and so searching for `Hawk' will return copies of books written
%% by `Stephen Hawking' (if such copies are in the system)
find_book_by_author(Author) ->
    handle_select(
        run_query(find_by_author,
                  [unicode:characters_to_binary(["%",Author,"%"])])
    ).

%% @doc Find books under a given ISBN.
find_book_by_isbn(ISBN) ->
    handle_select(run_query(find_by_isbn, [ISBN])).

%% @doc Find books with a given title. The matching us loose and searching
%% for `Test' may return `PropEr Testing'.
find_book_by_title(Title) ->
    handle_select(
        run_query(find_by_title,
                  [unicode:characters_to_binary(["%",Title,"%"])])
    ).
```

Elixir   code/Bookstore/elixir/bookstore/lib/bookstore/db.ex

```elixir
@doc """
Search all books written by a given author. The matching is loose and so
searching for `Hawk' will return copies of books written by `Stephen
Hawking' (if such copies are in the system)
"""
def find_book_by_author(author) do
  handle_select(
    run_query(
      :find_by_author,
      [IO.chardata_to_string(['%', author, '%'])]
    )
  )
end

@doc """
Find books under a given ISBN
"""
def find_book_by_isbn(isbn) do
  handle_select(run_query(:find_by_isbn, [isbn]))
end

@doc """
Find books with a given title. The matching us loose and searching
for `Test' may return `PropEr Testing'.
"""
```

```
def find_book_by_title(title) do
  handle_select(
    run_query(
      :find_by_title,
      [IO.chardata_to_string(['%', title, '%'])]
    )
  )
end
```

This should take care of everything. Run the tests and see:

```
$ rebar3 proper
«build output»
===> Testing prop_bookstore:prop_test()
................................................................
.......................
OK: Passed 100 test(s).

16% {bookstore_db,add_book,5}
15% {bookstore_db,borrow_copy,1}
15% {bookstore_db,find_book_by_title,1}
13% {bookstore_db,find_book_by_isbn,1}
13% {bookstore_db,return_copy,1}
13% {bookstore_db,add_copy,1}
12% {bookstore_db,find_book_by_author,1}
```

Right now, it seems like the calls tend to all succeed. We're now in a good position to start adding postconditions and to track state transitions, testing the system in more detail. We'll grow our model, track books, check availability, and refine our ability to look things up in the database.

Precise Stateful Modeling

It's time we use a model to dig deeper into what the system can or can't do. Once again, a critical property of models is that they are simpler but sufficient to represent the real thing. For our database, a map will prove sufficient to track all changes. But first, before we start to add postconditions, we may want to make an inventory of all kinds of operations we will want to check:

- Adding a book that is not yet in the system is expected to succeed.

- Adding a book that is already in the system is expected to fail.

- Adding a copy of a book that is already in the system is expected to succeed (and make one more copy available right away).

- Adding a copy of a book that isn't yet in the system should return an error.

- Borrowing a book that is in the system and available makes one less copy available.

- Borrowing a book that is in the system but unavailable returns an error saying it is unavailable.

- Borrowing a book that is not in the system would return an error saying it is not found.

- Returning a book that is in the system makes it available again.

- Returning a book that is not in the system returns an error saying it was not found.

- Returning a book that is in the system but for which all copies are accounted for returns an error as well.

- Looking up a book by ISBN should succeed if the book is in the system already.

- Looking up a book by ISBN should fail if the book is *not* in the system yet.

- Finding a book by author should succeed if the submitted name matches a part of or the full name of one or more existing books.

- Finding a book by title should succeed if the submitted title matches a part of or the full name of one or more existing books.

- Lookups of titles or authors for which we expect no match should return an empty result set.

The obvious way to go about validation is to just fill up next_state/3 callback clauses for each call in bookstore_db, stick all the checks into postconditions right there, and call it a day. The downside of this approach is that it will be difficult to gather metrics and know how many of our calls will hit each of the cases, or if most attempts will only hit the same case over and over again (such as inserting new records without errors). Similarly, it might be trickier to debug a failing test case if we need a lot of context to know what the actual operation was.

Using a Shim

A nicer approach is to force the model clauses to become more deterministic and explicit. The more determinism we have, the easier it will be to emphasize one type of operation over another one and to figure out what goes on. The best trick to make clauses deterministic (without affecting generation) is to use a *shim module*—a module that wraps regular operations with a known name to add more context—to make all other proper_statem callbacks simpler. Here's the implementation we'll use:

Erlang   code/Bookstore/erlang/bookstore/test/book_shim.erl

```erlang
-module(book_shim).
-compile(export_all).
add_book_existing(ISBN, Title, Author, Owned, Avail) ->
    bookstore_db:add_book(ISBN, Title, Author, Owned, Avail).
add_book_new(ISBN, Title, Author, Owned, Avail) ->
    bookstore_db:add_book(ISBN, Title, Author, Owned, Avail).

add_copy_existing(ISBN) -> bookstore_db:add_copy(ISBN).
add_copy_new(ISBN) -> bookstore_db:add_copy(ISBN).

borrow_copy_avail(ISBN) -> bookstore_db:borrow_copy(ISBN).
borrow_copy_unavail(ISBN) -> bookstore_db:borrow_copy(ISBN).
borrow_copy_unknown(ISBN) -> bookstore_db:borrow_copy(ISBN).

return_copy_full(ISBN) -> bookstore_db:return_copy(ISBN).
return_copy_existing(ISBN) -> bookstore_db:return_copy(ISBN).
return_copy_unknown(ISBN) -> bookstore_db:return_copy(ISBN).

find_book_by_isbn_exists(ISBN) -> bookstore_db:find_book_by_isbn(ISBN).
find_book_by_isbn_unknown(ISBN) -> bookstore_db:find_book_by_isbn(ISBN).

find_book_by_author_matching(Author) ->
    bookstore_db:find_book_by_author(Author).
find_book_by_author_unknown(Author) ->
    bookstore_db:find_book_by_author(Author).

find_book_by_title_matching(Title) ->
    bookstore_db:find_book_by_title(Title).
find_book_by_title_unknown(Title) ->
    bookstore_db:find_book_by_title(Title).
```

Elixir translation on page 334.

All possible cases from our prior list are represented within the shim module. This one is fairly straightforward, and as you can see, all variations of a given call directly call the same function. That's fine, since we'll just want to be able to *see* which use case we get in our properties.

Shim Modules

 Shim modules are the perfect place to do things such as turn an asynchronous interface into a synchronous one, capture side effects as if they were functional values, or to wrap nondeterministic values into a more deterministic format. They are helpers that always have access to runtime data and only run during real execution. Use them to shape and adapt your actual system to your model's needs.

We can then rewrite our command/1 callback to use the shim module:

Erlang	code/Bookstore/erlang/bookstore/test/prop_bookstore.erl

```erlang
%% Initial model value at system start. Should be deterministic.
initial_state() -> #{}.

command(State) ->
    AlwaysPossible = [
        {call, book_shim, add_book_new, [isbn(), title(), author(), 1, 1]},
        {call, book_shim, add_copy_new, [isbn()]},
        {call, book_shim, borrow_copy_unknown, [isbn()]},
        {call, book_shim, return_copy_unknown, [isbn()]},
        {call, book_shim, find_book_by_isbn_unknown, [isbn()]},
        {call, book_shim, find_book_by_author_unknown, [author()]},
        {call, book_shim, find_book_by_title_unknown, [title()]}
    ],
    ReliesOnState = case maps:size(State) of
        0 -> % no values yet
            [];
        _ -> % values form which to work
            S = State,
            [{call, book_shim, add_book_existing,
              [isbn(S), title(), author(), 1, 1]},
             {call, book_shim, add_copy_existing, [isbn(S)]},
             {call, book_shim, borrow_copy_avail, [isbn(S)]},
             {call, book_shim, borrow_copy_unavail, [isbn(S)]},
             {call, book_shim, return_copy_existing, [isbn(S)]},
             {call, book_shim, return_copy_full, [isbn(S)]},
             {call, book_shim, find_book_by_isbn_exists, [isbn(S)]},
             {call, book_shim, find_book_by_author_matching, [author(S)]},
             {call, book_shim, find_book_by_title_matching, [title(S)]}]
    end,
    oneof(AlwaysPossible ++ ReliesOnState).
```

Elixir translation on page 335.

That's very repetitive, but it's also simple. Simplicity is good in a model, so that's an acceptable tradeoff. You'll note that we've split the call generators in two segments: those that don't need to look at the state to make sense (all calls about unknown or new data, where random stuff is fine), and those that *must* have access to existing state and keys to work (because you can only find an existing book by reading a book from the state). The stateful calls are never generated if no state is available.

Here are the new generators we need to make this work:

```
Erlang                  code/Bookstore/erlang/bookstore/test/prop_bookstore.erl
```

```erlang
isbn(State) ->
    elements(maps:keys(State)).

author(State) ->
    elements([partial(Author) || {_,_,Author,_,_} <- maps:values(State)]).

title(State) ->
    elements([partial(Title) || {_,Title,_,_,_} <- maps:values(State)]).

%% Create a partial string, built from a portion of a complete one.
partial(String) ->
    L = string:length(String),
    ?LET({Start, Len}, {range(0, L), non_neg_integer()},
        string:slice(String, Start, Len)).
```

```
Elixir                  code/Bookstore/elixir/bookstore/test/bookstore_test.exs
```

```elixir
def isbn(state), do: elements(Map.keys(state))

def author(s) do
  elements(for {_,_,author,_,_} <- Map.values(s), do: partial(author))
end

def title(s) do
  elements(for {_,title,_,_,_} <- Map.values(s), do: partial(title))
end

# create a partial string, built from a portion of a complete one
def partial(string) do
  string = IO.chardata_to_string(string)
  l = String.length(string)
  let {start, len} <- {range(0, l), non_neg_integer()} do
    String.slice(string, start, len)
  end
end
```

This will allow for quick generation, but won't be sufficient for the model to hold up in all circumstances.

Enforcing Preconditions

Since all our shim calls map to the same underlying functionality, we can use preconditions to enforce the requirements for each shimmed function name. Also remember that preconditions are essential to enforce constraints when shrinking, so we'll need to double-check constraints as well:

```erlang
%% Picks whether a command should be valid under the current state.
%% -- all the unknown calls
precondition(S, {call, _, add_book_new, [ISBN|_]}) ->
    not has_isbn(S, ISBN);
precondition(S, {call, _, add_copy_new, [ISBN]}) ->
    not has_isbn(S, ISBN);
precondition(S, {call, _, borrow_copy_unknown, [ISBN]}) ->
    not has_isbn(S, ISBN);
precondition(S, {call, _, return_copy_unknown, [ISBN]}) ->
    not has_isbn(S, ISBN);
precondition(S, {call, _, find_book_by_isbn_unknown, [ISBN]}) ->
    not has_isbn(S, ISBN);
precondition(S, {call, _, find_book_by_author_unknown, [Author]}) ->
    not like_author(S, Author);
precondition(S, {call, _, find_book_by_title_unknown, [Title]}) ->
    not like_title(S, Title);
precondition(S, {call, _, find_book_by_author_matching, [Author]}) ->
    like_author(S, Author);
precondition(S, {call, _, find_book_by_title_matching, [Title]}) ->
    like_title(S, Title);
%% -- all the calls with known ISBNs
precondition(S, {call, _Mod, _Fun, [ISBN|_]}) ->
    %% to hell with it, we blank match the rest since they're all
    %% constraints on existing ISBNs.
    has_isbn(S, ISBN).
```

Elixir translation on page 336.

These preconditions mostly reencode the same restrictions we had in command/1. It's all repetitive and trivial, but that's a good sign: our constraints *are* trivial and straightforward. Tests that are easy to reason about are good tests; tests that are almost as tricky as your system can also be good tests, but they'll require more care and attention. Taking a more deterministic shim-based approach is exactly what creates this repetitive-but-simple code. If this annoys you and you prefer less repetitive code, you're free to avoid shims, but be aware that modifying, expanding, or debugging your tests may prove trickier later on.

You'll also note that pretty much all preconditions rely on the following helper functions:

Erlang	code/Bookstore/erlang/bookstore/test/prop_bookstore.erl

```erlang
%%%%%%%%%%%%%%%%
%%% Helpers %%%
%%%%%%%%%%%%%%%%
has_isbn(Map, ISBN) ->
    maps:is_key(ISBN, Map).
```

```erlang
like_author(Map, Auth) ->
    lists:any(fun({_,_,A,_,_}) -> nomatch =/= string:find(A, Auth) end,
              maps:values(Map)).

like_title(Map, Title) ->
    lists:any(fun({_,T,_,_,_}) -> nomatch =/= string:find(T, Title) end,
              maps:values(Map)).
```

Elixir	code/Bookstore/elixir/bookstore/test/bookstore_test.exs

```elixir
## Helpers
def has_isbn(map, isbn), do: Map.has_key?(map, isbn)

def like_author(map, auth) do
  Enum.any?(
    Map.values(map),
    fn {_,_,a,_,_} -> contains?(a, auth) end
  )
end

def like_title(map, title) do
  Enum.any?(
    Map.values(map),
    fn {_,t,_,_,_} -> contains?(t, title) end
  )
end

defp contains?(string_or_chars_full, string_or_char_pattern) do
  string = IO.chardata_to_string(string_or_chars_full)
  pattern = IO.chardata_to_string(string_or_char_pattern)
  String.contains?(string, pattern)
end
defp contains_any?(string_or_chars, patterns) when is_list(patterns) do
  string = IO.chardata_to_string(string_or_chars)
  patterns = for p <- patterns, do: IO.chardata_to_string(p)
  String.contains?(string, patterns)
end
```

The has_isbn/2 function checks whether the given ISBN is in the current state. The has_author/2 and has_title/2 checks are used for functions that wrap bookstore_db:find_book_by_author/1 and bookstore_db:find_book_by_title/1, which both use fuzzy-matching logic (LIKE "%string%" in SQL). This fuzzy matching means that we're not looking for full titles and author names, only partial ones, and so we must filter them explicitly.

The next step will be to drive state transitions forward.

Advancing the Model State

We can use the next_state callback to define state transitions:

Erlang   code/Bookstore/erlang/bookstore/test/prop_bookstore.erl

---

```erlang
%% Assuming the postcondition for a call was true, update the model
%% accordingly for the test to proceed.
next_state(State, _, {call, _, add_book_new,
                      [ISBN, Title, Author, Owned, Avail]}) ->
   State#{ISBN => {ISBN, Title, Author, Owned, Avail}};
next_state(State, _, {call, _, add_copy_existing, [ISBN]}) ->
   #{ISBN := {ISBN, Title, Author, Owned, Avail}} = State,
   State#{ISBN => {ISBN, Title, Author, Owned+1, Avail+1}};
next_state(State, _, {call, _, borrow_copy_avail, [ISBN]}) ->
   #{ISBN := {ISBN, Title, Author, Owned, Avail}} = State,
   State#{ISBN => {ISBN, Title, Author, Owned, Avail-1}};
next_state(State, _, {call, _, return_copy_existing, [ISBN]}) ->
   #{ISBN := {ISBN, Title, Author, Owned, Avail}} = State,
   State#{ISBN => {ISBN, Title, Author, Owned, Avail+1}};
next_state(State, _Res, {call, _Mod, _Fun, _Args}) ->
   NewState = State,
   NewState.
```

Elixir   code/Bookstore/elixir/bookstore/test/bookstore_test.exs

---

```elixir
# Assuming the postcondition for a call was true, update the model
# accordingly for the test to proceed
def next_state(
  state,
  _,
  {:call, _, :add_book_new, [isbn, title, author, owned, avail]}
) do
  Map.put(state, isbn, {isbn, title, author, owned, avail})
end
def next_state(state, _, {:call, _, :add_copy_existing, [isbn]}) do
  {^isbn, title, author, owned, avail} = state[isbn]
  Map.put(state, isbn, {isbn, title, author, owned + 1, avail + 1})
end
def next_state(state, _, {:call, _, :borrow_copy_avail, [isbn]}) do
  {^isbn, title, author, owned, avail} = state[isbn]
  Map.put(state, isbn, {isbn, title, author, owned, avail - 1})
end
def next_state(state, _, {:call, _, :return_copy_existing, [isbn]}) do
  {^isbn, title, author, owned, avail} = state[isbn]
  Map.put(state, isbn, {isbn, title, author, owned, avail + 1})
end
def next_state(state, _res, {:call, _mod, _fun, _args}) do
  new_state = state
  new_state
end
```

This one is much shorter, thanks to the shim. Only calls that we expect to be successful change the state, the rest of them leave it unchanged. Since we baked all conditions for success or failure in the function name (and through preconditions), we need to do very little dynamic detection to know how to update the state.

With transitions in place, validating that everything is correct is the last step.

Checking Postconditions

You'll find that the simplification due to shims also applies to postconditions, which we can write to all rely on pattern matching:

```
%% Given the state `State' *prior* to the call `{call, Mod, Fun, Args}',
%% determine whether the result `Res' (coming from the actual system)
%% makes sense.
postcondition(_, {_, _, add_book_new, _}, ok) ->
    true;
postcondition(_, {_, _, add_book_existing, _}, {error, _}) ->
    true;
postcondition(_, {_, _, add_copy_existing, _}, ok) ->
    true;
postcondition(_, {_, _, add_copy_new, _}, {error, not_found}) ->
    true;
postcondition(_, {_, _, borrow_copy_avail, _}, ok) ->
    true;
postcondition(_, {_, _, borrow_copy_unavail, _}, {error, unavailable}) ->
    true;
postcondition(_, {_, _, borrow_copy_unknown, _}, {error, not_found}) ->
    true;
postcondition(_, {_, _, return_copy_full, _}, {error, _}) ->
    true;
postcondition(_, {_, _, return_copy_existing, _}, ok) ->
    true;
postcondition(_, {_, _, return_copy_unknown, _}, {error, not_found}) ->
    true;
```

Elixir translation on page 337.

For all of these clauses, all we have to do is pattern match on functions and their result—we don't even need to look at the state (the first argument as '_') since we know what we want ahead of time.

Do note that most of these functions also turn out to be the side-effectful ones, those we expect will modify the state. Aside from getting the result telling us that they worked or not (ok or {error, _}), most write-only operations are not *observable* to the user; you have to trust the system. The impact of these functions is instead generally visible only by checking side effects (like logs or metrics), or when reading data back from the system.

And reading data is exactly what our next batch of postconditions worry about. This is what will make sure that the ok values returned by write operations are not just lies. Let's start with reads with an ISBN lookup:

Erlang	code/Bookstore/erlang/bookstore/test/prop_bookstore.erl

```erlang
postcondition(S, {_, _, find_book_by_isbn_exists, [ISBN]}, Res) ->
    Res =:= {ok, [maps:get(ISBN, S, undefined)]};
postcondition(_, {_, _, find_book_by_isbn_unknown, _}, {ok, []}) ->
    true;
```

Elixir	code/Bookstore/elixir/bookstore/test/bookstore_test.exs

```elixir
def postcondition(s, {_, _, :find_book_by_isbn_exists, [isbn]}, res) do
  res == {:ok, [Map.get(s, isbn, nil)]}
end

def postcondition(_, {_, _, :find_book_by_isbn_unknown, _}, {:ok, []}) do
  true
end
```

That's rather straightforward. The function looks for an ISBN, and we want to make sure the record we get from the model state (S) is the same stuff we get in the full Res result. An unknown ISBN just returns {ok, []} and that's it.

The two other reader functions have to do with matching a substring with the author and the title. We can do this using string:find(String, Pattern), which will tell whether Pattern is anywhere in String:

Erlang	code/Bookstore/erlang/bookstore/test/prop_bookstore.erl

```erlang
postcondition(S, {_, _, find_book_by_author_matching, [Auth]}, {ok,Res}) ->
    Map = maps:filter(fun(_, {_,_,A,_,_}) ->
                        nomatch =/= string:find(A, Auth)
                      end, S),
    lists:sort(Res) =:= lists:sort(maps:values(Map));
postcondition(_, {_, _, find_book_by_author_unknown, _}, {ok, []}) ->
    true;
postcondition(S, {_, _, find_book_by_title_matching, [Title]}, {ok,Res}) ->
    Map = maps:filter(fun(_, {_,T,_,_,_}) ->
                        nomatch =/= string:find(T, Title)
                      end, S),
    lists:sort(Res) =:= lists:sort(maps:values(Map));
postcondition(_, {_, _, find_book_by_title_unknown, _}, {ok, []}) ->
    true;
```

Elixir   code/Bookstore/elixir/bookstore/test/bookstore_test.exs

```elixir
def postcondition(
  state,
  {_, _, :find_book_by_author_matching, [auth]},
  {:ok, res}
) do
  map = :maps.filter(
    fn _, {_,_,a,_,_} -> contains?(a, auth) end,
    state
  )
  Enum.sort(res) == Enum.sort(Map.values(map))
end

def postcondition(_, {_,_,:find_book_by_author_unknown,_}, {:ok,[]}) do
  true
end

def postcondition(
  state,
  {_, _, :find_book_by_title_matching, [title]},
  {:ok, res}
) do
  map = :maps.filter(
    fn _, {_,t,_,_,_} -> contains?(t, title) end,
    state
  )
  Enum.sort(res) == Enum.sort(Map.values(map))
end

def postcondition(_, {_,_,:find_book_by_title_unknown,_}, {:ok,[]}) do
  true
end
```

Note that the result set in Res is *never* used to drive the results. The expected result set is entirely built from the model state S, and only then do we check whether the results from the actual system match. The model drives the test and validates the system, not the other way around.

Unimportant Ordering

 Whenever ordering is not important in a result set, use lists:sort/1 on both the model's result and the system's result so that their initial ordering is made irrelevant

---

Finally, all the cases not covered here are considered invalid:

Erlang	code/Bookstore/erlang/bookstore/test/prop_bookstore.erl

```erlang
postcondition(_State, {call, _Mod, _Fun, _Args}, _Res) ->
    io:format("~nnon-matching postcondition: {~p,~p,~p} -> ~p~n",
              [_Mod, _Fun, _Args, _Res]),
    false.
```

Elixir	code/Bookstore/elixir/bookstore/test/bookstore_test.exs

```elixir
def postcondition(_state, {:call, mod, fun, args}, res) do
  mod = inspect(mod)
  fun = inspect(fun)
  args = inspect(args)
  res = inspect(res)
  IO.puts(
    "\nnon-matching postcondition: {#{mod}, #{fun}, #{args}} -> #{res}"
  )
  false
end
```

This is a useful clause to have since all the direct matching on results in the previous clauses means whatever didn't fit before is caught here. The last catch-all clause always being false is your best shot at catching errors early on.

Think Like an Operator

If you find yourself in situations where you find it hard to write a model that works predictably without first poking at the running system, it means the people operating your system will likely have the same problem. Similarly, if you find it hard to validate the data you received in a postcondition because of lots of possible valid outputs, people debugging your system will feel the same pain. This is a good signal that you may need to rethink your approach a bit.

Think the way an operator would while debugging in production. If the system is too unpredictable, you can modify it to match a simpler model when possible, or broaden the model to be more relaxed. If relaxing the model feels unsafe and playing way too loose with your tests, that's how your operators would feel. Another option is to make the system more *observable*, meaning that you leave traces that make it easy for an operator to guess what the system's internal state is: should logs or metrics be produced and consulted? Can events be generated or messages sent? Can these be wrapped up and considered regular output? Take a holistic view of your system, consider what are valid inputs and outputs, and adjust the commands and make your tests work in a friendlier way, the way a human would enjoy it.

It can only result in more reliable and operable software for everyone.

With this done, our initial model is complete. We can run the tests against it and progressively refine both the model and the system until we trust it to do a good job in production.

Refining the Tests

We've got a complete rather deterministic model, with a complete piece of code to test. What we have to do now is just run tests until they fail—if they don't, that's a bit scary, so we should feel free to *cause* a failure ourselves—and then fix the problems as they come up. That step could save us from this kind of release cycle:

1. Write code.

2. Test code as usual.

3. Deploy or release the code.

4. A customer opens a ticket.

5. After scratching your head to figure out how in hell they get the problem, you finally reproduce it.

6. Fix the problem.

7. Go to 1.

Instead, we're now more likely to have this release cycle:

1. Write code.

2. Stateful property test the code.

3. Find a problem that the framework easily reproduces for you.

4. Deploy or release the code.

5. Wait a lot longer before getting a customer bug report. (It will still happen given enough time.)

6. ... and so on.

You have to expect bugs to still exist in the system, just fewer of them, and a much shorter bug-detection-to-bug-fixing cycle than you would otherwise have.

Order of Failures

Property tests are probabilistic. If you are following along, you may find different issues (or the same issues in a different order) than those in this text. This is normal, and rerunning the property a few times may yield different errors each time.

The first error in this section can't be reproduced easily in Elixir, where the string() generator is not exported by PropCheck. Instead, utf8() is used (also available in Erlang). However, utf8() more frequently returns well-formed Unicode data that doesn't cause the failure.

Let's see what kind of bugs we get with the bookstore:

```
$ rebar3 proper
«build and test output»
!
Failed: After 4 test(s).
«initial counterexample»
Shrinking (0 time(s))
[{set,{var,1},{call,book_shim,add_book_new,[<<57,55,57,45,57,56,53,45,54,56,
 55,45,54,48,51,45,56>>,<<>>,[0],1,1]}}]
History: [
  {#{},
   {error,
    {pgsql_error,
        [{severity,<<"ERROR">>},
         {{unknown,86},<<"ERROR">>},
         {code,<<"22021">>},
         {message, <<"invalid byte sequence for encoding \"UTF8\": 0x00">>},
         {file,<<"wchar.c">>},
         {line,<<"2017">>},
         {routine,<<"report_invalid_encoding">>}]}}}]
State: #{}
Result: {postcondition,false}
```

Running the tests then fails on unicode values of 0x00, meaning that the protocol likely uses null-terminated strings,[5] which causes failures. Anyone using this PostgreSQL driver needs to protect themselves against such strings.

For now, we'll assume that those invalid unicode values should either be filtered somewhere else (possibly at the same place that should validate that ISBNs have the right format) or that a bunch of other properties or unit tests will handle these, and we'll instead work around it by making sure our generators don't generate that data anymore. In fact, we'll find a lot of other troublesome characters: % and _ will influence PostgreSQL search in ways

---

5.   https://en.wikipedia.org/wiki/Null-terminated_string

that string:find/2 wouldn't, and \ will mess with escaping in SQL whereas our model won't care.

We have to ask ourselves whether what we want to test here is the minutiae of the SQL string handling, or whether these strings are a tool we use to validate the state transitions of our stateful model. This is the point where you can decide to split your property into two distinct properties:

1. One property to test the search patterns explicitly—to see if there are risky things happening with special characters

2. One property to test the state transitions and various matches

We'll focus on the second one, by ignoring all kinds of special characters in searches, titles, and authors:

Erlang	code/Bookstore/erlang/bookstore/test/prop_bookstore.erl

```erlang
title() -> friendly_unicode().

author() -> friendly_unicode().

friendly_unicode() ->
    ?LET(X, ?SUCHTHAT(S, string(),
                      not lists:member(0, S) andalso
                      nomatch =:= string:find(S, "\\") andalso
                      nomatch =:= string:find(S, "_") andalso
                      nomatch =:= string:find(S, "%") andalso
                      string:length(S) < 256),
         elements([X, unicode:characters_to_binary(X)])).
```

Elixir	code/Bookstore/elixir/bookstore/test/bookstore_test.exs

```elixir
def title(), do: friendly_unicode()

def author(), do: friendly_unicode()

def friendly_unicode() do
  bad_chars = [<<0>>, "\\", "_", "%"]
  friendly_gen =
    such_that s <- utf8(), when: (not contains_any?(s, bad_chars)) &&
      String.length(s) < 256
  let x <- friendly_gen do
      elements([x, String.to_charlist(x)])
  end
end
```

This makes sure that the character 0 never makes it through the generator, but also blocks backslashes and other troublesome characters. This will let us test our transitions without having to care about edge cases like that (which we decided should belong in another property). Let's run the test again and see what we get:

```
$ rebar3 proper
≪build and test output≫
!
Failed: After 7 test(s).
≪initial counterexample≫
Shrinking (2 time(s))
non-matching postcondition: {book_shim,return_copy_unknown,
                        [<<"99957-261-1-X">>]} -> {error, {{update, 0}, []}}
[{set,{var,1},{call,book_shim,return_copy_unknown,[<<57,57,57,53,55,45,50,
 54,49,45,49,45,88>>]}}]
History: [{#{},{error,{{update,0},[]}}}]
State: #{}
Result: {postcondition,false}
```

Interesting. So we fell through a case where return_copy_unknown returns an error for 0 updated rows. Our postcondition for this specific deterministic function instead expects this:

```
postcondition(_, {_, _, return_copy_unknown, _}, {error, not_found}) ->
    true;
```

The original code for this is in bookstore_db and can be fixed by adding one clause to handle_single_update/1 returning {error, not_found} as expected, and fixing all the functions using it:

Erlang	code/Bookstore/erlang/bookstore/src/bookstore_db.erl

```
handle_select({{select, _}, List}) -> {ok, List};
handle_select(Error) -> Error.

handle_single_update({{update,1}, _}) -> ok;
handle_single_update({{update,0}, _}) -> {error, not_found};
handle_single_update({error, Reason}) -> {error, Reason};
handle_single_update(Other) -> {error, Other}.
```

Elixir	code/Bookstore/elixir/bookstore/lib/bookstore/db.ex

```
defp handle_select({{:select, _}, list}), do: {:ok, list}
defp handle_select(error), do: error

defp handle_single_update({{:update, 1}, _}), do: :ok
defp handle_single_update({{:update, 0}, _}), do: {:error, :not_found}
defp handle_single_update({:error, reason}), do: {:error, reason}
defp handle_single_update(other), do: {:error, other}
```

We're good to run tests again. Let's see what we get:

```
$ rebar3 proper
«build output»
........!
Failed: After 10 test(s).
«initial counterexample»

Shrinking ..(2 time(s))
[{set,{var,2},{call,book_shim,add_book_new,[<<57,55,56,45,57,55,49,45,56,
  55,49,57,45,55,55,45,54>>,<<>>,[2,13],1,1]}},{set,{var,4},
  {call,book_shim,find_book_by_author_matching,[[13]]}}]
History: [{#{},ok},
          {#{<<"978-971-8719-77-6">> =>
                 {<<"978-971-8719-77-6">>,<<>>,[2,13],1,1}},
           {ok,[{<<"978-971-8719-77-6">>,<<>>,<<2,13>>,1,1}]}}]
State: #{<<"978-971-8719-77-6">> =>
             {<<"978-971-8719-77-6">>,<<>>,[2,13],1,1}}
Result: {postcondition,false}
```

This one's interesting. If we do the check by hand, things seem to be reasonable. We're looking for a book written by an author whose name contains the character 13 in it (that is U+000D, also known as *carriage return*, or \r). The database returns one book with that value, written by <<2,13>>, whereas our state contains the book author [2,13]. Those are the same author! We've just been hit by a bug in our test caused by our desire to support both UTF-8 binaries and character lists in the same interface.

Iterative Development

 Although we developed the model at once and then refined it in two distinct steps, this is mainly done for the clarity of text rather than an ideal workflow. Especially when getting started, you may find it easier to start modeling one piece of functionality at a time, and then test it end-to-end while refining it. With this done, you can start validating more functionality. A more iterative approach makes for a smoother learning curve.

The fix to this problem is to revisit our postconditions. We have to make sure that the string comparisons they contain won't care whether the string is a binary or a list of characters. We can devise some custom functions that will do that for us:

Erlang	code/Bookstore/erlang/bookstore/test/prop_bookstore.erl

```erlang
books_equal([], []) ->
    true;
books_equal([A|As], [B|Bs]) ->
    book_equal(A, B) andalso books_equal(As, Bs);
books_equal(_, _) ->
    false.

book_equal({ISBNA, TitleA, AuthorA, OwnedA, AvailA},
           {ISBNB, TitleB, AuthorB, OwnedB, AvailB}) ->
    {ISBNA, OwnedA, AvailA} =:= {ISBNB, OwnedB, AvailB}
    andalso
    string:equal(TitleA, TitleB) andalso string:equal(AuthorA, AuthorB).
```

Elixir	code/Bookstore/elixir/bookstore/test/bookstore_test.exs

```elixir
defp books_equal([], []) do
  true
end
defp books_equal([a | as], [b | bs]) do
  book_equal(a, b) && books_equal(as, bs)
end
defp books_equal(_, _) do
  false
end

defp book_equal(
       {isbn_a, title_a, author_a, owned_a, avail_a},
       {isbn_b, title_b, author_b, owned_b, avail_b}
     ) do
  {isbn_a, owned_a, avail_a} == {isbn_b, owned_b, avail_b} &&
    String.equivalent?(
      IO.chardata_to_string(title_a),
      IO.chardata_to_string(title_b)
    ) &&
    String.equivalent?(
      IO.chardata_to_string(author_a),
      IO.chardata_to_string(author_b)
    )
end
```

The first function takes two lists of books, and checks that all of its elements are the same, with the help of the second function (book_equal/2). The latter one tests the equality of all fields with a format known to be stable, and then uses string:equal/2 on the fields with varying unicode encodings to safely compare them for equality. The functions can be edited in our existing postconditions:

Erlang   code/Bookstore/erlang/bookstore/test/prop_bookstore.erl

---

```
«bunch of postconditions»
postcondition(S, {_, _, find_book_by_isbn_exists, [ISBN]}, {ok, [Res]}) ->
    book_equal(Res, maps:get(ISBN, S, undefined));
«bunch of postconditions»
postcondition(S, {_, _, find_book_by_author_matching, [Auth]}, {ok,Res}) ->
    Map = maps:filter(fun(_, {_,_,A,_,_}) ->
                                nomatch =/= string:find(A, Auth)
                      end, S),
    books_equal(lists:sort(Res), lists:sort(maps:values(Map)));
«bunch of postconditions»
postcondition(S, {_, _, find_book_by_title_matching, [Title]}, {ok,Res}) ->
    Map = maps:filter(fun(_, {_,T,_,_,_}) ->
                                nomatch =/= string:find(T, Title)
                      end, S),
    books_equal(lists:sort(Res), lists:sort(maps:values(Map)));
```

Elixir translation on page 338.

The first edit replaces one of our existing clauses and makes it use the new comparison function. The last two clauses work on lists and use books_equal/2 instead of book_equal/2.

Hopefully we're good to go now. We can run the tests again, crossing our fingers real hard:

```
$ rebar3 proper
«build output»
.......................
non-matching postcondition:
 {book_shim,borrow_copy_unavail,[<<"7-080930-26-5">>]} -> ok
!
Failed: After 25 test(s).
«counterexample and shrinking»
[{set,{var,1},{call,book_shim,add_book_new,[
    <<55,45,48,56,48,57,51,48,45,50,54,45,53>>,<<11,8,8>>,[20,10,2],1,1]}},
 {set,{var,5},{call,book_shim,borrow_copy_unavail,
    [<<55,45,48,56,48,57,51,48,45,50,54,45,53>>]}}]
History: [{#{},ok},
         {#{<<"7-080930-26-5">> =>
                {<<"7-080930-26-5">>,<<11,8,8>>,[20,10,2],1,1}},
          ok}]
State: #{<<"7-080930-26-5">> =>
             {<<"7-080930-26-5">>,<<11,8,8>>,[20,10,2],1,1}}
Result: {postcondition,false}
```

Good news, we have a failure. Have a look at the shrunken counterexample:

1. add_book_new(ISBNA, Title, Author, 1, 1) -> ok

2. borrow_copy_unavail(ISBNA) -> ok

It appears our problem is our model allows calling book_shim:borrow_copy_unavail/1 when the copy is in fact available. This is a problem with our preconditions not checking the right constraints. Currently, it is validated with this:

```erlang
%% -- all the calls with known ISBNs
precondition(S, {call, _Mod, _Fun, [ISBN|_]}) ->
    %% to hell with it, we blank match the rest since they're all
    %% constraints on existing ISBNs, no matter the number of arguments
    has_isbn(S, ISBN).
```

But it visibly doesn't check for book availability. Let's add clauses for this call specifically, and the bookstore_db:return_copy calls too, since they've the same problem:

Erlang   code/Bookstore/erlang/bookstore/test/prop_bookstore.erl

```erlang
precondition(S, {call, _, borrow_copy_avail, [ISBN]}) ->
    0 < element(5, maps:get(ISBN, S));
precondition(S, {call, _, borrow_copy_unavail, [ISBN]}) ->
    0 =:= element(5, maps:get(ISBN, S));
precondition(S, {call, _, return_copy_full, [ISBN]}) ->
    {_, _, _, Owned, Avail} = maps:get(ISBN, S),
    Owned =:= Avail;
precondition(S, {call, _, return_copy_existing, [ISBN]}) ->
    {_, _, _, Owned, Avail} = maps:get(ISBN, S),
    Owned =/= Avail;
«more clauses»
```

Elixir   code/Bookstore/elixir/bookstore/test/bookstore_test.exs

```elixir
  def precondition(s, {:call, _, :borrow_copy_avail, [isbn]}) do
    0 < elem(Map.get(s, isbn), 4)
  end
  def precondition(s, {:call, _, :borrow_copy_unavail, [isbn]}) do
    0 == elem(Map.get(s, isbn), 4)
  end
  def precondition(s, {:call, _, :return_copy_full, [isbn]}) do
    {_, _, _, owned, avail} = Map.get(s, isbn)
    owned == avail
  end
  def precondition(s, {:call, _, :return_copy_existing, [isbn]}) do
    {_, _, _, owned, avail} = Map.get(s, isbn)
    owned != avail
  end
«more clauses»
```

Let's try again, with one more run:

```
$ rebar3 proper
«build output»
.....................
non-matching postcondition: {book_shim,return_copy_full,
                             [<<"979-976-2-33736-X">>]} -> ok
!
Failed: After 23 test(s).
[{set,{var,1}, {call,book_shim,find_book_by_title_unknown,
            [<<9,2,4,7,10,7>>]}},
 {set,{var,2}, {call,book_shim,borrow_copy_unknown,
            [<<"978-90-8387-621-2">>]}},
 {set,{var,3}, {call,book_shim,add_book_new,
            [<<"979-976-2-33736-X">>,[7,12,17],<<1,33>>,1,1]}},
 {set,{var,4}, {call,book_shim,add_book_new,
            [<<"7-7662357-3-X">>,[2,4,25,1,10,10,4,16],[2],1,1]}},
 {set,{var,5}, {call,book_shim,find_book_by_isbn_unknown,
            [<<"979-977-879-375-2">>]}},
 {set,{var,6}, {call,book_shim,add_copy_new,[<<"978-7-2-1624032-X">>]}},
 {set,{var,7}, {call,book_shim,find_book_by_isbn_exists,
            [<<"979-976-2-33736-X">>]}},
 {set,{var,8}, {call,book_shim,return_copy_full,
            [<<"979-976-2-33736-X">>]}}]
«more output»
Shrinking
«shrinking»
===>
0/1 properties passed, 1 failed
===> Failed test cases:
prop_bookstore:prop_test() ->
  {'EXIT',
   {{badkey,<<"979-976-2-33736-X">>},
    [{maps,get,[<<"979-976-2-33736-X">>,#{}],[]},
     {prop_bookstore,precondition,2,
      [{file, "Bookstore/erlang/bookstore/test/prop_bookstore.erl"},
       {line,81}]},
«more stacktrace»
```

Now we've got a problem! Shrinking fails with a hard crash whereas the initial failure seemed legitimate. We'll have to go figure how to debug this property.

Debugging Stateful Properties

The previously failing property is interesting. If you look at the initial counterexample, it looks like a regular failure where our model or the system might have been wrong, but the shrinking totally imploded, and the source of failure isn't obvious. In this section, we'll revisit the shrinking mechanism of stateful properties to understand what goes on exactly and how to get PropEr to solve our problems for us.

Let's first compare the initial failing command set and then compare it to the shrunken one. The initial failure was caused by the following sequence of events:

1. find_book_by_title_unknown(_) -> {ok, []}

2. borrow_copy_unknown(_) -> {error, not_found}

3. add_book_new(ISBNA, TitleA, AuthorA, 1, 1) -> ok

4. add_book_new(ISBNB, TitleB, AuthorB, 1, 1) -> ok

5. find_book_by_isbn_unknown(_) -> {ok, []}

6. add_copy_new(_) -> {error, not_found}

7. find_book_by_isbn_exists(ISBNA) -> {ok, [BookA]}

8. return_copy_full(ISBNA) -> ok

So we might have a legitimate bug since we successfully returned a copy of a book that was never borrowed, but the shrinking isn't helping us since it appears it can't prune the irrelevant operations out of the list without crashing. This isn't great. How come shrinking failed us? The solution lies in the shrinking model.

In stateful properties, when we're given a sequence of commands [A,B,C,D,E,F] that yields a failure, shrinking will be done by progressively removing commands from the sequence to see if a shorter one can cause the problem as shown in the figure on page 275.

Then the framework might decide that [A,C,F,G] is the minimal sequence of commands able to reproduce the failure. The caveat with this approach is that if command B introduced the state required to make the precondition for D work, removing B will cause an inconsistency for D. In this previous illustration, the third list of commands may crash for the wrong reason and point toward a bug that doesn't actually exist, hiding the real one that triggered the initial failure. The distinction is very important:

- Deciding which commands to generate within command/1 works, but must be seen as an optimization to speed up generation.

- Encoding the constraints of command generation into preconditions is mandatory for shrinking to work.

In our case with the bookstore, the mistake we made was to base our preconditions for book borrowing and returning on the assumption that the requested ISBN will always be in the map, with calls such as maps:get(ISBN, Map), which crashes if ISBN isn't in Map. So we can take the full sequence of operations that led to a failure and randomly remove some of them to see if it still fails:

1.   ~~find_book_by_title_unknown(_) -> {ok, []}~~

2.   borrow_copy_unknown(_) -> {error, not_found}

3.   ~~add_book_new(ISBNA, TitleA, AuthorA, 1, 1) -> ok~~

4.   add_book_new(ISBNB, TitleB, AuthorB, 1, 1) -> ok

5.   find_book_by_isbn_unknown(_) -> {ok, []}

6.   ~~add_copy_new(_) -> {error, not_found}~~

7.   find_book_by_isbn_exists(ISBNA) -> {ok, [BookA]}

8.   return_copy_full(ISBNA) -> ok

We may get in a scenario where find_book_by_isbn_exists(ISBNA) was initially valid at step 7, but now can never be true again since we took out the addition of that book (third item of the list). Shrinking would then start misleading us.

Since *all* constraints must be repeated in the preconditions, we have to reedit our clauses:

Erlang	code/Bookstore/erlang/bookstore/test/prop_bookstore.erl

```erlang
precondition(S, {call, _, borrow_copy_avail, [ISBN]}) ->
    0 < element(5, maps:get(ISBN, S, {fake,fake,fake,fake,0}));
precondition(S, {call, _, borrow_copy_unavail, [ISBN]}) ->
    0 =:= element(5, maps:get(ISBN, S, {fake,fake,fake,fake,1}));
precondition(S, {call, _, return_copy_full, [ISBN]}) ->
    {_, _, _, Owned, Avail} = maps:get(ISBN, S, {fake,fake,fake,0,0}),
    Owned =:= Avail andalso Owned =/= 0;
precondition(S, {call, _, return_copy_existing, [ISBN]}) ->
    {_, _, _, Owned, Avail} = maps:get(ISBN, S, {fake,fake,fake,0,0}),
    Owned =/= Avail andalso Owned =/= 0;
```

Elixir	code/Bookstore/elixir/bookstore/test/bookstore_test.exs

```elixir
  def precondition(s, {:call, _, :borrow_copy_avail, [isbn]}) do
    0 < elem(Map.get(s, isbn, {:fake, :fake, :fake, :fake, 0}), 4)
  end
  def precondition(s, {:call, _, :borrow_copy_unavail, [isbn]}) do
    0 == elem(Map.get(s, isbn, {:fake, :fake, :fake, :fake, 1}), 4)
  end
  def precondition(s, {:call, _, :return_copy_full, [isbn]}) do
    {_, _, _, owned, avail} = Map.get(s, isbn, {:fake, :fake, :fake, 0, 0})
    owned == avail && owned != 0
  end
  def precondition(s, {:call, _, :return_copy_existing, [isbn]}) do
    {_, _, _, owned, avail} = Map.get(s, isbn, {:fake, :fake, :fake, 0, 0})
    owned != avail && owned != 0
  end
«more clauses»
```

By using default values that are fake and guaranteed to make the precondition fail in maps:get/3, we can ensure that removing a previously vital command for the current command will be seen as invalid by PropEr, and shrinking will only work on the actual bug. We can run the test one more time, and this time it should be able to shrink right:

```
$ rebar3 proper
«build output and similar failure as before»
Shrinking (3 time(s))
[{set,{var,2},{call,book_shim,add_book_new,
  [<<56,56,45,49,53,45,57,54,54,50,48,45,88>>,
  <<3,8>>,<<12,15,2,7,5>>,1,1]}},
 {set,{var,4},{call,book_shim,return_copy_full,
  [<<56,56,45,49,53,45,57,54,54,50,48,45,88>>]}}]
```

```
History: [{#{},ok},
         {#{<<"88-15-96620-X">> =>
               {<<"88-15-96620-X">>,<<3,8>>,<<12,15,2,7,5>>,1,1}},
          ok}]
State: #{<<"88-15-96620-X">> =>
               {<<"88-15-96620-X">>,<<3,8>>,<<12,15,2,7,5>>,1,1}}
Result: {postcondition,false}
```

Finally! A failure that makes sense, is not related to special characters, and appears to be in our actual system. Adding a book with one copy available, and then somehow returning that copy returns ok rather than the {error, _} tuple we expected. This points to the SQL query behind it all being wrong. You'll have to change the :return_copy query:

Bookstore/erlang/bookstore/priv/queries.sql
```sql
-- Return a copy of a book
-- :return_copy
UPDATE books SET available = available + 1
WHERE isbn = $1 AND available < owned;
```

If you run the tests once more, you'll find a problem with the function returning {error, not_found} rather than {error, unavailable}. The problem with this is that because of the WHERE clause in SQL, we don't know if an update operation fails because a book is not found, or because it is no longer available. To do so, we have to do two distinct checks:

Erlang	code/Bookstore/erlang/bookstore/src/bookstore_db.erl

```erlang
%% @doc Borrow a copy of a book; reduces the count of available
%% copies by one. Who borrowed the book is not tracked at this
%% moment and is left as an exercise to the reader.
borrow_copy(ISBN) ->
    case find_book_by_isbn(ISBN) of
        {error, Reason} -> {error, Reason};
        {ok, []} -> {error, not_found};
        {ok, _} ->
            case handle_single_update(run_query(borrow_copy, [ISBN])) of
                {error, not_found} -> {error, unavailable}; % rewrite error
                Other -> Other
            end
    end.
```

Elixir	code/Bookstore/elixir/bookstore/lib/bookstore/db.ex

```elixir
@doc """
Borrow a copy of a book; reduces the count of available copies by one.
Who borrowed the book is not tracked at this moment and is left as an
exercise to the reader.
"""
```

```elixir
def borrow_copy(isbn) do
  case find_book_by_isbn(isbn) do
    {:error, reason} ->
      {:error, reason}
    {:ok, []} ->
      {:error, :not_found}
    {:ok, _} ->
      case handle_single_update(run_query(:borrow_copy, [isbn])) do
        {:error, :not_found} ->
          {:error, :unavailable}
        other ->
          other
      end
  end
end
```

You can run the tests, knowing that it will now finally pass:

```
$ rebar3 proper -n 1000
«lots of periods»
OK: Passed 1000 test(s).
```

That was quite a bit of work for a rather straightforward application, but we found a few tricky bugs that would've been hard to find otherwise. We've also found interesting properties about the SQL protocol (it can't support NULL characters in strings) and further things to test with regards to escaping. We'll leave that for some other time, since now we'll get to try our system with parallel tests.

Parallel Tests

As with the last chapter, the parallel version of our system can be adapted by just declaring a new property and reusing the same model, to see if any glaring concurrency issue can be found.

You just have to add the parallel property to the same file:

Erlang	code/Bookstore/erlang/bookstore/test/prop_bookstore.erl

```erlang
prop_parallel() ->
    ?SETUP(fun() ->
        {ok, Apps} = application:ensure_all_started(bookstore),
        fun() -> [application:stop(App) || App <- Apps], ok end
    end,
    ?FORALL(Cmds, parallel_commands(?MODULE),
        begin
            bookstore_db:setup(),
            {History, State, Result} = run_parallel_commands(?MODULE, Cmds),
```

```
        bookstore_db:teardown(),
        ?WHENFAIL(io:format("=======~n"
                            "Failing command sequence:~n~p~n"
                            "At state: ~p~n"
                            "=======~n"
                            "Result: ~p~n"
                            "History: ~p~n",
                            [Cmds, State,Result,History]),
                aggregate(command_names(Cmds), Result =:= ok))
    end)
).
```

Elixir translation on page 339.

Once again, few changes are required aside from the name of the generator function and the one to run commands. We can run it, and see it pass:

```
$ rebar3 proper -n 1000 -p prop_parallel
《lots of periods》
OK: Passed 1000 test(s).
```

As we also saw in last chapter, the PropEr parallel tests are not necessarily great at finding concurrency issues, so we shouldn't take this as a proof of success. You can try to add erlang:yield() calls in multiple areas, but it won't necessarily uncover much. Careful analysis can always help clarify things.

It turns out that by default, any PostgreSQL query runs in an implicit transaction even if you don't specify one.[6] Those transactions run in *read committed* isolation levels, and are all simple SELECT and UPDATE queries with no external data and no need for reads from other queries. This means the operations are safe for concurrency.[7] The one case that could look funky is the last one we changed where we check whether a book exists before borrowing it. Since the two operations aren't in a transaction, there could be a risk of bad results where the wrong kind of error is returned, but no operation would succeed where it shouldn't.

In any case, these tests will help in case implementations change (say, using epgsql[8] instead of pgsql), or when some unsafe query usage or pooling takes place, rather than one connection per request like the project currently uses.

With all this, you now have nearly complete integration tests for the application's interactions with the database. Connectivity failures are still left untouched, but those may be more interesting to cover in another property, rather than adding to the complexity of this one.

---

6.   https://www.postgresql.org/docs/9.6/static/sql-begin.html
7.   https://www.postgresql.org/docs/10/static/transaction-iso.html
8.   https://github.com/epgsql/epgsql

Wrapping Up

In this chapter, we've been through a realistic integration test suite written as stateful properties. All we had was a model layer for a bookstore using a PostgreSQL instance, with no tests in it. We first started by drawing up the generators for our base data types, which helps do some broader testing to make sure the system works without throwing exceptions. That's where we encountered and resolved our first encoding bug.

With this out of the way, we established the initial model, using a wrapper module (a shim) to allow as much determinism as possible. As you've seen, this approach tends to create a bit more repetition with precondition-heavy code, but makes tests more decideable, and simpler to debug. You've also seen this at work as we refined the model through multiple failures and discovered yet more tricky aspects of using SQL.

Additionally, we've been through a round of debugging, seeing how PropEr shrinks stateful property command sequences to debug our models, before doing a final sanity check with parallel tests.

With this, you've seen most of what there is to see with stateful properties. The one exception is a specialization for systems that represent finite state machines, which you'll get to discover next.

## CHAPTER 11

State Machine Properties

If you've ever had a system that could do things differently based on context, you probably have an intuitive knowledge of what a finite state machine is. Finite state machines (FSM) are, informally speaking, an abstraction describing certain stateful programs. The program can be in only one of multiple known states at a time (such as a traffic light being red, yellow, or green), and *transitions* from one state to another based on specific inputs or events. Within each state, the program may behave differently.

Let's imagine a program that should take special measures—such as forbidding some actions or enabling new features—depending on whether network connectivity is good, bad, or entirely unavailable. Testing such a program with stateful properties while keeping them deterministic would create a kind of explosion of possible cases. If there are six possible events and three possible states, you quickly get at least eighteen possible combinations of calls versus states, and you have to do quite a bit of filtering in preconditions to hope to cover all kinds of transitions.

To help with this, PropEr provides *finite state machine properties*, which allow you to specifically model state machines: state names and transitions are made into first-class citizens, allowing you to properly explore their expected transitions in a less cumbersome manner than would be required with regular stateful properties or example tests.

Finite state properties are specifically useful when your users can interact with the system while perceiving multiple states, as opposed to just knowing that the system has a state machine internally. To put it another way, state machine properties are for when the model itself is a state machine, not the system. If there are no specific discernible states for the user—and therefore no specific discernible states for the model—then regular stateful properties are more appropriate.

In this chapter, we'll see the state machine properties' structure, and see how PropEr executes them. You'll find a lot of parallels with stateful properties, but we'll highlight all differences through testing a circuit-breaker[1] library, showing where this type of property really shines.

Laying Out State Machine Properties

State machine properties are very similar to regular stateful properties, conceptually speaking. They share the same the three major components:

- A model, which represents what the system should do at a high level.

- A generator for commands, which represent the execution flow of the program.

- An actual system, which is validated against our model.

Since FSM properties are really a specialization of stateful properties, the differences are subtle. If switching from basic to stateful properties was like trying an entirely new kind of food you had never seen before, learning about FSM properties should feel more like eating a new kind of spaghetti sauce.

The Model

The model for state machine properties keeps the same spirit as other models: it must be a simpler and straightforward version of your system, used to ensure the real system acts according to your expectations. For FSM properties, they're made of three parts:

1. A data structure that represents the expected state of the system—the data it should contain and that you'd expect to be able to get from it (the model's data).

2. The name of a state—either an atom or a tuple—representing the name of the modeled finite state machine, such as on or off as two state names for a light.

3. A function that transforms the model's data based on commands that could be applied to the system (named next_state_data).

The model is similar to stateful properties, but with state names as an extra thing to carry around and keep in mind.

---

1. https://en.wikipedia.org/wiki/Circuit_breaker_design_pattern

State and Data

When dealing with stateful components in Erlang and Elixir, we often refer to their "state" as the ensemble of data that is living within the component. In fact, "state" and "data" are often used interchangeably.

When dealing with finite state machines, we need to be accurate: *state* refers to the name of the state the FSM is in (a lock is in either locked or unlocked states), and *data* refers to actual information and records being held by the FSM. (The combination to open the lock is 3-13-37 and may be held in its data.)

The Commands

As with stateful properties, FSM properties have command generators. They work a bit differently, since they're based on the state. These command generators contain the following:

1. A list of functions sharing the name of the states, each of which returns a list of symbolic calls with generators defining their arguments, along with the name of the next state to transition to.

2. A series of preconditions defining whether a given symbolic call would make sense to apply according to the current model state and data.

3. An optional callback that defines the probability for a given state transition to happen; if no weight is defined, all transitions are equally likely.

Depending on your experience with stateful properties, this is rather straightforward, and examples will clarify everything. The last part needed is the validation.

The Validation

When it comes to validating our system against the model, we'll once again borrow a lot from stateful properties. The mechanism here relies fully on postconditions, with the one distinction that the state names involved in a transition are considered in the system.

Let's look at the execution model of FSM properties.

How State Machine Properties Run

PropEr divides the execution of a finite state machine test in two phases, one abstract and one real. The abstract phase is used to create a test scenario, only using the model and command generation callbacks, and call these to build out the sequence of calls that will later be applied to the system.

A graphical representation for it might look like this:

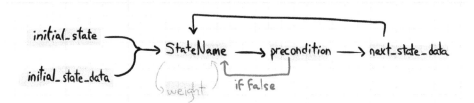

This should be familiar to you from stateful properties. The two big conceptual changes are for the initial state, now using both initial_state and initial_state_data, and an optional weight callback. Once the initial state and data are generated, the StateName callback is called, along with the optional weight function, to generate the next state transition and symbolic call to run.

That symbolic call is then passed, along with the data, to a precondition callback, which determines whether the call is valid or not. If the validation fails, PropEr tries again with a new generated command and state. Once a suitable command is found, the FSM generation moves forward.

The next_state_data function takes the command and the current state, and has to return a new data structure. Then the whole process is repeated over and over, until PropEr decides it has enough commands.

Once a full sequence of commands is generated, PropEr will start applying them against the real system:

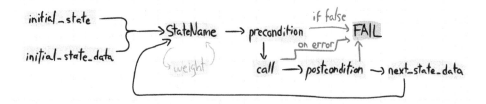

The rest of the mechanism is conceptually the same as for stateful properties. The preconditions are still reevaluated to ensure consistency so that if a generated precondition that used to work suddenly fails, the entire test also fails. If it doesn't fail, the next symbolic call in the list is executed, with its result stored. The postcondition is then evaluated, and if it succeeds, the state transition for the command is applied, the data is updated, and the next command can be processed.

Writing Properties

As with stateful properties, we can make use of the rebar3 plugin's templates to get a property suite within any standard Erlang project. Call the following within an existing project:

```
$ rebar3 new proper_fsm name=fsm
===> Writing test/prop_fsm.erl
```

The generated file contains the prop_fsm module, a test suite that is divided in two sections: one section for the state machine property we'll want to execute, and one for the model, which is a mix of callbacks and generators. Let's start by looking at the property:

Erlang

```
-module(prop_fsm).
-include_lib("proper/include/proper.hrl").

-export([initial_state/0, initial_state_data/0,
         on/1, off/1, service/3, % State generators
         weight/3, precondition/4, postcondition/5, next_state_data/5]).
prop_test() ->
    ?FORALL(Cmds, proper_fsm:commands(?MODULE),
        begin
            actual_system:start_link(),
            {History,State,Result} = proper_fsm:run_commands(?MODULE, Cmds),
            actual_system:stop(),
            ?WHENFAIL(io:format("History: ~p\nState: ~p\nResult: ~p\n",
                                [History,State,Result]),
                    aggregate(zip(proper_fsm:state_names(History),
                                  command_names(Cmds)),
                        Result =:= ok))
        end).
```

Elixir

```
defmodule FSMTest do
  use ExUnit.Case
  use PropCheck
  use PropCheck.FSM
```

```
property "FSM property", [:verbose] do
  forall cmds <- commands(__MODULE__) do
    ActualSystem.start_link()
    {history, state, result} = run_commands(__MODULE__, cmds)
    ActualSystem.stop()

    (result == :ok)
    |> aggregate(
      :proper_statem.zip(state_names(history), command_names(cmds))
    )
    |> when_fail(
      IO.puts("""
      History: #{inspect(history)}
      State: #{inspect(state)}
      Result: #{inspect(result)}
      """)
    )
  end
end
```

This property has a lot of exports. Many of them are variations on those for stateful properties, and we'll revisit them soon. Functions such as on/1, off/1, and service/3 are state-machine–specific and represent individual states: on, off, and a state called service. They will allow us to generate sequences of commands in a context-sensitive manner based on the FSM state.

At ❶ and ❷, special variations of stateful properties' command generators and runners are used. The rest of the property is mostly similar, aside from ❸, where a special zip/2 function (a specialized adaptation of lists:zip/2 made for FSM properties output that is autoimported by PropEr) is used along proper_fsm:state_names/1 to generate readable output in case of a test failure. The rest works as usual. Let's take a look at the callbacks, starting with the initial state and data.

Erlang

```
-record(data, {}).

%% Initial state for the state machine
initial_state() -> on.
%% Initial model data at the start. Should be deterministic.
initial_state_data() -> #data{}.
```

Elixir

```
# Initial state for the state machine
def initial_state(), do: :on
# Initial model at the start. Should be deterministic
def initial_state_data(), do: %{}
```

Both function calls must be deterministic. If the initial state name or the initial data are unpredictable, PropEr won't be able to know how to shrink a failing case, since every sequence being replayed may end up being entirely different. Once both values are chosen, data can be generated:

Erlang

```erlang
%% State commands generation
on(_Data) -> [{off, {call, actual_system, some_call, [term(), term()]}}].

off(_Data) ->
    [{off, {call, actual_system, some_call, [term(), term()]}},
     {history, {call, actual_system, some_call, [term(), term()]}},
     {{service,sub,state}, {call, actual_system, some_call, [term()]}}].
service(_Sub, _State, _Data) ->
    [{on, {call, actual_system, some_call, [term(), term()]}}].

%% Optional callback, weight modification of transitions
weight(_FromState, _ToState, _Call) -> 1.
```

Elixir

```elixir
# State command generation
def on(_data) do
  [{:off, {:call, ActualSystem, :some_call, [term(), term()]}}]
end

def off(_data) do
  [
    {:off, {:call, ActualSystem, :some_call, [term(), term()]}},
    {:history, {:call, ActualSystem, :some_call, [term(), term()]}},
    {{:service, :sub, :state},
      {:call, ActualSystem, :some_call, [term(), term()]}}
  ]
end

def service(_sub, _state, _data) do
  [{:on, {:call, ActualSystem, :some_call, [term(), term()]}}]
end

# Optional callback, weight modification of transitions
def weight(_from_state, _to_state, _call), do: 1
```

First, we have two simple states: on and off. These can generate a sequence of commands of the form {NextState, {call, Mod, Fun, Args}}. Here the on state can only transition to the off state through some_call. The off state can transition to the off state (basically meaning "stay in the same state") in one of two ways:

1. Through an explicit transition to the off state (at ❶).

2. Through an implicit transition by using the history state, which repeats the current state (at ❷)—a form that is useful when other functions are used to generate common calls used in all states, for example.

Following this, a transition can be made to a *nested state*, at ❸. A nested state is built as a tuple of the form {ParentState, SubState, SubSubState}, and the callback for it is shown at ❹: ParentState(SubState, SubSubState, Data). In the previous example, _Sub would be bound to sub, and _State to state. Any number of sub-states can be put in the tuple, as long as a callback generator function is in place to handle them all with the right arity.

Finally, the code sample shows the weight/3 callback, which lets us specify a relative probability for a given state transition or call. For example, if you wanted the transition from off to {service, sub, state} to be more probable than off to off, this callback lets you do that. It's entirely optional, and if omitted, all transitions are as likely as each other.

The remaining callbacks are more straightforward:

Erlang

```erlang
%% Picks whether a command should be valid.
precondition(_From, _To, #data{}, {call, _Mod, _Fun, _Args}) -> true.

%% Given the state states and data *prior* to the call
%% `{call, Mod, Fun, Args}', determine if the result `Res' (coming
%% from the actual system) makes sense.
postcondition(_From, _To, _Data, {call, _Mod, _Fun, _Args}, _Res) -> true.

%% Assuming the postcondition for a call was true, update the model
%% accordingly for the test to proceed.
next_state_data(_From, _To, Data, _Res, {call, _Mod, _Fun, _Args}) ->
    NewData = Data,
    NewData.
```

Elixir

```elixir
# Picks whether a command should be valid
def precondition(_from, _to, _data, {:call, _mod, _fun, _args}) do
  true
end

# Given that state prior to the call `{:call, mod, fun, args}`,
# determine whether the result (res) coming from the actual system
# makes sense according to the model
def postcondition(_from, _to, _data, {:call, _mod, _fun, _args}, _res) do
  true
end
```

```
# Assuming the postcondition for a call was true, update the model
# accordingly for the test to proceed
def next_state_data(_from, _to, data, _res, {:call, _m, _f, _args}) do
  new_data = data
  new_data
end
```

They are all pretty much adaptations of regular stateful properties, but with an additional pair of arguments which contain the current state (_From) and the next one (_To) if the call succeeds.

We'll put these callbacks in practice soon by seeing how we can model a circuit breaker with PropEr.

Testing a Circuit Breaker

Circuit breakers are one of the most interesting concepts in fault isolation for reliable systems. They are used to account for errors that happen over time in a part of the system. If the frequency at which the errors happen is considered too high compared to the successful cases, the breaker is tripped. Once tripped, further calls automatically fail before having a chance to reach the subsystem gated by the breaker. The idea is that failures tend to be costly and take a lot of time; and a failing system under heavy stress is even harder to get back into a usable state. The circuit breaker allows you to prevent the client from doing work that would result in expensive failures and directly turn them into a cheap failures, while letting the failing subsystem recuperate under less stress.

For this example, we'll use the circuit_breaker[2] library from Klarna,[3] and give it tests. But first, let's see how it works.

Understanding circuit_breaker

circuit_breaker is a library that has seen significant production use and has some unit tests, but nearly no documentation. So we'll go over how the library works and write tests for it.

The library can be used as a wrapper over a given function call. This wrapper looks at the return values and duration of each function call, and efficiently tracks various failure rates to figure out if the breaker should be tripped or not. Once tripped, the breaker prevents function calls from taking place. It can be untripped after either a cooldown period or a manual intervention. As

---

2. https://github.com/klarna/circuit_breaker/
3. https://www.klarna.com

a user, you can define a tolerance of how many errors per period of time are required to break the circuit, including acceptable error values and timeout thresholds. If the defined rate is crossed, the breaker trips. You can also trip the breaker manually to prevent any calls from taking place; this lets operators of a system selectively enable or disable features.

Here's what a circuit_breaker call looks like:

Erlang

```erlang
circuit_breaker:call(
❶    {myservice, SomeId},
❷    fun() -> some_call(State) end,
❸    timer:minutes(1),
❹    fun() -> true end,
❺    timer:minutes(5),
     %% Options
❻    [{n_error, 3},
      {time_error, timer:minutes(30)},
❼     {n_timeout, 3},
      {time_timeout, timer:minutes(30)},
❽     {n_call_timeout, 3},
      {time_call_timeout, timer:minutes(25)},
❾     {ignore_errors, [not_found]}]
).
```

Elixir

```elixir
:circuit_breaker.call(
❶   {:my_service, :id},
❷   fn -> 2+2 end,
❸   :timer.minutes(1),
❹   fn -> true end,
❺   :timer.minutes(5),
    # options
❻   n_error: 3,
    time_error: :timer.minutes(30),
❼   n_timeout: 3,
    time_timeout: :timer.minutes(30),
❽   n_call_timeout: 3,
    time_call_timeout: :timer.minutes(30),
❾   ignore_errors: [:not_found]
)
```

This is kind of a verbose function call, but it speaks to the flexibility of the library. The first argument (❶) is the *service identifier* for a given circuit breaker. Each service name is registered on its first use of circuit_breaker:call/6.

Through the service name, you could use one circuit breaker for all database calls in your system, or use one per _type_ of call, or one per account if you want. This identifier lets you specify the scope of each breaker since it's unrelated to the function call to be monitored, which is the second argument (❷). This function call can be anything at all; it will run within a dedicated process while circuit_breaker looks for failures or long delays—the timeouts of which are defined with the third argument at ❸.

Whenever the breaker is tripped, calls will automatically fail. It will take a given cooldown period (the fifth argument at ❺) before the circuit breaker goes back to a valid state, after which the fourth argument (❹) will be called, mostly for side-effect purposes.

The list of options defines what constitutes unacceptable error rates. The n_error and time_error values (❻) tell the maximal frequency for errors—in this case, three failures per half hour.

You can use the n_timeout option (❼) when the calls to monitor return the value {error, timeout}, such as when a socket call to gen_tcp:recv/3 takes too long and gives up. We won't test this one; instead, we'll focus on n_call_timeout (❽), which checks for the call taking too long to return according to a timer within the circuit breaker library. Finally, some errors can explicitly be ignored through the ignore_errors option, at ❾, which allows you to whitelist a bunch of values found in {error, Reason} tuples. In the sample call, {error, not_found} is considered to be a valid, nonerroneous return value.

But that's not all. The library also exposes a few more calls, namely circuit_breaker:block/1, circuit_breaker:deblock/1, and circuit_breaker:clear/1, which allows operators to respectively break the circuit with a manual override, go back to normal, or to clear circuit breaker trips that were automatically triggered by error rates. Those would be interesting to test as well.

With all of this, we can say that our model state machine should have three states:

1. The ok state, which is to be used when the circuit breaker has not been tripped and all systems are considered to be functional.

2. The tripped state, where too many failures have happened and the circuit breaker forces calls to fail.

3. The blocked state, which simulates operator-induced tripping of the circuit breaker as an attempt to prevent operations from taking place.

For the sake of simplicity, the finite state machine model we'll set up won't consider the time-handling aspects of the circuit breaker in terms of recovery, but only the manual clearing of its state with circuit_breaker:clear/1. This will allow us to go over the FSM properties' different mechanisms without making things too complex.

Testing Time-Sensitive Mechanisms

Testing a time-sensitive mechanism is always tricky, since time isn't very deterministic, and waiting through delays can take quite a while. In general, a few approaches are worth exploring:

- Make shim calls whose whole purpose is waiting until a predefined delay is over. You may need to couple that with a scaling of timers (making delays longer) to make it easy to keep everything as deterministic as possible. In general this approach is difficult to do well since it's hard to make delays predictable over long sequences of operations.

- When using synchronous calls (such as when calling passive sockets or gen_servers), mocking libraries such as meck may be used to simulate timeout results. Those can be tricky to make work well when only some of multiple calls must fail, so this approach tends to make most sense when time constraints are tested in isolation.

- Injecting timeout events tends to be the easiest way around. If the system you are testing uses built-in Erlang timers to send messages, you can often manually send the expected messages to simulate various timers firing whenever you want. You just have to configure the real timers to take long enough to ensure that only your fake messages will be active during the test. Injecting events that way will make time testing work well and fast.

Whenever you end up requiring timeout delays, experiment with any of these to see how it goes. Other approaches may be possible but might be application-specific and require clever solutions. For example, you may end up creating facilities to do fault injection in your production system, if only to ease testing.

With this information in hand, we can start implementing the actual model.

Modeling the Circuit Breaker

For stateful properties, we'd initially started our test suite by defining generators. We then needed to refine them when it came to writing the command generation, and ended up writing a shim module. This time around, we're going to start directly with the shim module. It's a good opportunity to revisit all kinds of possibile calls that can take place.

Since we're testing the circuit breaker itself, we'll want to cover these:

- Successful calls and their effect on the internal state of the breaker
- Calls ending in errors
- Calls ending in errors that are whitelisted, and therefore seen as successful
- Calls timing out
- Manual operations to trip and untrip the circuit breaker

Our first step is to ensure the libraries we need are all available to the project:

About the Code

 In the snippets that follow, code is labeled with both the language (Erlang and Elixir) and the file where you should put the code if you're following along.

Erlang   code/FSMProperties/erlang/circuit/rebar.config

```erlang
{erl_opts, [nowarn_export_all]}.
{project_plugins, [rebar3_proper]}.

{deps, [
    {circuit_breaker,
     {git, "https://github.com/klarna/circuit_breaker.git", {tag, "1.0.1"}}}
]}.

{profiles, [
    {test, [
        {deps, [
            {proper, "1.3.0"}
        ]}
    ]}
]}.
```

For Elixir, you'll instead need the following mix.exs file:

Elixir   code/FSMProperties/elixir/circuit/mix.exs

```elixir
defmodule Circuit.MixProject do
  use Mix.Project

  def project do
    [
      app: :circuit,
      version: "0.1.0",
      elixir: "~> 1.6",
      elixirc_paths: elixirc_paths(Mix.env),
      start_permanent: Mix.env() == :prod,
      deps: deps()
    ]
  end
```

```elixir
  defp elixirc_paths(:test), do: ["lib","test/"]
  defp elixirc_paths(_), do: ["lib"]

  # Run "mix help compile.app" to learn about applications.
  def application do
    [
      extra_applications: [:logger]
    ]
  end

  # Run "mix help deps" to learn about dependencies.
  defp deps do
    [
      {:circuit_breaker,
       git: "https://github.com/klarna/circuit_breaker.git",
       tag: "1.0.1",
       manager: :rebar3},
      {:propcheck, "~> 1.1", only: [:test, :dev]}
    ]
  end
end
```

Let's continue with the various calls within the shim module:

Erlang	code/FSMProperties/erlang/circuit/test/break_shim.erl

```erlang
-module(break_shim).
-export([success/0, err/1, ignored_error/1, timeout/0,
         manual_block/0, manual_deblock/0, manual_reset/0]).

-define(SERVICE, test_service).

success() ->
    circuit_breaker:call(
      ?SERVICE,
      fun() -> success end, timer:hours(1),
      fun() -> true end, timer:hours(1),
      options()
    ).

err(Reason) ->
    circuit_breaker:call(
      ?SERVICE,
      fun() -> {error, Reason} end, timer:hours(1),
      fun() -> true end, timer:hours(1),
      options()
    ).

ignored_error(Reason) -> err(Reason). % same call
```

```
timeout() ->
    circuit_breaker:call(
      ?SERVICE,
      fun() -> timer:sleep(infinity) end, 0,
      fun() -> true end, timer:hours(1),
      options()
    ).
```

Elixir translation on page 339.

The successful call returns success, the error-related calls return {error, Reason} (with Reason passed as an argument by the soon-to-be-written property), and all of them set all timeouts to one hour—which ensures timers won't accidentally interfere with our tests. The one exception is the timeout() call, which, at ❶, will sleep forever while setting a timeout value of 0, ensuring we will trigger a manual timeout there. Its cooldown period is still one hour, as set on the line after.

All options have been hidden within a function call, which is defined as follows:

Erlang	code/FSMProperties/erlang/circuit/test/break_shim.erl

```
options() ->
    [{n_error, 3},
     {time_error, timer:minutes(30)},
     {n_timeout, 3},
     {time_timeout, timer:minutes(30)},
     {n_call_timeout, 3},
     {time_call_timeout, timer:minutes(30)},
     {ignore_errors, [ignore1, ignore2]}].
```

Elixir	code/FSMProperties/elixir/circuit/test/break_shim.ex

```
defp options() do
  [
    n_error: 3,
    time_error: :timer.minutes(30),
    n_timeout: 3,
    time_timeout: :timer.minutes(30),
    n_call_timeout: 3,
    time_call_timeout: :timer.minutes(30),
    ignore_errors: [:ignore1, :ignore2]
  ]
end
```

They set all thresholds values to 3. We will have to remember this and keep it in sync in our model. It's an arbitrary value, but it should work. All delays for error rates are also set at thirty minutes, ensuring we won't have to play with time limitations for now.

Time and Circuit Breaking

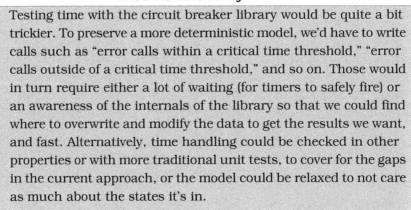 Testing time with the circuit breaker library would be quite a bit trickier. To preserve a more deterministic model, we'd have to write calls such as "error calls within a critical time threshold," "error calls outside of a critical time threshold," and so on. Those would in turn require either a lot of waiting (for timers to safely fire) or an awareness of the internals of the library so that we could find where to overwrite and modify the data to get the results we want, and fast. Alternatively, time handling could be checked in other properties or with more traditional unit tests, to cover for the gaps in the current approach, or the model could be relaxed to not care as much about the states it's in.

While this is all possible to do well, it'd be distracting from our objectives of learning about the finite state machine properties.

Finally, we can add the manual calls to finish it off:

Erlang	code/FSMProperties/erlang/circuit/test/break_shim.erl

```erlang
manual_block() -> circuit_breaker:block(?SERVICE).
manual_deblock() -> circuit_breaker:deblock(?SERVICE).
manual_reset() -> circuit_breaker:clear(?SERVICE).
```

Elixir	code/FSMProperties/elixir/circuit/test/break_shim.ex

```elixir
def manual_block(), do: :circuit_breaker.block(@service)
def manual_deblock(), do: :circuit_breaker.deblock(@service)
def manual_reset(), do: :circuit_breaker.clear(@service)
```

We can now get ready for the property itself. Add the test module to your project through the rebar3 template with rebar3 new proper_fsm break and let's set the property up:

Erlang	code/FSMProperties/erlang/circuit/test/prop_break.erl

```erlang
-module(prop_break).
-include_lib("proper/include/proper.hrl").

-export([initial_state/0, initial_state_data/0,
         unregistered/1, ok/1, tripped/1, blocked/1, % State generators
         precondition/4, postcondition/5, next_state_data/5]).
```

```erlang
prop_test() ->
    ?FORALL(Cmds, proper_fsm:commands(?MODULE),
        begin
            {ok, Pid} = circuit_breaker:start_link(),
            {History,State,Result} = proper_fsm:run_commands(?MODULE, Cmds),
            gen_server:stop(Pid, normal, 5000),
            ?WHENFAIL(io:format("History: ~p\nState: ~p\nResult: ~p\n",
                                [History,State,Result]),
                      aggregate(zip(proper_fsm:state_names(History),
                                    command_names(Cmds)),
                            Result =:= ok))
        end).
```

Elixir	code/FSMProperties/elixir/circuit/test/break_test.exs

```elixir
defmodule BreakTest do
  use ExUnit.Case
  use PropCheck
  use PropCheck.FSM

  property "FSM property for circuit breakers", [:verbose] do
    Application.stop(:circuit_breaker) # we take over that
    forall cmds <- commands(__MODULE__) do
      {:ok, pid} = :circuit_breaker.start_link()
      {history, state, result} = run_commands(__MODULE__, cmds)
      GenServer.stop(pid, :normal, 5000)

      (result == :ok)
      |> aggregate(
        :proper_statem.zip(state_names(history), command_names(cmds))
      )
      |> when_fail(
        IO.puts("""
        History: #{inspect(history)}
        State: #{inspect(state)}
        Result: #{inspect(result)}
        """)
      )
    end
  end
end
```

You can see the three generators in the Erlang version's -export attribute: ok/1, tripped/1, and blocked/1, and also a fourth one, unregistered/1. This generator will be added because manual calls aren't available until the circuit breaker's service id is registered, and this turns out to happen automatically on first use. This peculiarity will be encoded in the state machine itself.

You can also see that we're starting the circuit breaker process by hand, which is paired with a call to gen_server:stop/3 at ❶. The circuit breaker module doesn't expose a callback to terminate the breaker, usually preferring to let a supervision tree do that work. The gen_server behavior, however, exposes functions that let us bypass that by ordering the process to stop itself. Aside from this, the property is rather straightforward.

The model itself is where most of the complexity might live. The first set of callbacks we'll want to tackle are those that are initalizing the state and data for the state machine. We'll want to track the number of failures seen for each type, and the total number of failures we should expect before the breaker trips:

Erlang	code/FSMProperties/erlang/circuit/test/prop_break.erl

```erlang
-record(data, {
        limit = 3 :: pos_integer(),
        errors = 0 :: pos_integer(),
        timeouts = 0 :: pos_integer()
        }).
%% Initial state for the state machine
initial_state() -> unregistered.
%% Initial model data at the start. Should be deterministic.
initial_state_data() -> #data{}.
```

Elixir	code/FSMProperties/elixir/circuit/test/break_test.exs

```elixir
# Initial state for the state machine
def initial_state(), do: :unregistered
# Initial model at the start. Should be deterministic
def initial_state_data() do
  %{limit: 3, errors: 0, timeouts: 0}
end
```

We start by defining #data{} record.[4] The two callbacks then specify that we'll start in the unregistered state, with the data set to its default value. As mentioned earlier, the unregistered state lets us represent the fact that manual calls need the service to be registered (through normal calls) to be available.

Overall, our circuit breaker state machine should be able to transition as shown in the diagram on page 299. The most straightforward state is the first one, unregistered, which instantly transitions to ok through a successful call:

Erlang	

```erlang
%% State commands generation
unregistered(_Data) ->
    [{ok, {call, break_shim, success, []}}].
```

---

4. https://learnyousomeerlang.com/a-short-visit-to-common-data-structures#records

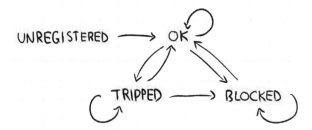

```elixir
# State command generation
def unregistered(_data) do
  [{:ok, {:call, BreakShim, :success, []}}]
end
```

The call to the shim should be successful, but we'll validate that in postconditions. The ok state itself is a bit more complex, with far more possible calls:

```erlang
ok(_Data) ->
    [{history, {call, break_shim, success, []}},
     {history, {call, break_shim, err, [valid_error()]}},
     {tripped, {call, break_shim, err, [valid_error()]}},
     {history, {call, break_shim, ignored_error, [ignored_error()]}},
     {history, {call, break_shim, timeout, []}},
     {tripped, {call, break_shim, timeout, []}},
     {blocked, {call, break_shim, manual_block, []}},
     {ok,      {call, break_shim, manual_deblock, []}},
     {ok,      {call, break_shim, manual_reset, []}}].
```

```elixir
def ok(_data) do
  [
    {:history, {:call, BreakShim, :success, []}},
    {:history, {:call, BreakShim, :err, [valid_error()]}},
    {:tripped, {:call, BreakShim, :err, [valid_error()]}},
    {:history, {:call, BreakShim, :ignored_error, [ignored_error()]}},
    {:history, {:call, BreakShim, :timeout, []}},
    {:tripped, {:call, BreakShim, :timeout, []}},
    {:blocked, {:call, BreakShim, :manual_block, []}},
    {:ok, {:call, BreakShim, :manual_deblock, []}},
    {:ok, {:call, BreakShim, :manual_reset, []}}
  ]
end
```

Notice something interesting in these operations. Successful calls and ignored errors are unsurprisingly remaining in the ok state (through the history atom), and the manual operations have the impact you'd expect them to have, but both errors and timeouts are there twice: once successfully, and once transitioning to the tripped state. It's odd because it doesn't sound like the same call could transition to any of two distinct states while remaining deterministic.

This is because PropEr handles generation in two steps. First it picks the call to run (such as break_shim:err/1), and then it sees, through preconditions, whether a single one of the target states makes sense. In the case above, we'll have to make sure that calls to break_shim:err/1 can unambiguously target only one or the other of the target states (ok or tripped) through preconditions and the FSM's data. If that's not done, PropEr will complain. Keep that in mind—we'll revisit it soon—but for now let's check out the other generators:

Erlang

```erlang
tripped(_Data) ->
    [{history, {call, break_shim, success, []}},
     {history, {call, break_shim, err, [valid_error()]}},
     {history, {call, break_shim, ignored_error, [ignored_error()]}},
     {history, {call, break_shim, timeout, []}},
     {ok,      {call, break_shim, manual_deblock, []}},
     {ok,      {call, break_shim, manual_reset, []}},
     {blocked, {call, break_shim, manual_block, []}}].
```

Elixir

```elixir
def tripped(_data) do
  [
    {:history, {:call, BreakShim, :success, []}},
    {:history, {:call, BreakShim, :err, [valid_error()]}},
    {:history, {:call, BreakShim, :ignored_error, [ignored_error()]}},
    {:history, {:call, BreakShim, :timeout, []}},
    {:ok, {:call, BreakShim, :manual_deblock, []}},
    {:ok, {:call, BreakShim, :manual_reset, []}},
    {:blocked, {:call, BreakShim, :manual_block, []}}
  ]
end
```

Manually resetting and deblocking should both return to the ok state. Aside from that, nothing for this state will go back to ok on its own since we disregard time for this property. Here's the last state to cover:

Erlang

```erlang
blocked(_Data) ->
```

```
   [{history, {call, break_shim, success, []}},
    {history, {call, break_shim, err, [valid_error()]}},
    {history, {call, break_shim, ignored_error, [ignored_error()]}},
    {history, {call, break_shim, timeout, []}},
    {history, {call, break_shim, manual_block, []}},
    {history, {call, break_shim, manual_reset, []}},
    {ok,      {call, break_shim, manual_deblock, []}}].
```

Elixir

```elixir
def blocked(_data) do
  [
    {:history, {:call, BreakShim, :success, []}},
    {:history, {:call, BreakShim, :err, [valid_error()]}},
    {:history, {:call, BreakShim, :ignored_error, [ignored_error()]}},
    {:history, {:call, BreakShim, :timeout, []}},
    {:history, {:call, BreakShim, :manual_block, []}},
    {:history, {:call, BreakShim, :manual_reset, []}},
    {:ok, {:call, BreakShim, :manual_deblock, []}}
  ]
end
```

This works the same and has the same requirements as the previous generators. Do note that once in the blocked state, no other command than manual_deblock can get you out of there. It overrides even clearing errors; the operator who ordered the breaker to be blocked is in total control.

We have two generators left to define, valid_error() and ignored_error():

Erlang

```erlang
valid_error() -> elements([badarg, badmatch, badarith, whatever]).
ignored_error() -> elements([ignore1, ignore2]).
```

Elixir

```elixir
def valid_error() do
  elements([:badarg, :badmatch, :badarith, :whatever])
end
def ignored_error() do
  elements([:ignore1, :ignore2])
end
```

These are based off the option() function in break_shim, which ignored both ignore1 and ignore2 errors, making them be perceived as a successful call.

With this in place, we can write the preconditions required for our case generation to work:

Erlang   code/FSMProperties/erlang/circuit/test/prop_break.erl

```erlang
%% Picks whether a command should be valid under the current state.
precondition(unregistered, ok, _, {call, _, Call, _}) ->
    Call =:= success;
precondition(ok, To, #data{errors=N, limit=L}, {call,_,err,_}) ->
    (To =:= tripped andalso N+1 =:= L) orelse (To =:= ok andalso N+1 =/= L);
precondition(ok, To, #data{timeouts=N, limit=L}, {call,_,timeout,_}) ->
    (To =:= tripped andalso N+1 =:= L) orelse (To =:= ok andalso N+1 =/= L);
precondition(_From, _To, _Data, _Call) ->
    true.
```

Elixir   code/FSMProperties/elixir/circuit/test/break_test.exs

```elixir
# Picks whether a command should be valid
def precondition(:unregistered, :ok, _, {:call, _, call, _}) do
  call == :success
end
def precondition(:ok, to, %{errors: n, limit: l}, {:call, _, :err, _}) do
  (to == :tripped and n + 1 == l) or (to == :ok and n + 1 != l)
end
def precondition(
      :ok,
      to,
      %{timeouts: n, limit: l},
      {:call, _, :timeout, _}
    ) do
  (to == :tripped and n + 1 == l) or (to == :ok and n + 1 != l)
end
def precondition(_from, _to, _data, _call) do
  true
end
```

You can see both calls to erroneous cases only being valid in mutually exclusive instances: (To =:= tripped andalso N+1 =:= L) means that the switch to the tripped state can happen if the next failure (the one being generated) brings the total to the limit L, and (To =:= ok andalso N+1 =/= L) means our state machine can only transition to the ok state if this new failure does not reach the limit. All other calls are valid, since they only transition from one possible source state to one possible target state, and the circuit breaker requires no other special cases. Using an FSM property simplified this filtering drastically compared to what we'd have with a regular stateful property.

The next step is to do the data changes after each command. For these, we mostly have to worry about error accounting:

Erlang	code/FSMProperties/erlang/circuit/test/prop_break.erl

```erlang
%% Assuming the postcondition for a call was true, update the model
%% accordingly for the test to proceed.
next_state_data(ok, _To, Data=#data{errors=N}, _Res, {call,_,err,_}) ->
    Data#data{errors=N+1};
next_state_data(ok, _To, Data=#data{timeouts=N}, _Res, {call,_,timeout,_}) ->
    Data#data{timeouts=N+1};
next_state_data(_From, _To, Data, _Res, {call,_,manual_deblock,_}) ->
    Data#data{errors=0, timeouts=0};
next_state_data(_From, _To, Data, _Res, {call,_,manual_reset,_}) ->
    Data#data{errors=0, timeouts=0};
next_state_data(_From, _To, Data, _Res, {call, _Mod, _Fun, _Args}) ->
    Data.
```

Elixir	code/FSMProperties/elixir/circuit/test/break_test.exs

```elixir
# Assuming the postcondition for a call was true, update the model
# accordingly for the test to proceed
def next_state_data(:ok, _, data = %{errors: n}, _, {_, _, :err, _}) do
  %{data | errors: n + 1}
end
def next_state_data(:ok, _, d = %{timeouts: n}, _, {_, _, :timeout, _}) do
  %{d | timeouts: n + 1}
end
def next_state_data(_from, _to, data, _, {_, _, :manual_deblock, _}) do
  %{data | errors: 0, timeouts: 0}
end
def next_state_data(_from, _to, data, _, {_, _, :manual_reset, _}) do
  %{data | errors: 0, timeouts: 0}
end
def next_state_data(_from, _to, data, _res, {:call, _m, _f, _args}) do
  data
end
```

Error and timeout calls both increment their count by 1, and deblocking and resetting turn them back to 0. Everything else should have no impact on the data we track.

The last part to cover before running the model and seeing if we have everything right (or if the circuit breaker is correct) is the postcondition/5 callback. This one is slightly trickier:

Erlang	code/FSMProperties/erlang/circuit/test/prop_break.erl

```erlang
%% Given the state `State' *prior* to the call `{call, Mod, Fun, Args}',
%% determine whether the result `Res' (coming from the actual system)
%% makes sense.
postcondition(tripped, tripped, _Data, _, {error, {circuit_breaker, _}}) ->
    true;
postcondition(_, blocked, _Data, {call, _, manual_block, _}, ok) ->
    true;
postcondition(_, blocked, _Data, _Call, {error, {circuit_breaker, _}}) ->
    true;
postcondition(_, ok, _Data, {call, _, success, _}, success) ->
    true;
postcondition(_, ok, _Data, {call, _, manual_deblock, _}, ok) ->
    true;
postcondition(_, _, _Data, {call, _, manual_reset, _}, ok) ->
    true;
postcondition(ok, _, _Data, {call, _, timeout, _}, {error, timeout}) ->
    true;
postcondition(ok, _, _Data, {call, _, err, _}, {error, Err}) ->
    not lists:member(Err, [ignore1, ignore2]);
postcondition(ok, _, _Data, {call, _, ignored_error, _}, {error, Err}) ->
    lists:member(Err, [ignore1, ignore2]);
postcondition(_From, _To, _Data, {call, _Mod, _Fun, _Args}, _Res) ->
    false.
```

The markers ❶, ❷, and ❸ appear in the left margin beside the clauses for `postcondition(_, blocked, _Data, {call, _, manual_block, _}, ok)`, `postcondition(_, blocked, _Data, _Call, {error, {circuit_breaker, _}})`, and `postcondition(ok, _, _Data, {call, _, timeout, _}, {error, timeout})` respectively.

Elixir translation on page 340.

The first clause validates that once the circuit breaker is tripped, all calls that keep it in the tripped state (success, err, ignored_error, and timeout) have no effect and see a circuit-breaker error.

The same is true of all calls that land you into the blocked state—first the manual tripping itself at ❶, and then all the other failing calls at ❷. Right after that are all calls to success that are expected to work and should end in the ok state, followed by calls that manually deblock and reset the breaker and also end up in ok.

Since all the error cases are already covered, the timeout clause at ❸ is guaranteed to be in the ok state and to "succeed" in timing out. Same for errors, where we do an additional check on whether the right category of error is used in either case. Any other return value is considered invalid.

You can now run the tests to see if we have it all right or all wrong:

```
rebar3 proper
===> Verifying dependencies...
===> Compiling circuit
===> Testing prop_break:prop_test()
.......................................................!
Failed: After 65 test(s).
«initial failure»
Shrinking ......(6 time(s))
[{set,{var,8},{call,break_shim,success,[]}},
 {set,{var,9},{call,break_shim,timeout,[]}},
 {set,{var,10},{call,break_shim,ignored_error,[ignore1]}},
 {set,{var,11},{call,break_shim,timeout,[]}},
 {set,{var,12},{call,break_shim,timeout,[]}},
 {set,{var,13},{call,break_shim,err,[whatever]}}]
History: [{{unregistered,{data,3,0,0}},success},
          {{ok,{data,3,0,0}},{error,timeout}},
          {{ok,{data,3,0,1}},{error,ignore1}},
          {{ok,{data,3,0,1}},{error,timeout}},
          {{ok,{data,3,0,2}},{error,timeout}},
          {{tripped,{data,3,0,3}},{error,whatever}}]
State: {tripped,{data,3,0,3}}
Result: {postcondition,false}
===>
0/1 properties passed, 1 failed
===> Failed test cases:
prop_break:prop_test() -> false
```

Let's figure out what we need to do to get it working.

Adjusting the Model

The first step of any stateful failure is to figure out what failing sequence exactly caused the problem. Shrinking does most of the job, but we still have to extract meaning out of it. We have the following:

```
[{set,{var,8},{call,break_shim,success,[]}},
 {set,{var,9},{call,break_shim,timeout,[]}},
 {set,{var,10},{call,break_shim,ignored_error,[ignore1]}},
 {set,{var,11},{call,break_shim,timeout,[]}},
 {set,{var,12},{call,break_shim,timeout,[]}},
 {set,{var,13},{call,break_shim,err,[whatever]}}]
History: [{{unregistered,{data,3,0,0}},success},
          {{ok,{data,3,0,0}},{error,timeout}},
          {{ok,{data,3,0,1}},{error,ignore1}},
          {{ok,{data,3,0,1}},{error,timeout}},
          {{ok,{data,3,0,2}},{error,timeout}},
          {{tripped,{data,3,0,3}},{error,whatever}}]
State: {tripped,{data,3,0,3}}
```

This creates a sequence of events and state transitions as follows:

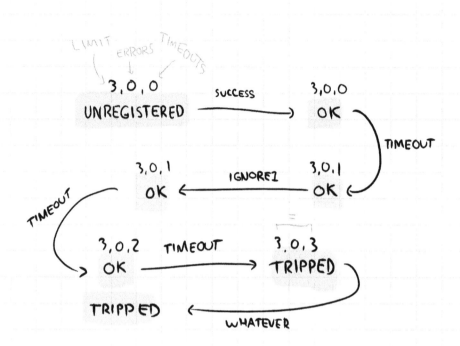

At least, that's the expectation from the history we have. But for the last error call, we expected to see {error, {circuit_breaker, _}} since we're in the tripped state. Instead the call returned {error, whatever}, which contradicts our expectations of the tripped state. This means our model's state machine and the real system are out of sync.

The underlying cause for this can be found in circuit_breaker's source code. After a code dive, you'll find that the actual circuit breaker doesn't just look for any N failures in a period of time, but instead decreases the counter by 1 on every successful call, first on errors, and then on timeouts, and only after some failures have been registered. So if, for example, every failing call is immediately followed by a successful one, as long as the breaker tolerates more than one failure, it will *never* trip. You'll need a higher ratio of failures than successful calls over time to trip it. This is a small but very important detail when defining failure thresholds.

The state machine should instead have behaved like this:

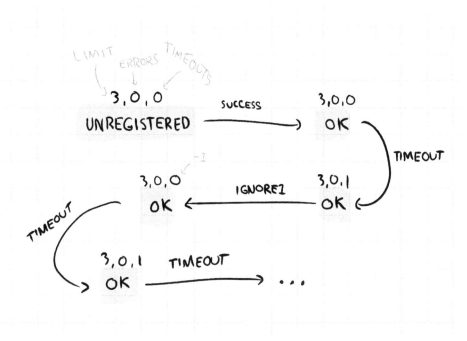

We can easily adapt the state transitions to work in a way that respects this:

Erlang	code/FSMProperties/erlang/circuit/test/prop_break.erl

```erlang
%% Assuming the postcondition for a call was true, update the model
%% accordingly for the test to proceed.
next_state_data(ok, _To, Data=#data{errors=N}, _Res, {call,_,err,_}) ->
    Data#data{errors=N+1};
next_state_data(ok, _To, Data=#data{timeouts=N}, _Res, {call,_,timeout,_}) ->
    Data#data{timeouts=N+1};
next_state_data(_From, _To, Data, _Res, {call,_,manual_deblock,_}) ->
    Data#data{errors=0, timeouts=0};
next_state_data(_From, _To, Data, _Res, {call,_,manual_reset,_}) ->
    Data#data{errors=0, timeouts=0};
next_state_data(ok, _To, Data=#data{errors=E, timeouts=T}, _Res,
                {call, _, F, _}) when F =:= success; F =:= ignored_error ->
    if E > 0 -> Data#data{errors = E-1};
       T > 0 -> Data#data{timeouts = T-1};
       E =:= 0, T =:= 0 -> Data
    end;
next_state_data(_From, _To, Data, _Res, {call, _Mod, _Fun, _Args}) ->
    Data.
```

Elixir translation on page 342.

The new clause is marked at ❶. On any nonfailure call to the circuit breaker, lower the errors by one. If the errors are at zero, then decrease the timeout counter instead, and only if it's above zero. This should cover and fix our problems:

```
$ rebar3 proper
===> Verifying dependencies...
===> Compiling circuit
===> Testing prop_break:prop_test()
......................................................................
.....................
OK: Passed 100 test(s).

12% {ok,{break_shim,err,1}}
12% {ok,{break_shim,timeout,0}}
8% {unregistered,{break_shim,success,0}}
7% {ok,{break_shim,manual_deblock,0}}
6% {ok,{break_shim,manual_block,0}}
6% {ok,{break_shim,success,0}}
5% {ok,{break_shim,manual_reset,0}}
5% {blocked,{break_shim,manual_block,0}}
5% {ok,{break_shim,ignored_error,1}}
5% {blocked,{break_shim,timeout,0}}
4% {blocked,{break_shim,err,1}}
4% {blocked,{break_shim,manual_deblock,0}}
4% {blocked,{break_shim,success,0}}
4% {blocked,{break_shim,manual_reset,0}}
3% {blocked,{break_shim,ignored_error,1}}
0% {tripped,{break_shim,ignored_error,1}}
0% {tripped,{break_shim,manual_deblock,0}}
0% {tripped,{break_shim,err,1}}
0% {tripped,{break_shim,manual_block,0}}
0% {tripped,{break_shim,timeout,0}}
0% {tripped,{break_shim,manual_reset,0}}
0% {tripped,{break_shim,success,0}}
===>
1/1 properties passed
```

That's good! But it feels like the statisics are kind of disappointing. The tripped state is rather poorly represented, with less than 1% calls for each of them.

This is not necessarily surprising since getting into the tripped state requires at least three more failures than successes, without having to accidentally get into the manual blocked state first. We can use the optional weight/3 callback to give a higher probability of failing into a tripped breaker:

Erlang   code/FSMProperties/erlang/circuit/test/prop_break.erl

---

```erlang
-export([initial_state/0, initial_state_data/0, weight/3,
         unregistered/1, ok/1, tripped/1, blocked/1, % State generators
         precondition/4, postcondition/5, next_state_data/5]).

«code»

weight(ok, tripped, _) ->
    5;
weight(ok, ok, {call, _, F, _}) ->
    case F of
        error -> 4;
        timeout -> 4;
        _ -> 1
    end;
weight(_, _, _) ->
    1.
```

Elixir   code/FSMProperties/elixir/circuit/test/break_test.exs

---

```elixir
# Optional callback, weight modification of transitions
def weight(:ok, :tripped, _) do
  5
end
def weight(:ok, :ok, {:call, _, f, _}) do
  case f do
    :error -> 4
    :timeout -> 4
    _ -> 1
  end
end
def weight(_, _, _) do
  1
end
```

The call raises the probability of any call forcing a transition from ok to tripped
and also increases the probability of all error calls in the ok state; the rest of
calls—such as error calls while already in the tripped state and manual
blocks—remain neutral in terms of probabilities.

Let's run the test again and see what we get:

```
$ rebar3 proper
===> Verifying dependencies...
===> Compiling circuit
===> Testing prop_break:prop_test()
................................................................
.......................
OK: Passed 100 test(s).
```

```
25% {ok,{break_shim,timeout,0}}
17% {ok,{break_shim,err,1}}
8% {unregistered,{break_shim,success,0}}
3% {ok,{break_shim,ignored_error,1}}
3% {blocked,{break_shim,success,0}}
3% {blocked,{break_shim,manual_reset,0}}
3% {blocked,{break_shim,manual_block,0}}
3% {ok,{break_shim,manual_block,0}}
3% {ok,{break_shim,manual_reset,0}}
3% {blocked,{break_shim,ignored_error,1}}
3% {ok,{break_shim,manual_deblock,0}}
2% {blocked,{break_shim,err,1}}
2% {blocked,{break_shim,manual_deblock,0}}
2% {blocked,{break_shim,timeout,0}}
2% {ok,{break_shim,success,0}}
2% {tripped,{break_shim,manual_block,0}}
2% {tripped,{break_shim,success,0}}
1% {tripped,{break_shim,err,1}}
1% {tripped,{break_shim,manual_deblock,0}}
1% {tripped,{break_shim,ignored_error,1}}
1% {tripped,{break_shim,manual_reset,0}}
1% {tripped,{break_shim,timeout,0}}
===>
1/1 properties passed
```

It's nothing amazing in terms of changes, but we get a much better distribution of tripped circuit breaker events than on previous runs.

Wrapping Up

In this final chapter, you've seen how to bring stateful properties to the next level in cases where the system under test can be modeled as a finite state machine. In such cases, FSM properties represent a useful specialization mechanism that lets you generate calls and data according to the state in which the system should be. We've been through the data generation model (both symbolic and real) for the property and have put it all in practice through tests for Klarna's circuit_breaker library. We came up with a multistate model, which proved to be ill-fitting for the actual library. We then went through the debugging steps required to fix the model and, through the statistics collected in the test execution—the step you should never forget!—rebalanced the possible generated events to get better transition coverage.

You now have all the knowledge required to use properties to find tricky bugs in all kinds of systems, from basic unit tests up to larger integration suites. You're ready to go on and start adding better tests to your software, to make your software better as well. Enjoy!

Solutions

Writing Properties

Question 1

proper_gen:pick(proper_type:Type())

Question on page 31.

Question 2

What the property is doing is validating the lists:seq(Start, Stop) function, which would be expected to return a list of integers in the range [Start, ..., Stop]. For example, running lists:seq(2,5) should return [2,3,4,5]. The property does the validation of this by looking at two aspects of such a list:

- The list should contain as many entries as the range covered by both terms (2..5 has 4 entries, or just (5-2)+1).

- To avoid having the test succeed on outputs such as [1,1,1,1], the increments/1 function is used to ensure that each number is greater than the next one.

Question on page 31.

Thinking in Properties

Question 1

Your answer could be any three of these strategies:

- Modeling—comparing the implementation with a simpler but obviously correct one

- Generalizing traditional tests by automating steps we would do by hand
- Finding program invariants to validate
- Using symmetric properties

Question on page 47.

Question 2

Two example solutions:

Erlang	code/ThinkingInProperties/erlang/pbt/test/prop_solutions.erl

```erlang
%% @doc this function tests that any lists of `{Key,Val}' pairs
%% end up being able to be sorted by the key by using `lists:keysort/2'.
prop_keysort1() ->
    ?FORALL(List, list({term(),term()}),
        begin
            %% is_key_ordered checks that all tuples' keys are ordered.
            is_key_ordered(lists:keysort(1, List))
        end).

is_key_ordered([{A,_},{B,_}=BTuple|T]) ->
    A =< B andalso is_key_ordered([BTuple|T]);
is_key_ordered(_) -> % smaller lists
    true.


%% @doc This function instead works by using random tuples with various
%% sizes, and picking a random key to test it.
%% This tests broader usages of lists:keysort, such as
%% `lists:keysort(2, [{a,b},{e,f,g},{t,a,n,e}])' yielding the list
%% `[{t,a,n,e},{a,b},{e,f,g}]', where the comparison takes place
%% on the second element of each tuple.
%%
%% While more complete than the previous one, this function
%% does not accurately portray the need for stability in the
%% function as documented: `[{a,b}, {a,a}]' being sorted will
%% not be tested here!
%% Those can either be added in a regular test case, or would
%% require devising a different property.
prop_keysort2() ->
    ?FORALL(List, non_empty(list(non_empty(list()))),
        begin
            %% Since the default built-in types do not let us easily
            %% create random-sized tuples that do not include `{}',
            %% which is not working with `lists:keysort/2', we
            %% create variable-sized tuples ourselves.
            Tuples = [list_to_tuple(L) || L <- List],
            %% To know what position to use, we're going to use
            %% the smallest, to avoid errors
            Pos = lists:min([tuple_size(T) || T <- Tuples]),
```

```erlang
        Sorted = lists:keysort(Pos, Tuples),
        Keys = extract_keys(Pos, Sorted),
        %% The keys returned by keysort have to be in the
        %% same order as returned by `lists:sort/1', which
        %% we now trust.
        Keys == lists:sort(Keys)
    end).

extract_keys(Pos, List) -> [element(Pos,T) || T <- List].
```

Elixir	code/ThinkingInProperties/elixir/pbt/test/solutions_test.exs

```elixir
property "pair keysort approach" do
  # This function tests that any list of {key,val} pairs
  # end up being able to be sorted by the key by using List.keysort
  forall list <- list({term(), term()}) do
    # is_key_ordered checks that all tuples' keys are ordered.
    is_key_ordered(List.keysort(list, 0))
  end
end

def is_key_ordered([{a, _}, {b, _} = btuple | t]) do
  a <= b and is_key_ordered([btuple | t])
end

def is_key_ordered(_) do
  true
end

# This function instead works by using random tuples with various sizes,
# and picking a random key to test it.
# This tests broader usages of List.keysort/2, such as
# List.keysort([{:a,:b},{:e,:f,:g},{:t,:a,:n,:e}], 2) yielding the list
# [{:t,:a,:n,:e},{:a,:b},{:e,:f,:g}], where the comparison takes place
# on the second element of each tuple.
#
# While more complete than the previous one, this function does not
# accurately portray the need for stability in the function:
# [{:a,:b}, {:a,:a}] being sorted in the same order will not be tested
# here!
#
# Those can either be added in a regular test case, or would require
# devising a different property.
property "multi-sized tuple keysort approach" do
  forall list <- non_empty(list(non_empty(list()))) do
    # Since the default built-in types do not let us easily create
    # random-sized tuples that do not include {}, which wouldn't work
    # with List.keysort/2, we create variable-sized tuples ourselves
    tuples = for l <- list, do: List.to_tuple(l)
    # To know what position to use, we're going to use the smallest,
    # to avoid errors
    pos = Enum.min(for t <- tuples, do: tuple_size(t)) - 1
```

```
        sorted = List.keysort(tuples, pos)
        keys = extract_keys(sorted, pos)
        # The keys returned by keysort have to be in the same order as
        # returned by Enum.sort/1, which we now trust.
        keys == Enum.sort(keys)
    end
end

def extract_keys(list, pos) do
    for t <- list, do: :erlang.element(pos + 1, t)
end
```

Question on page 47.

Question 3

The problem is with the model; sets don't generally allow duplicate elements. Here, the call that generates ModelUnion adds both lists together. This inadvertently maintains duplicate elements, which the actual sets module avoids.

If the call to lists:sort/1 is changed to lists:usort/1 (which removes duplicated elements) when handling ModelUnion, the property will adequately represent sets by removing duplicate elements and pass.

Question on page 47.

Question 4

The function is shaky because it validates only the keys portion of dictionary merging. The values resulting from the merge operation are untouched, and the test makes no mention of how it may resolve or report conflicts. To be safe, the property should either take into account the conflict-resolution function for merging, or a second property should be added to cover it.

Question on page 48.

Question 5

First the function:

Erlang   code/ThinkingInProperties/erlang/pbt/test/prop_solutions.erl

```erlang
word_count(String) ->
    Stripped = string:trim(dedupe_spaces(String), both, " "),
    Spaces = lists:sum([1 || Char <- Stripped, Char =:= $\s]),
    case Stripped of
        "" -> 0;
        _ -> Spaces + 1
    end.
```

```
dedupe_spaces([]) -> [];
dedupe_spaces([$\s,$\s|Rest]) -> dedupe_spaces([$\s|Rest]);
dedupe_spaces([H|T]) -> [H|dedupe_spaces(T)].
```

| Elixir | code/ThinkingInProperties/elixir/pbt/test/solutions_test.exs |

```
def word_count(chars) do
  stripped = :string.trim(dedupe_spaces(chars), :both, ' ')
  spaces = Enum.sum(for char <- stripped, char == ?\s, do: 1)

  case stripped do
    '' -> 0
    _ -> spaces + 1
  end
end

defp dedupe_spaces([]), do: []
defp dedupe_spaces([?\s, ?\s | rest]), do: dedupe_spaces([?\s | rest])
defp dedupe_spaces([h | t]), do: [h | dedupe_spaces(t)]
```

And next, the test, using an alternative implementation:

| Erlang | code/ThinkingInProperties/erlang/pbt/test/prop_solutions.erl |

```
prop_word_count() ->
    ?FORALL(String, non_empty(string()),
            word_count(String) =:= alt_word_count(String)
    ).

alt_word_count(String) -> space(String).

space([]) -> 0;
space([$\s|Str]) -> space(Str);
space(Str) -> word(Str).

word([]) -> 1;
word([$\s|Str]) -> 1+space(Str);
word([_|Str]) -> word(Str).
```

| Elixir | code/ThinkingInProperties/elixir/pbt/test/solutions_test.exs |

```
property "word counting" do
  forall chars <- non_empty(char_list()) do
    word_count(chars) == alt_word_count(chars)
  end
end
```

```
defp alt_word_count(string), do: space(to_charlist(string))

defp space([]), do: 0
defp space([?\s | str]), do: space(str)
defp space(str), do: word(str)

defp word([]), do: 1
defp word([?\s | str]), do: 1 + space(str)
defp word([_ | str]), do: word(str)
```

Question on page 49.

Custom Generators

Question 1

- collect(Term, BoolExpression) (in Elixir, BoolExpression |> collect(Term))
- aggregate([Term], BoolExpression) (in Elixir, BoolExpression |> aggregate(Term))

Question on page 83.

Question 2

?LET(Var, Generator, ErlangExpr); otherwise, the generators are abstract representations that won't be modifiable the way the generated data would be. The same syntax in Elixir is let var <- Generator do ElixirExpr end instead.

Question on page 83.

Question 3

Whenever a generator that may probabilistically choose multiple branches is called, using eager evaluation means that all alternative paths for it will be evaluated at once. If the generator is made recursive, this can quickly blow the size of the computation to very large levels. The ?LAZY(Generator) macro allows to only evaluate a given branch when required, ensuring faster execution with more predictable memory usage.

Question on page 84.

Question 4

The first step is to ensure the generator can terminate by using ?LAZY macros:

Erlang   code/CustomGenerators/erlang/pbt/test/prop_solutions.erl

```erlang
tree() ->
    tree(term()).

tree(Type) ->
    frequency([
        {3, {node, Type, undefined, undefined}},
        {2, {node, Type, ?LAZY(tree(Type)), undefined}},
        {2, {node, Type, undefined, ?LAZY(tree(Type))}},
        {3, {node, Type, ?LAZY(tree(Type)), ?LAZY(tree(Type))}}
    ]).
```

Elixir   code/CustomGenerators/elixir/pbt/test/solutions_test.exs

```elixir
def tree(), do: tree(term())

def tree(type) do
  frequency([
    {3, {:node, type, nil, nil}},
    {2, {:node, type, lazy(tree(type)), nil}},
    {2, {:node, type, nil, lazy(tree(Type))}},
    {3, {:node, type, lazy(tree(type)), lazy(tree(type))}}
  ])
end
```

Although the tree may terminate, finding a good balance can still prove tricky. The numbers have been modified a bit to fit better, but using the Size variable proves more effective to put a predictable boundary on growth:

Erlang   code/CustomGenerators/erlang/pbt/test/prop_solutions.erl

```erlang
limited_tree(Type) ->
    ?SIZED(Size, limited_tree(Size, Type)).

limited_tree(Size, Type) when Size =< 1 ->
    {node, Type, undefined, undefined};
limited_tree(Size, Type) ->
    frequency([
        {1, {node, Type, ?LAZY(limited_tree(Size-1, Type)), undefined}},
        {1, {node, Type, undefined, ?LAZY(limited_tree(Size-1, Type))}},
        {5, {node, Type,
            %% Divide to avoid exponential growth
            ?LAZY(limited_tree(Size div 2, Type)),
            ?LAZY(limited_tree(Size div 2, Type))}}
    ]).
```

Elixir   code/CustomGenerators/elixir/pbt/test/solutions_test.exs

```elixir
def limited_tree(type) do
  sized(size, limited_tree(size, type))
end

def limited_tree(size, type) when size <= 1, do: {:node, type, nil, nil}

def limited_tree(size, type) do
  frequency([
    {1, {:node, type, lazy(limited_tree(size - 1, type)), nil}},
    {1, {:node, type, nil, lazy(limited_tree(size - 1, type))}},
    {5,
     {
       :node,
       type,
       # divide to avoid exponential growth
       lazy(limited_tree(div(size, 2), type)),
       lazy(limited_tree(div(size, 2), type))
     }}
  ])
end
```

Although more verbose, it behaves much better.

Question on page 84.

Question 5

For morning stamps

The first implementation, while clear to its intent, is likely to be far less efficient as it is going to require dropping roughly half of all the generated terms to replace them with new ones, assuming a roughly equal distribution for digits between 0 and 23 for the H position.

By comparison, the generator with a ?LET uses a modulus to ensure that any hour greater than 11 starts over at 0. It will need to do one operation per generator, and will never have to retry. It is the better implementation.

For ordered stamps

Similarly in the second one, chances are roughly 50% that the first generator will need to be discarded because the probability that one stamp is greater than the other should be fairly even. Using the min/2 and max/2 functions gives a proper ordering without needing to generate newer stamps. The second solution is better.

For meeting hours

In this set of generators, there is no clearly defined way to use a ?LET to transform data that is't acceptable into data that is acceptable. The filtering done there is roughly the same as the one in ?SUCHTHAT and some ad-hoc procedure is used to generate alternative data. Because the range of restricted samples is fairly limited when compared to the whole problem space, the readability of the first solution is likely better in the long run.

Question on page 85.

Question 6

Using the provided wrapper functions, it's enough to export them and then use them with {'$call, ...} symbolic calls:

```erlang
Erlang                    code/CustomGenerators/erlang/pbt/test/prop_solutions.erl

file(Name) ->
    ?SIZED(
      Size,
      lines(Size, {'$call', ?MODULE, file_open, [Name, [read,write,raw]]})
    ).

lines(Size, Fd) ->
    if Size =< 1 -> Fd
     ; Size > 1 -> lines(Size-1, {'$call', ?MODULE, file_write, [Fd,bin()]})
    end.

bin() ->
    non_empty(binary()).
```

```elixir
Elixir              code/CustomGenerators/elixir/pbt/test/solutions_test.exs

def file(name) do
  sized(
    size,
    lines(
      size,
      {:"$call", __MODULE__, :file_open, [name, [:read, :write, :utf8]]}
    )
  )
end

def lines(size, fd) when size <= 1, do: fd
def lines(size, fd) do
  lines(
    size - 1,
    {:"$call", __MODULE__, :file_write, [fd, non_empty(utf8())]}
  )
end
```

The file is opened in both read/write mode to be more flexible to whoever will use it when running the test. The raw mode is entirely optional. It makes things go faster, but removes some flexibility when using the file module regarding encoding and buffering. Then the file is created. The generator asks for a name (which may or may not be a generator) and uses the Size parameter to know how big of a file to generate.

In the Elixir version, the raw mode is replaced with the utf8 mode and the binary() generator with utf8(). The reason for that is that the write wrappers for this solution use the IO module, which forbids using the raw mode.

By using shim functions, as many bytes can be added as desired over multiple calls. In this case, nonempty binaries are just sufficient, but the generator could as well have been written to let the user pass a generator for the data to file() and lines(), becoming fully configurable.

Question on page 86.

Shrinking

Question 1

- ?SHRINK(Generator, [AltGenerators, ...])
- ?LETSHRINK([Pattern, ...], [Generator, ...], Expression)

Question on page 176.

Question 2

?LETSHRINK always takes a list of arguments and generators, whereas ?LET takes any pattern and any generator in its first two arguments. When failing in a test case and needing a new simplified generator, one of the generators in the list will be used, but without the transformations being applied. A ?LET macro has no such rule and the transformation is always applied.

Question on page 176.

Question 3

The problem here is that the property expects a list coming out of the generator, but the way ?LETSHRINK works is that every single of the variable between Appetizer, Drink, Entree, or Dessert is an atom put in a list. During a failing test case, the shrinking attempt will fail as the property can't work through receiving an atom when it expects a list.

Instead, the generator should be reworked as follows:

Erlang	code/Shrinking/erlang/pbt/test/prop_solutions.erl

```erlang
meal() ->
    ?LETSHRINK([Appetizer, Drink, Entree, Desert],
               [[elements([soup, salad, cheesesticks])],
                [elements([coffee, tea, milk, water, juice])],
                [elements([lasagna, tofu, steak])],
                [elements([cake, chocolate, icecream])]],
               Appetizer ++ Drink ++ Entree ++ Desert).
```

Elixir	code/Shrinking/elixir/pbt/test/solutions_test.exs

```elixir
def meal() do
  let_shrink([
    appetizer <- [elements([:soup, :salad, :cheesesticks])],
    drink <- [elements([:coffee, :tea, :milk, :water, :juice])],
    entree <- [elements([:lasagna, :tofu, :steak])],
    dessert <- [elements([:cake, :chocolate, :icecream])]
  ]) do
    appetizer ++ drink ++ entree ++ dessert
  end
end
```

This ensures that every single variable is always a list, and the final result passed to the property in a successful case also remains a list. The elements generated should always have the same type as the one returned for ?LETSHRINK to work well.

Question on page 176.

Question 4

Since the special list and the price list are both required for the rest of operations, those two ?LET will be left alone. The third ?LET is where the merging takes place, and that's where we'll operate.

The gotcha here is once again that the types generated by the ?LET expression as a whole ({Items, Expected, PriceList, SpecialList}) don't match what the generators produce inside the ?LET ({{RegularItems, RegularExpected}, {SpecialItems, SpecialExpected}}). We can't just replace it wholesale for a ?LETSHRINK.

To do so, we must ensure that the values match. This can be done by adding an intermediary step where we use ?LETSHRINK to build the merged lists of items and the merged expected price, and use ?LET to join them in the final 4-tuple expected by the property rather than doing it all at once:

Erlang   code/Shrinking/erlang/pbt/test/prop_solutions.erl

```erlang
item_price_special() ->
    %% first LET: PriceList
    ?LET(PriceList, price_list(),
        %% second LET: SpecialList
        ?LET(SpecialList, special_list(PriceList),
            %% third LET: Regular + Special items and prices
            ?LET({Items, Price},
                %% Help shrinking by first trying only one of the
                %% two possible lists in case a specific form causes
                %% the problems on its own
                ?LETSHRINK([{RegularItems, RegularExpected},
                            {SpecialItems, SpecialExpected}],
                           [regular_gen(PriceList, SpecialList),
                            special_gen(PriceList, SpecialList)],
                           %% And we merge:
                           {RegularItems ++ SpecialItems,
                            RegularExpected + SpecialExpected}),
                {Items, Price, PriceList, SpecialList}))).
```

Elixir   code/Shrinking/elixir/pbt/test/solutions_test.exs

```elixir
def item_price_special() do
  # first let: freeze the price list
  let price_list <- price_list() do
    # second let: freeze the list of specials
    let special_list <- special_list(price_list) do
      # third let: regular + special items and prices
      # help shrinking by first trying only one of the
      # two possible lists in case a specific form causes
      # the problems on its own
      # and we merge
      let {items, price} <-
            (let_shrink([
                {regular_items, regular_expected} <-
                  regular_gen(price_list, special_list),
                {special_items, special_expected} <-
                  special_gen(price_list, special_list)
              ]) do
                {regular_items ++ special_items,
                 regular_expected + special_expected}
              end) do
        {items, price, price_list, special_list}
      end
    end
  end
end
```

This transformation ensures that the inputs and outputs of ?LETSHRINK are always 2-tuples that include a list of items and a price expected. The surrounding ?LET is in charge of taking the values and pairing them up in a 4-tuple with the price list and special list. Doing so, gives PropEr hints how to isolate whether the problem is with regular items, special items, or both at once.

Question on page 177.

Stateful Properties

Question 1

- The abstract phase contains: initial_state/0, command/1, precondition/2, and next_state/3

- The real interacting with the actual system contains: initial_state/0, command/1, precondition/2, next_state/3, and postcondition/3

Question on page 231.

Question 2

The pattern matching in the generator works fine to create an initial list of commands to run on the model system, but as soon as a failure happens—or a constraint needs to be enforced when parallelizing commands—the modification of the command list is done without regard to the initial patterns in command generations. Only the preconditions can be used to ensure the validity of the command sequence. Without preconditions, the framework isn't able to manipulate the sequence in any way, and parallelism and shrinking can't be effective.

Question on page 231.

Question 3

1. For the first one, the actual system will be started and stopped before every single test iteration.

2. The actual system will be booted once before the tests run, and the system instance will be shared for all iterations, before being shut down after the whole run.

3. The actual system will be started, then an abstract representation of the test case will be created. After this, the system will be stopped. But the test itself will not have run once at that point, so by the time the framework would try to execute the test, the actual system would have already shut down.

Question on page 231.

Question 4

The value must be treated as opaque since placeholders will be generated by the framework during the abstract phase of command generation. Symbolic calls may be added to the command when used in an actual execution context.

It is simpler to avoid it entirely, but one of the useful cases comes when interaction with the actual system relies on values it has returned and are not predictable. Those may include process identifiers, sockets, or any other unique, unpredictable, or transient resource. Whenever the system returns one of these and expects them back, you may not be able to plan the value ahead of time from the model state. The model is then better off holding a reference to that value without altering it.

Question on page 232.

Elixir Translations

Thinking in Properties

Putting It All Together

Here's the code for this whole chapter put together:

```
Elixir                 code/ThinkingInProperties/elixir/pbt/test/pbt_test.exs
defmodule PbtTest do
  use ExUnit.Case
  use PropCheck

  property "finds biggest element" do
    forall x <- non_empty(list(integer())) do
      Pbt.biggest(x) == model_biggest(x)
    end
  end

  def model_biggest(list) do
    List.last(Enum.sort(list))
  end

  property "picks the last number" do
    forall {list, known_last} <- {list(number()), number()} do
      known_list = list ++ [known_last]
      known_last == List.last(known_list)
    end
  end

  property "a sorted list has ordered pairs" do
    forall list <- list(term()) do
      is_ordered(Enum.sort(list))
    end
  end
end
```

```elixir
  def is_ordered([a, b | t]) do
    a <= b and is_ordered([b | t])
  end

  # lists with fewer than 2 elements
  def is_ordered(_) do
    true
  end

  property "a sorted list keeps its size" do
    forall l <- list(number()) do
      length(l) == length(Enum.sort(l))
    end
  end

  property "no element added" do
    forall l <- list(number()) do
      sorted = Enum.sort(l)
      Enum.all?(sorted, fn element -> element in l end)
    end
  end

  property "no element deleted" do
    forall l <- list(number()) do
      sorted = Enum.sort(l)
      Enum.all?(l, fn element -> element in sorted end)
    end
  end

  property "symmetric encoding/decoding" do
    forall data <- list({atom(), any()}) do
      encoded = encode(data)
      is_binary(encoded) and data == decode(encoded)
    end
  end

  def encode(t), do: :erlang.term_to_binary(t)
  def decode(t), do: :erlang.binary_to_term(t)
end
```

Translation of Erlang code on page 45.

Responsible Testing

This is the CSV module providing all of the parsing:

Elixir	code/ResponsibleTesting/elixir/bday/lib/csv.ex

```elixir
defmodule Bday.Csv do
  def encode([]), do: ""
```

```elixir
def encode(maps) do
  keys = Enum.map_join(Map.keys(hd(maps)), ",", &escape(&1))

  vals =
    for map <- maps, do: Enum.map_join(Map.values(map), ",", &escape(&1))

  to_string([keys, "\r\n", Enum.join(vals, "\r\n")])
end

def decode(""), do: []

def decode(csv) do
  {headers, rest} = decode_header(csv, [])
  rows = decode_rows(rest)
  for row <- rows, do: Map.new(Enum.zip(headers, row))
end

defp escape(field) do
  if escapable(field) do
    ~s|"| <> do_escape(field) <> ~s|"|
  else
    field
  end
end

defp escapable(string) do
  String.contains?(string, [~s|"|, ",", "\r", "\n"])
end

defp do_escape(""), do: ""
defp do_escape(~s|"| <> str), do: ~s|""| <> do_escape(str)
defp do_escape(<<char>> <> rest), do: <<char>> <> do_escape(rest)

defp decode_header(string, acc) do
  case decode_name(string) do
    {:ok, name, rest} -> decode_header(rest, [name | acc])
    {:done, name, rest} -> {[name | acc], rest}
  end
end

defp decode_rows(string) do
  case decode_row(string, []) do
    {row, ""} -> [row]
    {row, rest} -> [row | decode_rows(rest)]
  end
end

defp decode_row(string, acc) do
  case decode_field(string) do
    {:ok, field, rest} -> decode_row(rest, [field | acc])
    {:done, field, rest} -> {[field | acc], rest}
  end
end
```

```elixir
  defp decode_name(~s|"| <> rest), do: decode_quoted(rest)
  defp decode_name(string), do: decode_unquoted(string)

  defp decode_field(~s|"| <> rest), do: decode_quoted(rest)
  defp decode_field(string), do: decode_unquoted(string)

  defp decode_quoted(string), do: decode_quoted(string, "")

  defp decode_quoted(~s|"|, acc), do: {:done, acc, ""}
  defp decode_quoted(~s|"\r\n| <> rest, acc), do: {:done, acc, rest}
  defp decode_quoted(~s|",| <> rest, acc), do: {:ok, acc, rest}

  defp decode_quoted(~s|""| <> rest, acc) do
    decode_quoted(rest, acc <> ~s|"|)
  end

  defp decode_quoted(<<char>> <> rest, acc) do
    decode_quoted(rest, acc <> <<char>>)
  end

  defp decode_unquoted(string), do: decode_unquoted(string, "")

  defp decode_unquoted("", acc), do: {:done, acc, ""}
  defp decode_unquoted("\r\n" <> rest, acc), do: {:done, acc, rest}
  defp decode_unquoted("," <> rest, acc), do: {:ok, acc, rest}

  defp decode_unquoted(<<char>> <> rest, acc) do
    decode_unquoted(rest, acc <> <<char>>)
  end
end
```

Translation of Erlang code on page 103.

This code contains unit tests that cover content defined by examples in the CSV RFC:

Elixir	code/ResponsibleTesting/elixir/bday/test/csv_test.exs

```elixir
test "one record per line" do
  assert [%{"aaa" => "zzz", "bbb" => "yyy", "ccc" => "xxx"}] ==
           Csv.decode("aaa,bbb,ccc\r\nzzz,yyy,xxx\r\n")
end

test "optional trailing CRLF" do
  assert [%{"aaa" => "zzz", "bbb" => "yyy", "ccc" => "xxx"}] ==
           Csv.decode("aaa,bbb,ccc\r\nzzz,yyy,xxx")
end

test "double quotes" do
  assert [%{"aaa" => "zzz", "bbb" => "yyy", "ccc" => "xxx"}] ==
           Csv.decode("\"aaa\",\"bbb\",\"ccc\"\r\nzzz,yyy,xxx")
end
```

```elixir
test "escape CRLF" do
  assert [%{"aaa" => "zzz", "b\r\nbb" => "yyy", "ccc" => "xxx"}] ==
          Csv.decode("\"aaa\",\"b\r\nbb\",\"ccc\"\r\nzzz,yyy,xxx")
end

test "double quote escaping" do
  # Since we decided headers are mandatory, this test adds a line
  # with empty values (CLRF,,) to the example from the RFC.
  assert [%{"aaa" => "", "b\"bb" => "", "ccc" => ""}] ==
          Csv.decode("\"aaa\",\"b\"\"bb\",\"ccc\"\r\n,,")
end

# this counterexample is taken literally from the RFC and
# cannot work with the current implementation because maps
# do not allow duplicate keys
test "dupe keys unsupported" do
  csv =
    "field_name,field_name,field_name\r\n" <>
      "aaa,bbb,ccc\r\n" <> "zzz,yyy,xxx\r\n"

  [map1, map2] = Csv.decode(csv)
  assert ["field_name"] == Map.keys(map1)
  assert ["field_name"] == Map.keys(map2)
end
```

Translation of Erlang code on page 105.

Stateful Properties

Here's the code to make the cache code sequential:

Elixir	code/StatefulProperties/elixir/pbt/lib/cache_fixed.ex

```elixir
defmodule Cache do

use GenServer

## Public API ##
def start_link(n) do
  GenServer.start_link(__MODULE__, n, name: __MODULE__)
end

def stop() do
  GenServer.stop(__MODULE__)
end

def find(key) do
  case :ets.match(:cache, {:_, {key, :"$1"}}) do
    [[val]] -> {:ok, val}
    [] -> {:error, :not_found}
  end
end
```

```elixir
def cache(key, val) do
  GenServer.call(__MODULE__, {:cache, key, val})
end

def flush() do
  GenServer.call(__MODULE__, :flush)
end

## GenServer callbacks ##
def init(n) do
  :ets.new(:cache, [:public, :named_table])
  :ets.insert(:cache, {:count, 0, n})
  {:ok, :nostate}
end

def handle_call({:cache, key, val}, _from, state) do
  case :ets.match(:cache, {:"$1", {key, :_}}) do
    [[n]] ->
      :ets.insert(:cache, {n, {key, val}})

    [] ->
      :erlang.yield()

      case :ets.lookup(:cache, :count) do
        [{:count, max, max}] ->
          :ets.insert(:cache, [{1, {key, val}}, {:count, 1, max}])

        [{:count, current, max}] ->
          :ets.insert(:cache, [
            {current + 1, {key, val}},
            {:count, current + 1, max}
          ])
      end
  end

  {:reply, :ok, state}
end

def handle_call(:flush, _from, state) do
  [{:count, _, max}] = :ets.lookup(:cache, :count)
  :ets.delete_all_objects(:cache)
  :erlang.yield()
  :ets.insert(:cache, {:count, 0, max})
  {:reply, :ok, state}
end

def handle_cast(_cast, state), do: {:noreply, state}

def handle_info(_msg, state), do: {:noreply, state}
end
```

Translation of Erlang code on page 229.

Case Study: Bookstore

Introducing the Application

Script to initialize the database:

Elixir	code/Bookstore/elixir/bookstore/lib/bookstore/init.ex

```elixir
defmodule Bookstore.Init do
  def main(_) do
    # See: https://www.postgresql.org/docs/9.6/static/server-start.html
    File.mkdir_p!("postgres/data/")
    stdout = IO.stream(:stdio, :line)

    IO.puts("initializing database structure...")
    System.cmd("initdb", ["-D", "postgres/data"], into: stdout)
    IO.puts("starting postgres instance...")

    args = ["-D", "postgres/data", "-l", "logfile", "start"]
    case :os.type() do
      {:win32, _} ->
        spawn(fn -> System.cmd("pg_ctl", args, into: stdout) end)
      {:unix, _} ->
        System.cmd("pg_ctl", args, into: stdout)
    end

    # wait and pray
    Process.sleep(5000)
    IO.puts("setting up 'bookstore_db' database...")
    System.cmd(
      "psql",
      [
        "-h", "localhost",
        "-d", "template1",
        "-c", "CREATE DATABASE bookstore_db;"
      ],
      into: stdout
    )
    IO.puts("OK.")
    :init.stop()
  end
end
```

Translation of Erlang code on page 237.

Application Code

The bookstore module handling most operations related to databases:

Elixir	code/Bookstore/elixir/bookstore/lib/bookstore/db.ex

```elixir
defmodule Bookstore.DB do
  @doc """
  Create the database table required for the bookstore
  """
  def setup do
    run_query(:setup_table_books, [])
  end

  @doc """
  Delete the database table required for the bookstore
  """
  def teardown() do
    run_query(:teardown_table_books, [])
  end

@doc """
Add a new book to the inventory, with no copies of it
"""
def add_book(isbn, title, author) do
  add_book(isbn, title, author, 0, 0)
end

@doc """
Add a new book to the inventory, with a pre-set number of
owned and available copies
"""
def add_book(isbn, title, author, owned, avail) do
  bin_title = :erlang.iolist_to_binary(title)
  bin_author = :erlang.iolist_to_binary(author)

  case run_query(:add_book, [isbn, bin_title, bin_author, owned, avail]) do
    {{:insert, 0, 1}, []} -> :ok
    {:error, reason} -> {:error, reason}
    other -> {:error, other}
  end
end

@doc """
Add a copy of the book to the bookstore's inventory
"""
def add_copy(isbn) do
  handle_single_update(run_query(:add_copy, [isbn]))
end
```

```
@doc """
Borrow a copy of a book; reduces the count of available copies by one.
Who borrowed the book is not tracked at this moment and is left as an
exercise to the reader.
"""
def borrow_copy(isbn) do
  handle_single_update(run_query(:borrow_copy, [isbn]))
end

@doc """
Return a copy of a book, making it available again
"""
def return_copy(isbn) do
  handle_single_update(run_query(:return_copy, [isbn]))
end

@doc """
Search all books written by a given author. The matching is loose and so
searching for `Hawk' will return copies of books written by `Stephen
Hawking' (if such copies are in the system).
"""
def find_book_by_author(author) do
  handle_select(
    run_query(
      :find_by_author,
      [:erlang.iolist_to_binary(['%', author, '%'])]
    )
  )
end

@doc """
Find books under a given ISBN
"""
def find_book_by_isbn(isbn) do
  handle_select(run_query(:find_by_isbn, [isbn]))
end

@doc """
Find books with a given title. The matching is loose and searching
for `Test' may return `PropEr Testing'.
"""
def find_book_by_title(title) do
  handle_select(
    run_query(
      :find_by_title,
      [:erlang.iolist_to_binary(['%', title, '%'])]
    )
  )
end
```

Translation of Erlang code on page 240.

And the other functions that finalize database handling:

Elixir	code/Bookstore/elixir/bookstore/lib/bookstore/db.ex

```elixir
defp run_query(name, args) do
  with_connection(fn conn -> run_query(conn, name, args) end)
end

defp run_query(conn, name, args) do
  :pgsql_connection.extended_query(query(name), args, conn)
end

defp with_connection(f) do
  {:ok, conn} = connect()
  res = f.(conn)
  close(conn)
  res
end

defp connect() do
  connect(Application.get_env(:bookstore, :pg, []))
end

defp connect(args) do
  try do
    conn = {:pgsql_connection, _} = :pgsql_connection.open(args)
    {:ok, conn}
  catch
    :throw, err -> {:error, err}
  end
end

defp close(conn) do
  :pgsql_connection.close(conn)
end
```

Translation of Erlang code on page 243.

Precise Stateful Modeling

Here's the shim module for stateful modeling:

Elixir	code/Bookstore/elixir/bookstore/test/book_shim.ex

```elixir
defmodule BookShim do
  def add_book_existing(isbn, title, author, owned, avail) do
    Bookstore.DB.add_book(isbn, title, author, owned, avail)
  end
  def add_book_new(isbn, title, author, owned, avail) do
    Bookstore.DB.add_book(isbn, title, author, owned, avail)
  end
```

```elixir
  def add_copy_existing(isbn), do: Bookstore.DB.add_copy(isbn)
  def add_copy_new(isbn), do: Bookstore.DB.add_copy(isbn)

  def borrow_copy_avail(isbn), do: Bookstore.DB.borrow_copy(isbn)
  def borrow_copy_unavail(isbn), do: Bookstore.DB.borrow_copy(isbn)
  def borrow_copy_unknown(isbn), do: Bookstore.DB.borrow_copy(isbn)

  def return_copy_full(isbn), do: Bookstore.DB.return_copy(isbn)
  def return_copy_existing(isbn), do: Bookstore.DB.return_copy(isbn)
  def return_copy_unknown(isbn), do: Bookstore.DB.return_copy(isbn)

  def find_book_by_isbn_exists(isbn) do
    Bookstore.DB.find_book_by_isbn(isbn)
  end
  def find_book_by_isbn_unknown(isbn) do
    Bookstore.DB.find_book_by_isbn(isbn)
  end

  def find_book_by_author_matching(author) do
    Bookstore.DB.find_book_by_author(author)
  end
  def find_book_by_author_unknown(author) do
    Bookstore.DB.find_book_by_author(author)
  end

  def find_book_by_title_matching(title) do
    Bookstore.DB.find_book_by_title(title)
  end
  def find_book_by_title_unknown(title) do
    Bookstore.DB.find_book_by_title(title)
  end
end
```

Translation of Erlang code on page 255.

Here's the rewritten command/1 callback, which now uses the shim module:

Elixir	code/Bookstore/elixir/bookstore/test/bookstore_test.exs

```elixir
# initial model value at system start. Should be deterministic.
def initial_state(), do: %{}

def command(state) do
  always_possible = [
    {:call, BookShim, :add_book_new, [isbn(), title(), author(), 1, 1]},
    {:call, BookShim, :add_copy_new, [isbn()]},
    {:call, BookShim, :borrow_copy_unknown, [isbn()]},
    {:call, BookShim, :return_copy_unknown, [isbn()]},
    {:call, BookShim, :find_book_by_isbn_unknown, [isbn()]},
    {:call, BookShim, :find_book_by_author_unknown, [author()]},
    {:call, BookShim, :find_book_by_title_unknown, [title()]}
  ]
```

```
  relies_on_state =
    case Map.equal?(state, %{}) do
      true -> # no values yet
        []
      false -> # values from which to work
        s = state
        [
          {:call, BookShim, :add_book_existing,
           [isbn(s), title(), author(), 1, 1]},
          {:call, BookShim, :add_copy_existing, [isbn(s)]},
          {:call, BookShim, :borrow_copy_avail, [isbn(s)]},
          {:call, BookShim, :borrow_copy_unavail, [isbn(s)]},
          {:call, BookShim, :return_copy_existing, [isbn(s)]},
          {:call, BookShim, :return_copy_full, [isbn(s)]},
          {:call, BookShim, :find_book_by_isbn_exists, [isbn(s)]},
          {:call, BookShim, :find_book_by_author_matching, [author(s)]},
          {:call, BookShim, :find_book_by_title_matching, [title(s)]}
        ]
    end
  oneof(always_possible ++ relies_on_state)
end
```

Translation of Erlang code on page 256.

The initial set of preconditions for stateful tests:

Elixir	code/Bookstore/elixir/bookstore/test/bookstore_test.exs

```
# Picks whether a command should be valid under the current state.
# - all the unknown calls
def precondition(s, {:call, _, :add_book_new, [isbn|_]}) do
  not has_isbn(s, isbn)
end
def precondition(s, {:call, _, :add_copy_new, [isbn]}) do
  not has_isbn(s, isbn)
end
def precondition(s, {:call, _, :borrow_copy_unknown, [isbn]}) do
  not has_isbn(s, isbn)
end
def precondition(s, {:call, _, :return_copy_unknown, [isbn]}) do
  not has_isbn(s, isbn)
end
def precondition(s, {:call, _, :find_book_by_isbn_unknown, [isbn]}) do
  not has_isbn(s, isbn)
end
def precondition(s, {:call, _, :find_book_by_author_unknown, [auth]}) do
  not has_isbn(s, auth)
end
```

```elixir
def precondition(s, {:call, _, :find_book_by_title_unknown, [title]}) do
  not has_isbn(s, title)
end
def precondition(s, {:call, _, :find_book_by_author_matching, [auth]}) do
  like_author(s, auth)
end
def precondition(s, {:call, _, :find_book_by_title_matching, [title]}) do
  like_title(s, title)
end
# - all calls with known ISBNs
def precondition(s, {:call, _mod, _fun, [isbn|_]}) do
  has_isbn(s, isbn)
end
```

Translation of Erlang code on page 258.

The initial set of postconditions for stateful tests:

Elixir	code/Bookstore/elixir/bookstore/test/bookstore_test.exs

```elixir
# Given the state *prior* to the call {:call, mod, fun, args},
# determine whether the result (coming from the actual system)
# makes sense.
def postcondition(_, {_, _, :add_book_new, _}, :ok) do
  true
end
def postcondition(_, {_, _, :add_book_existing, _}, {:error, _}) do
  true
end
def postcondition(_, {_, _, :add_copy_existing, _}, :ok) do
  true
end
def postcondition(_, {_, _, :add_copy_new, _}, {:error, :not_found}) do
  true
end
def postcondition(_, {_, _, :borrow_copy_avail, _}, :ok) do
  true
end
def postcondition(
  _,
  {_, _, :borrow_copy_unavail, _},
  {:error, :unavailable}
) do
  true
end
def postcondition(_, {_,_,:borrow_copy_unknown,_}, {:error,:not_found}) do
  true
end
def postcondition(_, {_, _, :return_copy_full, _}, {:error, _}) do
  true
end
```

```elixir
def postcondition(_, {_, _, :return_copy_existing, _}, :ok) do
  true
end
def postcondition(_, {_,_,:return_copy_unknown,_}, {:error,:not_found}) do
  true
end
```

Translation of Erlang code on page 261.

Refining the Tests

Edited postconditions:

Elixir	code/Bookstore/elixir/bookstore/test/bookstore_test.exs

```elixir
«bunch of postconditions»
  def postcondition(
    state,
    {_, _, :find_book_by_isbn_exists, [isbn]},
    {:ok, [res]})
  do
    book_equal(res, Map.get(state, isbn, nil))
  end
«bunch of postconditions»
  def postcondition(
    state,
    {_, _, :find_book_by_author_matching, [auth]},
    {:ok, res}
  ) do
    map = :maps.filter(
      fn _, {_,_,a,_,_} -> contains?(a, auth) end,
      state
    )
    books_equal(Enum.sort(res), Enum.sort(Map.values(map)))
  end
«bunch of postconditions»
  def postcondition(
    state,
    {_, _, :find_book_by_title_matching, [title]},
    {:ok, res}
  ) do
    map = :maps.filter(
      fn _, {_,t,_,_,_} -> contains?(t, title) end,
      state
    )
    books_equal(Enum.sort(res), Enum.sort(Map.values(map)))
  end
«bunch of postconditions»
```

Translation of Erlang code on page 271.

Parallel Tests

The parallelized version of tests:

Elixir   code/Bookstore/elixir/bookstore/test/bookstore_test.exs

```elixir
property "parallel stateful property", [:verbose] do
  forall cmds <- parallel_commands(__MODULE__) do
    # No setup macro in PropCheck yet, do it all inline
    {:ok, apps} = Application.ensure_all_started(:bookstore)
    Bookstore.DB.setup()
    {history, state, result} = run_parallel_commands(__MODULE__, cmds)
    Bookstore.DB.teardown()
    for app <- apps, do: Application.stop(app)

    (result == :ok)
    |> aggregate(command_names(cmds))
    |> when_fail(
      IO.puts("""
      =======
      Failing command sequence
      #{inspect(cmds)}
      At state: #{inspect(state)}
      =======
      Result: #{inspect(result)}
      History: #{inspect(history)}
      """)
    )
  end
end
```

Translation of Erlang code on page 278.

State Machine Properties

Modeling the Circuit Breaker

First, the shim module:

Elixir   code/FSMProperties/elixir/circuit/test/break_shim.ex

```elixir
defmodule BreakShim do
  @service :test_service

  def success() do
    :circuit_breaker.call(
      @service,
      fn -> :success end,
      :timer.hours(1),
```

```elixir
      fn -> true end,
      :timer.hours(1),
      options()
    )
  end

  def err(reason) do
    :circuit_breaker.call(
      @service,
      fn -> {:error, reason} end,
      :timer.hours(1),
      fn -> true end,
      :timer.hours(1),
      options()
    )
  end

  def ignored_error(reason), do: err(reason)

  def timeout() do
    :circuit_breaker.call(
      @service,
❶    fn -> :timer.sleep(:infinity) end,
      0,
      fn -> true end,
      :timer.hours(1),
      options()
    )
  end
```

Translation of Erlang code on page 294.

And the circuit breaker postconditions:

Elixir	code/FSMProperties/elixir/circuit/test/break_test.exs

```elixir
# Given that state prior to the call `{:call, mod, fun, args}`,
# determine whether the result (res) coming from the actual system
# makes sense according to the model
def postcondition(
      :tripped,
      :tripped,
      _data,
      _call,
      {:error, {:circuit_breaker, _}}
    ) do
  true
end
```

```
① def postcondition(_, :blocked, _data, {_, _, :manual_block, _}, :ok) do
     true
   end
   def postcondition(
       _from,
       :blocked,
       _data,
       _call,
②     {:error, {:circuit_breaker, _}}
     ) do
     true
   end
   def postcondition(_, :ok, _data, {_, _, :success, _}, :success) do
     true
   end
   def postcondition(_, :ok, _data, {_, _, :manual_deblock, _}, :ok) do
     true
   end
   def postcondition(_, _, _data, {_, _, :manual_reset, _}, :ok) do
     true
   end
③ def postcondition(
       :ok,
       _to,
       _data,
       {_, _, :timeout, _},
       {:error, :timeout}
     ) do
     true
   end
   def postcondition(:ok, _to, _data, {_, _, :err, _}, {:error, err}) do
     not Enum.member?([:ignore1, :ignore2], err)
   end
   def postcondition(
       :ok,
       _to,
       _data,
       {_, _, :ignored_error, _},
       {:error, err}
     ) do
     Enum.member?([:ignore1, :ignore2], err)
   end
   def postcondition(_from, _to, _data, {:call, _m, _f, _args}, _res) do
     false
   end
```

Translation of Erlang code on page 304.

Adjusting the Model

The adapted transitions are as follows:

Elixir	code/FSMProperties/elixir/circuit/test/break_test.exs

```elixir
# Assuming the postcondition for a call was true, update the model
# accordingly for the test to proceed
def next_state_data(:ok, _, data = %{errors: n}, _, {_, _, :err, _}) do
  %{data | errors: n + 1}
end
def next_state_data(:ok, _, d = %{timeouts: n}, _, {_, _, :timeout, _}) do
  %{d | timeouts: n + 1}
end
def next_state_data(_from, _to, data, _, {_, _, :manual_deblock, _}) do
  %{data | errors: 0, timeouts: 0}
end
def next_state_data(_from, _to, data, _, {_, _, :manual_reset, _}) do
  %{data | errors: 0, timeouts: 0}
end
def next_state_data(
      :ok,
      _to,
      data = %{errors: e, timeouts: t},
      _res,
      {:call, _, f, _}
    )
    when f == :success or f == :ignored_error do
  cond do
    e > 0 ->
      %{data | errors: e - 1}
    t > 0 ->
      %{data | timeouts: t - 1}
    e == 0 and t == 0 ->
      data
  end
end
def next_state_data(_from, _to, data, _res, {:call, _m, _f, _args}) do
  data
end

def valid_error() do
  elements([:badarg, :badmatch, :badarith, :whatever])
end
def ignored_error() do
  elements([:ignore1, :ignore2])
end
end
```

❶

Translation of Erlang code on page 307.

Installing PostgreSQL

If you're using a Unix-like system, chances are your package manager already has prebuilt versions ready to go. You can just follow the instructions on the PostgreSQL download page,[1] or those found in common tutorials[2] until the init_db steps where you are asked to create a database, where we'll take over since they are common to both Windows and other operating systems.

If you're a Windows user, you'll need something a bit more convoluted. You can find the installer from the download page mentioned previously, grab a copy of the database (which takes around 150 megabytes), and then run through the following steps:

- Run the wizard.

    - Pick the command line tools options for our later setup scripts to work.
    - Pick a root password and note it down.
    - Leave the default port (5432) or note the new one down if you change it.
    - Stick with the default locale.
    - Wait for the install to complete.

- Add C:\Program Files\PostgreSQL\10\bin (make sure to pick a path that matches your installation) to your PATH environment variable so that the various PostgreSQL scripts are visible from everywhere.

    - See https://stackoverflow.com/a/44272417/35344 for a detailed walkthrough.
    - Restart your terminal session.

---

1. https://www.postgresql.org/download/
2. https://wiki.postgresql.org/wiki/Detailed_installation_guides

No matter the platform you use, you should be able to call the following command after installation to confirm that everything is installed and that command line tools are available:

```
$ initdb --help
initdb initializes a PostgreSQL database cluster.

Usage:
  initdb [OPTION]... [DATADIR]

Options:
«list of options»
```

If the command runs, then you know all the tools are available in your path and you're ready to go.

Generators Reference

Generator	Data Generated	Sample
any()	Any Erlang term PropEr can produce	Any of the samples below
atom()	Erlang atoms	'ós43Úrcá\200'
binary()	Binary data aligned on bytes	<<2,203,162,42,84,141>>
binary(Len)	Binary data of fixed length Len, in bytes	<<98,126,144,175,175>>
bitstring()	Binary data without byte alignment	<<10,74,2:3>>
bitstring(Len)	Binary data of fixed length Len, in bits	<<11:5>>
boolean()	Atoms true or false. Also bool()	true, false
char()	Character codepoint, between 0 and 1114111 inclusively	23
choose(Min, Max)	Any integer between Min and Max inclusively	choose(1, 1000) => 596
fixed_list([Type])	A list where all entries match a generator from the list of arguments	fixed_list([boolean(), byte(), atom()]) => [true,2,b]
float()	Floating point number. Also real()	4.982972307245969
float(Min, Max)	Floating point number between Min and Max inclusively	float(0.0, 10.0) => 5.934602482212932
frequency([{N, Type}])	The value matching the generator of one of those in the second tuple element, with a probability similar to the value N. Also weighed_union/1	frequency([{1,atom()}, {10,char()}, {3,binary()}]) => 23 (chances of getting an atom are $\frac{1}{14}$)

Generator	Data Generated	Sample
function([Arg], Ret])	An anonymous function	function([char(), bool()], atom()) => #Fun<proper_gen.25.96459342>
integer()	An integer	89234
list()	A list of terms, equivalent to list(any())	Any of the samples, as list elements
list(Type)	A list of terms of type Type	list(boolean()) => [true, true, false]
loose_tuple(Type)	A tuple with terms of type Type	loose_tuple(boolean()) => {true, true, false}
map(KeyType, ValType)	A map with keys of type KeyType and values of type ValType	map(integer(), boolean()) => #{0 => true, -4 => true, 18 => false}
neg_integer()	An integer smaller than 0	-1231
non_empty(Gen)	Constrains a binary or a list generator into not being empty	non_empty(list()) => [abc]
non_neg_float()	A float greater than or equal to 0.0	98.213012312
non_neg_integer()	An integer greater than or equal to 0	98
number()	A float or integer	123
oneof(Types)	The value created by the generator of one of those in Types, also union(Types) and elements(Types). In QuickCheck, oneof() shrinks toward a failing element, whereas elements() shrinks toward the first element of the list. PropEr does not make that distinction.	oneof([atom(), char()]) => a
pos_integer()	Integer greater than 0	1
range(Min, Max)	Any integer between Min and Max inclusively	range(1, 1000) => 596
string()	Equivalent to list(char())	"^DQ^W^R/D" (may generate weird escape sequences!)
term()	Same as any()	Any of the samples in this table

Generator	Data Generated	Sample
timeout()	Union of non_neg_integer() generator and the atom infinity	312
tuple()	A tuple of random terms	tuple() => {true, 13.321123, -67}
{T1, T2, ...}	A literal tuple with types in it	{boolean(), char()} => {true, 1}
utf8()	Generates to utf8-encoded text as a binary data structure	<<"□□₽3'"/utf8>> (may generate weird escape sequences!)
vector(Len, Type)	A list of length Len of type Type	vector(5, integer()) => [17,0,1,3,8]

Index

SYMBOLS

{} (braces) literal tuple generator, 23, 347

A

aggregate() function, 58–61, 185

anchors
    broad properties as, 153
    unit tests as, 44, 97, 106

annealing, simulated, 183–185, 189–191

any() generator, 23, 345

assertions, *see* unit tests

atom() generator, 23, 345

automated symbolic calls, 80–83

B

binary trees example, 186–193

binary() generator, 23, 345

bitstring() generator, 345

bookstore example, 233–279
    application code, 238–244
    broad stateful testing for, 247–253
    causing failures to refine tests, 265–273
    database for, 233, 237–244
    debugging properties, 273–278
    generators for, 245–247
    parallel tests, 278–279
    postconditions for, 261–265
    precise stateful testing for, 253–265
    preconditions for, 257–259
    project setup, 233–238
    shim module for, 254–257
    state transitions for, 259–261

boolean() generator, 23, 345

braces ({}) literal tuple generator, 23, 347

broad properties, 44, 153–156, 247–253

C

char() generator, 345

chardata type, 250

choose() generator, 23, 345

circuit breaker example, 289–310
    application code for, 289–292
    generators for, 297, 301
    modeling, 292–305
    preconditions for, 301
    state transitions for, 298, 306–310

code coverage metrics, 59, 127, 151

code examples
    binary trees, 186–193
    bookstore, 233–279
    circuit breaker, 289–310
    concurrent cache, 210–224
    conventions used in this book, xiii–xiv
    employee records, 92–132
    parallel executions, 224–230
    quicksort, 193–197
    supermarket, 133–166

collect() function, 54–58, 185

comma-separated-values (CSV) parser, 92, 95–106

command generation
    for state machine properties, 283
    for stateful properties, 203, 206, 209

commands
    mix new command, 13, 95
    mix test command, 16
    rebar3 new escript command, 94
    rebar3 new lib command, 11
    rebar3 new proper command, 14, 18
    rebar3 new proper_fsm command, 285
    rebar3 new proper_statem command, 205
    rebar3 proper command, 12, 21, 182

commands() generator, 206

Concuerror tool, 229

concurrent cache example, 210–224
    building model, 215–220
    implementing cache, 211–215
    tests for, 215–224
    validating system, 221–224

constraints on generators,
see filtering generators

counterexample, 29, 67, *see
also* shrinking

CSV (comma-separated-values) parser, 92, 95–106

D

data, generating, *see* generators

database, *see also* SQL
queries
in bookstore example,
233, 237–244
PostgreSQL, installing,
234, 343–344
transitioning from CSV
to, 117

doc meta-function, 182

documentation output for
failed tests, 182

E

elements() generator, 57, *see
also* oneof() generator

Elixir
properties, adding to
modules, 15–16, 19
properties, running, 16
repeating tests, 28
setting up for property-based testing, 12–14
targeted properties not
yet supported, 179

email templates, 128–130

employee records example,
92–132
CSV parser, 95–106
email templates, 128–130
employee module, 116–128
filtering records, 106–116
program structure for,
92–95

Erlang
properties, adding to
modules, 14, 18
properties, running, 15
setting up for property-based testing, 11–12
Unicode formats, 250

errors
errors on filtering, 68
order of errors received,
152, 266
warnings in shell, 24

example tests, generalizing
from, 37–38, 135

example-based testing, 7–10,
135

examples
binary trees, 186–193
bookstore, 233–279
circuit breaker, 289–310
concurrent cache, 210–224
conventions used in this
book, xiii–xiv
employee records, 92–132
parallel executions, 224–230, 278–279
quicksort, 193–197
supermarket, 133–166

?EXISTS macro, 185

ExUnit framework, 12

F

file structure, for modules,
18–20

filtering generators, 67–69

filtering records, 106–116

finite state machines, 281,
see also state machine
properties

fixed_list() generator, 345

float() generator, 23, 345

?FORALL macro, Erlang, 20–21

forall statement, Elixir, 20–21

?FORALL_TARGETED macro, Erlang, 180–182

frameworks, *see also* PropEr
framework; QuickCheck
framework
PropEr, library for, xiv
PropEr, setting up, 10–14
StreamData, 11
Triq, 10

frequency() generator, 69–72,
74–75, 345

function() generator, 345

functions for properties
naming, 19, 26
structure of, 20–21

fuzzing, 163

G

generalizing example tests,
37–38, 135

generators, *see also* shrinking
about, 17, 22

bookstore example, 245–247

circuit breaker example,
297, 301

default, limitations of,
51–53

default, list of, 23–24,
345–347

file structure for, 19

filtering, 67–69

grown by default, 61

manually generating data, 108–111

probabilities of, changing,
69–72

recursive, 72–80, 185

resizing, 61–65

for state machine properties, 283, 286

for stateful properties,
203–204, 206

supermarket example,
141–148

symbolic calls as, 80–83,
203, 283

targeted properties influencing, 179–197

transforming, 65–68

trying in shell, 24

for Unicode, 69

GPLv3 license, 11

H

helper functions, 19

hill climbing, 183–184

I

inputs, generating, *see* generators

installing PostgreSQL, 234,
343–344, *see also* setting
up PropEr

integer() generator, 23, 345

integration tests, *see also* stateful properties
stateful tests, 36, 211
vs. unit tests, 92

invariants, 38–42, 44

iolist type, 250

iolist_to_binary() function, 250

L

?LAZY macro, Erlang, 75–78

lazy() function, Elixir, 75–78

?LET macro, Erlang, 66–68,
75, 143–145

let statement, Elixir, 66–68, 75, 143–145

let_shrink() function, Elixir, 172–175

?LETSHRINK macro, Erlang, 172–175

libraries, *see also* PropEr framework
creating, 11
library project, creating, 11
mocking, 292
PropCheck, xiv

list() generator, 23, 26, 38, 345

loose_tuple() generator, 345

M

map() generator, 345

?MAXIMIZE macro, Erlang, 181

meck library, 292

mergesort, 193–195

messages
errors on filtering, 68
order of errors received, 152, 266
using timers, 292
warnings in shell, 24

meta-functions, 182

?MINIMIZE macro, Erlang, 181

mix build tool, 12

mix new command, 13, 95

mix test command, 16

mocking libraries, 292

model
circuit breaker example, 292–305
concurrent cache example, 215–220
for state machine properties, 282–283, 292–305
for stateful properties, 201–202, 207–210, 215–220

model checking, 201

modeling, 33–36

models, for stateful properties, 36

modules
file structure for, 18–20
properties, adding, 14–16, 18–19
shim modules, 254–257, 292, 294–296
as test suites, 19

N

neg_integer() generator, 345

negative testing, 152–166
broad properties, 153–156
calibrating negative properties, 156–159
relaxing constraints, 160–166

neighbor selection, 183–185, 189–193

nested states, for state machine properties, 288

new command, mix, 13, 95

new escript command, rebar3, 94

new lib command, rebar3, 11

new proper command, rebar3, 14, 18

new proper_fsm command, rebar3, 285, *see also* state machine properties

new proper_statem command, rebar3, 205, *see also* stateful properties

next_state function, 202, 209, 259–261

next_state_data function, 284

non_empty() generator, 23, 67, 345

non_neg_float() generator, 345

non_neg_integer() generator, 345

?NOT_EXISTS macro, 185

number() generator, 22–23, 345

O

oneof() generator, 57, 69–72, 345

online resources
PropEr documentation, xiv, 23
Quickcheck documentation, xiv, 23
for this book, xiv

operator, perspective of, 264

opts meta-function, 182, 195

oracle, for modeling, 36

order
error order, 152, 266
unimportant ordering, 263

P

parallel executions example, 224–230, 278–279

parser, CSV (comma-separated-values), 92, 95–106

pos_integer() generator, 345

postconditions
for state machine properties, 283
for stateful properties, 203, 209, 261–265

PostgreSQL, 234, 343–344, *see also* database

preconditions
for state machine properties, 283–284, 300
for stateful properties, 203, 209, 257–259

probabilities of generators, changing, 69–72

program structure, testability of, 92–95

project setup, 10–14, 233–238

prop_ modules, 14

PropCheck library, xiv

propcheck package, 12

proper command, rebar3, *see also* new proper command, rebar3
options for, 12
overriding options for, 182
using, 21

PropEr framework, *see also* properties; property-based testing
about, 10
documentation, xiv, 23
library for, xiv
setting up, 10–14

proper.hrl file, 21

proper_gen:pick() function, 22

proper_types:bool() function, 24

proper_types:float() function, 24

proper_types:function() function, 24

proper_types:non_empty() function, 24

proper_types:number() function, 22, 24

proper_types:range() function, 24

proper_types:term() function, 21

properties, *see also* state machine properties; stateful properties, targeted properties
  about, 7–9, 17
  adding to modules, 14–16, 18–19
  broad, 44, 153–156, 247–253
  documentation output on failure of, 182
  functions for, naming, 19, 26
  functions for, structure of, 20–21
  invariants, 38–42, 44
  number of, recommendations for, 46
  running, 15–16, 21–22
  stateful, 201–230
  stateless, 17, 24–31
  statistics from results of, 53–61
  structure of, 18–22, 44–46
  symmetric, 42–44, 97
  targeted, 179–197
  types of, 17
  unit tests as alternative to, 107, 111–116
  unit tests as anchors for, 44, 97, 106
  writing, generalizing examples for, 37–38, 135
  writing, iterative process for, 24–31
  writing, modeling for, 33–36
properties-driven development
  about, 133
  implementing features for, 148–152
  negative testing for, 152–166
  specification for, 134–135
  writing properties for, 135–145
property keyword, 26
property-based testing
  about, 8–9
  benefits of, 4–7
  compared to example-based testing, 9–10
  learning curve for, 4–5, 7
  when to use, 91

Q

queries, *see also* database
  in bookstore example, 237–244
  filtering invalid values for, 267
  testing, 277–278
QuickCheck framework
  about, 10
  concurrency testing with, 229
  differences with oneof() and elements(), 57
  documentation, xiv, 23
  example results from, 5–6
quicksort example, 193–197

R

range() generator, 23, 345
rebar.config file, 12, 182
rebar3 build tool, 11
rebar3 new escript command, 94
rebar3 new lib command, 11
rebar3 new proper command, 14, 18
rebar3 new proper_fsm command, 285, *see also* state machine properties
rebar3 new proper_statem command, 205, *see also* stateful properties
rebar3 proper command
  options for, 12
  overriding options for, 182
  using, 21
recursive generators, 72–80, 185
regressions, 106
resize() function, 61–63
resizing generators, 61–65
restrictions on generators, *see* filtering generators
reversible operations, testing, *see* symmetric properties
rules, *see* properties

S

search and variation, 191
search macros, 185
search_steps argument, 181
setup
  Elixir, 12–14

  Erlang, 11–12
  project, 10–14, 233–238
  PropEr, 10–14
  ?SETUP macro, 207, 248
  stateful properties, 207
?SETUP macro, 207, 248
shim module, 254–257, 292, 294–296
?SHRINK macro, Erlang, 168–172
shrink() function, Elixir, 168–172
shrinking, 167–175
  about, 27, 29
  choosing zero point for, 168
  dividing data for, 172–175
  failures in, debugging, 273–278
  re-centering with, 168–172
side effects, 93, *see also* integration tests; stateful properties
simulated annealing, 183–185, 189–191
?SIZED macro, Erlang, 63–65, 78–80
sized() function, Elixir, 63–65, 78–80
SQL queries, *see also* database
  in bookstore example, 237–244
  filtering invalid values for, 267
  testing, 277–278
state machine properties, 281–310
  circuit breaker example using, 289–310
  command generation for, 283
  components, 282–283
  execution phases of, 284–285
  initial state for, 284, 286
  model for, 282–283, 292–305
  nested states for, 288
  postconditions for, 283
  preconditions for, 283–284, 300
  state diagram for, 284
  state transitions for, 284, 287–289

validation for, 283
weight for, 284, 288, 308
writing, 285–289
stateful properties, 201–230
about, 17
bookstore example using, 233–279
command generation for, 203, 206, 209
concurrent cache example using, 210–224
debugging, 273–278
execution phases for, 204–205, 210
initial state for, 209
model for, 36, 201–202, 207–210, 215–220
parallel executions example using, 224–230
postconditions for, 203, 209, 261–265
preconditions for, 203, 209, 257–259
setting up and tearing down, 207
state diagrams for, 204
state transitions for, 202, 204–205, 210, 246, 259–261, 267–268
validation for, 203, 221–224
writing, 205–210
stateless properties, *see also* properties
about, 17
employee records example using, 92–132
writing, iterative process for, 24–31
statistics
gathering from test results, 53–61, 127, 151
target properties not allowing, 185
StreamData framework, 11
string() generator, 23, 345
such_that statement, Elixir, 67–69

?SUCHTHAT macro, Erlang, 67–69
supermarket example, 133–166
negative tests for, 152–166
specification for, 134–135
testing specials, 140–152
testing sums, 135–140
symbolic calls as generators, 80–83, 203, 283
symmetric properties, 42–44, 97

T

targeted properties, 179–197
binary trees example using, 186–193
Elixir not yet supporting, 179
limitations of, 185–186
quicksort example using, 193–197
search macros used by, 185
simulated annealing used by, 183–185, 189–191
syntax of, 180–182
TDD (test-driven development), xi, 133, *see also* properties-driven development
temperature, in simulated annealing, 184, 190–191
term() generator, 21–22, 345
test command, mix, 16
test suites, 19, *see also* modules
test-driven development (TDD), xi, 133, *see also* properties-driven development
testing, *see* example-based testing; integration tests; negative testing; property-based testing; unit tests
time-sensitive mechanisms, testing, 292

timeout() generator, 295, 347
to_range/2 function, 55
transforming generators, 65–68
Triq framework, 10
tuple() generator, 347

U

Unicode formats, Erlang, 250
Unicode generation, 69, 251–253
unicode:characters_to_binary() function, 251–253
union() generator, 57, *see also* oneof() generator
unit tests, *see also* stateless properties
about, 17, 92
as anchors for properties, 44, 97, 106
employee records example, 92–93
when to use instead of properties, 107, 111–116
?USERNF macro, 189
utf8() generator, 69, 266, 347

V

validation
for state machine properties, 283
for stateful properties, 203, 221–224
variation and search, 191
vector() generator, 347

W

warnings
errors on filtering, 68
order of errors received, 152, 266
warnings in shell, 24
weight, for state machine properties, 284, 288, 308

Thank you!

How did you enjoy this book? Please let us know. Take a moment and email us at support@pragprog.com with your feedback. Tell us your story and you could win free ebooks. Please use the subject line "Book Feedback."

Ready for your next great Pragmatic Bookshelf book? Come on over to https://pragprog.com and use the coupon code BUYANOTHER2019 to save 30% on your next ebook.

Void where prohibited, restricted, or otherwise unwelcome. Do not use ebooks near water. If rash persists, see a doctor. Doesn't apply to *The Pragmatic Programmer* ebook because it's older than the Pragmatic Bookshelf itself. Side effects may include increased knowledge and skill, increased marketability, and deep satisfaction. Increase dosage regularly.

And thank you for your continued support,

Andy Hunt, Publisher

Put the "Fun" in Functional

Elixir puts the "fun" back into functional programming, on top of the robust, battle-tested, industrial-strength environment of Erlang.

Programming Elixir 1.6

This book is *the* introduction to Elixir for experienced programmers, completely updated for Elixir 1.6 and beyond. Explore functional programming without the academic overtones (tell me about monads just one more time). Create concurrent applications, but get them right without all the locking and consistency headaches. Meet Elixir, a modern, functional, concurrent language built on the rock-solid Erlang VM. Elixir's pragmatic syntax and built-in support for metaprogramming will make you productive and keep you interested for the long haul. Maybe the time is right for the Next Big Thing. Maybe it's Elixir.

Dave Thomas
(410 pages) ISBN: 9781680502992. $47.95
https://pragprog.com/book/elixir16

Programming Erlang (2nd edition)

A multi-user game, web site, cloud application, or networked database can have thousands of users all interacting at the same time. You need a powerful, industrial-strength tool to handle the really hard problems inherent in parallel, concurrent environments. You need Erlang. In this second edition of the best-selling *Programming Erlang*, you'll learn how to write parallel programs that scale effortlessly on multicore systems.

Joe Armstrong
(546 pages) ISBN: 9781937785536. $42
https://pragprog.com/book/jaerlang2

A Better Web with Phoenix and Elm

Elixir and Phoenix on the server side with Elm on the front end gets you the best of both worlds in both worlds!

Programming Phoenix 1.4

Don't accept the compromise between fast and beautiful: you can have it all. Phoenix creator Chris McCord, Elixir creator José Valim, and award-winning author Bruce Tate walk you through building an application that's fast and reliable. At every step, you'll learn from the Phoenix creators not just what to do, but why. Packed with insider insights and completely updated for Phoenix 1.4, this definitive guide will be your constant companion in your journey from Phoenix novice to expert, as you build the next generation of web applications.

Chris McCord, Bruce Tate and José Valim
(325 pages) ISBN: 9781680502268. $45.95
https://pragprog.com/book/phoenix14

Programming Elm

Elm brings the safety and stability of functional programing to front-end development, making it one of the most popular new languages. Elm's functional nature and static typing means that run-time errors are nearly impossible, and it compiles to JavaScript for easy web deployment. This book helps you take advantage of this new language in your web site development. Learn how the Elm Architecture will help you create fast applications. Discover how to integrate Elm with JavaScript so you can update legacy applications. See how Elm tooling makes deployment quicker and easier.

Jeremy Fairbank
(250 pages) ISBN: 9781680502855. $40.95
https://pragprog.com/book/jfelm

Learn Why, Then Learn How with Elixir

Help introduce Elixir in your organization where it makes most sense, and dive into GraphQL for better APIs in Elixir. It's all here.

Adopting Elixir

Adoption is more than programming. Elixir is an exciting new language, but to successfully get your application from start to finish, you're going to need to know more than just the language. You need the case studies and strategies in this book. Learn the best practices for the whole life of your application, from design and team-building, to managing stakeholders, to deployment and monitoring. Go beyond the syntax and the tools to learn the techniques you need to develop your Elixir application from concept to production.

Ben Marx, José Valim, Bruce Tate
(242 pages) ISBN: 9781680502527. $42.95
https://pragprog.com/book/tvmelixir

Craft GraphQL APIs in Elixir with Absinthe

Your domain is rich and interconnected, and your API should be too. Upgrade your web API to GraphQL, leveraging its flexible queries to empower your users, and its declarative structure to simplify your code. Absinthe is the GraphQL toolkit for Elixir, a functional programming language designed to enable massive concurrency atop robust application architectures. Written by the creators of Absinthe, this book will help you take full advantage of these two groundbreaking technologies. Build your own flexible, high-performance APIs using step-by-step guidance and expert advice you won't find anywhere else.

Bruce Williams and Ben Wilson
(302 pages) ISBN: 9781680502558. $47.95
https://pragprog.com/book/wwgraphql

Level Up

From data structures to architecture and design, we have what you need for everyone on your team.

A Common-Sense Guide to Data Structures and Algorithms

If you last saw algorithms in a university course or at a job interview, you're missing out on what they can do for your code. Learn different sorting and searching techniques, and when to use each. Find out how to use recursion effectively. Discover structures for specialized applications, such as trees and graphs. Use Big O notation to decide which algorithms are best for your production environment. Beginners will learn how to use these techniques from the start, and experienced developers will rediscover approaches they may have forgotten.

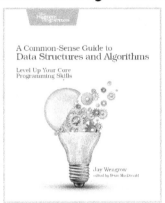

Jay Wengrow
(220 pages) ISBN: 9781680502442. $45.95
https://pragprog.com/book/jwdsal

Design It!

Don't engineer by coincidence—design it like you mean it! Grounded by fundamentals and filled with practical design methods, this is the perfect introduction to software architecture for programmers who are ready to grow their design skills. Ask the right stakeholders the right questions, explore design options, share your design decisions, and facilitate collaborative workshops that are fast, effective, and fun. Become a better programmer, leader, and designer. Use your new skills to lead your team in implementing software with the right capabilities—and develop awesome software!

Michael Keeling
(358 pages) ISBN: 9781680502091. $41.95
https://pragprog.com/book/mkdsa

Pragmatic Programming

We'll show you how to be more pragmatic and effective, for new code and old.

Your Code as a Crime Scene

Jack the Ripper and legacy codebases have more in common than you'd think. Inspired by forensic psychology methods, this book teaches you strategies to predict the future of your codebase, assess refactoring direction, and understand how your team influences the design. With its unique blend of forensic psychology and code analysis, this book arms you with the strategies you need, no matter what programming language you use.

Adam Tornhill
(218 pages) ISBN: 9781680500387. $36
https://pragprog.com/book/atcrime

The Nature of Software Development

You need to get value from your software project. You need it "free, now, and perfect." We can't get you there, but we can help you get to "cheaper, sooner, and better." This book leads you from the desire for value down to the specific activities that help good Agile projects deliver better software sooner, and at a lower cost. Using simple sketches and a few words, the author invites you to follow his path of learning and understanding from a half century of software development and from his engagement with Agile methods from their very beginning.

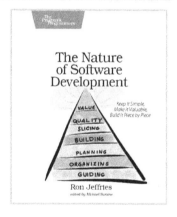

Ron Jeffries
(176 pages) ISBN: 9781941222379. $24
https://pragprog.com/book/rjnsd

The Pragmatic Bookshelf

The Pragmatic Bookshelf features books written by developers for developers. The titles continue the well-known Pragmatic Programmer style and continue to garner awards and rave reviews. As development gets more and more difficult, the Pragmatic Programmers will be there with more titles and products to help you stay on top of your game.

Visit Us Online

This Book's Home Page
https://pragprog.com/book/fhproper
Source code from this book, errata, and other resources. Come give us feedback, too!

Keep Up to Date
https://pragprog.com
Join our announcement mailing list (low volume) or follow us on twitter @pragprog for new titles, sales, coupons, hot tips, and more.

New and Noteworthy
https://pragprog.com/news
Check out the latest pragmatic developments, new titles and other offerings.

Save on the eBook

Save on the eBook versions of this title. Owning the paper version of this book entitles you to purchase the electronic versions at a terrific discount.

PDFs are great for carrying around on your laptop—they are hyperlinked, have color, and are fully searchable. Most titles are also available for the iPhone and iPod touch, Amazon Kindle, and other popular e-book readers.

Buy now at *https://pragprog.com/coupon*

Contact Us

Online Orders:	*https://pragprog.com/catalog*
Customer Service:	*support@pragprog.com*
International Rights:	*translations@pragprog.com*
Academic Use:	*academic@pragprog.com*
Write for Us:	*http://write-for-us.pragprog.com*
Or Call:	+1 800-699-7764

CPSIA information can be obtained
at www.ICGtesting.com
Printed in the USA
BVHW080841190319
543075BV00008B/147/P